Praise for Smokehouse Ham, Spoon Bread & Scuppernong Wine

"Joe's book makes my mouth water for Southern food and my heart hunger for Southern stories. Not since the Foxfire series has something out of the Appalachian experience thrilled me as much."
—Pat Conroy, *New York Times* bestselling author of *South of Broad*

"Joseph E. Dabney knows as much about the South as just about anyone…Don't read this heady amalgam of folklore, history, and literature on an empty stomach."
—Willie Morris, author of *My Dog Skip*, *North Toward Home*, and *New York Days*

"Joe Dabney's prize-winning book humanizes Southern food with its charming stories and interviews."
—Nathalie Dupree, cookbook writer and TV host

"It's the first 'cookbook' I've actually read from the top like a novel. It's a helluva book, and I haven't even taken it to the kitchen yet."
—Paul Hemphill, author of *Lovesick Blues: The Life of Hank Williams*

"This book is like a treasure uncovered in Grandmother's attic. Recipes and histories of their origin reminisce of the old days with such longing that even a Yankee will hanker for more."
—*Today's Librarian*

"This thang's so good it'll make you want to marry your cousin."
—Sam Venable, *Knoxville Sentinel*

"It's downright DEE-EE-EE-LI-CIOUS!!!!"
—Ludlow Porch, syndicated talk show host

SMOKEHOUSE HAM, SPOON BREAD & SCUPPERNONG WINE

Other Books by Joseph E. Dabney

Mountain Spirits

More Mountain Spirits

Herk: Hero of the Skies

The Food, Folklore, and Art of Lowcountry Cooking

SMOKEHOUSE HAM, SPOON BREAD & SCUPPERNONG WINE

The Folklore and Art of Southern Appalachian Cooking

10-Year Anniversary Edition

Joseph E. Dabney
Foreword by **John Egerton**
Foreword to the Tenth-Anniversary Edition by **Terry Kay**

CUMBERLAND HOUSE

F. Amaz. ⁸/₁₀   19.99

Published by Cumberland House, an imprint of Sourcebooks, Inc.
P.O. Box 4410, Naperville, Illinois 60567-4410
(630) 961-3900
Fax: (630) 961-2168
www.sourcebooks.com

Library of Congress Cataloging-in-Publication Data

Dabney, Joseph Earl.
  Smokehouse ham, spoon bread & scuppernong wine : the folklore and art of Southern Appalachian cooking / by Joseph Dabney. — 1st pbk. ed.
     p. cm.
  Includes bibliographical references and index.
  1. Cookery, American—Southern style. 2. Cookery—Appalachian Region, Southern. 3. Cookery—Appalachian Region, Southern—History. 4. Appalachian Region, Southern—Social life and customs. I. Title.
  TX715.2.S68D43 2010
  641.5975—dc22

                              2009050313

Printed and bound in the United States of America.
VP 10 9 8 7 6 5 4 3 2 1

Dedicated to the Memory of Martha Berry

whose motto, "Not to be ministered unto, but to
minister," has been a great inspiration to me over
the years since graduating from Berry College in 1949.

*I will lift up mine eyes unto the hills, from
whence cometh my help. My help cometh
from the LORD, which made heaven and earth.*

—121:1–2 Psalm KJV

(Martha Berry's favorite Bible passage)

Contents

Foreword to the Tenth-Anniversary Edition

My first sighting of Joe Dabney's *Smokehouse Ham, Spoon Bread & Scuppernong Wine* was in a bookstore in Athens, Georgia, and my thought was this: "Great title, Joe." Yet I am not sure I would have purchased the book if Joe's name—officially, Joseph E. Dabney—had not been emblazoned on the cover. There are a lot of books with clever, eye-catching titles that splash across the shelves of bookstores like colorful battle ribbons on the chest of literature. Few live up to the promise of their name.

But Joe is a longtime friend, and I read the works of longtime friends—not out of obligation but with affection and appreciation for the friendship.

In this case, I'm truly glad I know the man. If I had left this book on the shelf, it would have been a grievous omission in my reading experience, and my understanding of who I am would be far more muddled than it now is.

Simply put, Joe Dabney's book is, for me, the most magnificent inspection of life in Southern Appalachia that I have read.

That acknowledged, I will offer this:

Once, a young fellow in a public school class said to me that he thought of words as having wheels. I asked for an explanation. He replied, "Well, they take you places, don't they?"

I like the answer. It is how I consider the words of *Smokehouse Ham, Spoon Bread & Scuppernong Wine.* They take me on a tour of memory, traveling at a reading speed that invites pause and reflection.

By definition and by recognition, this is a cookbook (after all, it won the prestigious James Beard award), yet my trip on word wheels does not deliver me exclusively to my mother's kitchen or to the harvest of my father's fields; it takes me to their time and, of course, to my time with them.

It is, then, a history book for me. (In any event, I doubt seriously if I will include opossum or squirrel pie on the menu of future family gatherings, though the woods surrounding my home are abundant with the creatures.)

I could get maudlin with this. A book that begins with the arrival of people to take up permanent residence in a pristine wilderness and then ends with blessings (mealtime prayers) intoned by those people could be said to cover the gamut. And with Joe's book, it comes close.

My own people came out of Virginia through the Carolinas, meandering into Georgia. They brought with them the history of the British, the Scots, and the Irish, and intermingled it with the Cherokee. Throw in dabs of influence from the Germans, the Dutch, the French, and scatterings of other European centers, and over time, my people and others like them found their place in the foothills and in the valleys and high up across the ridges that would be known as Appalachia. With each generation, the people and the land settled whatever differences they might have had at first encounter, until the land became the people and the people became the land.

It's a long and shifting history, dotted now with deserted communities and forgotten gravesites. Stone chimneys stand like ancient statuary over faint leavings of cabins and tenant farmhouses. Where once there were fields muscled from forests, there are now forests covering fields, the only telltale sign being the ribbons of terracing made by two-horse turners.

Yet it's not as though history has vanished; it has simply changed. There are towns doing a brisk business by hawking antiques and flea-market memorabilia and mama's home cooking along the highways that snake through the mountains of the Appalachian range. On hillsides you can see fancy retirement homes rising up out of scrapped-down clearings, none of them having the right look for their location.

Every writer knows it's impossible to tell the complete story of such history. It's too expansive for words. The best a writer can do is distill it. Find something that reveals the quintessential portrait of the great view.

And it's what Joe Dabney does in *Smokehouse Ham, Spoon Bread & Scuppernong Wine*. He goes into the kitchens of Appalachian homes and tells us about the people who have lived there, somewhat in the fashion of the Foxfire books that he references with admiration. He gives us little stories that have the character of innocence and naiveté, often told with the wink and smile that comes with a tall tale—stories rendered by moonshiners and farmers and hunters and quilt makers and herb gatherers and hog butchers, stories so alive in the writing that we put down the book mesmerized.

Being mesmerized is as close to wonder as any of us will ever get. It makes near dreams of distant moments.

I am in my mother's kitchen as a boy—before electricity—and I again see her at her cabinets and at her wood-burning stove with the top warmer bins. She is cooking biscuits, as she did three times each day, and the smell of that baking lingers in the kitchen. All who knew my mother called her a fabulous cook. She had the practice for it, being the mother of twelve. She was a dab-of-this, pinch-of-that cook. When wisps of flour flew up over her mixing bowl, it was like watching the dust of a fairy's wand. Magic was in the place.

Joe doesn't know it, but he wrote that memory for me.

And he wrote the memory of hog killings and of fresh crackling cornbread and of pig's brains scrambled with eggs and of the football made from the pig's bladder.

And of slow-cooked beans and sassafras tea and dried apples and sorghum syrup and pickled watermelon rinds.

And of the sweet juice of peeled peaches on canning days at the canning plant.

And of potato hills made in Indian tepee fashion from cornstalks and pine needles and dirt.

Rabbit boxes and hoarfrost mornings.

Corn shuckings with a king snake in the crib to feast on mice.

All of these memories, Joe Dabney wrote for me. Many of them do not appear in his book but are from my own ride by on the wheels of words. And that's what a book of any sort ought to do: give the reader his or her own adventure.

But here is what I like most about *Smokehouse Ham, Spoon Bread & Scuppernong Wine*: talking about it. Saying to those who have some of the Appalachian blood in them, "I was reading this book by Joe Dabney and it brought to mind…Do you remember…? Did you ever…?" They'll talk you into the ground, these people will, and the tales they will pull out of memory (or fiction) will be like music.

Read it. You'll hear the merriment of the fiddles.

—Terry Kay

Foreword

Reading Joseph E. Dabney's sprawling, loquacious volume of Southern Appalachian cookery and culture caused me to go and look up something I remembered reading in a book called *Aunt Jane of Kentucky*, written a century ago by Eliza Calvert Hall. Aunt Jane, speaking in a mountain vernacular that rings clear and true, is telling her granddaughter how "piecin' a quilt's like livin' a life," and she allows as how she could use a patchwork quilt to preach a sermon on predestination and free will:

> You see, you start out with jest so much caliker. You don't go to the store and pick it out and buy it, but the neighbors will give you a piece here and a piece there, and you'll have a piece left every time you cut out a dress, and you take jest what happens to come. And that's like predestination. But when it comes to cuttin' out, why, you're free to choose your own pattern. You can give the same kind o' pieces to two persons, and one'll make a "nine-patch" and one'll make a "wild-goose chase," and there'll be two quilts made out o' the same kind o' pieces, and jest as different as they can be. And that's jest the way it is with livin'. The Lord sends us the pieces, but we can cut 'em out and put 'em together pretty much to suit ourselves—and there's a heap more in the cuttin' out and the sewin' than there is in the caliker.

This is not a treatise on the relative merits of store-bought calico or the technical fine points of quilt-making; it's a sage observation on the merits of individuality, the meaning of friendship, the importance of traditions and rituals. Aunt Jane was an expert quilt-maker, but ever so much more: she was a philosopher, a woman who knew something deep and meaningful about "livin' a life."

And so it is with the authentic characters who talk and cook and generally live life in Joe Dabney's evocative book. These pages are full of Aunt Janes (and Uncle Homers and Cousin Sades)—and there's a heap more in their curing and seasoning and distilling of good things to eat and drink than you could ever hope to find in the store-bought foods and beverages that now fill the fridges and pantry shelves of kitchens across the American landscape here on the cusp of the twenty-first century.

What Dabney sketches so clearly in *Smokehouse Ham, Spoon Bread & Scuppernong Wine* is closely akin to what Eliza Hall held dear: a mountain sensibility, suffused with language and lore, stories and songs, an abiding sense of place and, not least, dinner tables where families drawn by ageless tradition and an irresistible panorama of culinary gems linger to recite their history in stories—and in so doing, to nourish their social and cultural roots.

In place of the denigrating mythologies of Appalachia—the buffoonish Snuffy Smith–Lil' Abner–*Beverly Hillbillies* stereotypes—we see these salt-of-the-earth citizens for what they truly are: smart, industrious, creative, frugal, good-humored, and highly skilled, especially when it comes to putting great meals on the table.

Because he grew up at tables such as these in the southern arc of the Appalachian highlands—and remains close by even now—Joe Dabney knows how to re-create the atmosphere and the characters and the food in language that Aunt Jane and Eliza Hall would understand and embrace. Given his lifetime of keen observations and his professional skill as a journalist and writer (not to mention his natural abilities as a hunter, fisherman, gardener, and cook), Dabney is unquestionably the right person to pull together a big patchwork quilt of a book such as this.

He was born in the South Carolina mill village of Kershaw in 1929, a year before his father, a "mill hill" merchant, was swept into bankruptcy by a wave of customer credit when the mills closed in the Great Depression. Joe, the youngest of seven children, was barely two when the family left their home in the Piedmont for a rented farm in the Double Springs community of Greenville County, a hundred miles to the northwest. There, just below the eastern shadow of the Blue Ridge Mountains, the Dabneys rode out the Depression with unwavering faith, hope, and charity—in God, Franklin Roosevelt, and a support group of relatives and friends.

Back in the Kershaw area at the age of seven, Joe had already learned the code of the hills, and it would serve him well from then on. Like his forebears and his contemporaries, he mixed piety, honesty, and frugality with a respect for nature, an appreciation of independence and eccentricity, a sense of humor, and an abiding love of hill-country food.

Except for a tour of duty with the army during the Korean War, Dabney has lived most of his life in up-country South Carolina and north Georgia. He was raised a Baptist and an FDR New Deal Democrat; he graduated from Berry College in Rome (that's Georgia, not Italy); he worked for various newspapers in the region and for the Lockheed Corporation at its facility north of Atlanta. In 1974 he wrote a book on moonshining (*Mountain Spirits*, first published by Scribner and still in print in a regional paperback edition), and that volume, like this one, was more of a social-cultural history than a straight-out treatment of the ostensible subject. His interest in whiskey-making was more precisely an interest in whiskey-makers; likewise, his obsession with the foods of Southern Appalachia is really a love of the people who have raised, canned, cooked, and served the food since these wooded slopes were the sole possession of the Cherokees and their native kin.

And it is those people, the ancients and his own more recent kin and neighbors, whose voices echo through Dabney's smooth-flowing narrative. To be sure, this is a cookbook, and most of the talk is about food—or over it, at the table—but it is much more than that. It's about characters like whiskey-maker Theodore (Thee) King of Gum Log, Georgia, and Simmie Free of Tiger, Georgia, and ninety-year-old Nina Garrett of near

Cartecay, another Georgia hill-country community. (Turns out Miss Nina takes after her grandmother, "a good hand to bake biscuits.")

And Dabney's book is also about hog killing and smokehouses, about making lye hominy and gathering wild greens, about ramps and cushaws and leather-britches, about cracklin' bread and corncob jelly, whistle pig and poke sallet, apple butter and stack cakes. These are all elements of a food culture that once thrived in the mountains, and now faces a tenuous and uncertain future. One of Joe Dabney's many gifts in this big book is the documentation and preservation of a vanishing way of life, for the everlasting benefit of future generations.

All along the way, he is generous to a fault in giving credit to the great multitude of cooks and writers from whose works he has drawn. Not only in the hundreds of assembled recipes but in his narrative and in a bibliography of more than 250 books, Dabney repeatedly acknowledges with gratitude the many food-loving Southerners and others whose previous labors made his work easier. The end result is a highly readable volume, filled from cover to cover with priceless resources. As a reference book no less than a cookbook, *Smokehouse Ham, Spoon Bread & Scuppernong Wine* should have a long and useful life on library shelves and kitchen shelves wherever there survives a reverence for cookery and culture.

Aunt Jane and Eliza Hall and all the faithful denizens of Southern Appalachia must be properly honored by the arrival of this new contribution to the formal record of their time and place among us. And so should be all of us who believe in the merits of history.

—John Egerton

Preface to the Tenth-Anniversary Edition

It came as something of a shock, to say the least, when the dust jacket of this book was flashed on the big screen at the glittering 1999 James Beard Foundation awards ceremony in New York, and the presenter from KitchenAid announced that *Smokehouse Ham, Spoon Bread & Scuppernong Wine* was the winner of the cookbook of the year award.

It was then that I suddenly remembered that the Beard people had written me earlier, something to the effect that, if I should be lucky enough to win one of the prestigious awards, I would be expected to give a fifteen-second acceptance speech. As I looked up on the stage in the distance, there stood Jacques Pepin, holding the big James Beard medal, ready to hang it around my neck. *Lord have mercy!* For a country boy from Georgia this was indeed "high cotton."

After I composed myself, I said then what I would like to say again in the brief preface to this tenth-anniversary edition: I would like to once again express my heartfelt appreciation to the generous and always gracious people across the Southeastern hill country—upwards of a hundred of them—who opened their homes and their hearts to me, along with their hand-me-down recipes, their glorious food, and their ever-present expressions of kindness and goodwill. Without them, this book would never have seen the light of day.

I mentioned at the Beard ceremony what Chris Boatwright, then almost a hundred years old, of Holly Creek near the Cohutta Mountains had said to me as we were wrapping up an interview: "Well, Joe, have I learned you anything?"

The New York audience seemed puzzled. I guess I should have elaborated a bit, that with the Beard medal I would be able to tell Chris and all the others that they had, indeed, "learned" me a lot.

Chris Boatwright has since gone on to his reward, along, I regret, with so many of the others pictured herein. But I am happy that their stories and recipes will continue to live on in the pages of this book, which, thanks to Cumberland House president and publisher Ron Pitkin, is getting a great new lease on life. Thank you one and all and God bless.

—Joseph E. Dabney
July 2008

Acknowledgments

It would have been impossible for to me to have considered taking on a project like *Smokehouse Ham* without the knowledge that I could call on many old and new friends for interviews, recipes, photographs, and particularly for guidance and counsel.

I am grateful to a number of individuals who shared with me their knowledge of mountain lore and gave unstintingly in many ways. I am extremely grateful for the help that came from mountain man supreme Curtis Underwood of Resaca, Georgia, an enthusiastic connoisseur of all facets of Southern Appalachian life, including experience running a restaurant, hunting down wild hogs, operating a moonshine still, and getting to know many of the old-timers around the Blue Ridge Divide in Fannin, Gilmer, Lumpkin, and Dawson counties, particularly mountain patriarchs such as John Will Bailey.

Retired Western Carolina University professor Duane Oliver also was a great resource. Oliver's Appalachian roots run deep. His great-great-great-grandfather, John Oliver, in 1820 became the first white settler in Cades Cove, Tennessee. Duane Oliver himself grew up on fabled Hazel Creek, North Carolina, where his great-great-grandfather, Moses Proctor, had been the first non-Indian settler.

Several other individuals gave me valuable guidance and assistance from the very beginning: former state senator William G. Hasty Sr. of Canton, Georgia; Gilmer County native Mark Woody of Woodstock, Georgia; and my former Lockheed colleague Carl Dodd of Blue Ridge, Georgia. Another Lockheed retiree, Dan Westmoreland of Ellijay, Georgia, provided invaluable photo assistance and introduced me to Larry Davis of Ellijay, who helped me in so many ways I can't count them all, including locating people for me to interview in Gilmer County.

Several authors of books on the mountains and mountain cooking were especially helpful. Mark Sohn of Pikeville, Kentucky, author of *Mountain Country Cooking*, gave me valuable assistance, including reviewing part of the manuscript. Mark also shared several of his recipes with me. Other authors who shared advice, quotes, and recipes include my friend Nathalie Dupree, Atlanta's guru of public television cooking; historian John Egerton of Nashville, Tennessee, "the culinary mouth of the South"; Sidney Saylor Farr of Berea, Kentucky; Edna Lewis of Atlanta; John Rice Irwin of Norris, Tennessee; John Parris of Sylva, North Carolina; Rose Houk of Flagstaff, Arizona; Celestine Sibley of Atlanta; Kay Moss and Kathryn Hoffman of Gastonia, North Carolina; Marie Mellinger of Clayton, Georgia; former Georgia governor Zell Miller of Atlanta; John Martin Taylor of Charleston, South Carolina; Betsy Tice White of Marble Hill, Georgia; Nancy Blanche Cooper of Gatlinburg, Tennessee; Ronni Lundy of Louisville, Kentucky; Anne Dismukes Amerson of Dahlonega, Georgia; Kathy Thompson of Blue Ridge, Georgia; Walter Lambert of Knoxville, Tennessee; Lynda and Hank Kellner of Asheville,

North Carolina; Damon Lee Fowler of Savannah, Georgia; and Mrs. Earl Palmer of Christiansburg, Virginia.

Valuable "recipe testing" was provided by Diane Gibson of Smyrna, Georgia; Lib Dabney of Jackson, South Carolina; Jeanette Dabney of Rock Hill, South Carolina; Dottie Woody of Woodstock, Georgia; Michael Humphrey of Clarkesville, Georgia; Opal Gudger of Ellijay, Georgia; Charlene Terrell of Big Canoe, Georgia; Martha Hopkins of Ellijay, Georgia; and Frank Pressley of Lakeland, Georgia.

Scores of wonderful folk gave me valuable in-depth interviews.

I spent an enjoyable day plus numerous telephone interviews with Frank Pressley, who grew up at Cullowhee, North Carolina, and who now resides in Lakeland, Georgia.

The late Oscar Cannon, of Turner's Corner, who fiddled his way through the north Georgia hill country at the turn of the century and after (but never after midnight on a Saturday night), gave me an insightful overview of life in the hills eighty years ago.

An interview with seventy-six-year-old Hazel French Farmer, who plays Maybell in the mountain musical *Reach of Song*, was insightful. Hazel showed me that she not only puts up jellies, jams, fruits, and vegetables, she also knows how to handle firearms. She pulled out her shotguns to show me how she could yet today bring down wild turkeys or deer that venture out of the woods onto her pasturelands off north Georgia's Skenna Gap Road. "And by the way," she told me with a big laugh, "I still do leather-britches (beans)."

On Holly Creek Road, in the shadow of the Cohutta Mountain chain, Mr. and Mrs. Chris Boatwright shared details about how to get the most out of groundhog and a pot of fireplace-cooked beans. Chris, a onetime harmonica player, gave me his rendition of "The Groundhog Song."

Ninety-year-old Goingback Chiltoskey, the grand old man of the Cherokee Qualla Reservation, patiently gave me his time as he carved his wooden masterpieces at his elegant homestead on the banks of the Oconoluftee River that he occupies with his wife, the former Mary Ulmer. Mary—the gentle former educator and author—gave me permission to use some of the recipes from her book *Cherokee Cooklore*. Other North Carolinians who gave valuable interviews and assistance were Beuna Winchester, Bryson City; Bill Dwyer, son of the late Bil and Louise Dwyer of Highlands; Doug Reed, Cullowhee; Tom Dabney, Eleanor Hall, and Cynthia Bright, Asheville; Bill Millsaps, Robbinsville; Mrs. Georgia Tatum, Canton; Jean and Jim Hartbarger, operators of the Jarrett House, Dillsboro; Tom Robbins, Bryson City; and Doug and Barbara Brown, operators of the Nu-Wray Inn, Burnsville.

I will never forget the silver-haired, gentle, and mannerly Mrs. Azzie Waters of East Ellijay, Georgia, who gave me an interview and proudly showed off her wood-burning Home Comfort stove that comforted her with its warm glow on cold winter days. (That is, up until recently when she had to move in with her daughter next door.) Interviews, recipes, and help came from a number of other Gilmer County people, including Nina Garrett, Frances Gates Hill, Martha Hopkins, Rilla Chastain Nelson, Barbara Southern, Bess Dover Pache, Merle Weaver, Ophia Osborn McAmis, Bonnie Weaver Norris, Julia Evatt, Ernest Parker, James Lock, Frank Elliott, Ruby Mooney, Eva Sellers, Mrs. Dorsey Mulkey Jones, Sam Gates, and Arvil Wilson.

In Fannin County, Georgia, in addition to the aforementioned Carl Dodd, invaluable help came from Gary and Dawn Davis, Hattie Cochran, Loni Tuttle Millan, Jean Henry Zachary, Blue Ridge, and Mrs. Virginia Underwood, who shared a number of recipes from her recipe collection *Georgia Mountain Heritage*.

Other Georgians who gave valuable assistance include my brother, Dr. C. A. Dabney, Augusta; Dr. Sam Talmadge, Athens; John and Emily Anthony, Sautee; Mamie Atkinson, Flowery Branch; Leon Colwell, Blairsville; David and Betty Jo Bailey, Adairsville; J. R. Coker, Woodstock; Melvin and Ruth Swanson Hunter, Young Harris; Phil Hudgins, Athens; Ruth King Martin, Rome; the late Dallas Byess, Jasper; Marion Hemperley, Fayetteville; Jane Massey, Alpharetta; Bob Cloer, Atlanta; John LaRowe, Clarkesville; Wayne Daniel, Chamblee; Ethelene Dyer Jones, Epworth; John and Jane Fleetwood, Cartersville; Mrs Gene Wiggins, Dahlonega; George Houdeshel, Blairsville; Tim Howard, Chatsworth; Marilyn Pennington, Smyrna; John Humphrey, Talking Rock; Bill Kinsland, Dahlonega; Bobby Sutton, Douglasville; Evelyn Croft, Acworth; Susie Waters West, Ellijay; Ann and Maurice Farrabee, Blairsville; Don Shadburn, Cumming; Jack Stillman, Jasper; Dr. Charles Walker, Jasper; Vinnie Williams, Watkinsville; June Smith, Alpharetta; Mrs. Daisy Thompson, Norcross; Charles Jenkins, Blairsville; Johnny Vardeman, James Mathis, and Mrs. M. R. Perry, Gainesville; Jimmy Anderson, Dahlonega; Steve Whitmire, Cumming; Anne Dismukes Amerson, Dahlonega; Mrs. Ethel Spruill, Dunwoody; Virginia Underwood, Cherrylog; Bettie Sellers, the Georgia poet laureate, Young Harris; and Ronnie Silcox, University of Georgia Extension Service, Athens.

I am appreciative of the families of four deceased whiskey- and wine-makers who gave me interviews a decade or more ago: Simmie Free of Tiger, Georgia; Theodore King of Mars Hill, North Carolina; Buck Carver of Dillard, Georgia; and Maude Thacker of Tate, Georgia.

Valuable archival assistance came from historical societies, archives, and libraries. Special thanks are due to Annette Hartigan of the Smoky Mountains National Park, Gatlinburg, Tennessee; Ann Wright and Zoe Raine of the North Carolina room, Pack Memorial Public Library, Asheville, North Carolina; George Frizzell of the Hunter Library, Western Carolina University, Cullowhee, North Carolina; Norma Myers and Ned Irwin of the Sherrod Library, East Tennessee State University, Johnson City, Tennessee; Museum of the Cherokee Indian, Cherokee, North Carolina; John Rice Irwin, the Museum of Appalachia, Norris, Tennessee; Georgia Department of Archives and History, Atlanta;

historical societies of Gilmer County, Bartow County, and Union County, Georgia; Hurley Badders of the Pendleton, South Carolina, Historical Society; Anita Summers, librarian at the Gilmer County Library, Ellijay, Georgia; and the dedicated librarians in the DeKalb County Library System's branches at Dunwoody, Chamblee, and Brookhaven. Dr. Bobby Gilmer Moss, retired professor at Limestone College, gave me great help on the history of Scotch-Irish people who populated Southern Appalachia.

For the section on wild game, I am indebted to the University of Georgia Extension Service, and particularly to Jeffrey Jackson and Catharine Sigman, who compiled a comprehensive booklet of wild game recipes and directions for dressing game and fowl for cooking.

I greatly appreciate the kind assistance given me by Mrs. Evelyn Palmer of Christiansburg, Virginia, who graciously provided photos taken by her late husband, Earl Palmer, the great "photographer of the Appalachians." I also wish to thank Mrs. Martha Barnhill Horner of Gainesville, Florida, who granted permission for the use of the William Barnhill photos at the Pack Memorial Public Library in Asheville, North Carolina.

To my wife, Susanne, I appreciate beyond measure her dedicated proofreading and also her work in copying photos that were lent to me.

And to the dedicated staff at Cumberland House Publishing—led by president Ron Pitkin—who gave strong support for the manuscript from the very beginning and followed through with tender loving care, I am deeply grateful.

To these wonderful folk and to many others who are not singled out, my most sincere thanks and appreciation.

SMOKEHOUSE HAM, SPOON BREAD & SCUPPERNONG WINE

Introduction

One who has watched the family at fodder-pulling time, high up on the mountainside, and has heard floating down from that sunny space to the shadowed valley…the echoes of some hymn or song, feels himself apart in an enchanted land.

—*John C. Campbell,* The Southern
Highlander and His Homeland

~

There may well be as much to learn about a nation from the food and drink its people consume as from the laws it passes and the wars it fights… for food and drink are daily matters that intimately reflect the spirit and tastes of a people.

—Washington Post *review by Jonathan Yardley
of author's* Mountain Spirits

During the early 1930s—when the soul of the nation was drooping low and the Great Depression was beginning to take its economic and spiritual toll—my father, who had extended credit to the entire community, it seemed, was forced to give up what had been his flourishing grocery business in the little textile town of Kershaw, South Carolina.

Pushed into a heart-rending bankruptcy, and with a heavy heart, he closed the doors to his store building up the hill from the Springs mill, loaded his wife, Wincey, and five sons into his A-model Ford and a borrowed truck, and moved 150 miles to a Blue Ridge foothills farm northeast of Greenville. My brother Arthur, twelve at the time and ten years my senior, felt that the reason Dad took such a drastic step, hauling his big brood to what seemed to be the other end of the universe, was to get the family near our oldest sibling, Geneva, then in nurse's training at Greenville's General Hospital. Or perhaps to be near Uncle Gilmore, a Greenville insurance man, said brother Connie.

In any event, the place where we landed, the Spart Dill farm in the shadow of Paris Mountain and near South Carolina's "Dark Corner," became the savior of our family. Pretty soon my enterprising and hard-working father—with the help of my older brothers who ranged up to eighteen years in age—started making a bale of cotton to the acre on those rolling red clay fields and began harvesting bumper crops of corn and hay. Next to Dad's nice patch of roast'n'ear corn, probably the greatest boost to our bellies was his growing pen of pigs that would fill his smokehouse, plus his double-barrel twelve-gauge shotgun that brought us plenty of rabbits and squirrels from the nearby woods. That and my mother's steadfast and daily prayers, her milk cow, and her bountiful garden that yielded fresh vegetables galore—cabbage, tomatoes, beans, and the like.

> *W*ithin the boundaries of this [Southern Appalachian] territory are included the four western counties of Maryland; the Blue Ridge, Valley, and Allegheny Ridge counties of Virginia; all of West Virginia; eastern Tennessee; eastern Kentucky; western North Carolina; the four northwestern counties of South Carolina; northern Georgia; and northeastern Alabama. Our mountain region, of approximately 112,000 square miles, embraces an area nearly as large as the combined areas of New York and New England, and almost equal to that of England, Scotland, Ireland, and Wales.
> —John C. Campbell, *The Southern Highlander and His Homeland*

Within a couple of years, the tide was turned. As a Tennessee newspaper reported about the same time (1932), there may have been a depression going on across America, but not in our kitchen!

Thus, while cash was scarce on that first Christmas season at our weathered frame home in the Double Springs community, there was plenty of pork and squirrel meat to go around, and biscuits and fresh butter and corn bread and buttermilk and kraut and canned vegetables and sorghum syrup as well as an abundance of love and affection. Looking back, it was a wonderful combination for survival, and I thank the Lord above for such strong, loving, and persevering parents.

⁓

My quest for the quintessential Appalachian foods, their folk history, and Appalachian personalities with an ear for the past got its start—at least the idea came—when I pondered offering a piece for the Sunday "True South" column of my old paper in the 1960s, the *Atlanta Journal-Constitution*. It was a nice little feature that allowed southeastern freelancers to reminisce about and relish many subjects of our rural past, including time-honored Southern foods such as redeye gravy, butter beans, fried corn, and skillet-baked corn bread—foods that 90 percent of senior Southerners outside Atlanta grew up on. But the little column became a "gone with the wind" discard as the city geared up to host the 1996 Summer Olympics.

My musings set me to thinking about my own Scotch-Irish and French roots and the heritage of the people of the southeastern mountains, particularly how they and their foods came to be. During the subsequent three years, I learned a lot. This book is the result.

⁓

A sense of place sets Southern Appalachian people apart. Those who leave their ancestral homeplace for any length of time—such as those who go to the industrial cities up north—experience a bittersweet tug; their hearts and thoughts invariably return to their family roots—to where they grew up. Many return in person as often as possible.

As Sidney Saylor Farr noted in her eloquent *More Than Moonshine*, "What people who live in today's transient society don't seem to understand about us mountain folks is that it's possible to put one's roots down so deeply they cannot be satisfactorily transplanted anywhere else…take us anywhere in the world and there will always be pain in the missing part buried so deeply in hillside soil."

The Native Americans, particularly the Cherokees, were the first to develop a deep affection for the Appalachians. They called the area Shaconage—mountains of the blue smoke—and they wanted to live here forever. When the U.S. government told them to get out in the 1830s, they left kicking and screaming at the points of army bayonets. A thousand of them hid out in the far recesses of the Smoky Mountains and lived off nuts and roots until it was safe to come out. Their proud descendants today occupy the Cherokee reservation straddling the gentle, rock-bedded Oconoluftee River in the shadow of the Smokies.

The first white man to reach the Blue Ridge, in 1540, Spain's Hernando de Soto, was deeply impressed also. He loved the grandeur of the country around pres-ent-day Highlands, North Carolina. His troops forded the Little Tennessee River as they headed west to Franklin and beyond. De Soto called the mountains "Appalachees," and the name stuck, at least its derivative. With no gold evident, de Soto didn't linger long.

Eager European settlers who rolled down Virginia's Great Valley in the 1700s to occupy lands being reluctantly vacated by the Cherokees—land-hungry Scotch-Irish, war-saddened Germans, as well as English, Scot, and French descendants

I don't know how to tell you of its indescribable beauty. You are in the midst of hills in every direction. There seems no end to them. And as you drive slowly down the road, there are openings in the trees through which you look off over sweet, swelling valleys…On a clear winter day, when the trees are stripped bare of leaves, I can climb the slope back of our house and look out across five ridges, each rising a little higher than the one before, and I can see the sun glinting on the tin roof of a barn over on the last ridge. In between, the mists will be rising, like pale smoke, hugging close to the streams down in the hollows.
—JANICE HOLT GILES, *40 ACRES AND NO MULE*

moving inland from the seaboard—were visibly moved by what they found. Many wrote to relatives back home to tell of the "Cherokee Mountains" and foothills, a land even more magnificent than what they and their ancestors had left in the old country across the Atlantic. They found a world of rolling hills, verdant valleys, bold streams and virgin forests, a grandeur of hardwoods—hundred-foot-tall chestnuts, great walnuts, poplars, hickories, and oaks. "In the fall of the year," wrote Presbyterian missionary James Watt Raine, "the autumn foliage lights up these mountains with a many-hued magnificence… while above, in the magic blueness of a mysterious sky, the ever burgeoning clouds reflect all the silken tintings of the celestial hosts."

One writer called the half-billion-year-old weathered mountain chain "a glorious analogue of the true Scotch-Irishman's heart and nature." William Trotter rhapsodized even more eloquently in *Bushwhackers.**

> As you approach the western reaches of the central Piedmont, your eye is seduced, first by the hazy blue foothills, an almost melodic landscape. The farther west you travel the higher the land rises, and the more dramatic the vistas. Distances melt into further distances, and serried undulations of vast whale-backed ridges draw the eye and the spirit deeper into the mystery of the landscape. The land's pervading sense of antiquity is now serene, now brooding and dark. In places, the terrain is raw, harsh, plunging…indifferent to human frailty. In other places, the vastness is gentled and rendered into poetry by the time-worn roundness of its contours…No matter how beautiful is the spot on which you're standing, there is always another enticement of beauty somewhere beyond…Each receding wave of ridges seems to beckon like a promise whispered in a dream. Whatever the hungry soul yearns for—land, peace, beauty, the slowing of Time itself—the blue-veiled coves and crystalline streams, perfumed by the dark, emerald cold scent of balsam, fir and mountain laurel, must surely hold it…somewhere in its depths.

In my research and forays over the region, I received instructive insight into our Southern Appalachian foods, particularly the nourishing dishes we inherited from the Amerindians—those based on corn and beans and pumpkins and squash, just for starters. I learned the region's English and Scotch and Irish food heritage is also rich, particularly the puddings and stack cakes and pies, to say nothing of mountain folk's insatiable love for pork in all of its many dimensions. From the German migrants, of course, came wonderful dumplings and krauts, apple butters, deep-dish pies, and those wonderful Moravian cakes and cookies. I will go into details later.

What was perhaps the greatest joy that came from my Southern Appalachian odyssey

---

*John F. Blair, publisher

was getting to know a wonderful potpourri of people, descendants of the sturdy Scotch-Irish, English, and German pioneers who settled the region over two centuries before. People such as Chris Boatwright of Holly Creek, in north Georgia, who told me about timbering the Cohutta Mountains in the 1920s and who sang "The Ground Hog Song" for me. As I got up to leave following the last visit, Chris—nearing a hundred years old—asked sweetly, "Have I learned you anything, Joe?"

Scores of gracious folk such as Chris Boatwright shared with me their past lives and their foods and recipes. I already knew a lot about foothills cooking from my mother's Carolina kitchen and from having gorged on those great meals at Mrs. Donahoo's Boarding House on Cherokee Street in Cartersville, Georgia, during my misspent youth.

It was mid-summer, 1944, on this "two-horse farm" in Lancaster County, South Carolina. The author, Joe Dabney, then fifteen, admires the lush growth of cotton with his father, Wade V. Dabney. Fresh vegetables were abundant on the upstate farm.

Everywhere I visited during my three years of research—and I zeroed in quite a bit on Gilmer County, Georgia, with the valuable help of my friend Larry Davis—I found that food and cooking were and are basic elements of the "sense of place" among mountain people. Anyone who leaves the region soon yearns for the foods he grew up on. That was my experience when I awoke in my Pusan, Korea, Quonset hut on Christmas Day, 1951; my thoughts returned to my home and family in South Carolina and the luscious Japanese fruitcake that my mother always cooked for us. Plus, of course, all the pork dishes from year-end hog killings.

So while this book is basically about food, really it's about people.

I hope you enjoy these chapters and characters as much as I enjoyed researching them. As Simmie Free, my late, great *Mountain Spirits* friend from Tiger, Georgia, told me over two decades ago when I was writing an earlier book, "Joe, folks are shore going to enjoy it when you get that book built." I could have no fonder hope.

The Folklore

The People
America's Great Melting Pot

The Seasons
"To Everything There Is a Season"

The Social Life
From Work Frolics to "Bran Dances," a Spirit of Joy

The People
America's Great Melting Pot

March of the Celts Down the Great Wagon Road

On my father's side were Germans, blue eyes. On Mother's side they was a lot of them that was redheaded, most likely Scotch-Irish.
                        —*Ruth Swanson Hunter, Young Harris, Georgia*

~

Most of my people were Scotch-Irish. The Scotch-Irish have got a Presbyterian conscience. It won't keep you from sinning, but it'll keep you from enjoying your sin, and it will smite you unmercifully if you don't do what it tells you is right.
                        —*The late North Carolina U.S. senator Sam Irvin,*
                                in Mountain Voices *by Warren Moore*

~

Grandpa Raburn was Red Irish and Grandma Raburn was Black Dutch. 'Course she wasn't dark-skinned. That's just what they called them…Aunt Sara and Uncle Joe Raburn.
                        —*Hazel French Farmer, Union County, Georgia*

It was serendipity. Or perhaps an answer to an author's prayer. Just about the time I was about to give up my quest for a succinct metaphor to describe the human tide of European immigrants that poured down Virginia's Great Valley in the mid 1700s, a moonshiner from the north Georgia hills came to my rescue. His voice boomed forth from two decades before, via an audiotape. After I replayed it, I remembered the day Theodore (Thee) King told me his family history as we sat on the doorsteps of his home just off the square in Blairsville, Georgia.

"Joe," Thee told me, "where I take my flutter mill from—my tongue—is from my mother. She was a redheaded Scotch-Irishman with some German in her for good measure."

While Thee King's gift of blarney could be credited to a Gaelic grandparent, I wondered how it was that his hair was jet black and straight, having none of the Irish reddishness to it, and his skin bore the dark patina of a Lincoln, definitely not Scot ruddy.

"I'm quarter Cherokee," Thee King quickly told me. "My grandpa King was a thoroughbred Cherokee Indian."

Well now. Of course. I could see Thee's Indian-ness. He was tall and lanky and bony. And he had the gait of a Cherokee. It would be easy to picture him a few decades ago looking for a sign in the wilds leading up to Brasstown Bald, rearing up 4,780 feet of blue splendor just to the east.

But the moonshiner's story didn't end there. Thee King, now deceased, who loved to go by the nickname "Doc," wanted me to hear all about the roots of his family tree.

"My grandmother King," he said, "she was a thoroughbred Englishman... and my grandpa Pitt, he was a thoroughbred German." Looking up with a triumphant grin, Theodore winked at me and declared, "Joe, I'm four mixed up; I don't know where I take my sense of reasoning and what little common sense I got, but I believe it's atter the Germans!"

Wow. What a melting pot of a man, carrying just about all the strains of traditional Blue Ridge mountain stock, except perhaps a bit of the French as typified by "Nolichucky Jack" Sevier, Tennessee's first governor, and the Welsh, typified by the greatest American Welshman of all time, the Blue Ridge's own Thomas Jefferson.

I realized that here, in the person of Theodore King, sour mash whiskey-maker supreme, a native of Gum Log, Georgia, was a microcosm of the people who rolled down the Great Philadelphia Wagon Road, beginning around 1720, in their covered wagons—Scotch-Irish, German, and English.

Confederate veteran David Penland of Beech, North Carolina, holds a bucket of his own making, from green bark laced with bark thongs. He was typical of the tough, self-reliant people populating the Southeastern mountain country.

Thee King's Cherokee ancestry added another element to the Appalachian mix. It was the Indians—despite their bloody warrior reputation—whose benevolence provided the basis for many of the Appalachian foods, and whose lessons in hunting and fishing and farming and mountain living were crucial to the survival of the new Americans all the way from the first settlers at Jamestown.

The country we're talking about, of course, and the object of the human juggernaut of Celt migrants who invaded the colonial American interior in the 1700s, was the majestic Southern Appalachians—the country of rolling blue ridges, green valleys, swift flowing streams (by the hundreds), and dark coves by the thousands—all straddling the ancient mountains, a chain whose high peaks rise over six thousand feet, a magnificent complex of hills and valleys formed two million years ago at the beginning of the Pleistocene Ice Age.

*W*hiskey isn't the only thing that's been distilled in these hills. The people are a distillation too, a boiling down of good Scots–Irish stock, refined by mountain summers and winters, and condensed by hard times.
—CHARLES KURALT

The territory soon gained the nickname of "backcountry," particularly among the nouveau riche Tidewater planters who looked down their noses at the region and its settlers. Philadelphia's land speculators envisioned it as America's "Great Southwest" and so did the enthusiastic landseekers. They viewed the Appalachians as a wonderful world to conquer, the splendid and fertile Piedmont "foot of the mountain" country all the way from Pennsylvania down to north Alabama. And on the other side of the chain the verdant Indian hunting grounds that would become Tennessee and Kentucky. The region embraced the western section of Virginia and the future West Virginia, the western end of the Carolinas, and the mountain plateaus extending to Georgia and Alabama. Many mountain offshoots, plateaus, and valleys were part of the majestic mosaic—the Cumberlands, the Alleghenies, the Blue Ridge, the Smokies, the Cohuttas, and Sand Mountain southwest of Chattanooga.

The Great Philadelphia Wagon Road served as the eighteenth-century conduit for the tide of new Americans. Many would later follow Daniel Boone's lead through the Cumberland Gap on the Wilderness Road into Kentucky and south down the Holston and Watauga Rivers into Tennessee.

But the nation's busiest thoroughfare was the Wagon Road—a 435-mile stretch surveyed by Peter Jefferson from Philadelphia down the Great Valley of Virginia to North Carolina's Yadkin River. Generally, it followed the route of the Iroquois' Great Warrior's Path along the valley of the Shenandoah, "Daughter of the Stars" in Iroquois. The road picked up the Cherokee Trading Path from Salisbury, North Carolina, south on to Mecklenburg County and eventually to Augusta, Georgia.

Southbound traffic in the early 1770s soared to tens of thousands of wagons, horses, and humans, becoming the heaviest-traveled road in the continent.* As Carl Bridenbaugh wrote, the road "must have had more vehicles jolting along its rough and tortuous way than all other main roads put together," crowded with "horsemen, footmen, and pioneer families with horse and wagon and cattle."

The tide gained great momentum following the Cherokee defeat at the hands of the British in 1761.

Two years later, the French and Indian War, which had kept the frontiers tense, came to an end. In 1768, the Iroquois gave up land claims.

"Over the mountains, through the gaps, down the watershed they came," wrote Wilma Dykeman, Tennessee's eminent historian, "Scotch-Irish, English, German, low Dutch and occasionally French Huguenots...in their search of what they called the Southwest."

The late Simmie Free was happiest sitting on his front porch at Tiger, Georgia, admiring his valley and mountain spread. He was a descendant of Scotch-Irish migrants from Pennsylvania, Virginia, and North Carolina, typical of the hardy Europeans populating the Southern Appalachians in the eighteenth century.

Leading the eighteenth-century Celts on their relentless march southward were the Scotch-Irish from Ulster, Northern Ireland, or as some would call them, "Irish Protestants." Michael Frome characterized the early settlers as "a breed who loved their roving room, room to breathe, to hunt, to wander at will, who were democratic by nature, resenting implications of social superiority…"

By 1720, the Ulster Presbyterians were arriving at East Coast ports by the boatloads, especially at Philadelphia. Most all, it seemed, were eager to claim the cheap lands and taste the freedoms that America would give them. James Logan, soon to become Pennsylvania's governor, declared in 1725 that "it looks

---

*A Presbyterian clergyman in 1775 told of seeing "many every day traveling to Carolina, some on foot with packs and some in large covered wagons. The road here is much frequented."

as if Ireland were to send all her inhabitants…Last week there were no less than six ships…" Many of them came as indentured servants, pledging to work for a few years to pay for their passage, at which time they struck out to find land. Early arrivals liked what they found. On November 3, 1735, Benjamin Franklin's *Pennsylvania Gazette* gave page-one play to a letter from an American Scotch-Irish schoolmaster to his minister, Reverend Baptist Boyd back in County Tyrone:

> *These dark Smoky Mountains remember your name—*
> *remember when first the Logue family came—*
> *when Scots-Irish fiddles first shattered the still,*
> *as lonesome and high as these Tennessee hills.*
> *Those wild Celtic spirits from over the sea*
> *still wander these woods with the dark Cherokee.*
> —ROBERT ASHLEY LOGUE,
> SUMNER COUNTY, TENNESSEE

> I will tell ye in short, this is a bonny Country, and aw Things grows here that ever I did see grow in Ereland; and we hea Cows, and Sheep, and Horses plenty here, and Goats, and Deers, and Raccoons, and Moles, and Bevers, and Fish, and Fouls of aw Sorts…Ye may get Lan here for 10(Lbs) a Hundred Acres for ever, and Ten Years Time tell ye get the Money, before they wull ask ye for it…I wull bring ye aw wee my sel…fear ne the See, trust in God, and he wull bring ye safe to Shore.

The Scottish Lowlander ancestors had crossed the Irish Sea to Northern Ireland in the early 1600s at the behest of King James. He wanted them to conquer the "wild Irish," and extend his Calvinist Presbyterian faith. They proceeded to do just that, at the same time turning Ulster into a thriving and industrious land. But in the decades to follow, the Ulstermen turned bitterly resentful; they felt betrayed by British rulers who exacted severe "rack rents," and prohibited the Ulstermen from selling their woolen and linen goods to Britain. The worst insult of all, the state squelched their John Knox Presbyterianism.

Out of their persecution came an Ulsterman, according to Constance Lindsay Skinner, who arrived in America "high principled and narrow, strong and violent, as tenacious of his own rights as he was blind often to the rights of others, acquisitive yet self-sacrificing, but most of all fearless, confident of his own power, determined to have and to hold."

One of the prayers attributed to the Scotch-Irish was insightful: "Lord grant that I may always be right, for thou knowest I am hard to turn."

While their immediate objective in the new world was land, their overriding goal was total freedom. Yet they sometimes went overboard in their boldness. It was said of them that they were wont to "keep the Sabbath and everything else they could lay their lands on." Virginia's William Byrd—who sought unsuccessfully to recruit Swiss immigrants to his North Carolina lands—sought to shun the Scotch-Irish, comparing them to "the Goths and Vandals of old."

The Great Philadelphia Wagon Road, surveyed by Peter Jefferson, was the great population artery for European migrants—Scotch-Irish, Germans, and English—who rolled and walked south to claim land in the Shenandoah Valley, the Carolina Piedmont and mountain country, and through the Wilderness Road into Kentucky and Tennessee.

The aforementioned James Logan, an Ulsterman, advised William Penn in 1720 to send some Scotch-Irish to Pennsylvania's western flank as a shield against hostile Indians: "We were under some apprehension from the Northern (Iroquois) Indians…I therefore thought it might be prudent to plant a settlement of such men as those who formerly had so bravely defended Londonderry and Inniskillen as a frontier, in case of any disturbance."

A year later Logan had second thoughts. His Ulster countrymen, it seemed, in an "audacious and disorderly manner," swarmed onto a fifteen-thousand-acre tract in Conestoga and Gettysburg reserved for the Penn family. They declared it "against the laws of God and nature that so much land should be idle while so many Christians wanted it to labor on and raise their bread."

So down the Great Valley of Virginia they rolled in the decades to follow, "strong in wanderlust and individuality," riding their beribboned and belled Conestoga wagons in relentless pursuit of their dreams of absolute liberty. Thomas Jefferson expressed thanks for the Scotch-Irish who "formed a barrier which none could leap" in the valley between the Blue Ridge and the North Mountain.

While the Ulstermen were the dominant and boldest strain on the frontier thrust, being described as "the flying column of the nation," they shared the busy Wagon Road with thousands of Germans and English and Welsh who were headed south on the same mission.*

Destined to become the most famous Appalachian settler of English stock was a young lad

> *T*he Woodruff Family was Black Dutch…It's a term everybody in the mountains knows and identifies with tall, angular featured people like Pa and Abraham Lincoln.
>
> —FLORENCE COPE BUSH,
> DORIE: WOMAN OF THE MOUNTAINS

named Daniel Boone who had grown up in Berks County, Pennsylvania. His father, Squire Boone, son of an Englishman, and his mother, Sarah Morgan, of Welsh descent, took their family, including sixteen-year-old Daniel, on the Wagon Road south in 1750 after a dispute with their church. Two of Daniel's siblings had been ousted by the Quakers for marrying outside the church. A furious Squire Boone took his family to North Carolina's Yadkin River Valley.

Daniel himself, at age sixteen, already was showing signs of his explorer's bent. Before leaving Pennsylvania, he absorbed frontier lore from the Indians who patronized his grandfather's six-loom weaving shop. Upon receiving his first rifle at age twelve, he quickly became a skilled marksman on the hunt. Arriving in North Carolina, Daniel found himself in nature's wild heaven, a frontier full of game plus acres and acres of glorious hills, rivers, coves, and valleys to explore. In no time he assumed the Scotch-Irish wanderlust that took him deeper and deeper into the wilds. In later years, he opened up the Wilderness Road through the Cumberland Gap to Kentucky, always moving ahead of civilization.

While other "Appalachian Pilgrims" of English, Welsh, and Scot stock helped to fill up the Appalachian interior, it was the war-weary Germans—superior farmers, skilled craftsmen and expert gunsmiths who became the region's solid, sturdy backbone. Calling themselves "Deutsche" (German), they came to be known as "Pennsylvania Dutch." The term came to be used by many to embrace not only the Palatinate Rhineland Germans but also the Swiss and the French Huguenots who sailed to America at the invitation of William Penn.

---

*The Russell Sage Foundation found that of the thousands of settlers swarming into the North Carolina interior prior to the Revolution, the Scotch-Irish made up 30 percent of the total; the English, who were coming across from the coast as well as down the Wagon Road, made up another 30 percent, while the German immigrant settlers totaled 15 percent.

The Germans in particular were happy to get away from war. Their Rhenish region had repeatedly been run over by French troops as Louis XIV tried to seize Germany's Rhineland that is now part of Bavaria. Thousands were driven from their homes in the bitter cold of winter. Britain's Queen Anne—eager to get Protestants hostile to France and Spain in her colonies—invited the German war refugees to settle in America. Upward of 150,000 Rhinelanders headed to America, most to the port of Philadelphia.* Along with the poor who came in the mass exodus from Europe were some of Germany's finest citizens. Joseph Bach, a cousin of Johann Sebastian, arrived in America with his family in 1770 and later settled in Kentucky.

Strength of character shows in the faces of Henry Elbert (Ebb) and Melinda Emaline Blackwell of the Bucktown district of Gilmer County in north Georgia. They posed for this photograph around 1890.

The German refugees—nearly all devout Christians, Lutheran, German Reformed, or Moravian—found America's religious freedom and cheap frontier lands to be glorious gifts of God. They prayed often and with feeling, thanking the Almighty for their newfound homeland.

No one relished the religious freedom more than the Moravians who came to America with their "apostle," Count Zinzendorf, as missionaries to Native Americans. A pious religious sect, the Moravians moved from Pennsylvania to western North Carolina in 1752 to settle the magnificent 100,000-acre "Wachovia Tract." Soon there emerged an amazing business and religious community that they named Salem ("Peace"). The Moravians staffed their community with superlative professionals—physicians, teachers, merchants—as well as skilled craftsmen...weavers, spinners, cobblers, tinsmiths, gunsmiths,

---

*The mass exodus from Europe around 1720 was accelerated by events such as France's Revocation of the Edict of Nantes, subjecting European Protestants to renewed Catholic persecution, including by guillotine. Earlier, William Penn made a personal recruiting trip to Europe to encourage European immigration to Pennsylvania.

and potters, along with great cooks who built brick-lined ovens to turn out scrumptious loaves of bread and cakes for their religious love feasts…and to sell. These industrious folk—along with ministers and missionaries—became a great resource to people across the backcountry, including the Cherokees. The Indians loved to visit Salem, calling it a place "where there are good people and much bread."

The Moravian accomplishments—including an advanced waterworks system—gained widespread fame, including a visit from the peripatetic Anglican missionary from Charleston, Rev. Charles Woodmason. "The spot is not only Rich, fertile, and luxuriant, but the most Romantic in nature…delightfully charming! Rocks, Cascades, Hills, Vales, Groves, Plains—Woods, Waters all most strangely intermixt, so that Imagination cannot paint anything more vivid. They have Mills, Furnaces, Forges, Potteries, Foundries All Trades and all things in and among themselves…they are all Bees, not a Drone suffer'd in the Hive."

> *The North of Ireland has been occasionally used to emigration, for which the American settlements have been much beholden: But till now, it was chiefly the very meanest of people who went off, mostly in the station of indented servants and such as had become obnoxious to their mother country. In short, it is computed from many concurrent circumstances, that the North of Ireland has in the last five or six years been drained of one fourth of its trading class, and the like proportion of the manufacturing people. Where the evil will end, remains only in the womb of time to determine.*
>
> —LONDONDERRY JOURNAL,
> NORTHERN IRELAND, APRIL 1773

In the years leading to 1776, settlers continued to swarm into the Appalachian interior, "for the mospart Irish Protestants and Germans, and dayley increasing." In 1765 alone, more than a thousand immigrant wagons passed through Salisbury, and the population of the North Carolina interior rose to sixty thousand settlers. South Carolina's back settlements reached eighty-three thousand people, three-fourths of the colony's white population. By the time Thomas Jefferson penned his immortal words calling for severing the colony's ties to England, over a quarter million settlers had moved into the Appalachian interior. All told, from Pennsylvania to Georgia, Ulster Americans totaled nearly a half million hardy souls. Patrick "Give Me Liberty" Henry and his fellow Scotch-Irish led the backcountry rebellion, and lined up the Palatine Germans,

French Huguenots, and backcountry English to the Patriot cause. In 1772, the Watauga Association in east Tennessee adopted a Declaration of Independence that, according to Theodore Roosevelt, "was the first ever adopted by a community of Americans." Similar declarations followed in Abingdon, Virginia; Boonesboro, Kentucky; and, in 1775, in North Carolina with its Mecklenburg Resolves. The Scotch-Irish role in the revolution was critical. In London, King George III fumed that the resistance in the colonies was "a Presbyterian war."

As I wrote in my earlier book, *Mountain Spirits*, the Crown's strategy in seeking to squelch the revolution was to attack the colonies from the seaboard cities and use the Indians to contain the backcountry. The Indians needed no persuading. Their hatred for the Ulstermen was already at fever pitch for settler incursions into their borders. For two decades the frontier blazed with battles between the two. In the Watauga area of northeast Tennessee, a screaming band of Cherokees, led by Dragging Canoe and Oconostota, attacked frontier settlements. John (Nolichucky Jack) Sevier and Isaac Shelby led 210 mountain fighters in repulsing the attack. Sevier then took the offensive, becoming a mountain hero for his spirited leadership. As he would lead an attack, his yell, "Here they are! Come on Boys!" became a part of mountain folklore.

In 1774, farther north at Point Pleasant, a young Virginia Scotsman, Andrew Lewis, led a band of "long knife" riflemen in a crushing defeat of Chief Cornstalk and his Shawnees. Samuel Tyndale Wilson noted that in skirmishes from Georgia to Virginia, the frontiersmen "swept in retributive wrath upon the Tory-led Indians, and dealt them such a blow as extorted from them an unwilling but at least a temporary peace."

I'm Scotch-Irish; can't you tell? All Irish have black hair and red mustaches. My father had gray hair, but his mustache was red. Wasn't scared of nothing. My daddy, old man Early up here, and old man Madison, they all come to this country same time. Took two months to come across the water.

My daddy was always a farmer. All of us boys were farmers. Our pa loved to fox-hunt. He always kept seven or eight hound dogs all the time. Ever hear a fox hunt? Better than a gang of niggers singing. Yes, sir, I like to hear 'em.

The Indians were all gone when I was born. All run out. In one of our fields, there used to be an Indian ceremonial dance place. Had their furnace there. If any of them died,

While the frontiersmen played a major role fighting "the Rearguard of the Revolution" against the Indians, they won their greatest recognition at the Battle of Kings Mountain on the western Carolina border. It came during the fall of 1780, a sad period when George Washington had "almost ceased to hope." Lord Cornwallis had captured the South Carolina coast and was marching north from Charleston headed to the Patriot "hornet's nest" in Mecklenburg County, North Carolina. Concerned by the western frontier, he sent a band of a thousand Tories commanded by Scottish major Patrick Ferguson, to squelch the rebellion.

Ferguson marched his force deep into the North Carolina foothills and threw down the gauntlet to Sevier, declaring that if the mountaineers did not halt their opposition to the Crown, he would take his Tories over the mountains, hang the leaders, and lay waste to the country "with fire and sword."

The settler riflemen—having grown lean and tough on the frontier—were roused to action. The call for help brought volunteer riflemen from the headwaters of the Watauga, Nolichucky, and Holston Rivers. More than a thousand angry frontiersmen showed up at Sycamore Shoals on the Holston, wearing brimmed hats, buckskin shirts and britches, and walnut-juice-dyed gaiters, but armed with their own rifles and carrying bags of parched corn. The crowd swelled when another four hundred fighters came in from Virginia's Great Valley led by William Campbell. A Scotch-Irish Presbyterian preacher from Watauga, Rev. Samuel Doak, gave the Patriots a rousing Gideon's army sendoff, calling on them to use as their battle cry, "The sword of the Lord and of Gideon."

Ferguson, meanwhile, apparently started to worry and began a slow withdrawal toward the Cornwallis camp in Charlotte. On October 6, the frontier force—now having crossed

they brought them back here and had a party all night.

We had good times out on that farm. We'd always quit work at eleven, eat at twelve, and go swimming. Had to be back in the fields plowing at two-thirty. We'd run all the way to our wash hole. We went out there one night and every one of us was naked when we got back home...as naked as buck rabbits. 'Course it was dark. It come up a big cloud one day and went to raining. You know what we done? Pulled all our clothes off and stuck them under a log and got in the creek. All together!

—ALEX CHAPPEL OF SYLACAUGA, ALABAMA, AGE 100 WHEN INTERVIEWED BY THE AUTHOR IN 1975. HE DIED THANKSGIVING WEEK, 1979, AT THE AGE OF 104.

Whiskey making came with the Scotch-Irish and English migrants who populated the Appalachians in the 1700s. It became the common man's best money crop but went underground and became "moonshining" with the imposition of whiskey taxes in the late 1800s to pay off the Civil War. This photo, made before the turn of the century, shows Georgia moonshiners in the U.S. Annex of the Atlanta Jail. Note moonshine inmate at right holding his fiddle.

the mountains—learned that Ferguson and his Tories were near Kings Mountain. The mountaineers walked all night so they could launch their assault on the mountain early the next morning. Ferguson sent down words of defiance, declaring he would not be dislodged "by God Almighty and all the rebels out of hell."

As they prepared to ascend the hillside, Colonel Benjamin Cleveland of Wilkes County, one of the ten Patriot leaders, addressed his men:

> My brave fellows: We have beaten the Tories already and we can beat them again. They are all cowards; if they were not, they would support the independence of their country…I will show you how to fight by my example…Every man must be his own officer, and act from his own judgment. Fire as fast as you can, and stand your ground as long as you can. When you can do no better, run; but do not run quite off. Get behind trees, and retreat. If repulsed, let us return and renew the fight. We may have better luck the second time than the first.

Crouching and running up the wooded, gently inclined hillside in open formation, Indian-style, the frontiersmen opened fire. From the top, the Tory muskets exploded in a unison blast. The mountain blazed with volcanic thunder, flashing along its summit and around its base and up its sides in "one sulphuric blaze."

When the mountain men advanced up the mountain, Ferguson rode his horse back and forth, blowing his silver whistle, prodding his troops into action. The Tories launched two bayonet charges and drove the Patriots partway down the hillside, but only temporarily. The rebels counterattacked immediately, picking off the Tories one by one. As the Patriots surrounded the crest, Ferguson's silver whistle went silent. His horse went down, struck by eight shots. In less than an hour, the Rebel force had control of the mountain, with only 28 killed and 62 wounded. Tory losses totaled 224 dead, including Ferguson, and 163 wounded. The remaining 716 surrendered and were marched out as prisoners.

It was a stunning victory and revived the Patriot cause. George Washington called Kings Mountain "proof of the spirit and resources of the country." The British commander for North America, Sir Henry Clinton, said later the Kings Mountain defeat was "the first Link of a Chain of Evils that followed each other in regular succession until they at last ended in the total loss of America." And all accomplished by men Ferguson had called "backwater men…a set of mongrels." Yet they were men who, "without orders, without pay, without commission, without equipment, and without hope of monetary reward" struck an eloquent blow for the nation's independence.

Ironically, the Kings Mountain battle pitted Scotch-Irish against Scotch-Irish. Many South Carolina fighters recruited by the Tories were relatively new settlers who had come from Ulster through the port of Charleston.

As historian Dr. Bobby Gilmer Moss, Limestone College professor emeritus, would point out, Scotch-Irish settlers in the Carolinas fought on both sides in the Revolution, "sometimes father against son, brother against brother, and neighbor against neighbor."

In addition to the rebels' patriotic zeal, the victory at Kings Mountain was credited to the Patriots' superior German rifles, in contrast to the British smooth-bore, short-range muskets. That, along with the Indian style of fighting, a guerrilla tactic far removed from the British formation-style attacks, proved to be decisive.

~

With the end of the war, the new Americans pushed deeper into the frontier—into Kentucky and Tennessee and the mountain plateaus of the western Carolinas and north Georgia and Alabama.

They met up with many Cherokees—many still lingering in the coves and valleys after bruising defeats. Despite the seeming warring nature between the two, many romances resulted and intermarriage was not uncommon in the days following the war. A mountain descendant proud of his part-Cherokee ancestry is retired professor Duane Oliver of Hazelwood, North Carolina.

Men living across the Southern Appalachians in years past loved to wear overalls with a pocket on the chest for their watches. Walter McClure of Dawson County and Bud Davis of Lumpkin County were interested onlookers at the First Annual Ex-moonshiners and Revenuers Convention in Dahlonega, Georgia, in 1974.

While his ancestors were primarily English and "Black Dutch"—the Olivers and the Proctors, original settlers of Cades Cove, Tennessee—Duane Oliver has Indian roots. "I'm descended from Chief Oo-wah-hoo-kee, whose braves captured my great-great-great-great-great-grand-mother in 1760 in Burke County. She was a Birchfield and she and the chief's kids kept the Birchfield name with their descendants arriving in Cades Cove in the early nineteenth century."

William Jasper Cotter—whose grandfather immigrated from County Down, Ireland—remembered arriving as a ten-year-old lad in the 1830s in the Cherokee nation that was to become northwest Georgia. His family reached their destination—near the deep, rock-walled Coosawattee River valley—after wagoning in on the Federal Road from Gainesville. The newly built wagon road slashed diagonally through the heart of the Cherokee nation.

At the time, the Cherokees—whose capital of New Echota lay less than forty miles to the north—were working feverishly to hold on to their shrunken nation. But officials of the state of Georgia, in their capital city in Milledgeville, had other ideas. With encouragement from President Andrew Jackson, the state of Georgia on December 29, 1829, "annexed" the Cherokee nation's lands. Soon after, they dispatched surveyors to mark off 160-acre land lots that would be distributed to its citizens in a state lottery (except for 40-acre gold lots). In an autobiographical narrative published by his church, Cotter remembered it well:

The surveyors were there. I saw them running the lines, marking the station trees and corner posts, shaving off the outside bark of the trees, and making the figures telling the number of the lot of land...Mr. McDowell, a Baptist preacher, surveyed that district. He preached for us on a beautiful Sunday morning in May. These men had a hard time getting on in the wildwoods. On the side of a mountain a rattlesnake in his coil ready to strike looked them in the face. They reported that three days after the full moon in May and August was the best time to kill trees. A lick with a hatchet sometimes killed a chestnut tree...

Nature's surroundings were grand. On the east nearby was a ledge of mountains, in all other directions a rich and beautiful country. As time offered we fenced lots, built stables, and owned land. We bought chickens and a cow from an Indian who lived on Chicken Creek. He was well-to-do and had a large house with a hall, piazza and dining room. He took in travelers. At a supper there we had bear meat, clabber and honey. He had about a hundred bee stands. The gums were of hollow trees set on rocks or pieces of boards, two or three by a tree. The old people understood but could not speak a word of English. The younger ones could talk. His name was Calarxee and his wife's Takee and we named the cow Takee. When they left, mother bought her large washpot, a good article of English castings. I don't know how long it had been used by old Takee; but it rendered good service in our family for many years.

Cader B. Stancil (1810—1885) moved to Cherokee County, Georgia, in 1834. He married Lydia Nix on Christmas Day, 1837. They purchased 160 acres (Land Lot 266) in northern Cherokee County...and built a small cabin. Many of their neighbors were Cherokee Indians. Cader was a lieutenant in the State Militia and in May and June, 1838, had the unpleasant task of helping round up and remove the Cherokees from Georgia. Lydia, or "Granny Stancil" as she was known to many, lived to be 102 years old.

—JEFF STANCIL, NEW ECHOTA STATE PARK, GEORGIA, LYDIA STANCIL'S GREAT-GREAT-GRANDSON, IN *CHEROKEE COUNTY RECIPES AND RECOLLECTIONS*

A few years later, Cotter, who grew up to become a Methodist minister, recalled that when his family arrived in the Cherokee nation, "the wealthy mixed bloods received us cordially; but were all gone by 1835, and we felt our loss."

Three years later, Cotter watched in sadness as the remaining Cherokees were rounded up and marched west on their exodus to Oklahoma, the infamous "Trail of Tears."

Several hundred Cherokees hid in the deep mountain wilds of North Carolina, escaping capture by Federal troops. Many lived to establish what became the Cherokee Nation East. It became a federally protected reservation (Quala), with its capital in Cherokee, North Carolina.

～

With the 1838 departure of a majority of the Indians by force, the former Cherokee nation—centered in southeast Tennessee, north Georgia, and southwest North Carolina—became another "frontier" for the European migrants in the Southern Appalachian backcountry.

Many of North Carolina's Scotch-Irish and English and Germans now were ready to move on in a second or third migration. North Georgia received its share of these migrants. Gilmer County, Georgia, for instance, welcomed many of its citizens from Buncombe County, North Carolina.

Ben Sitton told the story of a party of twenty-seven people who made the autumn 1848 trek from the Asheville area to north Georgia. Sitton gave his family remembrances to George Gordon Ward, author of a splendid, fact-filled history, *The Annals of Upper Georgia Centered in Gilmer County.*

These Ulstermen and Germans who led the way into the Old Southwest were accustomed to short rations. Germans had not fully recovered from the devastation of the Thirty Years' War before it was stripped bare again during the wars of Louis XIV. Rhineland peasants were accustomed to danger, hardship, and hunger. In Scotland, peasants lived in one-room stone and turf huts with earthen floors, and they cooked and sought warmth at an open fire that was vented through a hole in the roof. In winter they shared the hut with any animals they were fortunate enough to own.

In northern Ireland the dwellings were no better and the Ulstermen lived in constant danger from the native Irish who had taken refuge in unsettled areas.

Traveling in seven ox-drawn covered wagons, jam-packed with their necessities, most family members either rode horses or walked, driving along their sheep, cattle, poultry, and hogs including a sow that gave birth to a litter of pigs en route. The men gave the mother hog a brief rest then boxed up the pigs and hoisted them into a wagon. Twice a day, the pigs were brought down for a mealtime rendezvous with their mama.

It took the party a month, traveling at a rate of three miles a day, to reach Ellijay, camping out along the way. Each morning, every person was allowed to take a swallow of corn whiskey to start off his day. Conrad Lowe and his wife, Patsy, with their baby in her arms, rode the mountainous route on their horse, a fine bay stallion.

"Ranging along wilderness streams, through rugged gaps, between mountain walls, the migrants pushed south and west. When a river in flood barred the way, they simply waited until it ran down."

Arriving in Ellijay on Christmas Day, they were welcomed with gourds of whiskey by a local merchant. The next day, the band rolled on into western Gilmer and settled in a valley at the foot of the Cohutta Mountains. Conrad Lowe was able to trade his horse for 160 acres of land.

The new migrants were sustained at first with milk from their cows and the game they shot in the forests—bear and deer and squirrels. Plus, of course, dried "leather-britches" beans and large earthen jars of kraut and pickled beans that they brought in their wagons. They also had available beef and mutton that had been dried Indian-style.

The late Edward S. Mauney told in a county history of the migrants who came into Union County, Georgia, from North Carolina:

Wolves constantly threatened their animals; English economic measures kept them on the verge of starvation. For these people, life on the [American] frontier, harsh though it was, was probably an improvement over what they had known. Obviously some people of English stock participated in this stage of the southern frontier, but more often, they let the Scotch-Irish and the Germans begin the clearing of the forest, fight the early decisive battles with the Indians, and make an area reasonably safe. Then they (English) went (south) west, armed with money instead of long rifles, and bought the land and the improvements made upon it by the true pioneers.

—JOE GRAY TAYLOR, EATING, DRINKING AND VISITING IN THE SOUTH

From 1832 until the Civil War, lumbering Connestoga wagons drawn by horses, mules and oxen made their way over the "gaps" from western North Carolina, South Carolina and East Tennessee, bearing human freight of frowsy-headed children staring at the new country, feather bedding, pots, pans, and provisions to populate the newly acquired land which was bought cheap from the Georgia owners. Cattle and sheep were driven along the wagon trains…They were a hardy, bearded, bewhiskered, heavily petticoated legion of pioneers…Their Bible was a sacred document. They were outspoken in their convictions. They believed in hanging for present punishment, fire and brimstone for future punishment, and herbs, teas and spirituous concoctions for all ills of life.

Frontier living was nothing new to them, but the settlers were delighted to find that much of the land had been cleared by the Cherokees, who annually burned off their corn and bean croplands. The new Georgians soon put in corn, potatoes, beans, and pumpkins, and set out apple and peach trees.

Their long rifles came in handy not only to bring home game but to ward off mountain wolves. Moravian bishop August Gottlieb Spanenberg—who came to the Tennessee/Georgia frontier to check out Cherokee missionary opportunities—recalled that "the wolves here give us music every morning from six corners at once, such music as I never heard."

To get their first log cabins, the settlers cut down and snaked logs to the home site, then invited their neighbors in for "a working." A customary bonus for the workmen was plenty of corn whiskey. To the housewives fell the task of cooking up a bountiful dinner and supper.

Their makeshift tables included strong frontier fare—quail, wild pigeon, wild turkey, bear, venison, squirrel; plus milk, cabbage, turnips, and cool glasses of buttermilk, a favorite of the Scotch-Irish all the way from Scotland and Ireland.

To pay their taxes, the new north Georgians picked up wild chestnuts, which they sold in towns such as Dalton, along with apples, walnuts, vegetables, and jugs of homemade apple brandy and corn whiskey. They carried their goods over the Cohutta gaps in wagon-train treks in the fall of the year. On the return trip, they brought coffee, salt, and sugar. These, along with nails and taxes, were the only items that required cash on the Appalachian frontier.

As Haw Creek, North Carolina, native Jack Brinkley told Warren Moore in *Mountain Voices*, "Our people lived off the land, and somehow it was instilled in us to have that same tenacious dig…to do and live."

Beuna Parton Winchester, of Bryson City, North Carolina, who for many years served as the farmstead commentator at the Great Smoky Mountains National Park's Oconoluftee Visitors Center, remembered that

> many people who come through these mountains occasionally sought to slight us a little bit 'cause we were brought up poor. They'd ask, "During the Depression, were you poor?" Well, I'd tell 'em, if we was, we didn't know it; we had just as much as anybody else did. We never did set down to a meal but what we didn't have somethin' on the table. We always had bread and meat. We raised our own meat; we raised our own vegetables; we worked like crazy, but we worked and made what we eat and eat what we made. Daddy had a cane mill; he would grind other people's cane and make their syrup for them. It was a day of trade and barter. What we didn't have, we could trade off what we had a surplus of to somebody had

a surplus of something else. So everybody didn't have to have everything. That's what you call a neighbor.

When we graduated to a mule, we were in high cotton. We was with people that had money. When I got old enough to cook, we got a wood stove, a big old Home Comfort wood stove. That's what I learned how to cook on.

Beuna Winchester

Beuna Winchester's story—typical of the descendants of the people who migrated into the Southern Appalachians two and a half centuries ago—is one that former Georgia governor and U.S. senator Zell Miller would appreciate. In his autobiography, the governor noted that the migrants brought "Anglo-Celtic qualities which formed the fundamental elements of pioneer American character— love of liberty, personal courage, capacity to withstand and overcome hardship, unstinted hospitality, intense family loyalty, innate humor, and trust in God…Above all," the governor concluded, "they loved their beautiful mountains as they loved the members of their families."

The Seasons

"To Everything There Is a Season"

Whippoorwill Spring to Hog-Killing Winter

The Dogwood trees are in bloom. Catfish will bite and the bed
bugs are ripe.
—*W. B. Townsend,* The Dahlonega Nugget

~

For, lo, the winter is past, the rain is over and gone; the flowers
appear on the earth; the time of the singing of birds is come.
—Song of Solomon 2:11–12 KJV

~

You can't have too much June, I say.
—*Celestine Sibley*

~

We'd get out of school in fodder-pulling time…the teacher couldn't say much
when your mom and dad said you had to stay home and pull fodder. Then
there was the excitement of storing up the apples under the floor so that the
whole house smelled like a party all winter long.
—*Jean Ritchie,* Singing Family of the Cumberlands

The sweetest song of spring came with the arrival of the first whippoorwills. Singing their hearts out through the late evening and early morning hours—WHIP-POOR-WILL!…WHIP-POOR-WILL!—the elusive songbirds just arriving from the south gave mountain people smiles of springtime hope.

Just as the Cherokee before him, the settler knew that the planting season was at hand, the arrival of earth's rebirth. "It's time to be getting our seeds in the ground," was the word heard over the land. "With each sunrise," wrote a schoolteacher in Oak Ridge, Tennessee, "spring changed the face of the beloved valleys. The snow was leaving, and in its place trillium and trailing arbutus were quick to follow."

The flutelike songs of the whippoorwills were liberating signs to youngsters, also; by May, perhaps, the kids could pull off their shoes and run lickety-split through the greening fields, maybe perhaps follow their fathers' footsteps as they plowed the warming earth, slicing open the ground for the planting of corn, beans, squash, and melons. In upstate South Carolina, I relished the chance to do just that, following barefoot in the furrows plowed by Dad and his half dozen "farm hands."

With the first warm winds of April, Larry Davis of Ellijay, Georgia, would test out his mother's barefoot resolve:

> It'd be a day like this [early April]. We'd be settin' around and we'd pull our shoes off and rub our feet in the dirt. If Mama stormed at us real loud, we'd have to put those shoes back on and bide our time. From then on, though, we kept testing her. Finally, on the day she remained silent when we rubbed our toes in the dirt, we knew *it was time!* Those first days, our feet would be so tender we couldn't walk on anything hardly more than where Daddy plowed. But by the fall, our feet would be so tough I'd even enjoy walking across gravel.

One mountain man developed leathery soles so hard he could strike matches on the bottom of his left foot to light his hand-rolled cigarettes.

The "green up" season also meant the time for a bracing round of spring tonics. Sassafras tea, made by boiling sassafras roots in water, was the common drink loved by all. At least they claimed they loved it. In the Big Creek community near north Georgia's "Blue Ridge (Continental) Divide," the late Jason Stanley, patriarch of the prolific Stanley family, insisted his children consume plenty of sassafras tea every April, sometimes for a week or more. "We were told that it was good for our blood," said Jason's son Reed, "and I guess it was. We drank it down even though it was a little bitter to swaller."

The first greens peeping through the earth gave another springtime signal. Welcome relief was coming after a winter of salty smokehouse meat and canned vegetables that were running low, anyway.

*G*rowing up in South Carolina, my sisters and I always looked forward to the blooming of the dogwoods.

"When will it be warm enough for us to go barefooted?" we would whine. Our mother, tired of our pestering, brilliantly decreed that we couldn't shed our shoes "until the dogwoods bloom."

—MARTHA WOODHAM,
ATLANTA JOURNAL-CONSTITUTION

On the Henry Grady Hasty farm near Waleska, Georgia, Montaree Hasty, like her counterparts across the Blue Ridge, would take her basket in hand to gather "a good mess of poke sallet" from nearby fields. She first parboiled the tasty wild greens, then fried them up with scrambled eggs for her eager family.

Celestine Sibley loved the "Aprilness" of such a spring day when her mother, "Muv," would walk up from her garden, bringing the season's first mustard greens and onions. "We'll have them wilted with bacon drippings for supper," Muv declared with joy.

On Gladys Russell's Tennessee farm in the Smokies, the springtime ritual called for the planting of most of the garden seeds on Good Friday, followed, after Easter, by several days of the planting of corn.

~

The inexorable turn of the earth toward summer and fall brought busy days in the fields as days got longer and hotter, moving toward getting crops "laid by."

Some felt they could almost hear the corn growing on warm spring mornings.

It was the time of year when tables groaned under the delights of the season: bounteous harvests of fresh corn and beans and tomatoes and June apples and plums and

Early May means that mountain children can shed their shoes and go barefoot. This school youngster from near Hayesville, North Carolina, carrying his lunch box, is enjoying one of spring's delights.

peaches. Sometimes the big dinners had not a single meat on the table, only vegetables in amazing abundance. I recall such days when we would come in for our noontime meal. Mother would present a table brimming with wonderfully delicious crowder peas, sliced tomatoes, fried okra, cream corn that Dad had picked that very morning, plus hot biscuits and sweet milk. After such a meal, during that hot time of day, my father would stretch out on the living room floor with a book under his head, and take a half-hour nap. Afterward, we would return to the fields refreshed and ready for an afternoon of plowing.

The grand finale of the summer season—"laying-by time," around July 4th—was a time of general happiness across the hill country. William G. Hasty of Cherokee County, Georgia, remembered that when the men gathered at the country store on a Saturday, "to be the first in the community to 'lay-by' your crops was a point of pride."

The July 4th weekend was also when farmers cut their first watermelons. At our home, following his annual ritual, Dad gave the youngest grandchild the honor of passing around the slices.

Revival time came the first week of August—a week of preaching and singing and "fellowshipping." One weekend would be dedicated to an old-fashioned "singing convention" with "dinner on the ground." Often the song leader—and here again my father was such a leader in the Baptist churches we attended at Double Springs, Charlesboro, Taxahaw, and Midway—would call on individuals to "come up here and lead the next song." The rafters would ring with old favorites such as "An Unclouded Day," "Rescue the Perishing," and "Hold to God's Unchanging Hand." It was a time of joy and thankfulness and a rededication to God and family.

In July, when the chestnuts and corn are green and full grown, they half boil the former and take off the rind; and having sliced the milky swelled long rows of the latter, the women pound it in a large wooden mortar...Then they knead them both together, wrap them up in green corn blades [shucks] about an inch thick and boil them well. This sort of bread is very tempting.

—JAMES ADAIR (1775)

As with spring, the birds signaled the coming closure of the hot season—no longer did they fly in mating pairs but joined together in flocks to sweep across the blue summer skies. Even the frogs in the millpond seemed to slow their songs of love, and the crickets and katydids carried forth with mournful concerts telling us that the long days of summer were drawing to an end. And you knew that fall was coming when the sumac turned a brilliant red and sourwood, black gum, and poplars began to take on the colors of autumn.

~

Fall's arrival brought a glowing pumpkin moon and the season of wine and gold—a time of cooking sorghum syrup and apple butter, of drying beans and peaches...and killing hogs. For the womenfolk, it was their busy season for drying and putting up the fruits of their gardens and orchards—beans, apples, corn. Another big task was processing the hog-killing-day meat and lard and getting the hams and shoulders and sausage salted down and smoked for the winter.

"Fall was the grandest time," recalled Mrs. Carl Brown of Robbinsville, North Carolina. "Mother put up everything in barrels—a barrel of kraut, a barrel of pickled beans, a barrel of beef in salt brine and a barrel of sulphur-smoked apples."

It was a time of squirrel-hunting also. "Mother would make dumplings with young squirrels in the fall that were out of this world," Bill Hasty remembered with relish.

Above all, noted Billy Joe Tatum, autumn was nutting time, with woods full of black walnuts and hickory nuts and butternuts. "You may be fortunate enough," Billy Joe said, "to fend off the squirrels and get your share of the almost forgotten chinquapins, which can be compared in flavor only to Old World chestnuts now that virtually all native American chestnut trees have died of blight."

It was the fall of the year in this Buncombe County, North Carolina, farm and youngsters were out for a joy ride as they hauled tow sacks of corn on the family sled. The oxen-drawn sled, an early version "pick-up," could conquer rough mountain terrain.

The Ritchies, the "Singing Family of the Cumberlands," loved to go hickory nut hunting on Saturdays. Jean Ritchie writes,

> We'd get up before the birds, take flour sacks and coffee sacks and stay all the long day rambling about the hills. Mom would go with us... We'd race and chase up ahead of her and get so winded that we'd have to fall down and rest...she'd [soon] be up with us. She'd never stop until she got to the top of the ridge, then she'd stand still and puff a little fanning herself with a cowcumber leaf...
>
> "Lord, children, look what a pretty sight it is. I guess it's Indian Summer. My dad allus said you couldn't find anything so fair as an Indian Summer day. The air right hazy soft and the sunshine yaller as firelight, and the hills all manner of fine colors."

Or as Henry Wadsworth Longfellow wrote,

The morrow was a bright September morn;
The earth was beautiful as if new-born;

There was that nameless splendor everywhere
That wild exhilaration in the air.

⁓

Winter had its pluses, too. For Celestine Sibley, it was "a time for soups and stews, of giant apple cobblers and buttery wedges of corn bread."

And to Atlanta's Edna Lewis, a Virginia transplant, the dead of winter meant "a great fire would be going in the fireplace and we would serve homemade cake and homemade wines."

The fireplace was indeed the friendliest symbol of February for me when I was growing up on a farm in upstate South Carolina. We loved to sit around the big fire on a cold night and watch the oak logs burning red hot, and talk about the next hog killing and about Easter upcoming and maybe even listen to the Major Bowes Amateur Hour on the battery-powered Sears Silvertone radio. As the night wore on, the big debate was which of the boys would be bold and generous enough to run to the cold bedroom and jump under the chilly quilts and "get the bed warm" for the rest.

The Franklin Hedden Dyer sorghum mill operated for years in the Choestoe District, Union County, Georgia. Blueford Elisha and Sarah Souther Dyer helped operate the mill, which used a mule to pull the cane-squeezer. Home in background was built in 1850, shortly after the departure of the Cherokee Indians.

(I was glad that many decades later, I was able to salvage the old home's fireplace mantel and sideboards, with telltale marks where my father scratched his matches to light his pipe and to start fires at four o'clock every morning, spring, summer, fall, and winter.)

On many winter nights, during the dark quiet before we went to sleep, and over in the mornings, we would hear the faint sounds of hounds yelping as they climbed the hills and ran down the valleys chasing a fox.

On the question of hog killing (described in detail in another chapter) the signs were a mighty important issue for people in the mountains during the chilly winter months. At age ninety-six, John Parris's grandfather was convinced that a "shrinking moon" (after it was full) was the time to slaughter swine. The proof, he contended, was in the meat. If the bacon curled up, you knew for sure that it was butchered the wrong time, in the light of a full moon, resulting in meat that "wouldn't give up its fat."

Fresh meat from a hog killing was one of the great bonuses of winter. Mother's sausages, containing a generous amount of fat meat along with the lean shoulder cuts, plus her sage that she dried over the kitchen stove, were so delicious that we enjoyed eating the patties for supper, along with biscuits, as well as for breakfast. Plus, of course, the delicious "eat-'em-now" cuts that hog-killing day brought—backbones and ribs, served with kraut. A few days later, souse meat would come on stream, a delicacy that mountain people waited for the whole year.

The Indian Moons

January—The Cold Moon

February—The Hunger Moon

March—The Crow Moon

April—The Grass Moon

May—The Planting Moon

June—The Rose Moon

July—The Thunder Moon

August—The Green-Corn Moon

September—The Harvest Moon

October—The Hunting Moon

November—The Frosty Moon

December—The Long-Night Moon

Fall and winter brought wild game meat, particularly rabbits and squirrels that could be turned into dumplings that would stick to one's ribs.

And, of course, winter was the time when the family dug into the vegetables and fruits that had been canned and dried back in the summer and fall.

Ronni Lundy remembered the fortifying "pots of full-bodied, bronze-hued shuck beans"—green beans her aunts strung on threads and hung up to dry every summer "just as their pioneer forebears had done." While the ancestors strung the beans for survival, Ronni noted, "my aunts did it because there is nothing in the world so addictively satisfying in winter as the robust flavor of shuck beans." The shuck beans, also called leather-britches by many, and soup beans also were always served with "real" mountain corn bread, that is, minus sugar and flour!

There is a notion that still prevails among the Cherokees of making a new fire every year. This is generally done in March. The fire is made by drilling in a dried grape vine...Seven persons are chosen to perform this with the conjurer. After this fire is made, each family in the town comes and gets a new fire, putting out all the old fire in their houses.

—ROBERT SPARKS WALKER,
TORCHLIGHTS TO THE CHEROKEES

During the chilly days of January and February, it was always a treat when I walked home from grammar school to find Mother waiting with a plate of hot corn bread and a glass of buttermilk. Kathy Starr enjoyed similar snacks when she came in from school hungry and cold. "If money was low, the most popular snack was sweetened water and white bread. You would put some sugar in a glass of water, then roll a slice of bread and dip it into the sweetened water."

It seemed to a youngster that the winter would never end. But there were ways to look forward to spring. I enjoyed poring over the Sears catalog by the hour, and Mama and Daddy checked the almanac and read the Bible. Edna Lewis's mother, eager for the Virginia spring, would line up eggshells on her windowsill and put a bean in each, along with a teaspoon of water. The arrival of April's first day of spring was a day of triumph when Mrs. Lewis could transfer the sprouted beans into the soil of her kitchen garden.

In time, the days started to get longer and a hint of spring would come in the warming winds from the south. Then the day that a shower came up accompanied by thunder, we knew that winter's days were numbered.

The Indians had a saying for it. Thunder, they said, meant that God was "breaking the backbone of winter."

The Social Life

From Work Frolics to "Bran Dances," a Spirit of Joy

"Y'all Come!"

Cider in the rain barrel, corn in the popper,
Shoats in the mast woods, mash in the hopper
Taffy in the window sill, rosen on the bow,
Grab your partners, boys, dance the "Do Si Do"!
—Louise McNeill, from Paradox Hill collection
as quoted in Voices from the Hills

~

At our corn-shuckin's, we had a big meal, all day.
—Frances Gates Hill, Mountaintown district,
Gilmer County, Georgia

~

People used to go walk for miles and sit down and talk to their friends and
neighbors for three or four hours at a time.
—Willard Watson of Deep Gap,
North Carolina, in Mountain Voices

To the European immigrants who peopled the Appalachians in the eighteenth century, the frontier was a magnificent new world to conquer.

And conquer it they did, in a splendid social style. Proudly riding and walking alongside their belled and beribboned Conestoga wagons, families jostled down the Great Philadelphia Wagon Road into Virginia's Shenandoah Valley, the rolling Carolina Piedmont and, a few years later—led by the boldest Englishman explorer of the lot, Daniel Boone—took the Wilderness Road through the Cumberland Gap into "the land of Kaintuck" and down the river trails into what was to become Tennessee.

They came in family and ethnic clusters—the sturdy Palatine Germans, the ruddy-faced, red-haired Scotch-Irish Presbyterians, the clever French Huguenot/English descendants such as Tennessee's John Sevier and, of course, the Virginia Anglo-Celts—the English, the Scots, and the Welsh—who decided to head to America's "great Southwest."

Despite the remoteness of the frontier wilds, a spirit of sociability spread across the mountain territory from the early days. First arrivals to settle the Piedmont backcountry initially put down roots near friends and families of like backgrounds. But soon clannishness gave way to cooperative Christian camaraderie as the newcomers joined hands to fight their common enemies—the tough frontier, the Cherokee tomahawk, and in time, the British Crown.

The tone of teamwork became the foundation for a country of constructive conviviality. The goodwill reflected itself in community barn raisings and later in corn-shuckings, apple cuttings, bean stringings, cane-strippings, hog killings, sorghum boils, and quilting bees, funerals, and weddings.

The social thread running through it all, down through the years, could be characterized in two words—y'all come! As an Englishman traveling through Virginia in 1746 wrote to a London magazine, "All over the (Virginia) Colony, a universal Hospitality reigns; full Tables and open Doors, the kind Salute, the generous Detention … Strangers are sought after with Greediness, as they pass the Country, to be invited."

It was no surprise that from this mélange of spirited generosity would emerge a bedrock bastion of down-home friendliness and hearty food, a strong work ethic, and yes, despite some failed religious attempts to suppress the fiddle, the cradle of country music.

"Work frolics" became the great social event. They began on the frontier when raising a house required swift communal action in the face of unfriendly Indians. But popularity of the "workings" went well beyond the end of the Indian wars.

Across the rolling Piedmont and hill country where each family had its own

> Neighbors helped each other out and had a good time doing it. Lots of hands made the corn shucking go a lot faster. Everybody wanted to hurry and get to the half-gallon jug of double-and-twisted whiskey at the bottom of the crib!
>
> Just about everybody made their own whiskey in the old days, including my granddaddy, John Will Saine…The family Bible got burned up in a fire, but he was ninety-five when he passed away. The Saines originally came from Germany and spelled their name "Sehn," or "Zurn." Other descendants spell their names "Sayne," "Sain," or "Seine."
>
> —Sam Saine of Lumpkin County, Georgia, in an interview with Anne Dismukes Amerson in *I Remember Dahlonega*

plot of land, averaging upward of three hundred acres, and unrestrained by society such as had existed in Ulster, the joys of the frolics knew no bounds. After working hard for weeks on end to tame the wilderness, the frontiersman exercised his periods of relaxation with great gusto, oftentimes dancing all night, feasting on squirrel pot pie, and getting high on homemade corn whiskey.

"When we had a corn-shuckin', a log-rollin', a house raisin', or any such frolic," recalled an early settler, "the whiskey just sloshed around like water...I should say so!"

In Kentucky and across much of the Appalachian hill country, a bran dance (that's right, a *bran* dance) was the great way folks celebrated, particularly following the erection of a new cabin. The owner would sprinkle corn bran over his new chestnut puncheon floor and then the dancers, with their shuffling shoes, would help polish the surface! (Kentucky historian Thomas Clark called later "barn dance" references "a great American folk typographical error...Pioneers never gave a 'barn' dance, but they were forever publicizing the 'bran' dances.")

Corn-shuckings became the liveliest of work frolics. In pioneer times, it was traditional for the host to stash a jug of whiskey deep in the unshucked corn pile. First shucker to reach the red ear won three swigs from the jug, or as they put it, "three bobs of his Adam's apple." As the jug made its round, subsequent imbibers were limited to only one Adam's apple bob.

When Doc Ledbetter died in Murfreesboro in the 1960s, the funeral was held in the old house his father had built...That day the house had the sweet smell of flowers and in the kitchen and dining room there was a reunion of relatives. There were several baked hams, along with congealed fruit salads and chicken salad. There were even chicken cutlets...Added to that was pound cake, sour cream cake, and coconut cake; chess pies, pecan pies, and apricot pies.

Why do Tennesseans cook so for funerals? No one knows for sure. But it gives thoughtful friends something visible to do for a loved family. It is more personal than sending flowers... Then there are the hugs and kisses and sympathy. The touching. The visit. As families care for one another in this way, over the years ties are cemented.

—Helen Exum's introduction to
The Original Tennessee Homecoming Cookbook

Corn shuckin's were great Appalachian social events up to the mid-1900s. This 1890 party, at the London farm near Dahlonega, Georgia, drew a big crowd. On occasions, the host would stash a bottle in the stack for a lucky participant. Finding a red ear allowed a man to kiss the girl of his choosing.

In later years, prizes for finding a red ear of Indian corn ranged from a ten-dollar bill all the way up to a milk cow.

"Corn-shuckin's was a mighty big day with people back in them times," recalled Ernest Parker, who grew up in the Bucktown district of Gilmer County, Georgia. A big October party would always take place at the Parker farm at the foot of George Parker mountain.

"People just piled their corn under the shed by the crib, you know. Just had a great big pile of it. They'd invite the whole community in. Be anywhere from fifteen to thirty-five people come in, gather around that pile and sit there and shuck it, throw the shucks back behind 'em and pitch that corn in the crib.

"Spend all day long at it. Stories you never heard the like, and a lot of 'em true! In the meantime, women of the community came in and helped the housewife cook dinner. They'd have everything you could think of that grew on the farm; they'd have it on the table for people to eat."

Corn-shuckings became a great place for a young man to find his future bride. If he lucked out on an ear of red Indian corn, he was allowed to bestow a kiss on the lass of his choosing.

In North Carolina, John Parris's grandmother "threw a conniption fit" she recalled later, when a young man reached the red ear and promptly surprised her with a slurpy smack on the cheek before the joyous throng.

"I burst out crying," she told her grandson later. "I thought I was ruined. It was the first time I had ever been kissed by a boy."

~

"Workings" included cutting roads through tortuous mountain land. In 1903, men from Gilmer and Fannin Counties, Georgia, launched a drive to construct a stretch of road from Cole Mountain through Allen Gap toward Cherrylog to provide a shorter trip to Ellijay and Blue Ridge. It became a long, arduous effort, requiring hand-to-hand combat with giant chestnut trees and rock outcroppings. Since dynamite was unavailable, sledgehammers were rock-busting instruments of necessity.

After a few weeks, morale flagged and prospects for completion seemed dim. That is, until Rick Stanley came up with an idea that roused the entire district to action—a squirrel barbecue. The plan blossomed quickly, recalled J. H. (Duck) Ray in an account published by George Gordon Ward in his *Annals of Upper Georgia Centered in Gilmer County:*

In lieu of paying taxes, many mountain people worked county roads. This is a road-working in Union County, Georgia, following the turn of the century.

On Friday evening and Saturday morning early we sent men into the woods…
A steady roar of guns brought the squirrels plopping to the ground. Meantime I
had mounted a mule and rounded up men on Persimmon Creek and through the
Garland settlement, and all along the Garland mountain I told everybody we'd
have a barbecue. I invited the women and the girls too.

On Saturday morning, the women and girls came in. They brought pots,
pans and other supplies. The hunters gathered in from the woods with more
squirrels. Soon, under the nimble hands of the women, there was spirited preparation of a meal…Hot coffee gave the atmosphere a homey aroma. New help
on the road added the energy of forty or more men and young fellows, which
along with the steady old hands, shot the whole project through with new life
and vigor.

At noon we served dinner at a big bold spring near the Allen Patch. I don't
remember how many squirrels we served. But we had all we needed, along with
the coffee, cakes, custards, and apple and pumpkin pies. We didn't finish our road
that day. But this new spurt assured us of our goal.

Hill country citizens found unique ways to amuse themselves during dark winters—candy pullings, box suppers, cake walks, and pound parties. The late Earl Dillard
of Rabun County, Georgia, enjoyed attending box suppers at the local school where
girls prepared fancied-up boxes of food with their names inside to be auctioned off to
the young men with the highest bids. "Naturally you didn't want some stranger buying your girlfriend's box…Sometimes they'd frame up on some old boy and run the
bid up."

Saturday night candy pullings (or "sorghum pulls") drew a lot of attention also.
"Sorghum surp" was cooked down on the stove until it reached "candy" stage. Then
boys and girls paired off, dipped their hands in lard so the candy wouldn't stick, and the
hilarity began. The boy would take one end of the three-foot-long candy loaf and the girl
would pull from the other. After the sugary goo was stretched several times, and turned
light in color, it was set aside to harden and become candy. Charles Hubert Watkins
recalled that "a boy considered it a great pleasure to pull the hot syrup and touch his best
girlfriend's hot sticky hands."

The norm of Southern pastimes in the mid-1800s, according to B. A. Bodkin in his
A Treasury of Southern Folklore, lay between such candy pullings, and the "sweaty, orgi-
astic fights, wrestling matches, gander pullings, and frolics of the time." To this could
be added cockfighting. Tennessee Governor "Singing Bob" Taylor rhapsodized on the
beauties of a candy pull: "In the bright, bright hereafter when all the joys of the ages
are gathered up and condensed into globules of transcendent ecstasy, I doubt whether
there will be anything half so sweet as were the candy-smeared, ruby lips of the country

maidens to the jeans-jacketed swains who tasted them at the candy-pulling in the happy long ago."

Azzie Fouts Waters recalled going to a "candy knocking" in the Faucette Lake district of Dawson County, Georgia, where she grew up. "It was at the John Turner place. A whole crowd of young folks were there, including a big crowd of Turner children. I went with one of my good friends. Candy was tied up on the loft and you marched around there and they gave you a stick to knock it down with."

The person who could knock down candy while blindfolded won a stick of candy. "We stayed up all night long," Mrs. Waters recalled. "We played games, then we'd eat a while, and go back to playing games. Somehow or another the night got by and I walked home the next morning. I reckon my parents trusted me; I wouldn't have done anything to betray that trust, you know, but we had a good time."

～

Nowhere was the spirit of sweet sociability more pronounced through the years than events revolving around churches, revivals, weddings, "all day singings and dinners on the ground," and yes, even cemetery cleanings and "decoration days." Churches proliferated throughout the valleys and coves of the region. By the mid-1800s, Fannin County, Georgia, typical of most, was blessed with a great variety—"Baptist, Missionary, Anti-Missionary, Methodist, and Presbyterian."

"Big meeting" revival time always came in the heat of late summer when an entire community's farming enterprises came to a joyous "lay-by time" halt; everyone joined together in a weeklong celebration of preaching and singing and praying. I remember as a wee lad being placed on top of the piano at the old Charlesboro Baptist Church in Lancaster County, South Carolina, to sing soprano during revivals and all-day singings. My father, "Mr. Wade," who taught "do-ra-mi-fa-so-la-ti-do"–shaped note music, would always lead the singing at our church, while Mama taught a Sunday school class. It was in the summer of 1940, at age eleven, to the strains of "Softly and Tenderly," that I "gave my heart to the Lord," became a Christian with other

> *I remember going to many a camp meeting when I was growing up. In those days, folks really got into the spirit of the occasion by shouting and crying. On one occasion, a woman named Mattie got to carrying on so loudly that one of my little cousins tugged at his mother's sleeve and asked, "Mama, what's the matter with that woman? Did a wasp get up her dress?"*
>
> —WESLEY DOCKERY IN *I REMEMBER DAHLONEGA*

kids my age, being accepted into a fold as a member of the church. At revival's end, the congregation gathered down at the creek out back, sang "Shall We Gather at the River," and looked on as Preacher H. J. Wood gave all us candidates a thorough Baptist dunking.

Methodist camp meetings—huge arbor "camp-outs" coming right after "lay-by time"—were heavily attended after the turn of the century. The fiery four-times-a-day "fire and brimstone" sermons would be broken up by rousing hymns such as "Standing on the Promises" and "On Jordan's Stormy Banks I Stand," and, of course, sumptuous meals under the trees.

In some mountain communities, day-long communion meetings also included the washing of feet. Rural churches in Cherokee County, Georgia, were among those carrying out the practice. "To me washing feet was one of the most humbling experiences a man could express to his fellow man," remembered former Georgia State Senator William G. Hasty. "Our people believed they should follow Christ's teaching in the 'upper room' the night before he was crucified."

Hasty remembered seeing the long white towels stacked up at the altar along with the bread and wine, and watching as each person draped a towel around his waist and gently washed and dried off his friend's feet. Both then arose to embrace or shake hands.

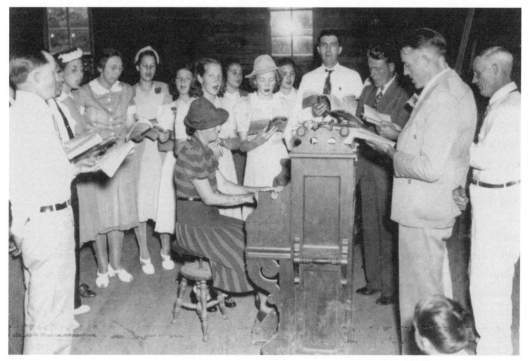

Members of a church in Pickens County, Georgia, gather around the pump organ after a service during the 1940s for a little singing.

Social highlight of all such events was the "dinner on the ground." Housewives would lay out a sumptuous spread on tablecloths draped across long outdoor tables under

the trees. My boyhood buddies and I soon learned to head to the tastiest puddings, chickens, ham, and vegetable dishes brought by the best cooks of the community.

"I'll never forget your mother's biscuits and pies," my grammar school buddy "Jib" Taylor told me decades later.

Romance often broke out during such gatherings as young people got acquainted, dated for the first time, walked together to the spring for water, sat together in church, and, if they were lucky, even held hands. Many met their spouses at

Bonneted southwest Virginia housewives put together a quilting frame in preparation for a quilting party.

such occasions. After the big dinner under the trees, members would often circle about and kneel and send up prayers for their church and country and for the community's "lost and unsaved."

Nineteenth-century community merrymaking reached a celebratory zenith at weddings. Fun events began with an Indian yell "run for the whiskey bottle" at the bride's home (where most early knots were tied), and ended with elaborate "infare" feasts featuring all of the frontier favorites—bear roast, venison steak, and wild fowl, along with generous dishes of vegetables plus plenty of liquid libations, pies, and stack cakes, with the ladies each bringing a stack for the bride's cake. And while revelers launched into a dance to the tune of fiddles, the bride's friends would capture her and tuck her into her wedding bed, followed by a group of men who installed the husband in bed beside her. Next day, the husband would take his wife home, the "infare" completed.

While many mountain churches officially condemned dancing, somehow the community's free spirits always found a way.

"We'd have a dance every week," Stanley Pope of Fannin County, Georgia, remembered when interviewed by students at West Fannin High School. "They would take all the furniture out of someone's house. There would be a fiddler, a banjo player, and a caller. The whole place would be full. No one got in trouble at church; they just kept their mouth shut."

To the east, at Turner's Corner, Georgia, Oscar Cannon fiddled his way through many a mountain dance. He was ninety-eight years old when I interviewed him in 1994. "We'd usually have a dance at somebody's house. I had a friend who picked the banjer, and we'd play together at the dances. But anytime they wanted me to play for a Saturday night dance, I told 'em I'd stay with them up 'til midnight but midnight was when the Lord's day started and I'd have to leave it with 'em."

*D*ancing had its place [in earlier days]. It was conducted after the Virginia-reel character, with set-callers, musicians and singing often interspersed. A variant was called "the North Carolina dance."...One favorite dance was known as "Charley." Dancers chose partners. Then all rose, a line of girls on one side of the room, a line of boys opposite...Bud Sellers generally called, "Swing." The first couple swung around each other once, then danced down between the lines. This continued till the girl had danced with every boy and the young man had done the same by every girl. Then followed the next couple. All sang as they went...

Oh Charley, he's a good old soul,
Oh Charley, he's a dandy,
Oh Charley he's the very lad
That drunk up Roper's brandy...

—GEORGE GORDON WARD, THE ANNALS OF UPPER GEORGIA CENTERED IN GILMER COUNTY

Today, the beat goes on. Carrying on the Appalachian "y'all come" tradition, north Georgia's Bailey family throws a magnificent autumn cookout for family and friends at their ancestral mountain farm near Double-head Gap. The site of Will Bailey's old homeplace, located in a verdant valley near the Blue Ridge Continental Divide, becomes a mecca for upward of three hundred people who join in the annual frolic.

At the first such cookout thirty years ago, Will Bailey and his son Homer, along with the entire Bailey clan, put on a feed "the way the Indians used to do it," serving barrels of barbecue plus turkey and ham and plenty of wild game—squirrel dumplings, bear steak, turtle stew, and even deep-fat-fried rattlesnake. In succeeding years, the big party got even more rambunctious and neighborly, with friends bringing in luscious loads of covered dishes—squash soufflés, bowls of butter beans, and heaping platters of fried okra and sliced tomatoes and golden pones of corn bread, plus pies and puddings and cakes aplenty, enough to break anyone's modern-day diet.

Another "Bailey tradition" has been the music. The family grew up picking and singing, and the young Bailey crowd loves to pick and sing Garth Brooks pieces, particularly "Friends in Low Places." One of the clan's legendary members, the aforementioned Homer Bailey, now deceased, "was often seen with a jug of moonshine in one hand and a banjo in the other," said Betty Jo Bailey, wife of David Bailey and herself a guitarist and fiddler. A bunch of local musicians always arrive with their instruments—Ebb and Jebb Collins, Gene Fox and Earl Neal (the "High Dial Pickers"), and the Harvey Blackstock Band. After the visitors play and sing several sets, the family takes over to pick and fiddle and sing and dance into the mountain night. They love to do the mountain clog (a Scotch-Irish hand-me-down dance) and the party often continues until five in the morning. Harvey Blackstock always gets requests to sing "The Bailey Cookout Song," which he composed with a little help from Philip and Terri Bailey and Eddie Tomlinson.

There's a gathering in the mountains
That comes once a year.
All the relatives come from far and near
It's an event they all talk about,
It's known as,
    THE BAILEY COOKOUT

When you leave home, you may ride
for awhile.
You'll come to a place known as
"High Dial."
"John Will" would be proud of such
a turnout
Up in the Mountains
    AT THE BAILEY COOKOUT

It's been going on for a pretty good while,
And sure makes everyone smile.
Nieces, nephews, cousins and friends
all about,
They all come up
    TO THE BAILEY COOKOUT

You'll never know what you might eat.
There could be fish, deer, bear or
    rattlesnake meat.
Phillip and Dan will cook anything from
ground hog to trout,
    UP AT THE BAILEY COOKOUT

We can't forget the girls in the crew,
There's Madeline, Terri, Betty Jo, Evalene
and Sue
They work real hard to make this all
come about,
    UP AT THE BAILEY COOKOUT

After supper we all pick and sing.
The music makes these mountains ring.
While Milus and Homer wouldn't
    have nothing to argue about,
With good times had by all
    UP AT THE BAILEY COOKOUT

After we eat we feel like stuffed hogs,
And Betty Jo's a-hunting a partner to clog.
There's David, Jack, and Darren hoping
they won't get picked out
To have to dance so early
AT THE BAILEY COOKOUT

Let us remember the ones who have gone on
To live with Jesus, in their Heavenly home.
They're probably up there right now
On a real tall cloud with our Father
AT A HEAVENLY COOKOUT

The ancestral home of the late Will Bailey, nestled in a valley near the "Blue Ridge Divide" in Fannin County, Georgia, is the site of the Bailey Family Cookout. Over 200 relatives and friends attend the reunion, which includes generous amounts of food and mountain music with Betty Jo Bailey on the fiddle (top).

The Art

The Art of Growing
God's Chosen People Tackle the Good Earth

The Art of Reading Signs
Tracking the Moon from Hog Killing to Moonshining

The Art of Mountain Cooking
From the Fireplace to the Microwave

The Art of Preserving
Smoking, Salting, Drying, Burying, and Canning

The Art of Growing

God's Chosen People Tackle the Good Earth

From the beginning, Southerners…were close to the soil. Their
lives revolved around the seasons, around sowing and cultivating
and harvesting.

         —*John Egerton,* Southern Food

~

[Pa] cleared new ground on a rolling hillside and made jokes about his
"perpendicular" garden. He said he was probably the only man
on earth who could fall out of his cornfield and break his neck. Ma
suggested that he stand in the door and plant his corn by shooting it into
the hillside with his rifle.

         —*Florence Cope Bush,*
     Dorie: Woman of the Mountains

Thomas Jefferson, the Blue Ridge's distinguished resident and early America's most illustrious farmer, hailed those who tilled the earth, calling them "the chosen people of God, if he had a chosen people."

The Appalachian pioneer's burning desire, as soon as he got his family safely ensconced in a cabin with a roof over their heads, was to get his farm going, that is, clear out the forests so he could plow his earth and plant some corn. Of course, he was happy to have the woods beyond; they were a perfect pigpen. He could turn his hogs loose (with identifying ear notches, of course) and they could live off the forest mast and build up plenty of meat for a Thanksgiving or Christmas hog killing.

But clearing "a Land which probably had never been ploughed since the Creation" was no easy task, unless he was lucky enough to inherit a tract that had been burned off every year by the Indians before him.* Fastest way was to girdle the giant oak, hickory, and chestnut trees. He did it by axing rings around the tree barks. The exertion of a lot of sweat and energy meant that a settler might—after a year of dedicated effort—clear

---

*Philadelphia-born botanist William Bartram—riding across a low-lying valley in the Appalachian Blue Ridge County in the late 1700s—land apparently burned over by the Cherokees—found wild strawberries so thick they stained his horse's legs up to his knees. His account was contained in his book Travels, published in 1791.

perhaps an acre of his thick virgin forest. Later, with the help of his neighbors, he would call for a logrolling and barn raising.

While girdling left "war zones" dotted with ghostly dead tree sentinels, it accomplished his purpose, opening up the forest to sunlight for the corn and beans, greens and squash, in turn providing green forage for pigs and cows.

In this 1938 scene in East Tennessee, a farmer does his spring plowing with his ox. Oxen were sure-footed on steep mountain fields.

As he cleared his land, the settler, using his muzzleloader or one of the more accurate "squirrel rifles" obtainable from German gunsmiths moving down from Pennsylvania, filled his family's meat hampers with wild game—turkey, bear, deer, squirrel, and pigeons.

While corn was destined to become his main crop, a patch of turnips was for many the initial vegetable of choice that first year on the frontier. That is if he could get them planted by the fall of the year. Considered by many to be the miracle plant of the mountains, turnips would mature within a few weeks of planting, giving the family some nourishing greens and fiber over the winter to go along with their wild game and wild fruit and nut diet.

In the meantime, in the face of the giant silver skeletons that stood sixty feet tall in his backyard a year or more after girdling, the settler learned from the Native Americans that he could plant hills of corn, beans, squash, and pumpkins right between the trees and stumps and roots of his new ground, using only a hoe. The runner beans could climb the cornstalks, and the squash and pumpkin vines could meander over the rough roots where they wished. This was perhaps the first example of intensified farming in America; it meant the farmer could harvest a bumper crop of food from a small plot, a vital necessity on a forested frontier. During this period, settlers learned to drop at least four grains of corn per hill, leading to the old folk saying:

One for the blackbird,
One for the crow,
One for bad weather,
And one to grow.

"Hoe farming"—while limited—assured a fairly diversified food crop from the small clearings that were typical of the early frontier farms of the eighteenth and nineteenth centuries. Corn and beans, fruits, nuts, and berries, and the milk from an old cow—plus pork from their wild pigs and meat from wild game—sustained the settler family as they conquered the wilderness.

In time, growing food in the Appalachian country became a reasonably successful enterprise. Those who claimed fertile valley lands straddling rivers such as the Shenandoah and the Tennessee, as well as the smaller streams, were able to create substantial farms; the black-soiled bottomlands produced mighty yields of corn, beans, and the like. Unlucky settlers who got the rough, rocky land higher up the hillsides and mountains, however, had a constant struggle to survive. Trying to grow crops on steep hills was a special challenge except for harvesting pumpkins. In the fall, all the farmer had to do was to roll his golden fruit down the hillside to his barn. On such steep land, oxen were preferred over horses or mules; while slower, they were more sure-footed.

Whether on good soil or bad, the common denominator was what the Indians called their "Mother Corn, Giver of Life."

Appalachian people's early attachment to corn was overwhelming. The native grain was the staff of life from early colonial days, providing the base for "the necessaries of life," ranging from bread to whiskey. As Harriette Arnow noted, a good crop of corn would translate into fat hogs, meat for the table, lard for biscuits, and grease for the lamp. Surplus corn meant whiskey while fodder and shucks would feed the family's milk cow over the winter.

Along with their axes and rifles and family treasures, the pioneers brought to Alabama the tales their forebears had heard in England, Ireland, Scotland, and Germany...

The farmer's earnest consideration is given to signs governing crop planting, the weather, fishing, hog killing and wood cutting...The lore-wise farmer knows one must not plant "eye crops"—potatoes, sugar cane, Jerusalem artichokes, and sweet potatoes—at night because the eyes will not be able to find their way to the surface. Cotton and grains should be planted during the light of the moon, while root crops do best when planted in the dark of the moon. For bulk and plenty of leafy growth, crops are planted on the growing of the moon, while for keeping qualities and weevil resistance, corn, peas, beans, and sweet potatoes should be seeded during the waning of the moon.

—WPA, The Alabama Guide (1941)

In contrast to other grains, corn not only provided four times the yield of wheat and oats, it seemed to possess a touch of the Almighty, having attributes that enabled it to grow quickly into a tall, strong plant, hoisting her ears well out of the reach of wild turkeys or raccoons. Also, her tightly wrapped ears were a great deterrent against smaller birds. And even when snow and ice came with corn still hanging in the fields, the corn's drooped and insulated ears were immune to the elements. Besides all this, the strong stalk provided a sturdy post for runner beans!

The love of corn went back to the early 1600s, when the Jamestown settlers were struggling to survive. It was maize that helped save them, thanks to the kind benevolence of Algonquin Indians who always kept a year's supply in storage.

Chief Powhatan early on was cooperative. As an Englishman reported, the chief was eager to "send some of his People that they may teach the English how to use the Grain of his Country." Emissaries of the chief and his daughter, Princess Pocahontas, delivered to Captain John Smith and his struggling newcomers a full-scale how-to course in growing, harvesting, grinding, and cooking the corn into soups, pones and hominy, and topped it all by teaching them how to fashion a glorious corn-bean succotash.

It was easy for settlers to understand why the Indians had venerated this grain [corn], but there seemed to be no end to the blessings it brought.

First of all, it provided them with a variety of food: cornbread, corn pone, johnnycake, Indian pudding, roasting ears, mush, popcorn, hominy, succotash, parched corn, dried corn, fresh corncakes, scrapple, stuffing, corn pudding, corn relish, corn soup, and other dishes...Corn fed the pigs and chickens, the horse and cow. Cornbread rewarded the faithful dog.

Pioneer homes used cornhusk mattresses, which were soft and comfortable...Settlers used corncobs as kindling and fuel. They used corncob pipes, corncob stoppers in jugs, and corncob fertilizer. The children made cornhusk and corncob dolls, played with hair, beards and mustaches fashioned of corn silk. Women made corncob syrup, a delicacy little known but still relished in the Kentucky mountain.

—ESTHER KELLNER, *MOONSHINE: ITS HISTORY AND FOLKLORE*

In time, and with a big push from Captain Smith, the first settlers came to realize that growing corn was a much more noble and essential pursuit than hunting for gold or attempting to grow silk. After all, corn yields quadrupled that of grains brought from England. To emphasize his point, John Smith himself planted forty acres in the native maize.

The amazing American corn thus became a near perfect crop for the new nation. By 1615, Virginia had more than five hundred acres in cultivation and in later years the colony was exporting corn to Massachusetts and even to the Caribbean. Thomas Ashe in 1682 put it this way: "Their Provision, which grows in the Field, is chiefly Indian Corn, which produces a vast increase, yearly, yielding Two plentiful Harvests, of which they make wholesome Bread, and good Bisket, which gives a strong, sound and nourishing Diet."

As corn production flourished, along with the fast-growing porker population that came with the introduction of swine from England, the basics of the Southern colonies' agriculture began to emerge: "Hogs and Hominy." The combination fit perfectly into Appalachian agriculture, and the foothill farmers of the Carolinas, Virginia, Tennessee, Kentucky, and Georgia were well on their way to self-sufficiency and beyond in the production of food and fiber.

~

A key element to the amazing Appalachian food story has been its wonderful array of gardens, which proved from the days of the early settlers to be a vital adjunct to each and every farmstead.

While garden patches required some initial plowing by the man of the house in the spring of the year, from then on it was in the hands of the housewife. Indeed the women were the sturdy "yeomen" of every farm, exerting tender loving care to

Family members tend the garden adjacent to their home in the Southern Appalachians.

the vegetable crop all the way from the first spring onions and greens, right up through the heavy-producing beans, tomatoes, okra, and the like.

"Mama worked her garden all the time," Chris Boatwright told me when I visited him at his beautiful valley farmstead in the shadow of north Georgia's majestic Cohutta Mountains. Chris was well past ninety years old at the time of my visit in 1995.

"Yes, Mama grew everything in her garden—pepper, okra, cabbage, tomatoes, beans—everything you could think of, crowder peas and field peas. We use to put up a sight of 'em."

In this 1930s scene, Western North Carolina farmers load up newly cut hay on their mule-pulled wagon.

While improved farming implements, plows and harrows, gradually came to the mountains, it was amazing, as noted earlier, what the housewives could accomplish with a hoe. As Rupert Vance reported in his *Human Geography of the South*, "A woman can take a…(hoe) in April and with a quart of seed plant a patch around a cabin and in six weeks she and her children can begin to eat roasting ears; and when it gets too hard for that, she can parch it."

The housewife maintained daily vigil against weeds and grass and made sure her plants received adequate water. During droughts it was her job to tote water from her well or spring to keep her plants alive.

Callie Henderson of Waleska, Georgia, planted a garden every season—spring, summer, fall, and winter. She gave her grandson Bill Hasty her secret to a good garden: "William, you must work your vegetable garden every day of the year if you expect to have produce to eat."

Azzie Fouts Waters, who now lives in East Ellijay, Georgia, remembered fondly the flourishing garden that her mother maintained at the Fouts farm in Dawson County, Georgia, not far from the southern end of the Appalachian Trail: "My daddy plowed the garden, but mother took care of it. She was proud of her garden…took real good care of it. Through the summer, we had fresh vegetables, plenty of cabbage and beans, okra and corn."

Life on the Fouts farm was always busy for the entire family:

We stored our corn in a hog house, and out from that was the log shuck house. After a corn-shucking, we would fill up the shuck house with feed for the cattle. I don't think we ever had a shucking party, but many people did. I remember going to a shuckin' they had at our neighbor's house. The men and the children shucked the corn while the women went in and helped prepare the dinner for the crowd. I remember the wives put on a big pot of turnip greens and some-how or another, with all of 'em buzzin' around, their dish rag got lost. Later on it showed up when they went to take up their turnip greens to put on the table. When they dipped the sau-cer down in the pot, there was the dish rag in their turnip greens!

My daddy grew wheat and rye. The threshers would come and spend a day or so in the summer… We'd take the wheat for grinding to Houser's mill on Shoal Creek right this side of Dawsonville. There would be the wheat bran for cow feed and the black shorts for hog feed and then the white shorts—they was all right to maybe make sweet bread out of—then there was the white flour.

> When "laying-by"…about the first week in July, the corn was so tall and the heat so intense, that life between the rows was almost intolerable. We were compelled to remove our trousers and plow in our shirt-tails, and even then, by the time our plows reached the end of the row, we were panting for breath, and so were our horses and mules; and they, like us, were soaked with perspiration.
>
> On such days, the water drunk from a wooden keg from the nearby Lowe Spring was the best that I have ever tasted in my lifetime. It was always cool…and had a pleasing and satisfying taste.
>
> —ROBERT SPARKS WALKER, CHATTANOOGA, TENNESSEE, *AS THE INDIANS LEFT IT*

We had a gristmill that ground our corn about a half mile from our home—the old Ruddell Mill. It was water-powered, turned by a water wheel from the waters of the Amicalola Creek.

At our home, we had a big old flour barrel and we had a meal gum, we called it. It was a big old hollowed out log. That's what we kept the meal in.

We had plenty out on our farm, such as it was, as good as anybody had at that time. The Faucette Lake community. That's where my grandfather grew up, and my mother. The post office was Johntown.

I hoed corn and pulled fodder on a lot of the ground that is under water now. Under the lake. It was a fine farm, bottomland. Where 136 road goes through. The bottom of the lake was a beautiful country land. Our farm was on one side and the Holden Densmore farm was on the other side. 'Course they put the lake right on the line between our farms. It was a good living. Our farm was around three hundred acres including the forests. My parents were good people. My father, Henry Fouts, carried the mail—a star route—about thirty-six years until his death in 1928. He traveled horseback [on his route] for several years. Then he had a two-seat road cart, then a buggy. In later years, he drove a car, a roadster, to deliver the mail.

Yes, our farm is no more, it's under the lake.

~

Fields of corn glisten in the sunshine in this turn-of-the-century photo as a wagon train of freight heads out from Dillsboro, North Carolina to Franklin. Note Indian mound at left.

The Art of Reading Signs

Tracking the Moon from Hog Killing to Moonshining

*It is a recognized axiom on moonology that hog meat killed on a
growing moon won't produce any grease [lard]...Killing on the wrong moon
also is a mighty good way to lose a hog.*

—*Herbert Wilcox of Elberton, Georgia*

~

Bathe only in the dark of the moon.

—*Bil Dwyer of Highlands, North Carolina,*
Thangs Yankees Don't Know

Early Celt settlers—the Scotch-Irish and the Scots and the Welsh—put great store in spirits, spells, and signs. Scots in particular were known to be blessed with a "second sight" of extrasensory perception that enabled them to predict the future and delve deeply into lunar "secret times."

It was no wonder that Gaelic myths, superstitions, and folklore that had been told and retold in the old country would take hold in the hollows and coves of eighteenth-century Appalachia.

The most popular manifestation of the powers of astrology—"checking the signs"—was a sacred absolute in colonial and pioneer days. Before having a baby, planting a crop, riving a roof,* or killing a hog, settlers pulled down their almanacs to check the zodiac status of the planets as they paraded across the celestial skies, particularly the phase of the moon.

"My daddy would plant his Irish potatoes only when the signs [were] in the feet, and the full of the moon...or as the moon started fullin'," declared A. L. Tommie Bass of Sand Mountain, Alabama. In his delightful account of turn-of-the-century

---

*Splitting oak boards with a froe, a type of ax.

life in the north Alabama hills, *Plain Southern Eating* (a tome recorded and edited by Professor John Crellin), Tommie religiously followed his father's wishes when it came to planting by the signs, come heck or high water. "He'd

tell me to go out and plow up the ground…I've done it when the water would follow the furrow, because he wanted to get [the potatoes] in…while the moon was right."

Kentucky's Dick Frymire, who created a far-flung cottage industry with his clairvoyant rooster, asserts that you should avoid planting potatoes in the new of the moon. If you do, they "will produce vines three feet tall, and the potatoes will come to the top of the ground and sunburn."

Before killing a hog, such as this one slaughtered at the turn of the century in Gilmer County, Georgia, farmers would pull down the almanac to see the status of the moon and stars. A bad sign could cause one to lose a hog or risk having an awful mess of fatback, lard, or cracklin's.

And of course everyone in the hill country knows that you should never attempt to kill a hog on a dark moon, otherwise some of your meat will just vanish. It's always best to slaughter your swine when the moon is shrinking. So the traditional thinking goes.

~

The supernatural science of "signs" astrology was said to have originated a thousand years before the birth of Christ, and confirmed in the Old Testament, in the third chapter of Ecclesiastes:

> To every thing there is a season, and a time to every purpose under the heaven: a time to be born, and a time to die; a time to plant, and a time to pluck up that which is planted. (vv. 1–2 KJV)

~

As soon as the first almanacs came out, in the 1700s, people of the Blue Ridge and other foothill areas of the Appalachians studied them closely, along with their Bibles, pondering the power of the planet positions within the twelve zodiac signs. The phases of the moon were particularly to be adhered to.

The basis for belief in astrology is that the planets, including Earth and its satellite moon, travel across an imagined highway in the heavens—a chart called the zodiac. Each of the twelve zodiac constellation signs, Gemini, Aries, etc., is assigned a part of the human body. Astrologers feel there is a strong link between the celestial clusters and the body. Therefore each part of the body—the head, the arms, the feet—is assigned a section of the celestial planet, together with a trait, such as being fertile or being barren.

Appalachian moonshiners checked the signs of the Zodiac before putting in a load of mash in preparation for a whiskey run. Among those who followed the moon in making corn whiskey was the late Theodore King of Towns County, Georgia, pictured here in one of his favorite poses.

But it's the moon and its phases that have attracted the most attention over the years. Even mountain moonshiners have looked to the moon for advice.

"I'll tell you about making whiskey, Joe," my late moonshiner friend Theodore (Thee) King of Hiawassee, Georgia, told me. "The weather and the time of year and the right phase of the moon is when you make whiskey. Don't never cook in a sweet mash on the new of the moon. If you do, it'll puke in your still and you'll never get it settled down. You want to cook it in the dark nights, on the dark of the moon.

"Cooking on the new of the moon you'll gain pot tails, hav'ta pour out some after ever' run. Cooking on the old moon, you'll lose pot tails, you'll have to add new meal, dang right you will!"

Confirming the commonly held belief that most illegal mountain whiskey was made by the light of the moon, Thee revealed that only a couple of times in his life did he recall stilling during daylight hours. And when he did, it felt uncomfortable to him. "We always cooked in of a night; it's good and cool and we just felt a little safer."

Planting of crops was considered best during the "fruitful" days of the month, such as those under the fertile "water" signs—Taurus, Cancer, Scorpio, or Pisces. Crops that would yield an aboveground harvest—such as beans, okra, tomatoes, and cabbage—were to be planted when the moon was waxing…getting brighter. The belowground crops—potatoes, beets, turnips—should be planted on the dark of the moon.

The Art of Reading Signs ⌢ 63

Many mountain people felt that the tender "eyed" vegetables—beans and peas and potatoes—needed to be in the ground by Good Friday. Otherwise they were sure to weep and even cry their eyes out over the Crucifixion.

As I grew up on a Blue Ridge foothills farm in the Double Springs community of Greenville County, South Carolina—in sight of Paris Mountain—I never heard my parents discuss signs. I do remember their reading the old faithful Grier's and Ladies Birthday almanacs. My father's big springtime goal was to make sure that all of his crops, particularly corn, were planted by April 15, a few days beyond the magic Good Friday planting date adhered to by many mountaineers for potatoes and other vegetables.

But the importance of signs was a strongly inherited gene in the makeup of most older-generation mountain people. Frances Gates Hill of the Mountaintown district of Gilmer County, Georgia, whose family always planted by the signs, declared flatly that it's an absolute no-no to attempt to make kraut or pickle beans when the signs are in the bowels. "It'll smell just like where you'd killed a hog, like a hog pen. We have tried it. They'll taste all right, but boy you can't stay in the house where they're making."

Even birds were considered by mountain people to be harbingers of things to come—probably an influence handed down by the Amerindians. Many mountain people told me that whippoorwills brought joy. When the shy songbirds started serenading them early of a spring morning, even if the chill of winter was still on the land, the birds were telling people to get their crop seeds in the ground. Cawing of crows in the morning was considered a good sign, foretelling the approach of Indian summer.

The blue jay, on the other hand, was a carrier of bad luck, a messenger from the devil, indeed described by some as a "bird of the devil." Stories were told of how the feisty jaybird's bent toward "devilment" was due to his having sold

> *During a blackberry winter, a cold spell late in the spring, Uncle France Wheeler, a hard-shell Baptist, was driving home from carrying a load of lumber to town. As he passed Les Baldwin's place, Nancy Baldwin was working in the garden, covering her early beans with old sacks and papers to prevent frost from killing them. Uncle France reprimanded her, "If hit's the Lord's will for your beans to get killed, they will, and if hit ain't they won't." Nancy quit covering her beans after she had protected two rows of the four. The next morning she had two rows of dead beans and two rows unharmed by the frost and the Lord.*
>
> —FLOYD E. AND CHARLES HUBERT WATKINS, *YESTERDAY IN THE HILLS*

his soul for a mere grain of corn. The jay's constant shuttling of sand and sticks meant that he was hauling them to hell to pay off the devil. Some went further, declaring the bird's primary mission was to spy on people and deliver a catalog of their sins to the man below.

Katydids were the forecasters of hog-killing weather. Within four months of the katydids' first cry, you could count on the arrival of a "killing frost." Not far beyond that, the temperature could be expected to drop low enough to enable a person to slaughter his swine.

When catbirds made their first appearance in the springtime, mountain youngsters whooped with joy. That's when mothers would let their kids go barefoot, but not before, according to Quay Smathers of Dutch Cove, North Carolina.

> *F*ather was always careful clearing a new ground, plowing the garden or field...He did not want to accidentally kill a toadfrog. He said if you killed a toad, your cow would give bloody milk. He and mother warned us to be careful especially during the Dog Days of early August because...dogs were likely to take fits and go mad. Snakes went blind during Dog Days and struck out wildly at anything which moved.
> —SIDNEY SAYLOR FARR, *MORE THAN MOONSHINE*

Weather forecasting seemed to be a natural role for birds. If you hear a dove holler, Berbie Harkins told author Ann Dismukes Amerson of Dahlonega, Georgia, you could count on rain to arrive within three days. Berbie had experience with screech owls also. She declared that if you hear one that sounds like a woman, "you can bet it will be raining inside of twenty-four hours."

The Cherokees had many signs and myths concerning birds, the most notable being that the mountains and valleys were formed by the dipping wings of the great buzzard as he swung low over the earth. Some Appalachian tribes gave crows high recognition and protection. They were considered the power that had brought them the wonderful gift of corn. Even pioneers gave credence to the rain crow as a rain forecaster.

Roosters, such the one Dick Frymire has used to predict the outcome of athletic contests, are considered supernatural in the hills. Emory University professor Floyd Watkins and his father, Charles, in their authentic book, *Yesterday in the Hills*, confirmed the role of a rooster: "General Wheeler often spoke of the crowing of the cock in the Bible. After a rooster crowed in an unusual way or at an unusual time of the night, something bad happened. If a neighbor was seriously sick, General would say, 'I wonder how old Tom Wilson is; you know that rooster crowed peculiar last night.' Crowing hens predicted calamity. People killed them because they were unclean agents of evil."

The wailing of dogs, the screeching of owls, and the ticking of a small insect "deathwatch" inside a wall were considered bad omens, perhaps a sign of death.

But astrological signs were what most mountain people gave credence to. The twelve divisions of the zodiac make up the "signs." The moon, according to the ancient astrologers, visits each sign two or three days each month. Therefore, the moon's impact on planet Earth—its people and their plants—varies from sign to sign, being advantageous to some signs and disadvantageous to others.

The "Ruling Days" of January were said to hold great significance.

Many old-timers celebrated "Old Christmas" on January 7, supposedly the precise date of Christ's birth. On that date, it was said, pokeweed would put forth sprouts and all the farm animals would kneel with their heads toward Jerusalem at "the first daybreak." That preliminary daybreak, sending up near brilliance of a real sunrise, would take place an hour early, followed by the dark, at which time the poke sprouts would fold over and wither.

> *We cut firewood and killed hogs on the shrinking of the moon. That's after it fulls—before it news. On the new moon or growing of the moon, the wood wouldn't burn good; it would fry at the ends...you could see juice coming out and you had to use a lot of dry kindling wood to make it burn. The hog meat and cracklin's, sides or middling or any other part would not fry out good. The cracklings would be spongy or rubbery if you killed the hog on the growing or new moon.*
>
> —FRANK PRESSLEY OF LAKELAND, GEORGIA, A NATIVE OF CULLOWHEE MOUNTAIN, NORTH CAROLINA

Most mountain people believed in the signs because the tradition came down from their fathers and grandfathers. As hill country native Walter Lambert of the University of Tennessee put it, "I simply know that because generations of my family have told me, that it is fair to plant in the head, good to plant in the arms or legs, and that cucumbers should be planted in the 'twin signs' of May."

But in his insightful book of reminiscence, *Kinfolks and Custard Pie*, Lambert reflects the growing modern-day ambivalence toward astrological forecasting. He admits that he doesn't much remember or follow the signs today. But with wry humor he nearly always takes note of just where he happens to be when the new moon emerges. That's supposed to have a bearing on one's fortunes.

"If you happen to be going up hill when you see the new moon, you are in for a good month. If you are on level ground, things will continue about the same. However, if you happen to be going down a steep hill, watch out!"

Even Sand Mountain's Tommie Bass admits that the era of signs may be near an end.

"Most people don't bother with signs now. Folks rely more on chemicals to get a crop."

Frances Hill hasn't given up on her almanac just yet. She always tries to get a Griers almanac every year but she's noticed that different almanacs have different predictions, and she's thinking that perhaps the weather has more to do with how crops fare than anything else.

"We always planted by the signs," she said, but sometimes credibility was stretched a bit. "Mama planted a row of beans one time when the signs was in the bowels, and Grandma said, 'Don't plant them beans! Just forget what you've already planted; plow 'em up, they won't do nothin'.' And you know what? That was the prettiest row of beans we ever did have."

Sweet potatoes were dug on the light of the moon and this saved them from rotting. Corn was planted on the light of the moon with the sign in the arms or thighs. If planted then, it should grow taller and produce bigger ears of corn. This was also the best planting time for beans. It was said that cabbage or mustard would have lice on them if planted when the sign was in the head. Cucumbers would bear to the ends of the vines if planted when the sign was in the feet.
—GLADYS RUSSELL, *CALL ME HILLBILLY*

Still today, many people in Gilmer County, Georgia—like those across Appalachia—pay heed to the signs.

Or as the beloved Aunt Arie of *Foxfire* fame declared: "Makin' apple butter on the new of the moon is best. But then really we couldn't always do that. We just made it when we could."

The Art of
Mountain Cooking
From the Fireplace to the Microwave

*"Honey," said Mother Mayberry with a pleased laugh as she seated the
minister's wife in a large rocker..."don't you know that nothing in the world
compliments a woman like the asking her for one of her cooking rules?"*
–Maria Thompson Davies of McMinnville, Tennessee,
quoted in Some Favorite Recipes *(1911)*

~

I'd a heap rather cook as t'eat.

—*Aunt Arie Carpenter,* Foxfire

~

*The North seldom tries to fry chicken and this is well: the art cannot be
learned north of the line of Mason and Dixon.*

—*Mark Twain*

I can see my mother now...she had a rack in her fireplace and she'd have her kettle
a'cookin' beans, 'specially shuck beans and green beans." Nina Garrett, now
ninety and living in her family's elegant old tin-roofed homeplace near Cartecay,
Georgia, remembers the mountain manner of hill country cooking in earlier days—
right in the fireplace.

For centuries, old settlers depended on their fireplaces for the cooking of their foods.
That is up until the end of the Civil War and the advent of the cast-iron and modern-
day stoves.

As we sat and rocked and talked on Miss Nina's front porch, she reminisced that
the food tasted better back then, around the turn of the century when she was a young
woman. Food had a full-bodied flavor because the meats and vegetables were cooked
more slowly. (It didn't hurt the flavor any that a nice chunk of fatback always shared the
pot with the beans and stews. And biscuits had a generous amount of lard.)

Hearty agreement came from neighboring mountain man supreme Curtis

Underwood, a former restaurateur, who confirmed that slow cooking was the key to much of the good eating that came out of Southern Appalachian kitchens over the years. He cited his mother-in-law, one-hundred-year-old Dessie Emma Kendall Tipton, who grew up at the foot of Brushy Mountain: "Miss Dessie cooked on an old wood-burning stove, but she slow-cooked everything. She didn't try to cook her beans or potatoes to death. Everything she cooked was fit to eat."

Ninety-year-old Nina Garrett of Gilmer County, Georgia, remembers fondly how her grandmother slow-cooked meats and vegetables in the fireplace, giving them a delicious taste.

Not overcooking vegetables was one of the great preachings of Southern cookbook writers of the past, such as Georgia's Annabella Hill, Virginia's Mary Randolph, and Kentucky's Lettice Bryan. Mrs. Randolph, in her 1824 tome, *The Virginia Housewife*, noted that asparagus "lose their good appearance and flavor if cooked too long." She added that "close attention and good judgment are necessary to know the proper time to take them up." In 1883, Estelle Wilcox, in her *Dixie Cook-Book*, advised that vegetables should not be cooked too long, "only till tender as too long cooking is very injurious." Tennessee's Martha McCullough-Williams also called for long-cooking caution.

On the other hand, even modern-day chefs like James Villas speak up for the old-time "thorough cooking" style. "Southerners are often accused of destroying some of the integrity of vegetables by overcooking them, but...what we might lose in texture and nutrient, we gain in sublime flavor." Similar thinking came from South Carolina's Ben Robertson: "We have never put much stock in the scalding school of vegetable cooking."

And while the early cookbooks seldom made it to isolated areas of the Appalachian "backcountry," it is interesting that their sentiments were shared and paid attention to where good cooking prevailed.

Key component of traditional, straightforward mountain fireplace cooking was the Dutch oven, a slow-cooking masterpiece if there ever was one. Having three legs and a flanged lid, it was, as Bil Dwyer loved to declare, "the pioneers' all-in-one cooking utensil." It could be suspended over an open fire, placed right in the fire, or ensconced in a bed of hot coals on the hearth. "It was at once a kettle, a frying pan, an oven, a pot, and sometimes even a stove."

Hazel Farmer, who played Maybell in the north Georgia mountain drama *Reach of Song*, prizes her grandmother Raburn's Dutch oven. "My folks baked potatoes in it and breads and cakes. Black cast iron with three legs. It was an all-purpose thing; I've cooked everything in it myself."

A confirmation came from the Cumberland foothills near Pulaski, Tennessee. Bessie Lard Llewellyn declared the Dutch oven food flavor was unequaled. "My grandmother on my mother's side had a big old Dutch oven, and she'd lotta times pour corn bread in that big old skillet and put the lid on it and then put coals on top of it. Didn't take long. We'd bake potatoes in it too. One thing that made it so good was having the lid on it; that kept the flavor in it. And such a wonderful flavor it was!"

> *There was no electricity in those days, so we carried oil lamps from room to room and cooked in the fireplace. Pots and pans hung from a wire over the fire, and corn bread and biscuits and even cakes baked in a Dutch oven set right in the hot coals. You used a pair of long tongs with a hook on the end to take the lid off to see if the bread was getting brown. When it got done, it was so good, it would melt in your mouth!*
>
> —LOIS SAINE, IN *I REMEMBER DAHLONEGA*

Speaking of flavor, there's no doubt that the obligatory piece of fatback provided flavor aplenty for any vegetable that went in the pot. Or as my friend Carl Dodd of Blue Ridge, Georgia, puts it: No fat—no flavor. This sentiment is echoed by the eminent food historian Karen Hess, who agrees that "cholesterol equals flavor."

(While high-fat diets draw severe present-day condemnation, there are many examples of people—dating all the way back to medieval Europe—whose high-fat diets did not affect their longevity. The Appalachians are full of old-timers who grew up on heavy regimes of mealtime pork yet who lived robust lives extending into their eighties and some topping a hundred. A key element in the Appalachians, of course—perhaps the perfect antidote or balance to such high-fat diets—was their physically active lifestyle, typical of life on a farm, particularly a mountain farm.)

> *"The bread's not browned. I ain't served brownless bread yet and I'm not going to take up shiftless ways."*
>
> —FROM THE NOVEL *LANDBREAKERS*, BY JOHN EHLE

Rhonda Boatwright, living on the Holly Creek prong of north Georgia's Cohutta Mountain range, still loves to put a pot of green beans over the fire in the old-fashioned way, along with "a big old piece of salted fatback and just let 'em simmer all day long, maybe boil a little bit. If anybody messes around with it, you might want to get the shotgun after 'em. It's good enough to kill for."

Farther north toward the Smokies, Ruth Swanson Hunter joined in the chorus. When I visited her Young Harris home and talked to Ruth and her husband, Melvin, Ruth said, "Corn bread tasted better back then, son, 'cause we were hungrier for it. You know hungry is the best meal you ever had. 'Course now that corn bread was good 'cause we cooked it in an oven in the fireplace. We called it an oven 'cause it had three legs and you put firecoals under it. It had a heavy led [*sic*] and you put firecoals on top of the led. Now we had a big pot hangin' in the fireplace on a chain. Mama cooked her green beans and pork in that pot, cooked 'em slow…a long time. They were good, too."

Much of the good cooking to come out of the Appalachians was due to slow fireplace cooking on a cast-iron Dutch oven with a flanged lid. Curtis Underwood of Resaca, Georgia, shows such an oven. Hot coals could be placed on top of the lid to allow vegetables, meats, breads, and cakes to be cooked slowly from underneath and above.

The unbeatable flavor from fireplace pots was confirmed by the irrepressible Martha McCullough-Williams, who, after a long hiatus as a writer in New York City, came back home to Tennessee at age sixty-five and wrote a marvelous tribute to country cooking in the old days in the old ways. She called her 1913 treatise *Dishes and Beverages of the Old South*.

"Ah me!" she reveled, "what savors, what flavors came out of the pots! Years on years I was laughed at for maintaining that no range ever turned out things to equal open-hearth cookery."

Harriet Beecher Stowe even linked the fireplace to American patriotism. "Would our Revolutionary fathers have gone barefooted and bleeding over snow to defend air-tight stoves and cooking ranges? I trow not. It was the memory of the great open kitchen-fire…its roaring, hilarious voice of invitation, its dancing tongues of flame, that called to them through the snows of that dreadful winter."

~

Appalachian cooking and foods carry a distinctive flavor and heritage from our English, Scotch-Irish, and German ancestors, but possibly even more important is the role played by the Amerindians who were here at the beginning of our nation's existence.

As Nashville food critic supreme John Egerton has stated, "The meeting of English and Indian people at Jamestown (in 1607) and the subsequent intermingling of their foods (with the Europeans) was the starting point for the region's distinctive food heritage."

While the British in time brought pigs, chickens, cattle, and sheep to supply the new American table, as well as grains, apples, cabbage, and turnips, the Jamestown pioneers received the generous help of the Iroquois/Algonquin Indians such as Chief Powhatan, who not only shared his tribe's stores of maize—the plant that would provide the base for much of colonial America's cuisine—but also peas and beans and pumpkins and native fruit. But over and above all this, the Indians trained the newcomers in the basics of growing, harvesting, grinding, and cooking up this amazing dish.

"It would be difficult to exaggerate the contribution of the American Indian to the diet of the South," stated Joe Gray Taylor in his masterful Southern food history, *Eating, Drinking and Visiting in the South*. It was from the Powhatans that the first settler wives received their "native food internships," learning how to identify and prepare available edible plants in the wild, such plants as pokeweed, persimmons, muscadines, and chestnuts and hickory nuts. Until swine became plentiful, bear grease and

Moravian cooking has a German heritage, for it was that heritage that was brought to Old Salem by the early settlers who came to this country from Moravia. The type of cooking is considerably like that of the Pennsylvania Dutch. Slight differences come from the fact that the Moravians in Pennsylvania settled among the Germans, whereas the Moravians in North Carolina settled among the English.

—BETH TARTAN, *NORTH CAROLINA AND OLD SALEM COOKERY*

walnuts and hickory nuts provided the cooking oils, thanks again, of course, to the friendly Indians, whose initial generosity was crucial to the settlement's survival (as well as the entire British colony up and down the seaboard).

Without doubt crucial help from the Indians came with the growing, harvesting, pounding, and cooking of corn. This was extremely important because the rye and wheat the first Britishers brought to Jamestown for their oatcakes failed to thrive in the virgin Virginia soil.

As ensuing years would confirm, corn became the region's single most important foodstuff. The *Progressive Farmer*'s Sallie F. Hill wrote in the magazine's 1961 *Southern Cookbook*, "Corn was the South's essential cooking ingredient. Aside from cornbread which many Southerners make at least once a day, we need 'meal' to fry fish or squirrel…We use meal in chess pie and most 'dressings' or stuffings. We use cornmeal dumplings for turnip greens and poke salad…and many will tell you that fried chicken must be dipped in cornmeal."

The Indians' storehouse of knowledge and propagation generosity extended to potatoes, beans, squash, peas, and green and red peppers. And while the Indians had tomatoes and eggplants under cultivation, most of the pioneer settlers refused to plant or eat them until the mid-1800s due to rumors of shade plant poison.

The Indians' food contribution was showcased in the 1940s at an annual feast put on by the Museum of the Cherokee Indian at Cherokee, North Carolina. The variety was impressive. The menus included broiled speckled trout, roast buffalo, roast deer, and stewed raccoon. A glorious array of bread was offered: bean bread, chestnut bread, hominy bread (corn bread), and molasses bread. Vegetables included boiled potatoes, roasted corn, hominy, beans cooked with fatback, wild greens, succotash, boiled Jerusalem artichokes, and ramps. Fruits and nuts were plentiful, fresh from the Smoky Mountain wilds: blackberries, huckleberries, wild

Powhatan and Cherokee cooks, following Algonquin and Iroquoian custom, always had food ready to serve if someone stopped by. In their households, a bubbling pot of soup or stew simmered at all times. Favorite recipes combined wild game—usually squirrel, rabbit, or turkey— with corn, beans, and tomatoes. However, like the delicious soups produced by French farmers' wives, the exact recipe for…stew depended on what leftovers were available to add to the pot.

—BEVERLY COX, SPIRIT OF THE HARVEST

strawberries, dewberries, gooseberries, raspberries, elderberries, plus wild plums, crab apples, persimmons, fox grapes, possum grapes, ground cherries, and nuts, including hazelnuts, hickory nuts, walnuts, and butternuts.

Intermingled with these Indian foods were the traditional foods from Europe that came with the settlers rolling down the Great Philadelphia Wagon Road in the 1700s. Particularly so were the great stick-to-your-ribs German dishes that arrived on the frontier—dumplings, krauts, apple butters, souses, and funnel cakes. As with the English and Scotch-Irish and French foodways, these were blended in with the Indians' "earth foods" found on the "Great American Southwest" frontier. The German migrants brought another cuisine contributor down the Wagon Road—their accurate long rifles. Thus wildlife such as bear and venison meat was more easily brought to the frontier table.

In 1778, a rousing feast occurred on the Ohio River, the present-day Louisville, Kentucky. Among the meats were bear, buffalo, wild turkey, venison, rabbit, and raccoon. These were accompanied by three kinds of corn bread: milk, butter, and homemade cheese. "The main attraction," Harnett Kane wrote, "was a very large possum, baked whole, and hanging by its tail from a piece of wood in the center of the table. While it lasted, the marsupial was the preferred meat of the feasters."

> German and Scotch-Irish settlers of the Piedmont Carolinas and Virginia added oats [oat cakes] to the Southern pantry of cereals. This simple old-fashioned cake refers readily to its highland homeland. In the winter it is welcome simply toasted and served with butter. In summer, serve it just warm with fresh raspberries and whipped cream.
> —BILL NEAL, *Biscuits, Spoonbread, and Sweet Potato Pie*

~

Southern Appalachian mountain cooking, while the subject of outsider jeers and criticism for the tendency of some wives to overcook and "overgrease" vegetables, nevertheless has had its advocates.

The aforementioned Mr. Kane, hailing from New Orleans, the most "gourmet" of Southern cities, wrote that "I can testify, from visits in Tennessee and Georgia, that mountain cooking—at Christmas or at any other time—can be memorable. Home-cooked ham with dark gravy, or pork ribs covered with their own fine drippings, or a simple cake still warm from the open fireplace…each has its own particular quality."

Indeed mountain food preparation has made great strides since the days of the fireplace Dutch oven, the crane, and the black pot. But with modern-day outdoor grills, particularly for barbecue and such, the rush is on to return to our pioneer roots, that of cooking by direct heat.

When all but the poorest Appalachian families of the nineteenth century graduated to cast-iron "wood stoves," it was, for each, a moment of quiet celebration. The most famous line of cookstove over the years was the old standard "Home Comfort," manufactured by the Wrought Iron Range Company of

"St. Louis, U.S.A." that began business in 1864. Various models are still to be found across the region. Mrs. Azzie Fouts Waters is one who prizes her Home Comfort stove that still graces the kitchen of her home in East Ellijay, Georgia. For years, she kept hers fired up most every day during winter months, using it not only to cook with—although she has an electric range/oven also—but as an extra heater for her frame home.

One of the great cooking instruments of the Southern Appalachians was the Home Comfort wood-burning stove, many of which are still used. Here Azzie Fouts Waters of East Ellijay, Georgia, makes up a batch of biscuit dough standing next to her old faithful "Home Comfort."

"When we started housekeeping in 1931 in Dawson County, I had a little four-eye cast-iron wood stove. It cooked good. We used that for several years. Poplar makes the best stovewood; it's cleaner for one thing, but my husband would cut up what was available. Then I had another stove with a warming closet on it. That one burned when our house burned. The neighbors came in and helped us build the house back, helped saw the logs, and had it back ready to move into within a month. Then we bought this Southern Comfort stove from a lady who wanted to sell her house."

Some stunning meals have come from such stoves over the years. At our home in upstate South Carolina during the thirties and forties, the cast-iron stove was our mother's pride and joy. Looking back, it seems a miracle how she managed to turn out such scrumptiously superlative meals week in and week out, including grand dinners for a roomful of guests. And she did it in such an efficient and masterly manner, using only that plain wood stove. Although at times she had the aid of a cook helper, her kitchen management skills were amazing. For a Sunday dinner, Mother had to cook everything from scratch, including killing the chickens, picking the fresh vegetables, making up the biscuits and dessert (usually a banana pudding), and getting everything cooked and ready, along with fixing up the ice tea, which required drawing water from the well on the back porch. How she also found time to attend Sunday morning Bible school and worship service on such days is beyond my comprehension. But of course, the triumph came after the blessing had been spoken by the preacher and we all sat quieted down and discovered anew her miracle of creation. Mama and Daddy would be greatly pleased, particularly Mama, when the good reverend asked for second helpings.

Frank Pressley, a native of Cullowhee, North Carolina, is proud of his Southern Comfort wood-burning stove that he fires up on occasion. He also uses cast-iron pots and pans.

Breakfasts were a special challenge since in those days (late 1930s), the first meal was many times the heartiest. When our family was growing up near Greenville and later in Lancaster County—and with a healthy gang of six children—our mother would cook up an amazing breakfast batch of forty-five biscuits (some to be held over for later meals)! Into the oven went a square pan that held twenty-five biscuits, plus two round pans of ten each. In addition to that, of course, Mother cooked up at least a dozen scrambled eggs, fried sausage, and fixed hot coffee and milk. For a breakfast dessert, we had a generous helping of sorghum syrup that we stirred with butter and then sopped with the biscuits.

Just how did mountain cooks such as my mother learn to cook? From their mothers, of course, and also from booklets put out by the stove manufacturers, such as the *Home Comfort Cook Book* and one published by the Rumford Chemical Company, the 1934 *Rumford Complete Cook Book*. Later Southern cookbooks from such names as Mrs. S. R. Dull of the *Atlanta Journal*, originally published in

1928, set the region's culinary standards for many years. People on Hazel Creek, North Carolina, in the early part of this century got many of their recipes from the friendly little *GRIT* newspaper, according to Professor Duane Oliver. I was glad to hear that, since as a young lad in South Carolina Piedmont I sold and delivered the old-timey tabloid that came to us from Williamsport, Pennsylvania.

The *Progressive Farmer* magazine also had a lot to do with cooking trends across the mountain South. In one of its old editions, a writer noted that "many wrecked homes, many divorces… have been traced directly to bad digestion, the result of wrong methods of cooking."

Nina Garrett had to use a little youthful persuasion to get her grandmother to teach her some cooking fundamentals.

Her grandmother Garrett "was a good hand to bake biscuits," Nina said. But a hand injury put her temporarily out of commission as a cook. It was that weekend that Nina's mother allowed her daughter to visit her grandmother. On their way, Nina's uncle said, "Nina, I'm awful glad your mama let you come home with us 'cause I'm wantin' some good biscuits in the morning."

"Well, I never had baked a single biscuit in my life! I was 'shamed to tell it but Mama had never let me learn. I didn't sleep none that night at Grandma's until I figured out how I'd do the next morning. So when we went to fixin' breakfast, I said, 'Grandma, I might not fix it right, since we have self-risin' flour at home, and you have plain, so you gonna have to help me a little." Well, Grandma turned and pointed to three big cans—two cans of the lard and a can of honey.

Musing on Measuring

Most cookbooks use explicit measurements in their recipes…[My husband] would say, "Billie, if you'll just measure, you'd be a better cook." My response: "I can't ever find the measuring spoons or the measuring cup." When you have little kids you'll give them anything…to play with, if it'll keep them happy. (One day I found my measuring cup in the boys' room with a live baby turtle in it. See?)…

In my recipes, when I say "teaspoon" I mean a small spoon. Unless I say "heaped" make it level…Don't give up; there's more:

A dab: Like a dab of butter. A heaping teaspoonful.

A glob: That's a heaping tablespoon.

A smidgen': That means a pinch, and a pinch is what you can hold between your thumb and index finger.

—BILLIE TOUCHSTONE SIGNER,
REDNECK COUNTRY COOKING

She said, 'Nina, honey, you get you a good wad of lard and grease the pan real good and you put plenty of that shortenin' in the flour; that's the way we like it.' So I did and mixed it in. Grandma put in the sodey and salt with her good hand and I kneaded the dough and pinched off the biscuits into the bread pan. You know the first ever biscuits I baked was as good as I've ever baked! So when I come back home the next morning, my brothers was ready to laugh at me but I was always tricky with 'em and I was ready. Miz Matthews was there, one of our neighbors. Mama said, 'Well, Nina, I reckon you got into it this mornin' a'tryin' to cook biscuits and you not knowin' the first thing about it.' And I says, 'Who's to blame, Mama, you wouldn't learn me. But I'm here to tell you, my uncle really enjoyed my biscuits; he said no one cooked better biscuits than I cooked this morning.'"

Everybody goes hog wild about my biscuits. I take a sifter of flour, to make say nine biscuits. Then I take about five spoonsful of lard or Crisco, put it in there, take a cup of buttermilk, work it up.
—AZILEE EDWARDS, *CABBAGETOWN FAMILIES, CABBAGETOWN FOOD* (1976, ATLANTA)

As we sat and rocked, Nina looked at me and smiled a gentle smile of satisfaction.

~

"Cookery is not chemistry," said X. Marcel Boulestin in *Petits et grands plats*, "it is an art. It requires instinct and taste rather than exact measurements."

And as Kentucky's Charles Patteson has written concerning cooking, Kentucky-style, "Nature doesn't operate with scientific exactness. If you were making an apple pie filling, you might want to combine apple slices, brown and white sugars, butter, cinnamon, nutmeg and perhaps other things. Exactly how much sugar to add or how much of the spices, is impossible to say, since the sweetness or tartness of the apples has a lot to do with it."

To this day, my favorite meal is fried chicken, field peas, green beans cooked all day with ham, fried okra, and corn bread.
—DEBORAH NORVILL, OF DALTON GEORGIA

Indeed. The key to good mountain cooking—to cooking in general—was enunciated also by the indomitable Margaret Lupo, for many years the legendary queen of Atlanta's Mary Mac tearoom. From the famed country food eatery on Ponce de Leon Avenue (one I frequent and love), Margaret declared that the two essentials to turning out great meals are "fresh ingredients and skillful cooks."

The cook's skill and loving attention to detail are where the "art" comes in. Reynolds Price, growing up on the edge of the Appalachian Piedmont, told it eloquently in his novel *Good Hearts*, recalling his mother and her approach to food:

"It was Mama's usual light touch—the turkey with cornbread dressing and cranberry sauce, country ham, corn pudding, snaps and little butterbeans she'd put up last July, spiced peaches, cold crisp watermelon-rind pickle, macaroni and cheese, creamed potatoes and gravy, then her own angel food cake and ambrosia. Every mouthful made the only way, from the naked pot upward by hand...Whenever I compliment her on it, she just says, 'It's the only way I know to cook.'"

Throughout the Southern mountains food and fixin's are held in tender reverence. Heirloom recipes for dried-apple stack cakes, stack pies, chicken and dumplings, roast venison, burgoo, wilted lettuce, apple butter, and fried liver are passed from generation to generation with loving loyalty. To say nothing of the myriad of special dishes made from the fruit of the land—from black walnuts, ramps, persimmons, pawpaws, fresh corn, shuck beans, sourwood honey, blackberries, and muscadine "bullaces."

"There is...something about the foodways of the mountains...that is undeniably compelling, even graceful," Eliot Wigginton noted in his intro to *The Foxfire Book of Appalachian Cookery.*

"Perhaps it has to do with the power of the experience, for older mountain women…as a rite of passage in their lives…

"Perhaps that compelling quality has something to do with the fact that food… became somehow a metaphor for the generosity and interdependence of life here that transcended the food itself…

"At Aunt Arie Carpenter's, cooking became an event, as opposed to a utilitarian task… There was not a single instance when she did not ask us, with more than a little… anticipation in her voice, 'Now will you'uns stay and eat with me?'"

The best cook in the mountains was Homer Bailey of Doublehead Gap, a confirmed bachelor. Homer cooked bear and groundhog to taste better than beef. He used a lot of dried red peppers and made good dumplings. He used to fry country ham in the morning so slow it would drive you crazy 'til it got done. But oh, was it good. Homer baked a chicken one time that my kids still talk about. He's the one that used to bury a pan and potatoes and onions in the mountains and when he went fishing out there, he'd dig it up and cook his fish and potatoes and onions on the spot.

—Betty Jo Bailey, Adairsville, Georgia

∽

In the following chapters, you will get a glimpse of the true dedication and loving approach Southern Appalachian women direct toward their foods. As my daughter Geneva (Llewellyn), a graduate nurse in Huntsville, Alabama, often declares,

"In the South, food is love."

∽

Cooking Advice for a Newlywed

My friend, the late Margaret Castleberry, who graced our newsroom at the Gainesville, Georgia, Daily Times on many occasions in the 1950s, passed on to newlywed wives a brilliant cooking suggestion.

She advised that in preparation for their husband's arrival at home each day—no matter what the planned menu—they should have a few onions sizzling in the skillet. "They smell so good and promising!" she said with her infectious laugh.

The Art of Preserving
Smoking, Salting, Drying, Burying, and Canning

Making relishes, chutneys, preserves, and marmalades may come close to a science,
but it is also an art—a row of these preserved fruits is a beautiful thing.
— *Camille Glenn,* The Heritage of Southern Cooking

~

One way people kept pumpkins from freezing was to bury them under fodder
in the barn loft; they stayed warm all winter.
— *Duane Oliver,* Cooking on Hazel Creek

~

A hornet's nest makes the finest place in the world to store hen eggs in wintertime.
Keeps 'em from freezin'.
— *Tlitha Messer of Jonathan's Creek, North Carolina,*
as told to John Parris in Mountain Cooking

Papa's daddy was half Indian; his mother was all Indian. I remember going to Aunt Martha's house, Papa's older sister. She'd have a pole across the porch; she'd cut pumpkins in big old rings and hang 'em up to dry on the pole. They made some of the best pies you could eat. You could fry 'em too, and put sugar on 'em." Thus spoke Bessie Lard Llewellyn, who resides in the hills of Tennessee.

When it came to preserving foods, mountain people displayed magnificent ingenuity. With only a springhouse to serve as their refrigerator—or perhaps just a lively branch of water or a well where they kept their milk and butter—they put up their foods in a superlative manner: pickling, drying, salting, smoking, spicing, burying, bleaching, sulphuring, fermenting, and, in time, canning.

Some hill folk even used hornets' nests to protect their eggs from freezing in mountain winters. As Tennessee's Willadeene Parton said in her autobiography, "We understood the true meaning of the term 'preserves.'"

"Putting-up" improvisations led to some of the great dishes of the region: "leather-britches" (dried snap beans—sometimes called shuckbeans or fodderbeans), sauerkraut, dried-apple stack cakes, smoked and salted pork, plus a vast array of jellies, jams, butters, pickles, and preserves. And let's don't forget smoked apples! Mark Woody remembered how he and his widowed mother, Laura Beaver Woody, sulphur-smoked apples at their homestead in the shadow of north Georgia's Whiskey Bill Mountain:

> Mother and I would slice up about twenty-five pounds of apples and put 'em in a flour sack. We'd take an empty whiskey barrel and set a three-legged skillet of hot coals down on the bottom. We'd pour a cup of sulphur on the coals and suspend that sack of apples over those smoking coals. That smoke would just boil; it would knock you out if you breathed it much. We'd throw a quilt over the barrel and let it set overnight. Next day, we'd pour the apples in a crock for the winter. We'd get the sulphur at the store, take a dozen eggs or so to buy such as that. The sulphur would penetrate those apples and preserve them as nice as you please. They'd keep all winter and they were tasty, 'course they had a little sharper whang [taste] than otherwise.

As public television's Nathalie Dupree has written, "Putting up food for later times, putting up food to be given away, putting up food just to have, is an important tradition in the South."

In the early hill country years, however, preserving food was a dire necessity, a major act of self-preservation, particularly when facing the feared dead-of-winter "starvation time."

John and Luraney Oliver, first white persons to settle in Cades Cove, Tennessee, survived on dried pumpkins during their initial winter there (1820). They arrived in the fall, too late to plant a crop, according to their great-great-grandson, retired Western Carolina University professor Duane Oliver. "That winter they would have starved had not the local Cherokees taken pity on them and given them dried pumpkin to get them through the winter."

Professor Oliver, inspired by his ancestors' stories of survival, has recorded his family's history in a fascinating narrative, *Remembered Lives*. His great-great-grandparents on his mother's side—Moses and Patience Proctor—were the first settlers on Hazel Creek, North Carolina. Based on his research and personal experience growing up on Hazel Creek (now partially covered by Fontana Dam), Duane Oliver found that mountain folk in the early settlement days worked extremely hard to store their foods. "By the time winter arrived, the smokehouse, corncrib, house, barn, and earth around the cabin contained almost all the pioneer family would eat in the winter, except for what the men shot in the woods."

~

Of all the preservation arts, drying was the most popular. In upstate South Carolina, Wincey Hunter Dabney (my mother) dried her red peppers by stringing them up on our back porch. After the peppers had shriveled up, she would take them in, chop them up—a few at a time—and use them in the kitchen, particularly in freshly ground sausage.

On Cullowhee Mountain, North Carolina, Iva Ashe Pressley "would hang shuckie beans around her old wood stove, to help dry 'em, and then she'd hang 'em out in the open," her son Frank remembered.

Some folk first dried their fruits in the oven. "Mama used to dry everything from blackberries and roastin' ears to apples and peaches and pumpkin," Berbie Robinson Harkins, told Dahlonega, Georgia, author Anne Dismukes Amerson. "She would put them in the oven and heat them just enough to keep them from souring. Then she laid them out on a long table in the sun and covered it with cheese cloth to keep the flies off."

Settlers learned bean- and pumpkin-drying techniques from the Amerindians. The drying of fruits and beans still continues. Even today, if you get off back-country roads in the Southern Appalachians, you can find evidence of this still-practiced art that includes dried beans, dried apples, dried peaches, dried berries, dried grapes, dried herbs, walnuts, peas, corn, sweet potatoes, and pumpkins, to name a few.

"They didn't can [their foods] back when I was growing up, they dried everything," Frank Norris told author Warren Moore in *Mountain Voices*. "Beans, corn, everything they grew they dried that couldn't be preserved in the ground…They had dry houses just like they had smoke houses." Some fortunate few built kilns to speed up the drying process.

I remember when people depended almost wholly on dried foods to survive [winters] in the cruel Depression years. Those who did not [dry their foods] or were not able to grow soup beans, bought them at the country store. If the farmer had the money he would buy a hundred-pound sack of beans. The Great Northern soup bean was the favorite, followed by the Pinto soup bean and the black-eyed pea.

—WILLIAM G. HASTY OF
CHEROKEE COUNTY, GEORGIA

Fruits are especially adaptable to drying. Apples, after getting a few weeks in the sun, turn a rich, rusty brown, and will "keep" for years, if hung in a dry place such as an attic.

With a little soaking, sugaring, and cooking, the dried fruit can be quickly turned into delicious dumplings, stack cakes, and pies.

As J. Hector St. John de Crèvecoeur wrote in his eighteenth-century memoir, "It is astonishing to what small size [apples] will shrink [when dried]. Those who have but a small quantity thread them and hang them in front of their houses. In the same manner, we dry peaches and plums without peeling them, and I know not a delicacy equal to them in the various preparations."

The formula for sun-drying fruits was an ancient one, having been accidentally discovered by the early Egyptians. They noticed that grapes left hanging on the vine in the sunshine lost their moisture and at the same time took on a sharply sweet new taste.

The Cherokees and other southeastern Indians squeezed persimmons into a pulp and spread the pulp out in half-inch-deep loaves. When dried, the pulp turned into delicious candy bars, much like "peach leather," a great deliciously chewy candy perfected by mountain pioneers. The Cherokees also sun-dried grapes, wild plums, and berries. They had an even quicker "outdoor kiln" drying method—hurdles, horizontal frames—which they erected with hickory saplings, and on which they spread their fruits. Underneath, fires were built to quick-dry the fruit.

My sister-in-law, Lib Dabney, recalled how her mother, Nannie Taylor Jones, who lived to age 104 in Greenville County, South Carolina, dried her peaches and apples. "Nannie had this little frame out in the backyard where it was in full sun. Every morning, she would take her sliced apples and peaches out there and put them on the rack and spread a net over them. If it started to rain, she'd run and bring 'em in. Then when they got to where they were near drying, she would put 'em in bags and store them in the basement. She made peach fried pies out of the dried fruit, little half-moon pies. Oh, they were good!"

Sometimes we'd have a scaffold outside; my daddy would put it up to dry apples on and sometimes we'd just break up [beans] and put 'em on a sheet or cloth and spread 'em out in the sun.

Sometimes we strung 'em. We took a needle and thread and strung 'em and hung 'em on a stick out in the sun. Let 'em stay out until they started drying and then put 'em back in the shade so they wasn't too dry, but keep it in the heat. They'd be yeller and bright, you know.

When you went to cook 'em, you'd take the beans off the string and break 'em up and put

North Georgia's Thelma Harmon Buice remembered her mother did the same thing, with the added note that she saved the peels and cores and turned them into jellies.

The smoking of fruit was a time-honored mountain technique. Frances Gates Hill, from north Georgia's Cohutta foothills, remembered her family's smokehouse filled with sulphurous smoke when the apples were being harvested. With a smokehouse full of apples, "Mother would set a saucer of sulphur in there and set it afire. She'd restart that fire two, three times a day. That preserved the fruit real well."

M. R. Perry of Gainesville, Georgia, gave me an old recipe for sulphur-bleaching of apples that left them "bone white."

> Prepare a large stoneware crock or wooden barrel. Line with white cloth (a worn sheet is fine). Peel tart apples and slice medium thin. Place 1 dishpan of apples in the barrel. Hollow out a cavity in the center of apples to set a small (1-quart) stoneware bowl to hold hickory coals. Have ready an airtight cover—old sheets or blankets to prevent smoke from escaping. Toss about 2 tablespoons of sweet sulphur on hot coals. Cover immediately. Do not inhale fumes! Let set 3½ hours. Repeat process until crock is full.

"Holing up" vegetables was a widespread practice—cabbage, potatoes, turnips, even apples. Cabbage preserved this way became white and tender, but apples took on the flavor of the earth.

On our upstate Carolina farm, every fall we built a "sweet potato hill" near the house, digging a six-foot-diameter "nest." We lined it with pine needles, packed in the tubers, then covered them with another blanket of pine needles. Final step was shoveling a half foot of dirt on top, mounding up a sharp cone top to allow rainwater to drain off. Many people hilled their Irish potatoes the same way, but we never did.

Chris Boatwright's father lined his potato hill with pine straw also. "Then he piled his taters in there," Chris recalled, "and covered 'em with a bunch of stalks where they'd get air down there but still be protected from those cold winds."

'em in a stew or whatever you were cooking. Or you could cook them separately; you'd soak them overnight and then you'd have a good piece of pork or sometimes a ham bone to put in and that would make it good. And some salt. Mother learned us girls not to put too much salt in to start with. Let 'em cook a while then you could kinda tell by tastin' it. That would be somethin' good to eat now, but you know I've not eat pork since I had my heart attack.

—NINA GARRETT, 90,
FROM NEAR CARTECAY, GEORGIA

To save cabbage for the winter months, many mountain people gave them an upside-down burial. They would yank up the heads of late cabbage from their gardens and bury them in a trench with the head down, leaving the root sticking up so the cabbage could be pulled out as needed. Around Christmastime, at Cullowhee, North Carolina, Iva Ashe Pressley could be heard to say, "Son, go out and get us a couple of heads of cabbage!" The son she was talking to, Frank Pressley, remembered how his mother would then boil the resurrected cabbage along with some fresh meat. "Boy, it was delicious," Frank said. He noted that "the outside leaves was what protected the cabbage heads. You'd pull off the discolored outer leaves and those heads were just as white and pretty, as sound and solid as a rock."

Many mountain farmers built root cellars, thick-walled rooms dug into hillsides or tunneled under farmhouses. Into the cellars would go barrels of apples, salted and pickled beef and beans, along with potatoes, onions, and other root crops. Being below the frost line, they kept the food from freezing in winter and from getting too hot in summer. Apples remained juicy and plump through the winter. Cellar-stored eggs were often cocooned in melted wax or straw, sometimes ashes.

> *With winter near, father would dig a three-by-four-foot hole in the ground. This was filled with crabgrass; the cabbage were cut and stacked up until they created a mound. Grass was again placed over them making air insulation, which would keep the cold. Last, but not least, the mound was covered with dirt. Believe it or not, those cabbage would keep the whole winter or until they were eaten by the family.*
>
> —WILLIAM G. HASTY,
> CHEROKEE COUNTY, GEORGIA

When spending the night with their grandparents near Canton, Georgia, young Alex and William Hasty would be taken by their grandpa down into his dark cellar underneath his house. "Daddy Hasty" would ask the boys what they wanted to eat. He let them pick from the rainbow array of vegetables and meats he had in storage—apples, cherries, tomatoes, relish, green beans, plus canned sausages, jams, and jellies.

Some vegetables such as onions were hung inside mountain homes. And the fruits—even those sun-dried and smoked—were stored in wooden barrels, baskets, and flour sacks. Crocks of pickled beans and kraut were usually close to the kitchen. As Duane Oliver recalled, "All these foods, sitting and hanging around, filled the air with their pungent aromas, getting mellower and mellower as the winter progressed."

~

Salt, when available, was the frontiersman's super-preservative. The practice came with the emigrants from Scotland, Ireland, England, and Europe. Salt was a crucial commodity that the settler was willing to pay his precious cash for, or more likely barter chestnuts or deerskins or corn whiskey for his salt—whatever it took.

Eighteenth-century writer Joseph Doddridge noted that "every family collected what peltry and fur they could obtain throughout the year for...salt and iron." North Carolina Moravians took butter, venison, hams, and the skins of deer and beavers to Charleston to barter for such necessities, including lead and powder. The settler, if he was lucky, obtained salt from salt springs or "licks." Sometimes he converted salt from the ashes of hickory wood or stream-weeds.

While the smokehouse became an essential building on every hill country farm for smoke-curing of pork, salt-curing became an even more effective method and eventually became the primary curing medium. Even though smoke-curing became passé, folk continued to call their meat buildings "smokehouses."

Salt brine was used a lot in the curing of pork and beef, by the barrelful. Even apples were kept by the salty method. Bil Dwyer's grandmother Phoebe would revive her wrinkled old apples by washing them in soda water, then placing them in a stone crock. Her brine mixture, a handful of salt mixed with three gallons of water, was poured over the apples and was changed every eight hours. She restored dry walnut meats by soaking them twelve hours in a solution of half water and half milk.

Sauerkraut was the salt-aged vegetable dish supreme

Barbecue, country ham, and grits all spring from Indian methods of preserving meat and corn by fire without the aid of salt. "For preservation, a barbecue is erected," a European traveler to the South wrote in the early nineteenth century, "and the fish are smoked over a fire." Since the discovery of salt, Europeans had preserved foods by pickling them in brine, but there were men who "barbecued" their game and fish by dehydrating them with mere smoke.

Smoke did for the southeastern tribes like the Catawbas and Cherokees and Creeks what the sun did for the tribes of the Southwest. A gathering of men around a raised platform of saplings above a fire pit to smoke the day's catch was a social occasion celebrating the gift of fire by which man tamed the wilderness and turned raw food to cooked before it rotted.

—Betty Fussell, I Hear America Cooking

for German settlers. In time, mountain people of all extractions grew to love the soured cabbage. They found it went well with wild game meat and pork. Most mountain homesteads put up at least one barrel of kraut every year. The contents would keep for a long time. I remember when kraut was one of our enjoyable dishes on the farm, with or without meat. Some neighbors turned turnips and corn into delicious krauts.

Salt water—brine—was the key to kraut, as well as the pickling of beans, beets, cucumbers, or the like. Actually, it was an art to know exactly how much salt to put in when making brine. And, of course, many folk checked the signs before attempting a kraut run, to make sure the moon was in a "waxing" (growing) mode. Otherwise the water wouldn't rise, they said. They also avoided making kraut if the signs were in the bowels or feet. According to the folk wisdom, kraut that fermented under the bowels sign would stink you out of your house and home! The same was said true for pickled beans.

This 1930s-era log smoke house, on display at the Georgia Mountain Fair grounds at Hiawassee, Georgia, was built by Charlie Cloer and his sons Ray and Ralph. Some mountain people refer to such a building as the "can house."

Before making kraut, mountain families went to a great deal of trouble scrubbing out their old faithful iron wash pots with Octagon soap. And of course, they sharpened up their "cabbage choppers," garden hoes straightened out for vertical action.

Ruth Swanson Hunter of Young Harris, Georgia, gave me her straight-forward directions for making kraut:

We always pickled our kraut in an earthen churn. You chopped your cabbage up real fine and put in about two handfuls in your churn along with a little salt, just like you was a-gonna eat it, you know, pack it down and put in more like that, layer by layer. When you got your jar full, you poured your water on it. You put a weight on that. We used a saucer or something that would go down in the jar and then we would get a rock and set it on that saucer and we would tie the churn up with a cloth and brown paper. Because when it goes to sourin' it'll get to workin' and the brine will go to runnin' all over the top if you don't have it weighted down. In earlier days, folks would use a hoe straightened out to chop the kraut, right in the barrel. Old folks would make kraut in fifty-gallon barrels and that's where the kraut stayed all winter, wherever they set it. Wouldn't be any left when summer come. Nowadays we just make it in a crock like that and take it out and can it.

Pickling of beans and cucumbers and other vegetables was another popular salt-based preservation method. Mrs. Gerrie Elsberry, in an unpublished narrative placed in the Georgia Archives, told how she pickled beans: "Green beans were…cooked a few minutes with a small amount of salt. Then they were placed in a churn or crock…to ferment or 'work' like kraut. They were canned in fruit jars like kraut, after nine days."

Mrs. Elsberry had an interesting account of how she pickled beets, using sugar:

> Women would cook a wash pot full of beets. They were then peeled and put into churns, and homemade syrup was poured over them. A thick cloth and brown paper was tied tightly over the top of the churn to keep out insects. The syrup would ferment into "vinegar" and pickle the beets. Wild grapes were picked from the stems, washed, and put up in syrup the same way.

As food writer James Villas has so aptly stated, none of the Southern culinary traditions are more sacred and respected than that of canning. And nowhere is this tradition carried out with such consistent continuity as in the Southern Appalachians.

Mountain housewives had been putting up fruits and vegetables in crock-type jars since early colonial days, usually with sugar or sweetenings such as honey or syrup. But around the turn of the century, easy-to-seal Mason-type glass jars became available for "home canning"; it was a boon to mountain homes.

If you want to see some of the greatest examples of the canning tradition, take a peek today into mountain country pantries; check out the rainbow kaleidoscope of colors in their jars of canned fruit, vegetables, pickles, and jellies. Such an example is to be found in the storage building at the farm of seventy-seven-year-old Hazel Farmer in Union County, Georgia. Long shelves of fruits and vegetables reflect the bounty of Hazel's garden and her handiwork and skill in putting up the food.

Jars made by Mason and Ball—brought into production earlier in this century—provided housewives improved preserving capability.

Cooks like Mrs. Farmer continue to consider pickling, preserving, and jelly-making an important family enterprise. Another example is the aforementioned Frances Gates Hill. She received her "putting up food" training from her mother, Tamer Sumner

Gates, who every year canned hundreds of jars of fruits, vegetables, applesauce, soups, jellies, and meats, including sausage.

Frances recalled that "Mama and Daddy had a place outside and they would take a big old wash tub and build a fire under it and put the jars in that tub and cook hundreds of jars in a day. Put the jars in the tub full of water, like they do now at a cannery. Mason jars. We had the zinc lids and rubber that sealed 'em down."

But one day, Mrs. Gates got a special canning challenge. She had a brother-in-law from North Carolina who loved to hunt—James Page. James and Willard Hill, Frances's husband, brought home to Mother Gates ninety-eight squirrels they bagged in that day's trip to the woods.

"Mama canned them every one," Frances recalled with a laugh. "Yes she did; the men skinned and washed 'em good and cut 'em up in pieces and Mama put 'em in jars and cooked 'em; I believe five hours was what she cooked the meat in those big old cookers."

Colorful jars of fruits, vegetables, juices, and jellies line the cellar at Hazel Farmer's homestead in Union County, Georgia. Note crocks and churns on bottom shelf used in an earlier era to preserve kraut and other foods for the winter.

The Foods

Breads
Corn Bread & Biscuits

Mountain Beverages
*Moonshine, Eggnog, Syllabub, Wine, Beer,
Cider, Sassafras Tea & Buttermilk*

Meats & Gravies
*Hog-Killing Day, Smokehouse Ham, Barbecue,
Mountain Gravies, Brunswick Stew,
Burgoo & Wild Game*

Fresh, Fresh Vegetables
*Corn, Greens, Ramps, Irish Potatoes, Indian Squash,
Cabbages, Sweet Potatoes, Leather-Britches,
Hominy, Grits, Mush, Soups & Relishes*

A Cornucopia of Fruits & Nuts
*Apples, Peaches, Berries, Persimmons, Grapes, Pawpaws,
Nuts, Jellies, Jams, Preserves & Apple Butter*

Desserts
Pies, Puddings, Cakes, Sorghum Syrup & Honey

Introduction

> MOUNTAIN WIFE: Won't you stay for supper? We're having leather-
> britches, bear meat, gritted cornpone, poke sallet, and sourwood honey.
> VISITOR: I believe I will; I'm partial to poke sallet.

This exchange, supposedly spoken in the 1800s on Hazel Creek in North Carolina's Great Smoky Mountains, was offered by Professor Duane Oliver, a Hazel Creek* native, as typical for the time.

Once established on their homesteads, people in the Southern Appalachian frontier ate fairly well. Their daily bread was a hearty blend of homegrown foods—corn and pork and vegetables—and foods gathered from the wild, such as bear meat, venison, honey, chestnuts, and ramps, "creasy greens," and muscadine grapes.

"Pigs were easy to raise," said Oliver. "Actually they raised themselves out in the woods, feeding on the forest mast, the nuts and berries that abounded. Wild greens were well loved by the settlers, particularly poke and cresses."

Up until recent decades, Appalachian mountain foods reflected an amazing continuity from the days of the earliest settlers in the 1700s. Yet there were times that tried the mountaineers' souls—and their stomachs. Next to the Civil War, the most wrenching challenges came with the Great Depression. Even during that difficult episode, in the 1930s, resourceful mountain people met the situation head-on.

"Growing up poor" brought deprivation in many ways, but most who had a garden and a milk cow and a few pigs generally fared well at the dinner table.

As the late Ben Robertson remembered in his engaging memoir, *Red Hills and Cotton*, about life in northwest South Carolina's Blue Ridge foothills, "No matter how hard the times were, we always had more than we needed to eat…there was an air of happiness about our boards." His experiences were repeated in Gilmer County, Georgia, where breakfast was a big event in the Dover home as recalled by Bess Dover Pache:

> Mother would get up every morning; there were five of us kids. She had to
> fix a big pan of biscuits. We always had plenty of chickens, plenty of eggs. She
> would fry us all an egg apiece. My daddy, a schoolteacher, used to like his fatback
> meat crispy. He wanted us to have meat on the table every time. Once or twice

---

*Hazel Creek was the same area to which Horace Kephart fled in 1904 and was the setting for his Appalachian epic, Our Southern Highlanders. A Little Tennessee River tributary, Hazel Creek was partially covered by the waters of Fontana Lake in 1944.

Hog meat and chicken were our meats. My mother would wring a chicken's neck; it's quicker and easier that way, but sometimes she would lay the head on a chop block and cut the head off with an ax. Mother would fry young chickens. Old chickens, she would stew them and make dumplings or gravy.

Chickens were better to eat back when they ran out in the yard. They're not good these days, I don't eat 'em no more. I just got turned against 'em. This fast-growing feed they eat is just not good. People of today eat too much junk food to be healthy.

—RUTH SWANSON HUNTER, YOUNG HARRIS, GEORGIA

a week, Mama would fry a chicken for breakfast, or make a chicken pie. Now I loved that cream gravy with hot biscuits and ended up with honey and butter and homemade syrup. We always had a pitcher of syrup and a big bowl of honey set on the table all the time.

We wasn't allowed to drink coffee when we was kids. Papa drank coffee but not us. We had to drink milk. We had about four gallons of milk a day, milking two cows, and Mama churned and made the butter.

Farther north, at Young Harris, on the North Carolina line, Melvin and Ruth Swanson Hunter remembered that even on their hardscrabble turn-of-the-century mountain farms, mealtimes were happy times.

"We didn't go hungry, that's for sure," declared Mrs. Hunter, pointing from her living room window down Swanson Road to her father and grandfather's farm, a tract her family has occupied since the mid-1800s.

'Course we didn't have dainties, but we had good food…potatoes and beans and greens, and our meat and our chickens and eggs and our milk and butter. We would dry fruit and cook it in the fireplace in a stone jar. It would be on the hearth with coals of fire under it and next to it, and mother would bake sweet potatoes in a lidded Dutch oven on the hearth. She had another'un that she cooked our corn bread in and that was delicious.

Ruth's favorite meat was pork, particularly on hog-killing day. "That was a greasy day, rendering lard. But that night, oh boy, we enjoyed the cracklin' bread and tenderloin and fried ribs. Spare ribs are awfully good fried."

Their meals through the year were a nice blend of homegrown meats and vegetables:

For breakfast we would have meat and gravy, sometimes oatmeal and butter. We had good old fresh butter that was homemade. I loved fried apples too. We usually fried Red or Yellow Delicious. If you used a real sour apple, it would mush up and wouldn't fry in whole pieces. Put them in there with a little butter and sugar and put a lid on the pan. We had coffee for breakfast. My parents let me drink it early. We had biscuits most of the time for breakfast.

Dinnertime (at noon) was our big meal. We'd have our garden stuff, cabbage, beans, and potatoes and greens. And we always had corn bread at dinnertime and suppertime. That growed healthy people, boy.

We drank a lot of milk for supper. It's gonna sound funny, but I fixed up my milk half and half—a half a glass of sweet milk and a half a glass of buttermilk. Boy that's good. I never did like sweet milk and I don't like buttermilk by itself because it's too sour. I like to crumble corn bread in it. That's good and if you'll cut up a tomato and some onion in it, you got a good mess. I love onions, eat 'em every day, raw. I hardly ever had a cold."

For most mountain people, supper was usually a simple meal, a time for leftovers or simply a cool glass of milk from the nearby creek or springhouse, a practice that came all the way from lowland Scotland and Northern Ireland. Again we turn to the eloquent Ben Robertson:

We sat down to [supper] at dusk, tired out from the long greatness of the summer day, and often all we would have would be milk, cool from the springhouse buckets, cornbread, sliced thin and almost sizzling hot; soft salted fresh butter and sorghum molasses. Soon after supper we washed our feet and went to bed. We believed we slept better if at our last meal we had eaten but little.

～

In the recipes that follow, you will find a refreshing simplicity to most—honest, straightforward, and direct—reflecting solid foods that sustained lives lived across the Appalachians from the days of the early settlements.

Many of the key recipes were tested by a dedicated cadre of friends across the region. My primary objective was to include dishes that could be relished and enjoyed.

～

Southern food is not just food cooked south of the Mason–Dixon Line. It is a product of time and people as well as place.

—BILL NEAL'S SOUTHERN COOKING

I remember as a boy spending a night with my grandparents; they lived just over the ridge there in the Bucktown district. Grandfather Parker was a Primitive Baptist preacher. Next morning when I woke up, I smelt meat a–fryin'. Grandmother was making up her biscuit dough in one of them old handmade bread trays, and my grandfather was frying ham in a skillet in the fireplace. When he got the meat fried, he took the ham out and made brown gravy. Then Grandma put her biscuits in the same pan and baked 'em right there in the fireplace.

Before we went to the table, my grandfather pulled a jug of homemade syrup from under his bed and poured up a glassful and set it on the table. He showed me how to mix the syrup with that gravy, and we sopped it up with those biscuits and ate the ham. Boy that was something good; it was fitten to eat. I can remember that just as well.

—ERNEST PARKER, 90, OF CANTON, GEORGIA

Corn Bread

Mountain Staff of Life

Some people in the mountains view corn bread as a gift from God.
It compares to the manna that sustained the Israelites for forty years
in the desert.

—*Mark Sohn,* Mountain Country Cooking

~

Biscuits were biscuits and wheat bread was "light bread." But when we said,
"Pass the bread," we meant corn bread.

—*Will Campbell, Mount Juliet, Tennessee*

Nothing is more authentically Appalachian than a steaming, hot-out-of-the-oven pone of corn bread, radiating its earthy, nutty aroma and supreme mountain taste. Especially when served with a plate of fresh vegetables and a cold glass of milk.

From the lowly ash cake of early pioneer days to the elegant spoon bread perfected in Virginia's Tidewater, corn bread has served for more than three centuries as a constant and luscious link to the region's ancestral past, as vital to the Appalachian diet as salt. Mountain people particularly love to dip chunks of corn bread into "pot likker," the wonderful byproduct of turnip greens, cabbage, and the like (more about pot likker in an upcoming chapter on greens).

The Blue Ridge's ubiquitous Thomas Jefferson, who grew to love French cuisine while serving as ambassador to France in the late 1700s, never lost his love for corn bread; he even grew corn in his garden in Paris!

Having grown up in the Piedmont foothills, I can testify to the region's limitless love of corn bread in its many variations. I yet today love a light supper consisting of nothing but corn bread and a glass of buttermilk. Sometimes I embarrass my grandkids when I spoon out corn bread from a glass, à la trifle.

And yes, corn bread has even been served as a sweet treat. In earlier years, devotees would split open a piece of hot pone, slather it with butter, then smother it with sorghum syrup. To be truthful, it became one of my favorite childhood snacks!

When you get down to the Blue Ridge basics, from the early days of the European immigration—and long before during the Native American era—corn bread has been the region's basic food mainstay, the key element of its everyday meals.

> To grind the corn and wheat they grew on their (Appalachian) farms, Europeans introduced gristmills to the mountains. With abundant sources of flowing water for power, mills both small and large were located on streams throughout the Smokies. The basic principle involved pouring grain down onto two large round stones, called buhrstones, with sharp beveled edges. The top, or runner stone, turned while the bottom, or bed, stone stayed stationary. The space between the rocks determined the coarseness or fineness of the meal...Mill day was a community event in the mountains. People loaded sacks of corn and wheat onto wagons or horses, made the journey to the mill and, while waiting for their "turn," spent the time visiting with others doing the same.
>
> —ROSE HOUK, FOOD AND RECIPES OF THE SMOKIES

While the Indians for centuries had honored maize as their "sustainer of life," the grain didn't go over too well with the first Englishmen who landed in Virginia in 1607. They were just off the streets of London and were more interested in finding ways to wealth. Gold perhaps? But over time, with pressure from John Smith and others, the newcomers came to realize that maize was a key to survival. And besides that, they reluctantly began to actually like the new bread. With the kind help of Pocahontas and her father, Chief Powhatan, the new Americans soon learned the Indian method for pounding the native grain into a course meal for their ash cakes and "conahaney" hominy.

From this basic grain—pulverized in tree stump "hominy blocks"—came a multitude of breads, ranging from cornpones, muffins, bannock bread, corn cakes, corn dodgers, ad infinitum, right up to cracklin' bread and hushpuppies and, topping the corn bread throne, scrumptious spoon bread.

Benjamin Franklin became an ardent fan. From London in 1766, he wrote home to his wife, asking her to ship him Indian cornmeal and buckwheat. Later that year, he fired off an angry letter to the London *Gazetteer*, challenging an anti-corn letter published earlier: "Pray let me, an American, inform the gentleman, who seems ignorant of the matter, that Indian corn, take it for all in all, is one of the most agreeable and wholesome grains in the world…and that johny or hoe-cake, hot from the fire, is better than a Yorkshire muffin."

To begin at the beginning, America's Indians had been growing maize and consuming corn breads well over 2,500 years before the arrival of the first Europeans. The basic Indian cornpone was called "appone" or "suppone." The native people mixed the cornmeal with water, wrapped the batter in oak leaves or corn husks and placed them in the hot ashes of the fireplace. Colonialists called the dish ash cakes.

Scotch-Irish Presbyterians who arrived in the Appalachians in large droves from the 1720s—learned to transition to corn bread from the oatcakes eaten by their ancestors in Scotland and Ireland. The same held true for the British and Welsh immigrants as well as Scot highlanders who drifted to the mountains in later years from the North Carolina coast.

The simple meal, water, and salt–type ash cake was an Appalachian mainstay for many decades. A variation was "hoecakes," a flattened-out fritter. Some said the name originated on farms where workers baked

Smiles indicate a good corn crop for this family in western Virginia, which means plenty of corn bread in the coming year.

bread on their metal hoes. A more plausible explanation came from a frontiersman who said they used a type of flattened hoe blade to scoop up the flat cakes from fireplace hearths.

My friend Celestine Sibley, the beloved *Atlanta Journal-Constitution* columnist, noted that "in the old days, a real corn bread virtuoso merely swept a clean place on the hearth, lined up the cakes or pone and covered them with hot ashes." Celestine's modern fireplace technique at her Sweet Apple cabin is to wrap each dollop in tinfoil.

In the 1800s, Nancy Caroline Densmore, who lived near Tesnatee Church on Town Creek in north Georgia, used cabbage leaves in cooking ash cakes.

According to her granddaughter Mamie Atkinson, she would start off by laying a large cabbage leaf down on the hot hearth. On top of the leaf, she would pour a heaping spoonful of corn bread batter. She then would cover the batter with another cabbage leaf and cover the top leaf with hot ashes. Voilà! A wonderful meal.

Fireplace corn bread cooking became an Appalachian art form with the use of three-legged iron "spider" type skillets and Dutch ovens—utilizing hot coals that enabled mountaineers to bake their breads top and bottom. One of these was the late Mrs. Laura Beaver Woody who lived near Jeff Top Mountain south of Blue Ridge, Georgia. While she had a cast iron stove, she did most of her winter cooking in her fireplace, using her old faithful three-legged skillet.

Mrs. Woody's son Mark Woody recalled, "The three legs helped keep the skillet stable, since rock hearths in the mountains weren't always level. We didn't have a fireplace swing-arm to hang kettles like many people did. We'd generally rake out a bed of live coals and set the skillet on top then put hot coals on the lid. The corn bread had a super taste."

> *Muv feels about true cornmeal the same way some people feel about wine. The wine bibber, tasting and smelling, seeing a "bouquet," turning his glass between his fingers in the light...hasn't got a thing on Muv and cornmeal.*
>
> *She, too, uses all her senses on meal, rubbing it between her fingers for texture, shaking out a little the better to see the color, smelling for freshness, and tasting for whatever it is you taste in raw meal.*
>
> *And I have it on Muv's authority that the world is in a bad way for decent meal. "Bought meal!" she scoffed when she saw the package in my cupboard. "Honey, have you come to this?" She read the label and gave me that dark, bright-eyed glance which said as plain as words that her own flesh and blood was betraying her. "Self-rising!" She threw the word at me as if it were a moral indictment.*
>
> —CELESTINE SIBLEY,
> *THE CELESTINE SIBLEY SAMPLER*

As the frontier shifted westward and living standards rose, the region's corn breads also climbed in stature. Housewives began adding lard, eggs, sweet and sour milk, baking powder and soda, even eggs.

By the middle of the 1800s, according to Damon Lee Fowler in his authoritative *Classical Southern Cooking*, corn bread "had evolved into the bread that is legend: cornmeal mixed with salt, rendered fat and butter-milk, then baked in a heavy preheated iron pan. It changed little until well in the twentieth century and is still one of the most satisfying breads in the world."

How to make a great corn bread? Virtually all cooking experts agree that authentic Appalachian corn bread requires the use of whole grain, unbolted (unsifted) cornmeal, meal that is ground slowly and coarsely (on a stone mill if possible).

Mark Sohn treasures coarse stone-ground corn meal "because it is rough-textured and full flavored and includes the hull and the germ." To reach corn bread nirvana, true corn bread fanatics have been known to arise early enough to be first in line at the mill so their corn could be ground on cold stones! Many feel that modern-day grinding on high-speed hot steel buhr mills removes much of the true corn taste, along with important mineral elements. My personal preference is to use a wholesome stone-ground meal from a mill such as Nora Mills in Helen, Georgia, whose machinery leaves in the grain husks and germ.

Then, for many mountain folk, white corn is essential. The late William Riley Tallent of Sylva, North Carolina, loved to say that "white corn is for folks, yellow for critters." Marion Flexner of Kentucky went further, declaring white corn resulted in a corn bread "crisp and crunchy on the outside, moist inside...not as dry and duffy as the Northern yellow corn bread." Atlanta's Edna Lewis, a Virginian by birth

Hubert Sullivan pours shelled corn into a hopper at the John Cable Mill at Cades Cove, Tennessee. The cornmeal there is ground on the same hand-sharpened stones installed when the mill was built between 1870 and 1874. The mill is operated by the Great Smoky Mountains Natural History Association.

and beloved guardian angel of traditional Southern cooking, comes down on the side of white corn, declaring it "has a clear, clean taste that's a little sweeter."

Third, connoisseurs agree that cast-iron cookware is an absolute must. Before pouring in the batter, preheat your bacon-greased skillet and get it good and hot, around 450 degrees, so that when the batter hits the hot pan, it will begin a sensuous sizzle leading to a delectable golden-brown crust.

Now to the matter of sugar and flour. Many mountain purists say no and a thousand times no! They would never in a coon's age surrender to such a flatlander indulgence. Kentucky's Ronni Lundy states flat out that "corn bread is the holy grain of the mountains and it's never puffed up and self-important with sugar or flour." East Tennessee native Betsy Tice White, in her book on mountain food, says, "For mercy's sake, don't put any sugar in your corn bread. That's like trying to eat grits with sugar and cream. A Yankee strays down this way and tries it once in a while, but it's a pitiful thing to see."

> *B*ack in my day, you put a pone of bread on the table and passed it around for everybody to break 'em off a piece.
>
> I can remember we'd be working in the fields and we'd get tired and hungry in the afternoon, we'd go by the garden and get us some onions and Mama'd get some glasses and some corn bread and we'd go down to the spring, pour us out some buttermilk, and eat corn bread and buttermilk and onions for our evening snack. It was good, right there at the spring. Take a spoon to stir it up. That was a good snack.
>
> —Hazel Farmer, Upper Young Cane community near Blairsville, Georgia

Yet I must hedge a bit here and note that I have known some honorable mountain cooks (well, two or three) and several cookbook compilers who have jumped the traces of supposed Appalachian tradition and have opted for a pinch or two of sugar just to sweeten the corn taste a tad. Same for flour. But not to the extent of that done by cooks in the Plantation South, or the "Yankee North." Marjorie Kinnan Rawlings, who sought to reflect authentic country cooking in her *Cross Creek Cookery,* opted for flour in her oven corn bread and sugar in her corn bread muffins.

In any event, this is how you go about making mountain corn bread—as summarized for me by ninety-year-old Ernest Parker of Gilmer County, Georgia: "First you sift the cornmeal to get the bran out of it, then you break it up with buttermilk or plain water and put salt and soda in it, along with an egg and some lard, and put it in the oven and bake it, or in the fire place if not in the stove. When you finish, you'll have somethin' good to eat, I'll tell you…that corn bread!"

Curtis Underwood, a onetime north Georgia restaurateur—and ex-moonshiner—confirms that using a good sour buttermilk is always important. Some years ago he discovered that corn bread can be made even more sharp and tangy by using moonshine mash—distillers' beer—as a substitute or supplement for milk!

"When it's nearly worked off, that fermented mash gets real sour," sayeth Curtis, "and it gives corn bread an even more wonderful taste."

In this connection, the aforementioned John Parris—North Carolina's much-loved "poet of the mountains" who recently retired from his column-writing for the *Asheville Citizen-Times* after a distinguished career of more than four decades—shared with his readers a home method for fermenting corn meal: Boil your meal in salted water into a mush. Add a half cup of sugar, three-quarter cup of lard, and enough dry meal to make a stiff batter. Cover it and set it aside for two to four days until it ferments. It is then ready to be cooked in a hot iron skillet.

Now for some recipes.

> *E*ven if we only had soup and beans, fried potatoes and greens to eat, as long as we had a pan of hot corn bread, it was a fine meal.
> —SIDNEY SAYLOR FARR,
> MORE THAN MOONSHINE

Buttermilk Corn Bread

Berry College's founder, the late Martha Berry, had a beloved cook at her ancestral home on the Oostanaula River in the Appalachian foothills near Rome, Georgia—"Aunt Martha" Freeman. Long deceased, Aunt Martha was a legend in the area for her cooking wizardry. Although she never wrote down her recipes, some Berry friends did. Here is Aunt Martha's basic buttermilk corn bread recipe as preserved by the Daughters of Berry, with my personal thanks to Lillian Farmer, assistant director of the Martha Berry Oak Hill Museum. Her recipe calls for a wee three tablespoons of flour, which admittedly is a mountain no-no. But Martha Berry, a belle of the mountains in her day, gave the recipe high marks.

Aunt Martha's Buttermilk Corn Bread

3 tablespoons all-purpose flour	1 cup buttermilk
1¼ cups cornmeal	2 small eggs
1 teaspoon salt	2 tablespoons shortening
¾ teaspoon baking powder	½ teaspoon baking soda

Preheat oven at 450°F. Mix flour, cornmeal, salt, and baking powder. Add buttermilk to beaten eggs. Melt shortening. Cut into dry ingredients. Add baking soda dissolved in a little water. Pour in hot greased skillet or pan and bake at 425°F until done. Serves 6.

Cracklin' Bread

As noted previously, a wonderful variation of corn bread is cracklin' bread, utilizing tasty morsels left over from the rendering of lard and usually served at the beginning of the hog-killing season. (Thanksgiving Day was the usual hog-killing

*C*racklin' bread? My mother made it, and it was good. No matter how much she cooked, it was all gone when the meal was over. I make it this way: I take 1½ cups of self-rising meal, a good heaping cup of cracklin's and a cup of buttermilk. And I put in maybe a fourth of a teaspoon of baking soda. And if that buttermilk don't make it up like you want it, you can add a little water.

We growed our corn and took it to the gristmill up on the creek over here. Usta be a roadway up there but the old road's growed up now. My great-grandfather Fowler used to run the mill. As a kid, I usta like to look down there and watch that big old wheel. They had a pole and when they pulled it, that let up the gate and the water run under there (down the sluice). That mill was in operation until the early fifties.

—RUBY FOWLER MOONEY, GILMER COUNTY, GEORGIA

date four decades ago, but with the modern-day onslaught of environmental warming, the arrival of cold "hog-killing weather" today is totally unpredictable.) But memories of cracklin' bread season are still strong in the land, such as those retained by former Cherokee County State Senator William G. Hasty of Canton, Georgia: "I knew I was in for a treat when the fragrant aroma of Mother's cracklin' bread met me at the front door."

For cracklin' bread, along with other corn bread ingredients, you simply mix in a cup of cracklin's for each cup of meal. Here's a recipe that comes from Professor Duane Oliver's wonderful western North Carolina recipe collection, *Cooking on Hazel Creek*. Located in the southeast side of the Great Smoky Mountains National Park, Hazel Creek is the remote mountain valley to which writer Horace Kephart fled in 1904, and where he wrote his Blue Ridge Mountain opus, *Our Southern Highlanders*. Professor Oliver was born in the same vicinity. He obtained many of his traditional mountain recipes from his mother, grandmother, and other Hazel Creek old-timers who settled the remote valley.

Hazel Creek Cracklin' Bread

1½ cups cornmeal	¼ teaspoon salt
¼ cup all-purpose flour	1 cup buttermilk
½ teaspoon baking soda	1 cup finely diced cracklin's

Preheat oven at 400°F. Mix and sift together dry ingredients. Add milk, stir in crack-lin's. Pour into greased pan, and bake at 400°F for 30 minutes or until done.

~

Here is an older cracklin' bread recipe from Professor Oliver's collection that calls for no sugar.

Old-Timey Cracklin' Bread

1 pint cracklin's   *1 teaspoon baking soda*

1 quart cornmeal   *Big pinch of salt*

1 pint buttermilk

Crush cracklin's with a rolling pin. Make a dough of cornmeal, buttermilk, baking soda, and salt. Heat the cracklin's, and stir them into the dough, which must be stiff enough to mold well. Mold the bread with your hands into small, oblong pones about 3 inches wide. Bake in a hot, well-greased pan.

Indian Cake (Bannock Bread)

As mentioned earlier, sorghum sweet Indian cake, called "bannock bread" by some, was an early favorite. Housewives placed the batter on a board at the front of the hearth near the fire at a 60-degree angle. Lydia Maria Child, in her 1832 book, *The American Frugal Housewife*, offered the following directions:

> Indian cake, or bannock, is sweet and cheap food. One quart of sifted meal, two spoonfuls of molasses, two teaspoonfuls of salt, a bit of shortening half as big as a hen's egg, stirred together; make it pretty moist with scalding water, put into a well-greased pan, smooth over the surface with a spoon, and bake it brown on both sides before a quick fire. A little stewed punkin scalded with meal, improves the cake.

What to do with left-over corn bread was solved by turning it into something called Poor Do or Fried Bread. To make this dish, take day-old, or older, corn bread, slice it and fry the cut sides in a little grease until brown. Then add enough milk to about half cover the bread and simmer for awhile. This dish lingered on and had a revival in popularity during the Depression years when people all over the country sometimes made an entire meal from it.

—DUANE OLIVER, *COOKING ON HAZEL CREEK*

Corn Bread Fritters

Fritters are another mountain favorite. The late Bil Dwyer of Highlands, North Carolina, offered his friends the following recipe handed down from Appalachian old-timers in his book *Southern Appalachian Mountain Cooking*. Highlands, incidentally, is one of the premier Appalachian Blue Ridge mountain resorts, having been frequented by summer visitors from the seacoast since the 1800s.

Highlands Corn Bread Fritters

1 cup cornmeal	*2 teaspoons baking powder*
1 cup all-purpose flour	*1 egg*
½ teaspoon salt	*Milk for stiff batter*

Mix dry ingredients together. Beat egg, and add enough milk to make a stiff batter. Drop from teaspoon into deep hot fat, and cook until golden brown. Drain on paper.

Corn Dodgers

Corn dodgers were popular in the Appalachians and throughout the South in the eighteenth century. Many people made corn dodgers by forming the cornmeal batter into balls and dropping them into hot grease to make a type of dumpling. Modern-day versions call for the addition of a quarter cup of chopped onions with each cup of meal and three-quarter cup of hot water. This virtually turns the dodger into a modern day "hushpuppy."

Cornmeal Batter Cakes

Cornmeal batter cakes have been a perennial favorite in the mountains since pioneer days. The following recipe comes from a Haygood Mill collection published by the Pendleton, South Carolina, Historical Society. Built in 1825, the famed old water-powered Haygood Mill—located in the far northwest corner of South Carolina—has been lovingly restored by the historical society and is open to the public.

Michael Humphrey, operator of The Book Cellar on the Square in Clarkesville, Georgia, tested this recipe (along with other corn bread recipes). His batter cakes "came out great." He substituted cooking oil for bacon drippings and served the cakes with honey instead of syrup.

Haygood Mill Cornmeal Batter Cakes

1 cup cornmeal	*2 eggs, beaten*
½ teaspoon baking soda	*1½ cups buttermilk*
¼ teaspoon salt	*2 teaspoons bacon drippings*

Sift meal, baking soda, and salt together. Add beaten eggs, then buttermilk. Stir until smooth. Add bacon drippings, and mix well. Drop a tablespoon of batter onto a hot greased skillet. Let brown on bottom. Then turn quickly, and lightly brown on other side. Serve with butter and syrup, or with vegetables as a corn bread.

Corn Muffins

Muffins and corn sticks rate high with mountain people. As on all corn breads, cast-iron pans should be used. Among the designs for these are pans with corn ear motifs, some with round molds. Here's an adaptation of a muffin recipe offered by Maynard Murray of Sylvan Falls Mill, Georgia, and published in the book *Somethin's Cooking in the Mountains*. My thanks go to the publisher, Jay Bucek, operator of the Mark of the Potter located at the converted Grandpa Watts gristmill on north Georgia's Soque River north of Clarksville.

Sylvan Falls Corn Muffins

1 cup cornmeal	*1 cup all-purpose flour*
¼ cup sugar	*2 eggs*
½ teaspoon salt	*1 cup milk*
4 teaspoons baking powder	*⅓ cup melted butter or oil*

Preheat oven at 400°F. Sift dry ingredients into bowl. Add eggs, milk, and shortening. Beat with fork until smooth. Do not overbeat. Cook in greased muffin tins for 25 minutes at 400°F.

My friend Elliott Miller was hospitalized. During his recovery, one of the first meals he ordered from the hospital menu was buttermilk and corn bread. He poured his milk into a bowl, crumbled his corn bread into the milk, and ate with relish. I was surprised—didn't he pour his milk over his corn bread? He looked at me equally stunned. "Pour buttermilk on corn bread?" he asked scornfully.

For a...rational intermediary, we turned to his uncle Joe Elliott, who has been eating corn bread and buttermilk since he was a farm boy. He was amused by our dispute. "There were twenty to feed on our farm," he said, "morning, noon, and night. When the women made the corn bread, they made at least four pans of it. With luck there was some left over when we came home from school.

"We would pull out the largest mixing bowl we could find, and one would crumble the corn bread into pieces and the other would pour buttermilk into it or the other way around. We would take it around the house with spoons for all and lie sprawling out on our stomachs on the ground facing it, all digging into the same bowl, until it was all gone."

—NATHALIE DUPREE, *SOUTHERN MEMORIES*

Cornmeal Dumplings

The late Bill Neal described cornmeal dumplings as "about as close as we get to native cooking." It was from the Indians that the first settlers in the Carolinas and Virginia learned the corn dumpling art.

Many mountain people like to fix corn bread dumplings in turnip and other greens, in chicken broth and soups and stews. Here's a recipe offered by the aforementioned Haygood Mill of Pickens, South Carolina:

Pickens County Cornmeal Dumplings

8 cups stew vegetables with
    liquid or beef stock
1 cup cornmeal
¼ cup all-purpose flour
1 teaspoon baking powder
½ teaspoon salt
2 eggs

½ cup sweet milk
1 tablespoon melted butter
½ teaspoon onion powder
½ teaspoon lemon pepper
¼ teaspoon thyme
¼ teaspoon celery salt

Have the broth hot and simmering while making the dumplings. Sift together the meal with flour, baking powder, and salt. Set aside. In a bowl, beat 2 eggs to a froth, add milk, and blend in cornmeal mixture. Mix thoroughly, stirring in melted butter. Drop batter from a teaspoon into boiling stock, cover, and cook exactly 12 minutes. Move to back of stove, and simmer 3 more minutes. Lift the lid, and remove dumplings to a platter. Add to broth the onion powder, lemon pepper, thyme, and celery salt.

Gritted Corn Bread

Some mountain people swear gritted corn bread is the tastiest variant of the corn bread art, being a blend of corn bread, spoon bread, and creamed corn. The late William Riley Tallent of western North Carolina declared that when that (gritted) bread comes from of the oven, "all crisp and brown and steamin', it makes a body's mouth water."

True gritted bread can be baked only during a brief period, usually in October when corn reaches "grittin' size." That's when the grains have hardened a bit but still retain some thin milk in their ears.

Old-time mountain folk "milked" the corn with homemade "gritters," tin sheets punched with nail holes—providing a nice, sweet, milky corn pulp, and almost always guaranteeing a scrumptiously tasty bread.

This is adapted from a recipe used by the Saylor family in eastern Kentucky and published in Sidney Saylor Farr's authentic classic, *More Than Moonshine*. Sidney does not sift her gritted meal, feeling the extra fiber is good for the bread.

Kentucky Gritted Corn Bread

1¼ cups gritted meal	2½ teaspoons baking powder
½ cup all-purpose flour	2 tablespoons bacon grease
1 teaspoon salt	

Preheat oven to 450°F. Combine meal, flour, salt, and baking powder. Add bacon grease and water to form a soft dough. Mix ingredients thoroughly, stirring until mixture is smooth and creamy, about the thickness of gravy. Pour into a 10-inch iron skillet or an 8-inch square pan that is 2 inches deep. Bake until done.

There are still plenty of people who think that corn bread is more American than apple pie. And to us "ole timers," there is nothing like water-ground meal when it comes to making corn bread.

—GRACE HARTLEY, FORMER FOOD EDITOR OF THE *ATLANTA JOURNAL*

Grandfather Kimmons liked his corn bread made with plain meal...didn't want no seasoning put in it. He fried it on top of the stove, a little thin cake, flip it over like pancakes. I liked mine like Mother used to fix it, with buttermilk and salt and sody, and plenty thick.

—RUBY FOWLER MOONEY, GILMER COUNTY, GEORGIA

Spoon Bread

Southern food critic supreme John Egerton describes spoon bread as "the lightest, richest, most delicious of all corn bread dishes, a veritable corn bread souffle."

And while most people today think of spoon bread as a suppertime dish, that was not the case in Thomas Jefferson's time (early 1800s). At his magnificent "Monticello" home in Virginia's Blue Ridge foothills, his cooks served spoon bread throughout the day, all the way from early morning breakfast through late evening light suppers.

Spoon bread is a reported descendant of suppawn, a Native American cornmeal/milk pudding whose meaning derives from the Algonquin "nasaump" (cornmeal "softened by water"). Virginians, using whipped egg yolks and whites, finessed the cooking of the delicacy to a fine art, giving it a nice brown crust with an inside soft enough to dip out and eat with a spoon. It is to be served, of course, with a generous dollop of butter. White corn is the preferred base.

Jefferson's files yielded his own spoon bread recipe that called for scalding a quarter of milk and salt (quarter teaspoon). Into this was to be sprinkled (slowly) one cup of cornmeal, followed by a double-boiler cooking for an hour. Butter (three teaspoons) and eggs (three) then were stirred in. The mixture was then placed in an oven for forty-five minutes of baking.

Spoon bread goes well with many Appalachian dishes—vegetables, chicken, ham and gravy, and various stews, including rabbit and squirrel, plus hot fruit dishes and even salads.

The late beloved Mary Alice Barnes, who for many years gracefully reigned over Catherine Hall on Berry College's original turn-of-the-century log cabin campus, offered the following spoon bread recipe to the Daughters of Berry. It is named for the college's Lavender Mountain on top of which Martha Berry built her "House of Dreams." The mountain is named for George Lavender, a Tennessean of German descent who in the early 1800s operated a trading post on the Oostanaula River with Cherokee chief Major Ridge. It was located across the river from what later became the farmland of Colonel Thomas Berry, Martha Berry's father.

Lavender Mountain Spoon Bread

2 cups milk

¾ cup sifted meal

1 teaspoon salt

3 tablespoons butter

3 eggs (separated)

Heat milk in double boiler until steaming. Add meal slowly. Stir and cook until thick like thick white sauce. Add salt and butter. Beat egg yokes and stir into cornmeal mixture. Then fold in stiffly beaten egg whites. Pour into buttered baking dish and bake in moderate oven for 30 minutes.

~

Here is a second spoon bread recipe that comes from Martha Lawson of Rossville, Georgia. This recipe turned out "very good…very light and smooth" when baked for the first time by the aforementioned Michael Humphrey of Clarkesville, Georgia. Michael took the spoon bread to his family's Easter dinner and came home with an empty dish. Rossville takes its name from John Ross, the chief of the Cherokee Nation who led his people on the Trail of Tears to Oklahoma. One of his earlier homes is located in Rossville, just outside Chattanooga, Tennessee.

Rossville Spoon Bread

1 cup cornmeal

¼ teaspoon baking soda

Dash of black pepper

1 tablespoon flour

½ teaspoon salt

2 cups water

1 stick butter

4 eggs (separate yolks and whites)

2 cups milk

Preheat oven at 375°F. Mix dry ingredients. Add water and cook until soft mush. Add melted butter; mix well. Mix together beaten egg yolks and milk. Add to mush. Beat egg whites until stiff and fold into mixture. Bake at 375°F for 1 hour. Use large oiled Pyrex dish for baking.

~

You can still find spoon bread in Berea, Kentucky, at the Boone Tavern on the Berea College campus.

There are no statistics on this, but cornmeal must account for at least 10 percent of the weight of your average natural-born Southerner. The only living creatures that eat more corn surely have hooves.

—Jim Auchmutey, Atlanta Journal-Constitution

Katherine Anne Porter's Old-Style Cornpone

These directions for making "Old-Style Cornpone" are adapted from a recipe authored by the late Katherine Anne Porter. Miss Porter said these "two-ounce" pones, "very crusty outside, tender and melting inside" should be served hot with butter and are "ideal with cold buttermilk or sweet milk with thick soups (split pea, black bean, black-eyed pea, potato) and meant to go with all sorts of good country messes, such as turnip greens, beet tops, boiled bacon, with stewed fresh tomatoes."

Cornpone, Old-Style

2 cups white cornmeal	1½ to 2 tablespoons bacon fat
¼ teaspoon salt	2 cups boiling water

Preheat oven to 450°F. Have baking tin ready, greased. Sift meal into bowl with salt. Add bacon fat. Scald with the boiling water, stirring with large spoon and pouring water slowly to avoid lumps. If necessary add a little more water to make a heavy batter, but not quite dough. Let stand to expand and soften until cool enough to handle. Form into small egg-shaped pones. Press two fingertips into each one to make two dents (this is standard...custom...I don't know why but I wouldn't think of not doing it). Place on baking sheet and put in oven. Turn heat to 350°F at once, leave to bake 40 minutes or until a bright, smooth brown. But look at them now and then to make sure.

(*Author's note*: Miss Porter died in 1980 at the ripe old age of ninety. She was noted among friends as quite a cook.)

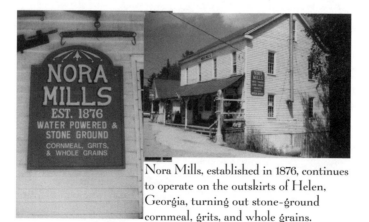

Nora Mills, established in 1876, continues to operate on the outskirts of Helen, Georgia, turning out stone-ground cornmeal, grits, and whole grains.

Biscuits

And Butter 'Um While They're Hot!

Served with blackberry jam or ham gravy [good biscuits] are mighty apt to put men folks in a good humor with the world.

—*Maria Thompson Daviess of Warren County, Tennessee, 1911*

~

If there's any doubt in your mind that hot, light fluffy biscuits are important in the South, just remember that a duel was once fought between two families over…their biscuit recipes.

—*Joni Miller,* True Grits

I never in the world thought that anyone could surpass my dear Scotch-Irish South Carolina mother, Wincey Hunter Dabney, when it came to baking biscuits. Hers were so satisfyingly stout and yet so fluffy and down-home delicious—particularly when she showed me how to dip them into breakfast coffee for what she called "coffee soakee."

I loved Sundays, when, with a table full of company, Mama would proudly present her steaming platter of buttermilk biscuits and declare, "Take two, Preacher Wood, and butter 'um while they're hot."

But in June of 1945, at the tender age of sixteen, when I took that steam-powered Seaboard train from Hamlet, North Carolina, down to Atlanta's grand old Terminal Station and then on to Rome, Georgia, I was about to enter a new realm of gustatory experience. In Berry College's Greek-columned Blackstone Hall there was unveiled to me a larger-than-usual biscuit that I must confess outdid (perhaps ever so slightly) the breakfast delicacies that came from my mother's oven.

The author's mother, the late Wincey Hunter Dabney, was rated by her children as an excellent cook, covering the entire gamut of country foods—particularly in breads and desserts. She possessed "the light touch" in baking.

There, in the Blackstone kitchen, Berry's grand chefs, Vernie and Floyd Nabors, turned out Sunday morning biscuits that melted in one's mouth. Particularly if you opened one up and added fresh butter along with a generous portion of the Berry-made apple butter. (More later about apple butter.)

One of my classmates put it for me in hushed tones: "What you see there, Joe, is what we call the Cathead Biscuit, the gift of an all-knowing and benevo-

This basket of cathead biscuits, tested by Charlene Terrell of Big Canoe, Georgia, was rated excellent in taste. Catheads gained fame—along with white gravy—among timber workers in the Great Smoky Mountains in the early part of this century.

lent God." Mountain people, he explained, were particularly partial to the giant-size biscuits, which were destined by the Almighty to go with milk-enhanced sawmill gravy, another mountain favorite. (More about that later, too.)

Indeed the "cathead"—an Appalachian phenomenon—was the precursor to the even larger size biscuits offered today by chains such as Hardee's and Mrs. Winner's. The big difference between regular-size buttermilk biscuits and the catheads was that with most "cats," the cook pinched off handfuls of dough rather than rolling it out and using a biscuit cutter. Radio humorist Ludlow Porch had fun with a caller who wanted to know what all the fuss was about cathead biscuits and how they came to be so named:

> LUDLOW: A cathead biscuit? It's called a cathead biscuit because it's almost as big as a cat's head.
> CALLER: What size cat?
> LUDLOW: I would say a medium-size female. They're soft and fluffy and almost fall out of your hands into your mouth. You can't get them buttered with one daub of cow butter, takes two daubs.

Berry Academy graduate Ophia Osborn McAmis of Cartecay, Georgia, a student helper in the Berry kitchen, recalled for me the Berry biscuit recipe. The numbers were so staggering they defied extrapolation attempts by my supreme biscuit recipe-tester, Diane Gibson. But for your own amazement, Ophia remembered that the recipe for eleven pans of biscuits called for twenty pounds of flour, one pitcher each of buttermilk, sweet milk, and water, plus five pounds of lard, one cup of salt, and three and a half cups of baking powder.

A more manageable recipe was offered by mountain cook par excellence Beuna Winchester of Bryson City, North Carolina, for many years the popular interpretive commentator at the Oconoluftee Visitors Center on the eastern edge of the Great Smoky Mountains National Park. My tester on this recipe, Charlene Terrell, found Beuna's recipe an excellent one and described the resulting big biscuits to be "very light and tasty." Charlene, by the way, is author of the splendid history of the Big Canoe area in north Georgia, *Wolfscratch Wilderness: A Backward Walk in Time.*

> *Do you know the ultimate test of a good biscuit?... Whether it tastes like your mama's.*
> —LUDLOW PORCH, HUMORIST AND RADIO TALK SHOW HOST

Bryson City Cathead Biscuits

2¼ cups flour	2 teaspoons baking powder
⅓ teaspoon baking soda	5 tablespoons lard
1 teaspoon salt	1 cup buttermilk

Preheat oven to 475°F to 500°F. Sift and mix dry ingredients then blend with lard. Add buttermilk. For each biscuit, pinch off a portion of dough about the shape of a large egg and pat out with your hands. Bake in a 350°F oven in wood stove about 10 minutes. In a modern electric or gas stove, bake at 475°F to 500°F.

My longtime friend, Atlanta columnist Celestine Sibley, who started baking biscuits at age eight under her mother "Muv's" watchful eye, became something of a connoisseur of Southern cooking with a special interest in the cuisine of north Georgia's Appalachian foothills where she has a cabin. Celestine came to admire the biscuits of the late Miss Kitty Jarrett of Ellijay, Georgia. Miss Kitty, along with her sisters, ran a wonderful two-story boarding house near Ellijay's old train station.

Typical of many mountain housewives, Miss Kitty would stay on her feet during mealtimes, walking around with a pan of hot biscuits in hand. On occasion, visitors who arrived late were plain out of luck. "I'm not serving cold biscuits to anybody," Miss Kitty would say.

My research has revealed that, next to serving the morsels hot out of the oven, the key to soft and fluffy biscuits—large or small—lies in the wheat flour used.

"Don't ever use that old hard northern flour," was the blunt advice offered by legendary cook Martha Pearl Villas, mother of food writer James Villas of Charlotte, North Carolina. Mrs. Villas went further to recommend White Lily or Red Band, "or any good, soft Southern flour."

Self-rising flours so popular in the mountains—topped by products from the 115-year-old White Lily mill in Knoxville, Tennessee—are, indeed, milled from soft winter wheat, low in gluten, providing biscuits an airy fluffiness that makes them perfect with butter, gravy, jellies, or whatever. (With regular "all-purpose" flour, you can make your own "self-rising" by adding one teaspoon salt and one tablespoon of baking powder to two cups of flour.)

Buttermilk Biscuits

As the late Mrs. S. R. Dull, the South's food writer supreme, pointed out, "The Southern housewife has always prided herself in the whiteness and fluffiness of her biscuits."

Undoubtedly the most popular all-time biscuit across Appalachia was the one called "the buttermilk biscuit." This was because buttermilk was readily available while sweet milk often was in short supply. Also buttermilk simply provided a nice sour tang to biscuit dough.

To get an authentic recipe for this traditional biscuit, I turned to the maker of the famed "Home Comfort" wood-burning stoves that served people across the Appalachians and the South so nobly during the decades before and following the Great Depression.

Published by the St. Louis Stove Co., *The Home Comfort Cook Book* was a household word wherever the beloved stove was sold, which was practically everywhere, particularly south of the Mason-Dixon Line. Anyway, this was their buttermilk biscuit version (before the advent of self-rising flour).

I might mention further that the tester of most of these biscuit recipes, Diane Gibson of Smyrna, Georgia, wife of my Lockheed colleague Jack Gibson, remembered the buttermilk biscuit as "the biscuit I grew up on—as did our daughter. When these morsels were left over, we made 'thumbey biscuits'…you would poke your thumb in one side and fill the hole with molasses. Leftover biscuits also were good as pie crust cookies."

Home Comfort Buttermilk Biscuits

2 cups all-purpose flour	*2 tablespoons shortening*
½ teaspoon salt	*½ teaspoon baking soda*
½ teaspoon baking powder	*1 cup buttermilk*

Sift flour, salt, and baking powder together into a mixing bowl. Add shortening, and rub it lightly into flour mixture; add baking soda to buttermilk, and stir thoroughly until it effervesces, then add to flour, gradually working it into a stiff dough. Turn onto floured board, and knead lightly until smooth; roll out slightly more than a quarter-inch thick. Cut out biscuits, and bake on a greased pan in hot oven 12 to 15 minutes.

Angel Biscuits

Sometimes called "high biscuits" or "cream biscuits," angel biscuits are small-scale tender biscuits that have many qualities of a yeasty roll. That's because yeast is added and the dough is allowed to rise before placing it in the oven.

One of the nicest recipes for angel biscuits that I could find is one offered by Kindness Nelson Beaird of Mount Berry, Georgia, the beloved wife of Berry's great farm director for many years, the late Arthur "Pap" Beaird. This was Kindness's recipe that she offered the Daughters of Berry and which they shared with me, thanks to Mrs. Lillian Farmer, assistant director of Berry's famed Oak Hill Museum:

Kindness Beaird's Angel Biscuits

4 tablespoons sugar	*4 cups self-rising flour*
1 packet yeast	*¾ teaspoon baking soda*
2 tablespoons warm water	*1½ cups buttermilk*
1 cup shortening	*(room temperature)*

Preheat oven to 400°F. Dissolve sugar and yeast in warm water. Combine flour and baking soda and cut in shortening. Add buttermilk and yeast mixture. Knead about 2 minutes. Let stand and rise before baking. Bake at 400°F. Makes 40 biscuits. These biscuits will keep well in refrigerator for a week.

A shorter version was offered by Regina Hill of the Gates Chapel community in west Gilmer County, Georgia, in a cookbook put out by the Gates Chapel United Methodist Church. Diane and Jack Gibson declare that this was the very best biscuit of all the recipes they tested.

Regina's Angel Biscuits

1 package active dry yeast	*1 tablespoon sugar*
½ cup warm water	*⅔ cup shortening*
4¾ cups self-rising flour	*1¼ cups buttermilk*

Grease baking sheets. Preheat oven to 400°F. Soften yeast in warm water; set aside. In mixing bowl, combine flour and sugar. Cut in shortening until mixture resembles coarse crumbs. Add softened yeast and buttermilk. Stir just until dough clings together. Knead gently on lightly floured surface, l0 to 12 strokes. Roll or pat dough and cut with biscuit cutter. Place on baking sheets. Bake at 400°F for 15 to 20 minutes.

Beaten Biscuits

My first inclination in considering this biscuit chapter was to omit any mention of "beaten biscuits," since they appeared to be more of an upper-class tidewater status symbol dish that depended on a lot of labor, a commodity lacking in most Appalachian households.

My reticence was overcome, however, when I came across references that the unleavened, wafer-size critters were a popular delicacy in the mountain interior among quite a few homes during the 1800s and perhaps long before. Eastern Kentucky's Sidney Saylor Farr remembered that while her mother never made beaten biscuits, their neighbors did. Several accounts tell of such biscuits in households in Tennessee and the Carolinas.

"People…who enjoy a physical relationship with their doughs," author and restaurateur Bill Neal wrote, "should be in heaven here. There is no getting around the activity. Fifteen minutes of heavy, consistent abuse is the minimum." A 1776 recipe collection called for cooks to place the dough "on a smooth flat surface of a tree stump and beat it with an iron pestle or side of a hatchet until the dough raises little blisters of air and is smooth and satiny." Or as Philadelphia's Eliza Leslie wrote, "Beat 500 times for company, 300 times for family…"

One of the earliest recipes on record for beaten biscuits was published in 1824 by Mary Randolph in her pioneering Southern cookbook The Virginia Housewife or Methodical Cook:

Apoquiniminc Cakes

Put a little salt, one egg beaten, and four ounces of butter in a quart of flour—make it into a paste with new milk, beat it for half an hour with a pestle, roll the paste thin and cut into round cakes; bake them on a gridiron, and be careful not to burn them.

Beaten Biscuit Critic

This is the most laborious of cakes, and also the most unwholesome...We do not recommend it; but there is no accounting for tastes. Children should not eat these biscuits—nor grown persons either, if they can get any other sort of bread. When living in a town where there are bakers, there is no excuse for making Maryland [beaten] biscuits...Better to live on Indian cakes.
—Eliza Leslie, *Directions for Cookery in its Various Branches* (1837)

Kentucky historian Thomas Clark, in his lively history, *The Kentucky*, called the beaten biscuit "a somewhat mysterious and temperamental creation, and as crusty as the sole maiden survivor of a proud family." His recipe for beaten biscuits started off with a pint of (plain) flour, to which he added "...a tablespoon of lard, a good pinch of salt, and then cold milk which is mixed into a stiff dough. Work one hundred and fifty times through a kneader. Roll into sheets one-half inch thick, cut out or make with hands, pick with a fork and bake in a hot oven."

From this, Tom declared, would come "a flinty biscuit which people brag on publicly, but which, if the truth be known, they wonder privately whether it is really worthwhile after all."

Sally Lunn Bread

A molded bun-type of tea bread, Sally Lunn bread caught on through part of the Appalachian interior in the 1700s. Those who like a romantic angle to such matters tend to love the story about a British lass who concocted and served the unique bread to the upper-crust customers coming to her tea shop in Bath, England. Unfortunately, there seems little substance to the story.

Another version, also shrouded in mystery, says "Sally Lunn" is based on the French words, *soleil-lune*, or "sun and moon." Whatever its ancestry, the fact is that the yeast bread did indeed spread in popularity across the South, including the Blue Ridge and over the mountain interior, before and after the Revolutionary War. The first solid reference we get of it showed up in the cookbook published in 1820 by the famed Mrs. Annabella Hill and later came from the pen of Sarah Rutledge in *The Carolina Housewife*, published in 1847.

This is an adaptation of an Appalachian Piedmont recipe handed down by the Cowan family of Salisbury, North Carolina (first used by Mrs. Thomas L. Cowan), and passed on by Mrs. Charles Lambeth. I am indebted to the *Old North State Cook Book of Charlotte, North Carolina*, for the basic recipe. Tester Diane Gibson found this to be a nice cakelike bread that can be sliced and buttered for serving with jellies or jams.

Sally Lunn Bread

1 yeast cake, dissolved in ½ cup lukewarm water	*3 large eggs*
	4 cups all-purpose flour
½ cup shortening and ½ cup butter, mixed	*2 teaspoons salt*
	1 cup milk (lukewarm)
3 tablespoons sugar	

Preheat oven to 325°F. Put yeast in warm water to dissolve. Set aside. Melt the shortening and butter, and combine with sugar, mixing it until creamy. Add the beaten eggs. Add the flour and salt to the mixture then add the dissolved yeast and milk. Beat thoroughly and set aside in warm place until risen to double in size (about 3 hours). Then beat, beat, beat. Pour into a greased cake pan (funnel), and let rise again for 1½ to 2 hours. Bake at 325°F for about 45 minutes, then increase to 375°F and bake until golden brown. Serve with butter.

Sweet Potato Biscuits

Served with sourwood honey, sweet potato biscuits, according to Pikeville, Kentucky, television personality and author Mark Sohn, are "classic mountain, country to the core…a show-stopper, a flag-raising treasure, a topic of conversation." Wow. My tester for this recipe, the aforementioned Charlene Terrell of Big Canoe, agreed, and declared the resulting biscuits "were great."

This is adapted from the recipe Mark offered in his book, *Mountain Country Cooking*. He starts off with a sweet potato casserole mix that defines the biscuit flavor: Purée 4 cups well-cooked and mashed sweet potatoes. Mix in ¼ cup brown sugar, ¼ cup orange juice, ¼ cup butter, ½ teaspoon salt, and ¼ teaspoon cinnamon.

Pikeville Sweet Potato Biscuits

¼ cup butter, plus 3 tablespoons	*1½ teaspoons salt*
1 cup all-purpose flour	*1 cup casserole mix*
2 teaspoons baking powder	

Preheat oven to 400°F. Melt 3 tablespoons of the butter and place in 8 x 8-inch baking tin. In separate bowl, combine flour, baking powder, and salt. Mix the butter into the dry ingredients followed by the sweet potato mixture (use a pastry blender if available).

A s far as I can recollect, I was ten years old when I run away from my mother to the white people's home, where she worked, Mr. Billy Barfield's. I ran away because my stepfather treated me mean. The Barfields took me in just like I was one of the children.

I helped 'em sweep the yards, get up eggs, milk the cows, and pick cotton. Billy Barfield made me a bed right in the house. It was a big old slavery-time log house. Dem days they had these old rope beds. And they was high. At night they would pull my little bed out and every day they would slip it back under the big bed.

Of course, way back in dem days they called you, "My little ole Nigger..." I didn't care nothin' about that. All I wanted was to get them biscuits and ribbon cane syrup. Butter and bread. Mix up the butter with the syrup!

—108-YEAR-OLD JOHN I. HALL ALLEN, INTERVIEWED IN 1976
BY JOE DABNEY AT HIS HOME AT SUNNYSIDE, GEORGIA

Mix and knead the dough on a floured surface. Pat out dough to ½-inch thickness, and cut 2-inch diameter biscuits with a cutter. Place biscuits in the buttered tin. Bake 12 to 15 minutes or until brown on edges. Broil to brown the tops. Serves 8.

~

I end this chapter with a learned word on great biscuits from Public Television's cooking queen and author, Nathalie Dupree of Atlanta.

The ideal Southern biscuit, Nathalie declares, is feathery light "with a light brown crust on the top and a moist interior…Although it may be made with lard, butter or some other fat, it is most often made with shortening and a minimum of low gluten flour and baking powder to ensure a texture generally referred to as fluffy."

Nathalie prefers a biscuit not too thick; she enjoys the brown outside as much as the inside and she feels it doesn't require an overly amount of baking powder which could kill the taste.

"Finally," she sums up, "…to make true Southern biscuits requires what my colleagues and I call a touch a grace—a gift that some people are blessed with."

Well said, Nathalie. And so, so true.

When I was a boy, my grandparents introduced me to country ham and beaten biscuits, and my life was immeasurably enriched thereby. More than a mere taste for these delicacies, more than an appetite, they gave me an ancient ritual and a deep cultural experience.

It was in the little town of Cadiz, Kentucky...that I received my initiation into the fellowship of country ham and beaten biscuit devotees. My grandfather had a backyard smokehouse there in which he cured and aged and stored hams and other pork cuts. He also kept in fine running order for my grandmother a contraption called a biscuit brake, a kneading device designed to transform a ball of dough into a slick, glossy ribbon of raw pastry...

Just as the curing of hams was my grandfather's responsibility, the making of the beaten biscuits belonged in my grandmother's domain. Her biscuit brake consisted of a marble slab mounted like a table top on a wrought-iron sewing machine base...At first glance, the machine looked like a cross between a Singer and a wringer, a device for both sewing and washing clothes...

It turned out that a machinist in St. Joseph, Missouri had marketed such machines for years after the Civil War. Joseph DeMuth, while serving in the Union army, had seen women in Kentucky and Tennessee struggling to make a certain kind of hard, unleavened biscuit that required repeated pounding of the dough with a heavy mallet. These so-called beaten biscuits had the virtue of lasting for days without becoming stale, and thus made good pocket bread for people on the move. DeMuth went home after the war and...assembled his first dough-kneading machine and put it on the market.

In the 1940s, when my brother and I were finally old enough to turn the crank, the old machine was still running like a top...In the winter...Grandmother made up a batch of dough and we dutifully manned the crank, dreaming all the while of paper-thin slices of aged ham heaped high between halves of a smooth and tender biscuit. Then as now, I recognized that inspired combination made in culinary heaven.

—JOHN EGERTON, SIDE ORDERS

From Buttermilk to Bourbon and Spring Water Galore

The Stills will be soon at work for to make Whiskey and Peach Brandy...Now will come their Season of Festivity and Drunkenness...In this both Presbyterians and Episcopals very charitably agree.

—*Rev. Charles Woodmason*

~

Whiskey and freedom gang thegither.

—*Bobby Burns*

In 1775, the Church of England dispatched its Charleston-based "foreign missionary," black-frocked Reverend Charles Woodmason, into the Carolina backcountry—the lands beyond the sand hills fall line—to convert the immigrant infidels to Christianity or to bring back into the fold those who had fallen from grace.

Riding his horse into Camden and points north, the stony-faced cleric soon found himself hot under the ecclesiastical collar with the rowdy, unchurched Scotch-Irish settlers he encountered in the rugged interior. Woodmason pointedly objected to their food and drink, or, as he often pictured it, the lack thereof.

"As for Tea and Coffee," he wrote in his journal, "they know it not. These people are all from Ireland, live wholely on Buttermilk, Clabber, and what in England was given to Hogs and Dogs."

Although there may have been a bit of merit in Woodmason's initial anger, some historians feel he was too quick to judge, or perhaps too impatient to try out the authentic and utilitarian beverages of America's "Great Southwest" of the time.

Had he come down a bit from his imperial high horse, and lingered longer with the common folk, he might have acquired a taste for nutritious buttermilk, a hand-me-down peasant tradition from Ireland and Scotland and England. Buttermilk was an ideal beverage for the people filling up America's remote hill country frontier. Unlike fresh-from-the-cow "sweet" milk, buttermilk was relatively immune to spoilage, and it provided frontier housewives with a tangy corn bread cooking medium. The secondary result of a "churning"—butter—was essential for cooking, for spreading on one's bread, and in time for mixing with sorghum syrup.

While tea and coffee were scarce in the pre-Revolutionary backcountry, most mountain settlers fortunately found themselves with plenty of water. This proved to be a blessed basic beverage resource. Pioneers checking out places to settle felt their prayers answered if they could quickly locate a site with plenty of water.

Young Roy Davenport totes a bucket of water from a spring at Greenbrier Cove in East Tennessee in this 1926 scene.

Housewives routinely placed pitchers of water on the table at mealtimes. Even whiskey drinkers took water with their meals and held off their serious drinking until later.

The good Reverend Woodmason, accustomed to wines and teas of England, grudgingly reconciled himself to drinking "naught but water" during his backcountry jaunts. This was quite galling to him, remembering that in Europe, many water courses even then were quite polluted.

The earliest European settlers exhibited a strong partiality to their own spring or well, be it limestone, sulphur, soapstone, or freestone. Most all were clear and cold, clean and pollution-free. "Hit bubbles right out'n the ground, hit's bound to be puore," an early settler told Presbyterian Reverend James Watt Raine.

To bring the Appalachian water story up to date, Ernest Parker, ninety, who writes a weekly column for north Georgia's *Ellijay Times-Courier*, remembers the delicious spring water of his youth near Amicalola Falls.

"We had a spring, it was not far from the house. That was the best spring. Oh Lord, you wouldn't have to put no ice in that, if you'da had ice. That water was so cold, coming right out of the side of the mountain."

Even when coffee became the popular breakfast beverage in the early 1800s, mountain people clung to their love of fresh water. Retired professor Duane

Oliver recalled that people who had to evacuate Hazel Creek, North Carolina, grieved that they were leaving behind their favorite springs.

"They all bubbled up at the foot of mountains, never in a meadow, and perhaps that had something to do with their coldness and flavor. Near the Proctor School was a spring that everyone said had the best water in the creek, and sometimes people would walk to it just to get a drink.

"Close to our home was a spring that bubbled up at the foot of the mountain; it was wonderfully cold and flavorful, and was a little warmer in the winter than in the summer."

Water was a vital beverage to the settlers on Cullowhee Mountain, North Carolina, remembered Frank Pressley.

> Everybody in our family drank coffee for breakfast except Pop. He had to have his hot water the first thing when he got up. After he'd get out and feed his mule, he'd come in and wake Mama to get breakfast. He'd go to the water bucket over there on the cook table. We always kept three or four buckets there for Mama. We'd catch the water out of that spring next to the house. We used gourd dippers to drink with. By the time Ma got to the kitchen, Pop had the water hot on the stove. He'd cool it, temper it down, and drink it as hot from his mug as he could. He did that every morning, That was his way of doin'.

Many mountain people put their drinking water in cedar buckets, along with a drinking dipper. Cedar kept the water cold and gave it a good taste, was the feeling of most people.

Robert Sparks Walker, whose book *As the Indians Left It* was published by the Chattanooga Audubon Society, relished the opportunity to slurp cool spring water at every break when "laying by" corn on steamy July days in the Chickamauga River valley. Walker remembered water bubbling from the Lowe spring. He found it to be "the best that I have ever tasted in my lifetime. It was always cool and had a pleasing and satisfying taste."

*M*ountain people...highly valued a cold, good-tasting spring, and when they had to go to the "flat lands" always returned home complaining about how warm and awful-tasting the water was. Dock and Liza Jones, who lived fairly near (Hazel) Creek's mouth, had a springhouse and anyone who passed by and was thirsty knew they could stop and have a drink of ice cold water or some of Liza's good buttermilk.
—DUANE OLIVER, *COOKING ON HAZEL CREEK*

Eventually, coffee made its way from the seaboard into the interior and received great acceptance as the early morning mountain beverage. Coffee became one of the few "necessaries" for Piedmont and mountain people, an object they would willingly fork over their scarce cash to pay for at the settlement store, along with sugar and salt. The Moravian Love Feasts conducted by the Germans who settled the great Wachovia tract in North Carolina had a great dependence on coffee. Beth Tartan noted that they would tie a pound of coffee in a bag and drop it into three gallons of boiling water, then after a quarter hour would stir the bag through the water with wooden paddles. When the coffee reached the necessary strength, the coffee-maker would remove it and serve it in love feast mugs.

Coffee should be black as the Devil, hot as Hell, pure as an Angel, sweet as Love.
—COURT MAURICE DE TALLERAND-PERIGORD

My father, Wade V. Dabney, loved his coffee steaming hot. I remember he would pour his morning coffee into his saucer and then blow it a bit to cool it off. Although most kids were expected to drink milk in the morning, I was fortunate that my mother indulged me a bit with coffee when I was growing up on a farm near Travelers Rest, South Carolina, and later on a farm along the Lynches River in South Carolina. She allowed me to enjoy a delightful "coffee soakie" treat with our ham and eggs breakfasts. "Soakie" was a dip—dunking biscuits into a cup of coffee.

Many mountain people loved a "honey drink" pickup "when a body was tired"—usually a mixture of two-thirds cup of honey to a quart of water. A variation was offered by the late Ferne Shelton of North Carolina in her Pioneer Cookbook. Ferne noted a frontier family would keep their jug of the drink cool by placing it in a spring or well.

Sweet-Sour Refresher

Mix ½ cup honey with 1 cup cider vinegar. Stir well and keep covered. When ready to drink, mix four tablespoons with a glass of water.

Until the 1940s, mountain folk bought their coffee in raw bean form. "Most of those coffee beans were green," recalled Ernest Parker. "We had to parch 'em. We'd put 'em in a pan and stick it in the oven. Every few minutes we'd reach in with a cloth and stir them around where they wouldn't burn. When they turned brown, just right, we'd grind them in a coffee mill. Some of the folks held the mill in their laps as they turned it, but most had theirs fastened to a wall."

Nina Garrett remembered seeing her grandmother Stover parch green coffee on her fireplace hearth near Cartecay, Georgia. "She had a long paddle; she'd put on her bonnet and she'd stir that coffee and parch it. Later on we had our coffee grinder nailed up on the back porch. That was my sister's job of a'morning, to grind coffee. They let us all drink coffee if we wanted it."

In north Alabama's Sand Mountain area, a favorite practice was to take the white of an egg and stir it into coffee as the beans were parched and brown. Folk said this gave the beverage a glazing and would help keep the coffee grounds down in the bottom of the pot.

In time, with the first apple and peach trees, hard ciders began showing up on backcountry tables. Fermented apple cider rose in popularity, serving not only as a well-loved mealtime beverage, but also as a key element in weddings, funerals, barn raisings, and corn-shuckings.

> *outherners like stronger, blacker coffee," Miss Charlotte said. "...Maybe it's partially because of all the substitutes we had during The War, like parched sweet-potato peel, or parched this and parched that. I like it black, and strong. Also, maybe it's because very strong coffee goes so well with our very sweet desserts."*
>
> —Eugene Walter,
> AMERICAN COOKING, SOUTHERN STYLE

Many went on to distill their fruit "pummies." "Apples and peaches were turned into brandy," wrote Georgia's Rev. George Gilman Smith. "Everybody drank in those days, except a few very strict Methodists."

As night follows day, it was inevitable that the Appalachians—the landing spot for the Scotch-Irish and Germans and English who were pouring in a human tide down the Great Philadelphia Wagon Road—would give birth to a great gusher of grain whiskey. The pioneers who came from Northern Ireland and Scotland, Wales and England, brought with them alcoholic appetites and whiskey recipes and found plenty of expert craftsmen ready and willing to build copper pot stills and condenser "worms" just like those in the old country.

Soon distilleries began firing up in every mountain and foothill community, utilizing the great American grain, maize, which substituted nicely for the barley that had been the base of Irish and Scotch whiskeys. Soon the use of liquor became commonplace. Hewson L. Peeke noted that "a libation was poured on every transaction at every happening in the community...the drawing of a contract, the signing of a deed, the selling of a farm, the purchase of goods." When a person died, the community went into mourning, and spirits circulated freely at the home of the deceased.

John Egerton confirmed that most cookbooks coming out of the South in the 1800s—including those from Methodist and Baptist churchwomen—commonly offered alcoholic drinks, wines, brandies, beer, claret, cider, eggnog, and syllabub as well as the less common shrubs, bounces, slings, flips, toddies, and the like.

Court records in Tryon County, North Carolina, to the west of Charlotte, showed that the hotels in the mid-1700s advertised not only "Lodging in a good feather bed, clean sheets," but such refreshments as cider, brandy, toddy, grog, port, and whiskey. An innkeeper near Charlotte offered "egg nogg and nip punch" on his list of available beverages.

But in the Kentucky hill country beyond the Cumberland Gap—and down in Tennessee's Smoky Mountain and Cumberland foothills—were being nursed into creation great new corn whiskeys that were destined to become the all-American alcoholic beverages, eclipsing the whiskeys of Scotland and Ireland in the hearts of the people populating the young American republic.

~

The Moravians shared with all their neighbors (their) penchant for coffee. In times of scarcity, Southerners sought substitutes wherever they could find them: grains, sweet potatoes, acorns, and the seeds of persimmons, okra, and watermelon. In good times, though, each day's coffee was roasted in the morning, kitchens filling with the aroma. It's a satisfying step backwards to roast coffee in a skillet on top of the stove.

—Bill Neal, *Bill Neal's Southern Cooking*

Moonshine

Mountain Water of Life

There's nothing that will life you up like a dram of corn liquor in the morning.
—*Kentucky mountain ballad*

~

If you needed to talk to one of the moonshiners, all you had to do was whistle like a bobwhite as you approached the still…It's a wonder the revenuers never learned the signal.
—*Wesley Dockery, Lumpkin County, Georgia,*
in I Remember Dahlonega

~

There's a lot of nourishment in an acre of corn.
—*William Faulkner*

~

When I was in Virginia, it was too much whiskey—in Ohio, too much whiskey—in Tennessee, it is too, too much whiskey!
—*Anne Royal, traveling across the country*
in a stagecoach in the 1800s

Mountain people had an old saying years ago that humorously captured their love for liquid corn:

Here's to old corn whiskey,
Whitens the teeth,
Perfumes the breath,
And makes childbirth a pleasure.

A mountain character, Gid Moon, who lived during the early part of this century in the mysterious "Dark Corner," a moonshining stronghold in the foothills northeast of Greenville, South Carolina, expressed it even more succinctly: "Aye Goddd, drinkin Cokee Coley and smoking cigarettes are going to be the ruination of this country. Now this corn-cob pipe and a morning swig of corn whiskey—they are absolute needcessities."

Indeed, corn whiskey played a key dietary role across the Appalachians. "Americans in Andrew Jackson's day," declared historian W. J. Rorabaugh, "believed that God had made corn for America and Americans for corn; thus they thought of whiskey as their national drink."

~

Nina Estelle Garrett was nearing ninety when I visited her for the first time in 1995 at her mountain home in the Cartecay/Big Creek Road area of Gilmer County, Georgia.

> *Hey George, your corn's looking good; how much you think you're going to make to the acre?"*
> *"Oh, about a hundred gallons."*
> —QUOTE FROM AN EX–GEORGIA
> MOONSHINE TRIPPER

Daughter of a large mountain family, Miss Garrett lives in a modest but proud, tin-roofed frame home in the rolling mountain country near the Blue Ridge Continental Divide. Mountain to the core and wearing her long dress typical for hill country old-timers, Nina was not hesitant to tell me about corn whiskey's role in mountain life. She confirmed that, like Scottish clans of old, many mountain families produced corn liquor as a base for medicines and to earn money for family necessities.

Yet while whiskey runs deep in their genes, the vast majority of mountain people—contrary to the Snuffy Smith image—have exercised moderation in their drinking habits over the years, respecting the power of distilled spirits. "We make it to sell, not to drink," was the oft-repeated dictum of many moonshiners that I heard throughout the mountains.

Miss Nina's recollections about her grandmother Nancy Brookshire Garrett were insightful:

> Grandmother Garrett always kept a little whiskey on hand. People used to, they'd fix liquor up in medicine, put herbs in it. Grandmother was a weakly woman, and she worked hard. That whiskey, it give her strength. You know that's not wrong to drink it when you're drinkin' for your health.
>
> When Grandmother'd go to eat breakfast of a morning, she'd take her a little sip of whiskey, about a teaspoonful. And every time she'd eat she'd take her a little sip of corn whiskey. It was just made out of corn and nothin' added to it and it adulterated.
>
> Lot of people wouldn't drink it, though, but sold it. Back then, the boys—my brothers—made whiskey and sold it. But my Daddy never made it.

Miss Nina's feelings about the virtues of corn whiskey as a routinely consumed beverage—particularly for its medicinal value—were repeated to me many times as I crisscrossed the Appalachian South.

Higher up near the Smokies, on Cullowhee Mountain, North Carolina, the late Robert Daniel Pressley downed "two or three swallers" of corn liquor every afternoon when he came in from his mountainside fields. Pressley kept a jug of whiskey on the kitchen table "but it wasn't for the family; he kept that on hand for medicine," a son recalled. When a wagon train of twenty-seven migrants moved from Buncombe County, North Carolina, into north Georgia in 1848, the rule was that each adult could drink a swallow of corn liquor from the common jug every morning before they began that day's journey. On arrival in Ellijay, they were met by a merchant who welcomed them with a barrel of whiskey.

Jesse James Bailey, the late legendary sheriff of Buncumbe County and Madison County, North Carolina (on separate occasions), told author Wilma Dykeman

The late legendary Jesse James Bailey, who served as sheriff of both Buncombe and Madison counties, North Carolina, over his illustrious career, is pictured with a few stills he cut down in one year.

that when a person got elected sheriff in a remote mountain county he automatically became the county's corn whiskey prescription agent. He showed Wilma this prescription sheet that came to him from a local doctor:

> Sir—Hollis Mason is very sick and I have advised him to use whiskey. If this is legitimate, consider me as prescribing for him as often as he sends for it. —M.D.

When Bailey completed his two-year term as Madison County sheriff, his desk drawers bulged with twenty-three thousand whiskey prescriptions! "Seemed like every time you made a raid the whole county got sick," Jesse James told Mrs. Dykeman.

While Frank Pressley was advised by his Cullowhee Mountain papa to drink moderately, occasionally he would visit a friend's still. He recalled taking a nip of high-proof whiskey as it trickled out of the copper worm. As a dipper, he used a galvanized fruit jar lid lined with a white dish.

In the north Alabama foothills, the late Alex Chappel was a moderate corn whiskey imbiber from his childhood days, taking two toddies a day until he was past one hundred years old.

My granddaddy made whiskey,
His granddaddy did too.
We ain't paid no whiskey tax
Since 1792.

We just lay there by the juniper
While the moon is bright;
Watch them jugs a–fillin'
By the pale moonlight.

—OLD FOLK SONG

"My daddy kept whiskey on the table when we were all little. Big old white jug with the handle broke on it. But you better not drink too much; you get your britches tore up."

Alex recalled that back in Alabama's Bullgate mountains, nearly everybody in the settlement made corn whiskey. Their primary utensil, of course, was a Scotch-Irish–style copper pot still and a copper worm condenser. Alex was a spry one hundred and one years old when I interviewed him in 1975 at the home of his daughter, Catherine McCaa. He spoke lovingly of freshly distilled white whiskey:

"All likker is made white, and it's colored later (in aging). I don't like that coloring in it. I want pure old homemade."

In researching my earlier book, *Mountain Spirits: A Chronicle of Corn Whiskey*, I met scores of "retired" copper pot moonshiners. One of my personal favorites was Simmie Free of Tiger, Georgia, a lively Scotch-Irish leprechaun with a wonderful sense of outrageous humor. Shortly after my first visit to his home near Lake Burton, Sim pointed to an oval tintype of his father on the wall, and with a mischievous grin declared, "That's my father; he lived to be a hundred nine years old, and you know the old scudder fooled around and let likker kill him!" With a wink, he added, "That's the story me and the preacher tell on him."

God invented whiskey to keep the Irish from conquering the world.

—BUMPER STICKER

~

Appalachian mountain people have a split personality when it comes to hard spirits. The strong religious turn of most mountain communities has caused many people to increasingly frown on moonshining and on heavy drinking. Thus it is not uncommon to find most mountain counties "dry," a tradition handed down over scores of decades. Bourbon County, Kentucky, for instance, where Rev. Elijah Craig invented bourbon whiskey in the 1700s, is still today a dry county, except for the county seat of Paris. The same is true for Moore County, Tennessee, home of the famous Jack Daniels distillery.

Yet the making and consumption of spirits are built into mountain psyches, handed down from previous generations, going back to Scotland and Ireland and Wales.

> *The north of Ireland was settled by Scotchmen...who had been imported by James I...They learned how to make poteen in little stills, after the Irish fashion, and to defend their stills, after the Irish fashion. By and by these Scotch-Irish fell out with the British government, and large bodies of them emigrated to America...They were a fighting race...They brought with them, too, an undying hatred of excise laws.*
>
> —HORACE KEPHART,
> *OUR SOUTHERN HIGHLANDERS*

It was in Scotland that the word *whiskey* came into being. Scottish Gaels called it *usquebaugh*, Gaelic for the Latin *aqua-vitae*, or "water of life." As Janet Warren pointed out in *A Feast of Scotland,*

> It was during the seventeenth century that Scotland's most famous product was properly developed...whisky. Aqua vitae was in fact distilled in religious establishments as early as 1494, but it was not until much later that the practice became widespread...Before this the Highlander drank either the fresh burn water, or milk and its by-products, such as buttermilk and whey.
>
> Surplus barley would be malted and turned into usquebethea (the Gaelic for "water of life") in a pot still over a peat fire. Clansmen would carry scallop shells with them to use as tumblers for their whisky, and drank it copiously. So rapidly did home distilling spread throughout Scotland that whisky assumed a great importance in the Scottish economy and was used as barter for rent, servants' wages and general purchases.

From *usquebaugh* it became *uisgebetha*, then *uisge* and simply whiskie. Scots, always economy-minded, elected to spell it whisky while the Irish, being more generous, added an "e" to call it whiskey. America—with its Kentucky and Tennessee whiskeys—sided with the Irish.

The expression "moonshiner" also came from Britain. During the 1600s, smugglers of brandy from France and Holland to the British coast were called "moonlighters"—those who smuggled spirits by the light of the moon. *A Classical Dictionary of the Vulgar Tongue*, published in 1785, offered this definition of the beverage: "The white brandy smuggled on the coasts of Kent and Sussex is called moonshine." The term is thought to have been picked up in America following the Civil War, with the imposition of excise taxes on whiskey. This caused many mountain whiskey-makers to go underground. In the Smoky Mountains, moonshiners were called "blockaders" and their product was called "blockade whiskey." Both are thought to relate to blockade-running during the Civil War.

It is a fact that most mountain moonshine was made at night. The late "Thee" King of Hiawassee, Georgia, confirmed it: "Only a couple times in my life did we cook whiskey mash in the daylight. We always cooked it of a night. It's good and cool. I don't know, it's just safer. You're always looking for somebody that don't want to see you and they won't hardly ever come in on you of a night."

The Appalachian mountaineer considered whiskey-making a mere extension of his farming operation, and a way to convert some of his corn and fruits into a salable product.

Operators take time to pose at their moonshine still near Porter Springs in Lumpkin County, Georgia in 1899. The Dahlonega Signal referred to their product as "mountain razzle dazzle." Moonshiner on left has a mash stir stick in his hand while man in middle holds a proof vial to "check the bead." The copper still pot is to the left of the man with axe. All mash barrels have hickory strip bands.

Former Georgia governor Zell Miller, who grew up in mountainous Towns County, known for its strong moonshining heritage, noted in his autobiography that Anglo-Saxon and Celt settlers brought the whiskey tradition with them to the Blue Ridge, "and it was only natural that the distilling of whiskey should become an integral part of their transplanted…way of life."

Even George Washington had a distillery at Mount Vernon. His Scot distiller turned out roaring rye whiskeys and brandies on his Dogue Creek still. LaFayette was astounded at the "swift authority" of the Mount Vernon spirits.

In addition to serving as a superb income supplement for cash-strapped mountain people, moonshine whiskey helped finance many Appalachian counties. "When taxes were due," wrote Betty Ridley in a Gilmer County, Georgia, history, "it is said that there was a haze of smoke in every hollow in Gilmer County." Corn whiskey was the currency of the Appalachians, "stronger than the continental dollar, easily divisible and always improving with age." With a few barrels in the 1800s, you could buy yourself a nice farm. That's exactly what Abe Lincoln's father did when he moved from Kentucky into Illinois.

The two whiskey makers in middle had just been caught by revenuers when this photo was made, probably in the late 1800s when the federal government launched an all-out war against illicit whiskey stills across the Appalachians. The cap was off the 30-gallon still at photo bottom. Wife of one of the moonshiners stands on the left.

And when turnpikes were cut through the mountains in the 1800s, the taverns that followed—providing drovers with food and a place to sleep—white lightning corn whiskey became the drink of choice, being powerful and cheap. Scores of such taverns lined the Buncombe Turnpike that ran from Greeneville, Tennessee, to Greenville, South Carolina, by way of Asheville, North Carolina. In the year 1826 alone, hard-drinking drovers moved 200,000 hogs down the pike from Tennessee and Kentucky to Charleston, South Carolina.

Thousands of corn whiskey recipes and variations have evolved over the years. Basically they call for cornmeal as the mash base, along with water and, depending on the whiskey maker, varying amounts of sugar, corn, barley or rye malt, and sometimes yeast. The original copper-pot, pure-corn craftsmen scorned sugar. But later generations found sugar, along with yeast, added speed and pizzazz to the process.

In time, the traditional Scotch-Irish "singlin' and doublin'" copper pots gave way to multiple "thump kegs," upright steamer stills, groundhogs, and giant pan stills. Plus, of course, sugar and yeast.

Here's a simple corn whiskey recipe that is easy to understand. This one is posted next to a copper pot still at the Great Smoky Mountains National Park Oconoluftee Visitors Center. It's similar to the "double and twisted corn liquor" produced through the mountains before the era of the "thumper kegs." Double and twisted meant that the whiskey was run through the still on a second "doubling," high-proof run, and then did a final twisting dance through the copper coil condenser before emerging from the "money piece."

Smoky Mountain Corn Likker

80-gallon still
60-gallon barrel
½ bushel malt (sprouted
  corn dried and ground)

4 bushels ground corn (not too fine)
¼ bushel of rye, ground coarse

Mix together, scald, and pat like dough. Let stand 24 hours. Then put in barrel, and fill with water. Let it work 18 days or until cap falls off. Makes 2 gallons to the bushel.

This recipe, by the way, tells only how to ferment the mash, producing the still beer. The subsequent and equally important step is that of placing the beer in the still pot and boiling it at a temperature of not much higher than 173°F (alcohol's boiling level), extracting the spirits from the water, which, of course, boils at the much higher 212°F.

$\sim$

Here's an adaptation of a more modern eastern Kentucky moonshine recipe. It's an "old family recipe" that appeared in a delightful reminiscence, *More Than Moonshine*, by Sidney Saylor Farr of Berea, Kentucky. While old-time mountaineers preferred "pure corn" whiskey, made of only corn and cornmeal and rye malt, with water, of course, this version contains sugar and yeast. These ingredients found their way into mountain whiskey recipes in the early 1900s:

Kentucky Moonshine

1 peck shelled corn (for malt)
25 pounds cornmeal

25 pounds sugar
⅓ pound yeast

Put shelled corn in cloth sack, pour warm water over it, and store in warm place. Wet it down several times each day. When sprouts reach about 2 inches in length, spread out on flat spot to dry. This is corn malt. When dry, grind the malt, and add it to the cornmeal, sugar, and boiled water to make a mash. After the mixture cools, add yeast to a gallon of lukewarm water and pour into the mash. Add enough water to make 30 gallons of mash. Fermentation will take around 4 days in summertime, perhaps a day more in winter. Distill.

Bourbon Whiskey

Bourbon whiskey, the most distinguished outgrowth of the corn whiskey art, came into being in Kentucky in the late 1700s under mysterious circumstances. Most historians agree, however, that a Baptist preacher, Rev. Elijah Craig, was probably its primary catalyst. The good minister and his brother had settled in central Kentucky after wagoning their hymn-singing "traveling church" through the Cumberland Gap and Wilderness Road. It was a fortunate move since the area was rich in soft limestone water, a prime whiskey prerequisite.

In 1789, at the Craig-Distillery, Preacher Craig, so the story goes, produced and distilled a unique corn/rye/barley malt mash. By chance Craig stored a batch of his distilled product in some oak kegs that had been unintentionally burned on the inside. The aging in the burned oak barrels gave the whiskey a nice mellowness. The Kentucky

This moonshine distillery was in operation on a hillside in the Tickanetley area of Gilmer County, Georgia around 1920. The copper still pot itself can be seen just to the right of the tree on left.

Revenuers used every means available to find stills...cars, boats, and airplanes, and staked out roads that had suspicious early morning or late night traffic. They had two things going for them. One was the distinctive [mash] odor, which was impossible to disguise. The other was the informer. When a man had a grudge against another, he would turn him in. The informer was described by one man as "the lowest man I ever knowed." Many times a wife who had tired of her husband's drunkenness would tell the revenuers where the still was hidden.

Hiding the still was one thing, but hiding the product before selling was another ingenious act. Hollow logs, thickets, cellars, and barns were common hiding places. One man kept his jugs submerged in a lake. Another kept his jugs in his bee gums. Most folks steered away from bees, so no one bothered his jugs.

—BETTY RIDDLE, THE HERITAGE OF GILMER COUNTY (GEORGIA)

whiskey became a big hit and was named for Craig's home county. (Almost two centuries later, in 1964, the U.S. Congress passed a resolution calling bourbon a "distinctive product" of the United States.)

While corn whiskey, by government definition, should contain at least 80 percent corn, bourbon, by act of Congress, requires a fermented mash of not less than 51 percent corn and aged a minimum of two years in unused charred barrels made of white oak.

Tennessee whiskeys that came later on the Cumberland Plateau, such as Jack Daniels and Dickel, were actually closer to corn whiskey in content than bourbon, and developed ardent and loyal devotees over the country and world.

Fruit Brandies

Fruit brandies found their way into mountain beverage lore right behind corn whiskeys. Apple brandy, as well as spirits made of plums, muscadines, and peaches, became very popular across the Appalachians. When he was Georgia's lieutenant governor, Zell Miller found that the fiery beverage was a unique breath sweetener.

"[Brandy] makes you belch," he told writer Steve Oney. "And after a drink of it, you belch all evening and each belch tastes like apples. It's best on a cold night before a dance. One swallow will do it. It's strong enough that you only want one shot. And then you belch, a lot. And it smells sweet on your breath."

Another take on apple brandy came from a resident of Sugar Valley, Georgia, who gulped down what he thought was a jar of plain moonshine.

"I must have farted fire!" he recalled.

Brandy-making was commonly practiced in the foothills before World War II. Floyd Watkins, in his book, *Yesterday in the Hills*, told of a Cherokee County character, Bud Wheeler, who was called up to court as a witness to a knifing. The lawyer asked Wheeler when the knifing occurred.

WHEELER: It was brandy time.
ATTORNEY: Tell the jury what you mean.
WHEELER: I don't have to tell 'em…It's when the peaches get ripe.
I thought all smart lawyers knowed when brandy is made.

An old time brandy-maker by the name of Judge John I. Hall Allen of Sunnyside, Georgia, reportedly 109 years old when I interviewed him in 1975, remembered that "the way I learned to make whiskey…way back yonder they had government stills; we'd haul our peaches to this government still and make peach brandy; Mr. Bates run it. I decided to try it, too, when times got so hard."

When researching *Mountain Spirits*, many sources for Appalachian fruit brandies were opened up to me. One of my favorite bootleggers—who lives near the foot of Georgia's Amicalola Falls—peddled a superb and distinctive apple brandy. I shared a snifter with a friend from Washington, a top aviation magazine editor. He fell in love with the Amicalola brandy and called every fall to request a new batch.

The aforementioned late Simmie Free was an expert in making brandy as well as whiskey. His preference for brandy base was super-sour "streaked June" apples. Simmie set out four streaked June apple trees on his hillside farm near Tiger, Georgia, and dedicated them to brandy-making. Here's Simmie's recipe for making ten gallons of "high-falutin plumb good brandy" from a fifty-five-gallon barrel of apple pomace:

"There's a difference in apples. Some use as much again [sugar] as others…they're sour. I got four trees I set out purpose to make brandy out of, Streaked June. They take more sugar than Delicious…And you get a better turnout when you beat 'em, get a better taste of brandy, but don't run it [distill] too soon. You've got to wait 'til it gets ready and then make it. And then you've got a mild taste and it's strong as the dickens too. Makes you want to just keep drinkin' it. After a while, you'll be layin' down, wantin' to move, and can't. Yeah, that brandy'll knock your eyes out, if you ain't used to it."

Anybody with a grain of knowledge about moonshining wouldn't think of setting up a still on a branch with touch-me-nots. They denote hard water and hard water won't make corn whiskey.
—NORTH CAROLINA OLD-TIMER, AS QUOTED BY JOHN PARRIS

Simmie Free's Streaked June Apple Brandy

(In Simmie's own words)

Get you a long hickory pole and make you a maul on the end. Take your maul and beat up your apples real good. You can set in a chair and just beat the devil out of 'em. You don't have to pull it up. That there hickory pole will come back up every time. When you get your beater full, pour the pomace over in the 55-gallon wooden barrel. That pomace would be eight inches deep in the barrel. Then get you some good homemade rye meal and then sprinkle it on top like putting face powders on it. Do the same thing with the next batch. Keep on until your barrel is two-thirds full. When you beat the last'un, just put it in without any rye on top. Leave it be until the next morning. Then add a quart of corn malt and 50 pounds of sugar. Stir the batch up real good. Then the last thing you do, put in your water, fill it up almost to the top, along with a quart of rye meal. Fermentation time depends on the weather. When it's worked off, get you a sled and take it to your still and distill it. When you run it, it'll be way up yonder, over a hundred proof, as high as white lightnin'. But it'll be good. Temper it with water to taste.

Cherry Bounce

The most interesting historical corn whiskey character I ran across in my research was a post–Civil War moonshiner named Amos Owens of Rutherford County, North Carolina. He was known over the Piedmont country as "the cherry bounce king."

A jolly, red-faced Irishman, Amos had a distinctive "whiskey tenor voice." And like most of his peers, he believed it was his inalienable right to convert his fruit and grain into brandy and liquor without being licensed, taxed, or inspected by the government.

During his half century of liquor-making, Owens gained fame for his bounce—fermented cherry juice fortified with high-proof corn whiskey. Every year on the second Sunday of June, to celebrate the arrival of his new crop of black heart cherries, Amos would host a popular "cash bar" party for his friends and neighbors.

On the appointed day, the grounds around his mountaintop estate echoed with the sounds of boisterous good times. The crowd often got rowdy as the revelers partook of his cherry/alcohol concoction and paid for the opportunity to dance and engage in available amusements including a "grab the greased goose" horseback competition.

Amos Owens, "Cherry Bounce King"

While Amos's recipe unfortunately did not survive him, the late Bil Dwyer of Highlands, North Carolina, came out with a cherry bounce recipe in his *Southern Mountain Mountain Cooking*, named for Owens' home county. Here is an adaptation of that recipe:

Rutherford County Cherry Bounce

Mash cherries in a barrel or crock. Do not break the pits. For each gallon of fruit add a gallon of water. Let ferment. When bubbling stops, press the liquor out, and place in a cask, along with 2 pounds of honey for each gallon of mash. Also add 1 ounce of tarter for every 5 gallons of mash. Stir well, and place in cask. Take 10 to 12 pits for each gallon of mash, and crush them, placing them in the cask. Also add 2 gallons of corn whiskey for every 5 gallons of mash. Reseal cask. After 4 months, bottle and cork your bounce.

An old-time nineteenth-century bounce recipe was published by Lettice Bryan in her wondrous 1839 book *The Kentucky Housewife*, republished by the University of South Carolina Press in 1991:

Cherry Bounce

Mix together equal proportions of black hearts and morella cherries, which must be very ripe and full of juice. Extract one half of the stones, and break up the other half with the cherries. Weigh the whole, and to each six pounds add one gallon of rectified whiskey. Put it in a cask, stop it closely, and let it set in a cool place for two months, shaking it up frequently for the first month. Then draw off the liquor, strain it, dissolve in it one pound of loaf sugar, or of sugar candy, to each gallon, and bottle it for use.

Let me end this treatise with a warning about the power of cherry bounce. The afore-mentioned Bil Dwyer was the one who declared that a drink of real cherry bounce had been "known to snap a person's suspenders and stop his watch." So you are forewarned.

You also need to be forewarned that while you can ferment around three hundred gallons of wine and beer each year for home consumption, it is a federal offense to distill or sell hard spirits. So the alcohol recipes listed herein are offered primarily for their humor value. We suggest you leave the production of the hard stuff to the professionals—particularly those in Kentucky and Tennessee. After all, they have the best water… limestone soft!

Mint Julep: Bourbon's Genteel Descendant

Bourbon's most famous offshoot is the mint julep. A fairly simple concoction, the julep supposedly originated in Kentucky, although Virginia has claimed it for its own. Richard Barksdale Harwell, in his 1975 book, *The Mint Julep*, stated flat out that the drink originated in the northern Virginia tidewater, "spread soon to Maryland, and eventually all along the seaboard and even to transmontane Kentucky."

Kentuckians see it differently. They trace the julep's origins to their state, noting that young congressman Henry Clay was one of its most ardent promoters in the 1800s.

There's no doubt that Kentuckians lovingly embraced the julep and put it on a pedestal along with their pretty women and fast horses. In 1890, Judge Soule Smith offered a humorous recipe for the much-loved libation:

Kentucky Mint Julep

Take from the cold spring some water, pure as the angels are; mix with it sugar till it seems like oil. Then take a glass and crush your mint in it with a spoon—crush it around the border of the glass and leave no place untouched. Then throw the mint away—it is a sacrifice. Fill with cracked ice the glass; pour in the quantity of bourbon you want. It trickles slowly through the ice. Let it have time to cool, then pour your sugared water over it. No spoon is needed, no stirring allowed. Just let it stand a moment. Then around the brim place sprigs of mint so that one who drinks may find taste and odor at one draught. When it is made sip it slowly. August suns are shining, the breath of the south wind is upon you.

Some attribute the lighthearted quote to Kentucky humorist Irvin Cobb. In my opinion, it came from the judge's pen and was later quoted by Cobb, who added his endorsement with the affirming words, "…and that's a helluva mint julep."

In a more serious frame, the late North Carolina restaurateur Bill Neal offered in his book *Bill Neal's Southern Cooking* a nice julep recipe with a few more specifics. This is an adaptation:

Mint Julep

2 teaspoons sugar	*⅜ cup finely crushed ice*
2 teaspoons water	*2¼ ounces bourbon*
8 to 10 mint leaves	

Combine the sugar, water, and mint leaves in the bottom of a silver goblet or tumbler. Crush the mint gently with the back of a spoon; it is not necessary for the sugar to dissolve. Add approximately ⅜ cup dry, finely crushed ice, and pour the bourbon over. Do not stir or shake, but let stand a few minutes until the container frosts over.

Eggnogging and Syllabubing

Eggnog is a rich English cousin of boiled custard, at least as old and just as simple and straightforward.

—John Egerton

~

Syllabub à la Hate
Put into a bowl a bottle of red or white wine, ale, or cider, sweeten it and grate in nutmeg or cinnamon; then either hold it under the cow and milk into it, till it has a froth on top, or heat new milk as hot a[s] if fresh from the cow.
—Devereux ms (1842), Raleigh, North Carolina,
as published in The Backcountry Housewife

Year-end eggnog and syllabub celebrations have carried down to many Appalachian homes.

In 1866, a Britisher visiting Baltimore wrote that Christmas "is not properly observed unless you brew 'egg nogg' for all comers, everybody calls on everybody else, and each call is celebrated by a solemn egg-nogging."

As originated in England, the drinks were made with a stout ale—the Brits called it a "nog." Southerners naturally substituted bourbon or brandy when the tradition reached our shores. In making his nogs, George Washington was said to have used whiskey, sherry, brandy, and rum!

In the Southern interior, eggnog took on a mystical charisma. Noted food writer James Villas, a North Carolina native, recalls that no one loved eggnog more than his maternal grandmother.

"Even when Maw Maw was confined to a nursing home at age ninety-three," Villas wrote in his book, *My Mother's Southern Kitchen*, "the one thing she always asked Mother to bring at Christmastime was a jar of this spirited concoction 'with plenty of whiskey.'"

Christmas Eggnog

In many a mountain homestead, people felt it would be unlucky to greet Christmas morn without downing a hearty cup of eggnog. The mixing and serving of the nog was a ritual traditionally reserved for the household's elder male. He would be expected to burst forth with a lyrical toast to his family and friends.

The late Rush Wray, scion of a distinguished Blue Ridge family and for many years operator of the famed Nu-Wray Inn at Burnsville, North Carolina, followed his father's tradition in serving Christmas morning nog. The household would join him in lifting their cups and drinking the nog. Then he would invoke God's blessings.

Until his death, Rush continued the tradition, using his father's recipe. The inn is now owned and operated in the same down-home mountain tradition by Doug and Barbara Brown. And the old-timey nog recipe is still carried in the Nu-Wray Inn's *Old-Time Recipes* booklet. I am happy to reproduce it with thanks to the Browns. Rush Wray urged the use of a fork or wire whisk rather than an eggbeater in whipping up the nog:

Christmas Eggnog

6 eggs (separate the yolks
    and whites)
6 teaspoons sugar
1 pint milk

12 teaspoons brandy (The Wrays used
    peach or apple brandy, which they
    felt was smoother than whiskey.)
Nutmeg

Beat the yolks well, gradually adding the sugar until it is creamy. Pour in the milk slowly, beating all the time, next the brandy, and last, the well-beaten whites. Fill glasses, grating a little nutmeg, and serve at once. If richer eggnog is desired, add a cupful of cream to the milk. More or less brandy may be used according to taste. Serves 6.

⌒

Virginia's Martha McCullough-Williams, the turn-of-the-century writer, suggested that people wanting an early morning "Nogg" celebration should prepare for it the night before. This included beating the yolks and blending them with sugar and placing the mixture in a cool place overnight along with the egg whites. In the morning, the only additions needed were the liquor and the stiffly whipped egg whites.

Syllabub

Running a distant second to eggnog in the frothy "alcoholic milk shake" category was that of syllabub. This is a good holiday drink even today for those wishing to avoid the use of raw eggs.

British in origin, the syllabub was extremely popular among Elizabethans during the 1600s. It gained favor in the colonial Virginia tidewater and spread to the Appalachian interior, along with eggnog. Some mountain people preferred the bubbly "bub" to eggnog at year-end.

Froth is the key to the syllabub, its inspiration being the milking of the cow. Indeed,

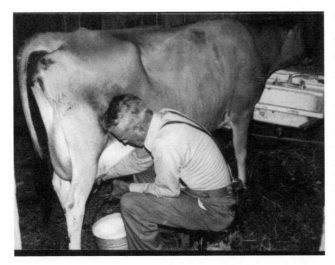

Milk fresh from the cow was just what many mountain people used for their syllabubs. Sometimes they ran the stream of sweet milk straight from the cow's teat into the syllabub container. This picture was shot in Southwest Virginia.

the Oxford English Dictionary defines syllabub as "a drink or dish made of milk (freq. as drawn from the cow)."

Along this line, Mrs. L. R. Ernst of Alabama recalled for students of Alexander State College that, "just before milking time," you start off by mixing a pint of fine cider or wine with one-half pound of white sugar and a bit of grated nutmeg. "Then take it to the cow and squeeze about three pints of milk into the mixture, stirring it occasionally with a spoon." The bub, Mrs. Ernst asserted, had to be "beaten and eaten" before the froth subsided.

"Mrs. Julia" Wray was ninety years old at the time she was interviewed by John Parris (1975) on the subject of syllabub. "Back in the old days," she told John, "folks sometimes

Syllabubs, possets, and nogs live in a no-man's land situated somewhere between dessert and drink. All three are hearty, alcoholic confections rich in cream or eggs, or both...

They also exist in the annals of English medicine. Possets, likely the most antique of the three and written of in 1440, were the common remedy for the common cold. James Howell, British author and diplomat, prescribed the syllabub as part of the country cure in 1645: "Leave the smutty Ayr of London, and com hither...wher you may pluck a Rose, and drink a Cillibub."

Nogs were part of the comforting domestic pharmacopoeia. In 1896, Harper's magazine reassured the invalid: "Mrs. Baker was holding a foaming glass to the sick man's lips. 'There; take another sup of the good nog,' she said...In 1872, Dr. Cohen's Diseases of the Throat advised, "I would rely chiefly on eggnog, beef essence, and quinine."

—BILL NEAL, *BISCUITS, SPOONBREAD AND SWEET POTATO PIE*

made syllabub right at the table. They had little churns, some attractive hand-painted china containers. Others were made of tin with a small wooden dasher."

The Wrays' syllabub recipe is still carried in the hotel's recipe booklet. This adaptation is with my thanks again to Doug and Barbara Brown.

Nu-Wray Syllabub

1 quart cream (24 hours old)
1 cup sugar
1 teaspoon vanilla
¼ cup sherry wine

1 cup fresh milk
½ cup grape juice or ¼ cup
* orange juice*
1 cup sugar

Place all ingredients, cold, in a large bowl. Beat with an eggbeater until frothy. Serve immediately.

～

There are variations of this recipe, of course. One such old recipe as told by Mrs. Lucile Watson of Clemson, South Carolina, reverses the milk and cream portions listed above, with this substitution for brandy: "Four tablespoons rye whiskey that's really old, sure enough moonshine, or ½ cup sherry wine."

Solid Syllabub

A delicious variation of the syllabub art, the solid syllabub, has been a favorite through history. Most recipes called for the mixture to be poured into glasses and set aside in a cool place twenty-four hours before serving. A primary ingredient of this South Carolina recipe for solid syllabub, published in the *Back Country Housewife*, called for mountain wine:

Take a pint of thick Cream & three quarters of a pound of sugar & half a pint of mountain Wine with the juice of two Lemons & peel of one grated in mix them together & beat it one way till the whisk will stand upright, they will keep a fortnight in a cool place from flies.

Floating Island

An interesting syllabub variation, called "floating island," was described by Mrs. Mary Randolph in her 1836 book, *The Virginia Housewife*. Eggs were the key additions:

> Have the bowl nearly full of syllabub, made with milk, white wine, and sugar; beat the whites of six new laid eggs to a strong froth—then mix with it raspberry or strawberry marmalade enough to flavour and colour it; lay the froth lightly on the syllabub, first putting in some slices of cake; raise it in little mounds, and garnish with something light.

Coffee Syllabub

During colonial days, a coffee version of syllabub was served at the Governor's Palace in Williamsburg, Virginia. This may have been a little "highfalutin" for most interior settlers, but we reproduce it here since, with Kentucky bourbon as a key ingredient, such recipes doubtless reached many homes in the mountains.

Virginia Coffee Syllabub

1½ cups strong brewed coffee, chilled	½ cup milk
	1 cup aged bourbon whiskey
1 cup heavy or whipping cream	¼ cup sugar, or to taste

Combine the coffee, cream, milk, and whiskey. Beat the mixture with a rotary beater until it is well blended. Sweeten with sugar to taste and chill thoroughly. Beat the syllabub again before pouring it into small cups or sherry glasses. Serves 8.

~

Since North Carolina was a totally dry state when Mother was growing up, every summer her mother and grandmother would make big crocks of potent scuppernong and blackberry wine, store it in the cellar, and use it not only for drinking and all-purpose cooking but for making this delicate drink called syllabub. Little did they know...that syllabub, prepared as a much more dense, puddinglike dessert, had been part of English gastronomy for centuries before evolving in the American South as a drink...Mother says she never saw my grandmother so furious as when Maw Maw once placed her syllabub on the back porch to cool, only to have the family cat lap every last ounce from the bowl.

—JAMES VILLAS, *MY MOTHER'S SOUTHERN KITCHEN*

Wines, Beers, and Ciders

Maude Thacker's Elderberry Magic

A glass of scuppernong wine is better for a body than a shot of penicillin.
—Arvil Wilson, Mountaintown District,
Gilmer County, Georgia

~

Persimmon beer is the poor relation of champagne—with the advantage that
nobody is ever the worse for drinking it.
—Martha McCullough-Williams, 1913

Nineteen hundred and seventy-seven was a vintage year for elderberry wine produced in Pickens County, Georgia.

I know it firsthand; it was in December of 1977 that I took my first sip of Maude Thacker's freshly fermented elderberry wine. I realized immediately that here was an honest piece of work, truly Appalachian. While Maude's 1977 wine—aged in the smokehouse behind her little home in Tate—had a modest lavender color, it exuded a sweet elderberry bouquet along with a subtle earthy bite that caused me to sit up and take notice and remember it to this day.

Maude Thacker—what a character!—possessing a personality and yodeling mountain voice equal to her wines. Slim and rangy, old-timey from her plaited pigtails and bonnet to her long dresses, Maude learned wine-making after she was grown. But she had a good raising for it, having worked as a still-hand for her moonshiner father, Eli Fields.

In the 1920s and 1930s, Eli Fields was a copper pot craftsman, one of north Georgia's major independent moonshiners, turning out hundreds of gallons of corn whiskey and fruit brandies every year. The Fields farmstead covered 130 acres at the foot of Hendricks Mountain, now part of the Bent Tree mountain resort near the south end of the Appalachian Trail. Maude not only helped make moonshine, she plowed a mule, snaked logs out of the mountains, and hauled sugar to Eli's stills. When she left home, she married a Baptist preacher and later got into wine-making for the pure pleasure of it.

Maude Thacker—Legendary Winemaker

The late Maude Thacker produced splendid fruit wines in her smokehouse at Tate, Georgia. Her elderberry wine was especially popular. As a young girl, Maude helped her father, Eli Fields, make moonshine whiskey at his stills at the foot of Hendricks Mountain near the present Bent Tree mountain resort.

Maude became something of a local celebrity in the late 1970s when Ed O'Neal, publisher of my book *More Mountain Spirits*, placed her likeness on the book's cover. It showed Maude, long pigtails and all, holding up bottles of her finest product. And as usual, her sweet smile showed through her leathery mountain wrinkles, every one of them well earned.

A year or so later, Maude became a national personality when Charles Kuralt found her, with a little help from me. She not only told the CBS-TV on-the-road man all about wine-making, she played her pump organ and sang a few of the old English ballads such as "Barbara Allen," as handed down from her ancestors.

It was in the merry month of May
When the green buds they were swellin'
Young Willie on his deathbed lay
For the love of Bar-bra Allen.

Maude, who died in 1993 at the age of ninety-two, stayed active to the end. Every springtime she would roam the dark coves and sun-splashed hillsides of her native Pickens County looking for wild greens. Then in the fall of the year she would climb Burnt Mountain and Oglethorpe Mountain to pick wild elderberries and foxgrapes as well as blackberries and dewberries.

As a testimony to Maude's wine-making wherewithal, one taste of her elderberry wine led my wife, Susanne—great-granddaughter and great-great-granddaughter of South Carolina Baptist preachers—to abandon her teetotaling ways.

Maude's Elderberry Wine
(In Maude Thacker's own words)

After you pick the elderberries off of them big bunches, the berries are about the size of a bird's eye. I wash 'em good and put 'em in glass gallon jugs, sometimes in a churn. I get them nearly filled with elderberries and then I put in the sugar. I don't measure the sugar, just add it till it tastes right—sorta sweet, but not too sweet—and pour warm water over them and put a lid on it, but not tight. I set the jars down there in the smokehouse and let them work. Sometimes it takes months to work off. But if you cook your berries out, it'll work off nearly in a month. I use three wine-makers. When the mash quits bubbling, I know it's worked off. I strain the berries twice; I first strain them through a sifter, then when they work off, I strain them through a cloth. After it quits bubbling, I take the wine out and seal it in a jar and put it in the 'frigerator.

Cherry Wine

Arvil Wilson roams the wilds from his valley home near north Georgia's towering Cohutta Mountains seeking wild berries and fruits with which to make wine. A jolly outdoorsman, he's known to his friends as "Crockett," in recognition of his frontier approach to life.

Rocking on his front porch on a hot summer afternoon, Arvil awes visitors with stories about hunting wild hogs and critters of all description. "'Course I'm better at tellin' stories late in the evenin' when I'm tarred and relaxed, with a little rhythm music in my belly." Wilson produces wines from muscadines, scuppernongs, grapes, strawberries, blackberries, and blueberries. But the blueberry, he confesses, "is no good by itself. It has a little funny taste. I don't know how to describe it. But I usually make about half and half—blackberry and blueberry." Other fruits yield bracing spirits under his dexterous hands—apples, plums, pokeberries, parsnips, and rhubarb. His favorite is muscadine or scuppernong wine. A friend with high cholesterol amazed his doctor by reducing his clogged arteries with a daily drink of muscadine wine.

When I first visited Arvil, in March of 1995, he was making cherry wine. "Usually, this time of year," he told me, "you got cherries in the freezer. When everything else plays out you fall back on your cherries. This cherry wine I got here now I racked it up this morning." He handed me a sample. It tasted smooth.

Arvil's recipe is fairly simple. He takes the cherries out of the freezer and thaws them out and runs them through a blender. He then places about 4 to 5 pounds of cherries in a 5-gallon container. In a second container, he dissolves about 10 pounds of sugar in 4½ gallons of lukewarm water. "You don't want to boil your water in the runnin' and fermentin' of it," he says.

How Wild Strawberry Wine Revived Horace Kephart, Author of the Mountain Classic Our Southern Highlanders

One day in 1904 Granville Calhoun, the young squire of Hazel Creek (North Carolina), came down from the hills to the railroad depot at Bushnell to meet a fellow named Horace Kephart...

Granville waited at the depot with a pair of mules for the stranger Kephart. He had received word from a friend that Kephart wanted to get as far back into the hills as he could.

The train arrived on schedule from Asheville. Granville watched a dozen or so passengers dismount and go their way. Finally only one remained. "I'm the man who came to meet you," Granville said to him.

"Oh, I was sort of thinking about getting back on the train," Kephart replied strangely...He was pale and weak looking, like a very sick man, afflicted with tuberculosis. "Can you ride a mule?" Granville asked.

"I'll try anything in the way of horseflesh," Kephart answered; but after struggling into the saddle all he could manage was to clutch the horn—riding with scarcely any control.

When they arrived at the house, Granville had to carry him and thought he had a dead man on his hands.

He works hard to keep bacteria out of the mix. "Buddy, you just got to be perfect with your cleanliness. If your wine gets sick [infected with bacteria] either your yeast didn't work or the containers weren't sterilized."

Arvil mixes up his ingredients and lets the batch set for "better than 12 hours" (sometimes up to 24 hours) before adding 2 tablespoons of yeast pre-dissolved in lukewarm water. "It'll start working in a couple to three hours," he says. "Then it'll hold a good workin' all the way through it."

In about 5 or 6 days, "you lift that top to see if it's weakening up. I always have a plastic bag over a 5-gallon bucket where it'll blow up like a balloon. When that balloon starts going down you know it's finished working and it's time to cork it and put it in a wine rack." You can drink it right then. It don't have to set long, 'cause I don't put in a lot of ingredients usually called for, just yeast and sugar."

Wilson uses only a 5-gallon container. "I usually don't want it full," he says. "You don't want much air in your container. You don't want your wine thick, like syrup. If so, it'll make you sick. Other words, it won't work right. You don't want your wine to lay there long like some-

He offered the stranger supper, but all he would eat was a cracker with sugar and water.

"You need a stimulant," said Granville, pouring a half glass of wild strawberry wine mixed with a little sugar...His hand shook reaching for the glass.
"If it helps, I'll give ye a little more," said Granville...Kephart downed the wine in three gulps and held out the glass. His eyes brightened; for the first time he seemed more alive than dead; then he fell away to sleep.

In an hour, Granville woke him with a glass of milk, but Kephart pointed a finger beyond the milk, silently pleading for more wine. "No, you try this sweet milk," insisted Granville.

So it went for three weeks, Granville spoon-feeding Kephart, first milk, then bread and butter and fish from the stream, while Kephart arose very slowly from his torpor and tremens, the long hangover, the flight away from himself and the world he knew before.

Then he entered a new world where he found his place, on the Little Fork of Sugar Fork of Hazel Creek, where his life became the life of the mountain people and he their chronicler as no one before or since.
—Condensed from Strangers in High Places by
Michael Frome, University of Tennessee Press, 1966

thin' dead. That's the reason I wait twelve to twenty-four hours before putting yeast in, and then it takes off."

Blackberry Wine

Wine is looked upon by Appalachian mountain folk as a great tonic for whatever ails you, particularly ailments involving the intestinal tract as well as arthritis. This thesis is attested to by Rilla Nelson, a gospel singer and guitarist who lives on the banks of the beautiful Cartecay River in eastern Gilmer County, Georgia. From her living room window she can look out at the site of the old Chastain gristmill run by her late father, Harley Chastain, and her grandfather, "Blue Mountain Joe" Chastain.

Former Gilmer County Commissioner Larry Davis introduced me to Rilla. She treated us not only to samples of her wines but played her guitar and gave us a plate of shuck beans, or as the Indians named them, "leather-britches." These are string beans that are dried after picking and then later resurrected by being soaked and then boiled with a hunk of salted fatback. (More about leather-britches later.)

Famed locally for her wines and herbs, Rilla passes out her concoctions free of charge to her friends and neighbors as a gesture of goodwill. "You can be throwing up or have diarrhea," says Rilla, "and you can just take a spoonful of blackberry wine every ten minutes and it will stop it. Blackberry's real good for that."

Rilla doesn't go by exact measurements but here is her method for making blackberry wine. On this recipe, Rilla sometimes adds a packet of yeast and additional sugar to help the batch work faster.

Rilla's Blackberry Wine

Get a gallon of fresh blackberries. Add a small amount of water, and heat for a few minutes enough to melt sugar. Place in 5-gallon crock along with 2 to 3 cups of sugar, tasting it to get it to your desired sweetness. Put aside. When bubbles stop, berries will rise to top. Strain it out and put in bottles. Refrigerate.

Pokeberry Wine

Beuna Parton Winchester of Bryson City, North Carolina, for many years the interpretive commentator at the Oconoluftee Visitors Center leading into the Great Smoky Mountains Park, is a great advocate of pokeberry wine. She says that to make the poke wine, you ferment the berries the same way as you do in making blackberry wine. Many mountain people, including wine-maker Cub Hodgen of Nelson, Georgia, declare pokeberry wine a good medicine for treating arthritis. Curtis Underwood had a neighbor in the north Georgia mountains who made pokeberry wine for his rheumatism.

Scuppernong Wine

Atlanta food and wine writer Jane Garvey declares muscadine wine, boasting a powerful grape character, "exerts a magnetic attraction for Southerners." Indeed.

Muscadine's cousin, the bronze, juicy wild scuppernong, also makes a powerful wine that has been quite popular through the Appalachians for centuries. Thomas Jefferson proudly compared wines made from North Carolina scuppernongs to the finest wines from Europe.

The word scuppernong derives from the Indian word ascuponung, the Sweet Bay tree found growing along North Carolina's Scuppernong River.

The following recipe is adapted from one published in the *Foxfire Book of Winemaking* and produced by the students at Rabun County High School in northeast Georgia. The basics were offered by Clarence Lusk, whom the students interviewed.

Rabun County Scuppernong Wine

3 gallons mashed scuppernongs	*1 large churn*
5 to 6 pounds sugar	*1 packet yeast*

Wash the grapes, mash them, and place in churn. Add water until grapes are just floating. Place a cover on churn, and allow to ferment for around 8 days. Use a wine strainer and strain out the juice in small amounts, discarding the pulp. Add 3 pounds of sugar for each gallon of juice. Add the yeast. Put a cloth over the churn and let ferment for 9 to 10 days, until fermentation stops. Bottle the wine with a loose top and put in a cool place.

Appalachian Beers

Across the Appalachians, homemade beers have had a great following over the years. Corn beer was highly esteemed. Most moonshiners, for instance, kept gourd dippers hanging on their mash boxes so they could sample the beer before it was shifted to the still pot.

"Ever' time I'd go by," Curtis Underwood told me, "I'd rake that foam back and get me a gourd of that beer."

But it was persimmon beer that tickled the fancy of many. People across the mountains and Piedmont foothills considered persimmon beer a marvelous Christmas season treat. Some housewives even substituted persimmon beer for milk when their cows went dry.

My *Atlanta Journal* correspondent in the '60s in Elberton, Georgia, Herbert Wilcox, described for me the region's deeply felt affinity for persimmon beer. Herbert quoted his Elberton neighbor Charlie Smith as saying that "a few glasses a day of persimmon beer tones you up for the cold of winter."

In making his annual persimmon beer run, Charlie Smith's only ingredients were persimmons and honey locusts that he picked in his backyard, plus water. Other beer-makers would add cornmeal, sweet potatoes, or sorghum syrup to their persimmon mash, but not Charlie. In his wooden barrel,

*T*he cider flow from the press was one of the best-tasting experiences that a young boy could ever have.
—BILL HASTY, CANTON, GEORGIA

Charlie placed on the bottom a layer of broomstraw filtering, then a layer of locust pods, topping it with persimmons and water. He covered the barrel with a clean bag that admitted air but excluded insects. After about two weeks of autumn weather, "there would trickle from Charlie's spigot a drink that is in a class by itself," Herbert Wilcox recalled.

The following recipe gets its name from a pleasant community located northwest of Elberton. In 1900, Postmaster Jack Christian was pondering what name to give his post office. About that time, his daughter walked in and gave him a dew-covered rose. Prayers answered. In this recipe, note that honey and sugar are substituted for locust pods, which are difficult to find today.

Dewy Rose Persimmon Beer

3 gallons persimmons
1 large kettle of hot water
3¼ pounds sugar
1 (5-gallon) wooden keg or crock.
2 pints honey (locust substitute)

Harvest your persimmons only after they have been kissed by at least one good frost. Slice the persimmons in half, removing seeds. Place the fruit in a crock, filling it about half full. Pour in enough hot water to cover. Let stand for about 3 days. Add 2 pounds of sugar along with honey. Let ferment until bubbling ceases. Add the remaining sugar and stir it daily, checking the taste, adding a bit of sugar if too bitter and allowing mash to resume fermenting. When bubbling ceases, strain the beer through cloth strainer. Put in jars and seal.

Peach Beer

Tall and bearded Thee King of Hiawassee, Georgia, was a peach beer fanatic. An Abraham Lincoln look-alike, Thee tended the moonshine still at Georgia Mountain Fair for many years. "Yessir," Thee told me, "peach beer is pretty tasty stuff. Dee-licious… best drink in the world."

The late Buck Carver of nearby Rabun County agreed: "When it gets just about ready to run (distill into brandy), by Ned, it'll knock your pillars out from under you. We'd use hollow bugle weeds and drink the beer from the brandy mash barrels…get as drunk as a fiddler's fice."

Buck Carver's Peach Beer

(In Buck's own words)

1 50-gallon barrel   *40 pounds white sugar*

7 bushels of peaches (beginning to rot)

The more rotten your peaches, the better. First, squeeze the kernels (seeds) out or take a close mesh scoop on a pole and dip them out. Place the peaches in the barrel, and let 'em set there until they rot. Some people stir the pomace. I loved to get down barefooted in the barrel like Italians would and just stomp 'em good. Let that set around 72 hours or so, souring. Then throw in the sugar. When your bubbling stops, take some screen wire and strain the beer into a bucket. Now you talk about pigs in a bucket! We lapped her up. You need to drink the beer quick or cover it up and put in a cool place.

Mountain Ciders

Apples and apple cider have been big through the Appalachians since colonial days when seeds were brought over from England with the first settlers. Apple seeds found fertile locales in western Virginia's Great Valley, in Henderson County, North Carolina, and north Georgia. Apple cider proved popular not only as a beverage but for treating many ailments, including use as a medicine to gargle for laryngitis and sore throats.

"We used to make a lot of hard cider there at Big Creek on the Blue Ridge Divide," recalled the late Reed Stanley of Ellijay, Georgia. Reed's father, Jason Stanley, the family patriarch, promoted hard cider as a beverage good for the stomach. Reed himself favored cider and vinegar.

The Stanleys and other mountaineers kept crocks of the hard stuff available to friends and neighbors, with a friendly gourd hanging on the barrel. "We gave it to everybody who lived around close," Reed said. "We hand-ground those apples in our cider mill and put 'em in our press. Then we put that juice in a barrel and let it work. We didn't let the pomace in, like for brandy…just the juice. Adding sugar will make it really work. It would get as sharp as a brar."

A cider/honey drink called "switchell" was popular as a thirst-quencher during the hot summer months. A spoonful of the concoction, made of equal amounts of cider and honey, would be added to a gourd or dipper of water.

The late Reed Stanley of Cartecay, Georgia, recalled his father, Jason Stanley, making barrels of apple cider at their homeplace in the Big Creek area of Gilmer County.

We made cider for our own use every year when I was growing up at Cullowhee [North Carolina]. It was sweet when it was fresh. We would chill it in the spring water and drink it for several days. But then we would also let it ferment, and it would be kinda like beer; it would have a kick to it.

—FRANK PRESSLEY, LAKELAND, GEORGIA

Georgia's premier apple country centers on Gilmer County, high on the Appalachian plateau. There, apple cider is one of the great treats for visitors and homefolks alike when the Yellow and Red Delicious varieties hit, along with Rome beauties, Stayman and Winesaps, and ten or so other varieties. Out-of-towners checking out the colorful apple barns can purchase only fresh sweet cider today, a far cry from what came from the cider barrels a half century ago. Here is a hard cider recipe named for the Stanleys' home community in Gilmer County, Georgia.

Big Creek Hard Apple Cider

2 bushels crushed apples	5 pounds sugar
50-gallon barrel	

Grind your apples, and put the pulp in a press with the handle on top. Press all the juice out (discarding the pulp), and put the juice in the barrel along with sugar. When it's working, it gives off a fine bubble all over. Get down close and you can hear it poppin'. It works off usually in 7 days. When it quits working, it has a sharp taste. Pour it in a clean 5-gallon crock. Tie a cloth over the crock; don't seal it. The longer you keep the cider, the harder and sharper it gets.

Mulled (Hot) Cider

Fortified with butter, spices, and sugar, sweet cider makes a wonderful hot drink, popular from pioneer days. Many names are attached to the drink—hot apple cider, spiced cider, hot mulled cider. Mulled cider is perhaps most descriptive because mull means to sweeten, heat and flavor with spices. This was a typical recipe that is still good today.

Buttered Spiced Hot Cider

4 quarts apple cider	¼ cup brown sugar
2 (3-inch) cinnamon sticks	3 tablespoons butter

Put cider and cinnamon sticks in pot or kettle. Bring to hot but not to boiling. Add sugar until it is fully dissolved, then add butter. When serving in mugs, sprinkle with powdered nutmeg and cinnamon.

Metheglin

I cannot leave this chapter without including one of the sweetest and most popular fermented beverages of the Appalachian country—hand-me-downs from the Saxons and the Greeks—honey-based metheglin.

Botanist William Bartram was a great admirer, as well as William Alexander, who wrote in his diary of soothing "methegalum." Its popularity was high throughout the colonial interior country. In 1649, a Virginian wrote of a farmer who kept bees and "made excellent Matheglin, a pleasant and strong drink." Oldmixon's *History of Carolina* (1708) notes that "the bees swarm there six or seven times a year, and the metheglin made there is as good as Malaga sack."

Martha Washington, in her early 1700s *Booke of Cookery*, offered this recipe for the honey drink. The Martha Washington cookbook, incidentally, was brought to life by noted food historian Karen Hess, who meticulously transcribed the old text.

To Make Metheglin

Take a quart of honey and 6 quarts of water. Let it boyle ye third part away, and boyle [with] it 3 races of ginger. When it is cold, put it in a pot which hath a spiket, & put yeast into it & let it stand 3 days, then bottle it up and put into ye

Cider-making was my favorite time...The men began preparation for cider making several days before. For months, they had been looking for the right size of poplar tree to make the cider press. After they found the tree, they took horses into the woods to haul it home. Limbs, leaves and bark were stripped from the trunk, which was hollowed out about halfway through, making a trough. Near the bottom of the log, a small hole was bored, with a spout to let the apple juice drip into a bucket.

A round mallet made from hickory was used to pound the apples into pulp. When the apples were sort of like coarse sand, a press was put on them to force all the juice out. The juice was strained through a cloth to get out the tiny bits of pulp. Fresh cider didn't last long. We had a way to preserve it. It soon fermented and became hard cider and then vinegar. Hard cider can make you as drunk as moonshine.

—Florence Cope Bush, *Dorie: Woman of the Mountains*

bottles a little leamon & a stick of cinnamon & a few raysons of ye sun & let it be a fortnight before you drink it.

~

Here is a simplified recipe for metheglin, thanks to Kay Moss and Kathryn Hoffman, authors of a great folk history, *The Backcountry Housewife: A Study of Eighteenth-Century Foods*, published by the Schiele Museum in Gastonia, North Carolina:

Mountain Metheglin

Take one quart honey, 5 quarts water, a ginger root long as your hand and one lemon, chopped. Simmer for about half an hour. Let it stand overnight. Strain. It will "work up" (ferment) in about four days.

~

There is something of a controversy in the mountains over whether aging improves metheglin's taste. One school says that you should drink it right after the fermentation. The other school says let it age in the crock for at least six months.

(*Author's note*: Wine-making is not illegal in federal terms if you produce your wine for the use of your family and friends. A head of household, however, must limit his annual production to three hundred gallons.)

It was in the late 1930s when I was working some moonshine stills in Lumpkin County, eight miles north of Dawsonville, Georgia. We were in the Mill Creek district down below Nimberwill Gap. We had four groundhog stills dug into the creek banks and they took 1,600 pounds of sugar. We sledded in everything...sugar, meal, gallon cans.

We had a mule we called Kelly—she'd been bought around 1912; Kelly pulled our sleds. Every time we'd go in to the still site, I'd bring out a bucket of still beer and give it to ole Kelly. She would drink every drop of that four-gallon bucket and boy, would she belch!

Now you take that corn beer...it was good. The groundhog still beer would be a stronger proof than what you find in today's import beer. I used to bring it home from the still and the old lady would make corn bread out of it; you talk about some good corn bread, oooo-weeee!

—Curtis Underwood of Resaca, Georgia

Sassafras Tea

Spring Tonic Supreme

*Drink sassafras tea during the month of March and you won't need a doctor
all year.*

—Old mountain saying

~

*[Ginseng tea] cheers the Heart even of a Man that has a bad Wife, and makes
him look down with great Composure on the Crosses of the World.*
—William Byrd of Virginia

Sass Tea? My Lord, yes, we made it!" Frank Pressley, hardy scion of the western North Carolina mountain country, was remembering the heady "growing-up" days of his youth on four-thousand-foot-high Cullowhee Mountain.

"We'd get the roots of the sassafras, and my mom would boil it for medicine. Some people liked to drink it as a tea. They all said it would thin the blood and refresh the spirit. But to me, that dark red drink had a sickening taste."

Sassafras tea is still popular across the Appalachian South. Dick Frymire of Kentucky is one of its great advocates. He says that not only will sassafras tea pick you up, chewing on a sassafras root will calm you down. Besides that, Frymire claims the versatile wild root will whiten your teeth! And to top it all, sayeth Mr. Frymire, if you want to give your flower plants more vigor, sprinkle some strong sassafras tea on them.

The hardy pioneers pouring down the Great Philadelphia Wagon Road to settle the Appalachians used many plants, leaves, roots, and barks for hot and cold beverages. But sassafras was the most popular.

There was a little ditty used to promote the sassafras tonic in earlier days:

In the spring of the year,
When the blood is too thick,
There is nothing so fine
As a sassafras stick.
It tones up the liver,
And strengthens the heart,
And to the whole system
New life doth impart.

~

The first Spanish explorers in America considered sassafras not only a fine beverage, but a powerful cure-all for ailments that ran the gamut. The British traders and settlers who came later agreed. They got the idea from the Indians who used the root to treat fevers, rheumatism, and to strengthen women following childbirth. The Indians used powdered sassafras as a great drug to treat wounds and venereal infections.

Newton Hylton totes his newly dug and washed sassafras roots home to be brewed in a delicious sassafras tea spring tonic.

From the areas around Jamestown in the 1600s, Captain John Smith and others sold shiploads of the roots to England and Europe. It was touted as a cure, all for whatever ailed you, from sore eyes to stinking breath, from dysentery to gout. The sass roots fetched a fancy price—upward of a thousand dollars a ton. But after a few decades, Europeans slowly determined that the highly acclaimed root was not all that it was cracked up to be. Across the Appalachians, however, sass's popularity as a tasty pick-me-up and as a year-round beverage waned only slightly. It remained the beverage of choice to be consumed cold in summer and hot in winter. Later on, sass tea was taken to combat obesity. The old saying went,

> *I got so thin on sass-fras tea*
> *I could hide behind a straw.*

The late Robert Sparks Walker of Chattanooga, whose book *Torchlight to the Cherokees* gave a classic account of the New England Protestants who came to the Appalachians in the early 1800s as missionaries to the Cherokees, recalled that sassafras tea "was not only beautiful in color, but was always a favorite beverage at mealtimes."

~

A small shrubby tree, sassafras usually is found in patches in light woods and overgrown fields. It is also known as the "mitten tree" because some of its leaves are shaped like mittens—oval with thumb-shaped leaves. Some leaves have two "thumbs," some none.

For tea purposes, folk dig the roots early in the spring while the trees are still dormant and when the bark peels off easily. The small sapling roots make excellent tea, rich red in color, but later in the year, when the sap rises, the roots give off a bitter taste.

The aforementioned Arvil Wilson told me that "any herb you dig from the ground—sassafras included—will have a funky taste if you boil it before you dry out the roots. 'Course it's all right if you want to chew the sassafras, for your gums. Like yellowroot. They're good for your mouth, for ulcers in your stomach, ever what ails you in your stomach and intestines."

> *I never did become a coffee drinker. We did, however, like very much the fragrant tea made of the spicebush that grew in great abundance on the banks of the Chickamauga (river). The sassafras tea, made of the roots of the red sassafras, was not only beautiful in color, but was a favorite beverage at meal times with us...The deep crimson berries of spice-bush were popular substitutes for spices of commerce when the store-bought spices were difficult to obtain.*
>
> —ROBERT SPARKS WALKER,
> *AS THE INDIANS LEFT IT*

Mountain folk say that to boil up a good-flavored root tea, avoid metal pots. First job is to clean the roots and scrape off the bark. If the roots are big, they need to be pounded a lot with a hammer. Cut the roots into small pieces and dry them near a fire or in an oven for two or three hours. The bark can be reused several times or can be stored for use throughout the year.

Sassafras tea has been a favorite from pioneer days in Sevierville, Tennessee, named for the great patriot and Indian fighter, John "Nolichucky Jack" Sevier, who became Tennessee's first governor.

Some time ago, as I was walking through my woodland, I found a thrifty sassafras tree about three inches in circumference...You must recollect the fragrance which the blossoms of our wild vine afford. There is none in the southern countries that equal it. They perpetually exhale the most odoriferous smell...

Next year I intend to send you some of the sassafras' blossoms properly dried. I think their infusion far superior to the Chinese tea. Alas, had the Chinese exclusively possessed the sassafras, we would think it voluptuous to regale on it; but because it grows wild in our woods, we...overlook it, and, like fools, we poison our bodies, lessen our pockets in purchasing those far-fetched Chinese leaves.

—J. HECTOR ST. JOHN DE CRÈVECOEUR, *LETTERS FROM AN AMERICAN FARMER*

Sevierville Sassafras Tea

1½ quarts water   *½ cup dried, chopped roots*

As noted earlier, dig the roots in late winter or very early spring while the sap is low. Process the roots as indicated earlier by cleaning, pounding, and drying. Bring the water to near boiling and drop in the roots. Simmer around a half hour. Serve with sugar, honey, or sorghum syrup (or, for modern folk, a little sugar or artificial sweetener).

In addition to sassafras, mountain folk popularized a number of other natural teas such as spicewood, tansy, dried persimmon leaves, catnip, sweet birch, yellowroot, and others.

Spicewood Tea

"Spicewood tasted good," Pressley recalled. "We'd scrape the bark off just like sassafras and soak it in cold water and drink it. Oh, was it delicious. Grew in little clumps, never did get any bigger in trunk size than your finger, and would grow five or six feet high" usually along the banks of creeks and branches.

Some folks made spicewood tea even more palatable by adding honey or molasses. Many drank it with cracklin' bread. While Pressley limited his spicewood recipe to soaking, others boiled the roots and shavings just like you do sassafras.

Birch Tea

Birch tea—using syrup tapped from birch trees—was also popular in pioneer days and up through the depression era. Tall, slim trees, they are found on mountain slopes in the Appalachian foothills. Recipes called for combining the birch sap with an equal amount of water, heat to boiling, and then reduce to a simmer. As with other teas, they would be sweetened with honey. A similar tea was made using the juice from maple trees. In some cases, the sap was fermented to make birch beer.

Another sweet birch tea recipe calls for cutting small twigs of the sweet birch tree (also known as black or cherry birch), putting them in a pot of boiling water, and boiling them until they reach a pale pink color. Others added birch sap to the boiling mixture.

Other herb teas once popular in the mountains were those made from mint, sage, ginseng, chestnut leaf, yellowroot (with a lot of sweetening), pine tops (new needles), wild ginger, honey locust, possum grapes, and a tea popular with the Cherokees, made from red sumac berries.

Sumac Lemonade

While lemons were seldom seen throughout the Appalachian country in the 1800s, ingenious mountain people came up with a wonderful substitute, sumac. In *Foxfire 3*, the Rabun County students reported that the base was the berries found on the fiery red-leafed sumac bush seen throughout the mountains. Sumac lemonade not only had a delicious taste—with a tangy, lemon flavor—it was said to reduce fever and lessen fatigue. As for other herb drinks, you crush the sumac berries, put them in boiling water and steep them until they reach a strong color. The juice is strained through a cloth, sweetened with honey or sugar, and served cold.

My friend Arvil Wilson said yellowroot tea is made up much like sassafras tea. "The root should be dried real good, then pounded and boiled into a drink. Bitter? Yes, it's supposed to be bitter." (But of course, honey or sorghum syrup was often used to sweeten it a bit.)

Throughout this narrative, you will notice that generally I have bypassed the subject of medicinal herbs; that's a book subject of its own. But I must make mention here about a few Appalachian teas that have proved to be something of a medicine drink as well as a beverage.

And again we turn to Arvil Wilson who makes a "peach tree tea" that he claims will cure one of hiatal hernia. "I made some for a friend, a half a gallon, and she's not had another lick of trouble with high hernia.

Years ago when I first started cooking mountain foods, two good friends came to our house to play bridge. They brought us a gift: sassafras roots. The three large sassafras roots were fresh, partly debarked, and tied with a red ribbon. We removed the ribbon, popped the roots into a pot of boiling water, boiled them for ten minutes, and spent the evening playing bridge and drinking tea.
—MARK SOHN, *MOUNTAIN COUNTRY COOKING*

"You take the bark of the peach tree to make the tea. Cut a limb off and scrape the bark and dry it. You can dry peach tree bark in a day or less. Then you boil it; put you a little salt in it for a preservative. Drink that and it'll do you good."

Maypop Tea

The Cherokees made a drink by boiling maypops, the passion fruit. They squeezed the soft pulp of the fruit through a strainer and drank it hot. Historian Charles Hudson also told of a sweet-sour honey locust beverage the Cherokees loved to drink both hot and cold. It's one that is still made today. The recipe calls for cutting the locust pods in two, soaking them in hot but not boiling water, and straining through a cloth.

And how could I fail to mention catnip? Over the years it has been very popular across Appalachia, indeed over the South. Some folks living on Sand Mountain in northern Alabama once drank it every morning as we do coffee. And in north Georgia, Betty Jo Hughes Bailey, who married David Bailey of the Big Creek area of Fannin County, says, "Grandma Lou Bailey gave catnip to my fussy babies. It worked.

"And she gave us boneset tea for the flu and put a little whiskey in it. It tasted terrible but it made you sweat; boy did it make you sweat."

A. L. Tommie Bass of Sand Mountain, Alabama, agreed that boneset and yellowroot tea were well liked but that he considered them too bitter.

"Ground ivy's another one," he declared in his book, *Plain Southern Eating*. "After I give talks these days, folks come up and tell me they drink ground ivy tea…It's a good tonic; I don't know how many minerals it's got—iron, magnesium, iodine and others—real nutritious. It'll kill a headache graveyard dead."

∼

Many's the time I've made [birch tea]. I'd go out into the woods with a sharp pocketknife and scrape off the bark of a sweet birch. Then I would carry it home and put it in a glass and pour cold water over it, put in some sugar, and let it set for a couple of hours. It made a delicious drink.
—Mrs. Ila Gurley of Yancey County, North Carolina, as quoted by John Parris in *These Storied Mountains*

Cool, Tangy Buttermilk

With Corn Bread Crumbled In, Elvis-Style

There now, don't you cry,
Hush your crying by and by
Then we'll make the butter fly
Mommy's baby don't you cry…
Churn, churn make some butter
For my little girlie's supper…

—Jean Ritchie, Singing Family of the Cumberlands

If you had a good milk cow…that would make plenty of milk and butter, that
cow would set your table.

—Quay Smathers, Dutch Cove, North Carolina,
quoted in Mountain Voices

There is no finer way to quench a summer thirst than with a glass of buttermilk flecked with butter flakes."

Thus spoke former Georgia governor Zell Miller in his auto-biographical tome, *The Mountains Within Me.*

The good governor—mountain to the core—is not alone.

Appalachian folk swear by buttermilk. A cool glass of sharp, tangy buttermilk is sometimes the only thing many old-timers need for supper, with perhaps a square or two of corn bread. The latter to crumble into the milk, like Elvis Presley did, all to be eaten with a spoon.

Ever since ancestor days in Scotland, Ireland, Wales, and England, mountain folk have relished freshly churned butter-milk, with its full-bodied, buttery tang, complete with the flecks of butter, as the governor noted, a taste that is near impossible to duplicate in today's pasteurized world.

In my case, I have "been a fool about buttermilk" from childhood. In 1932, as a three-year-old residing with my family in Greenville County's Double Springs community, our doctor

Former Georgia governor Zell Miller, a native of Young Harris, Georgia, in mountainous Towns County, loves his buttermilk with crumbled corn bread.

took me off sweet milk and told my parents to substitute buttermilk. This was after he diagnosed me as having colitis. Not only was it a blessing to my tummy and taste buds, it saved my life and gave me an appreciation for authentic buttermilk that has carried down to this day.

Like the pioneers of old, I love to pour a tall glass of cold buttermilk as a snack, along with a hunk of corn bread. Some mountain folk like to complete the snack with a slice or two of fresh onion. Some even chop up the onion in the milk.

Mrs. Julie Stapp milks the family cow while her husband, John Stapp, waves off the flies. This was in the 1920s at their farm on Beaver Ruin Road near Norcross, Georgia.

One reason for buttermilk's delicious taste in earlier days was that cows were allowed to graze at will in the woods and open spaces. One of my daily chores was fetching our cows home in the late afternoon from their woodsy pasture. I knew I was getting close when I would hear their tinkling bells. The free range had a generally flavorful effect on the milk and butter, except when the cows found a patch of bitterweed or, heaven forbid, the white snake root that could cause "milk sickness." (Such an illness proved fatal on the frontier in 1818 to Nancy Lincoln, the future president's mother.)

"[Butter] has a more pleasant taste…[from free range cows]," wrote J. Hector St. John de Crèvecoeur in his 1782 volume, *Letters from an American Farm*. He told of plans "to send you a firkin [of butter] that your friends in England may judge whether or not I am right. This is one of the principal advantages which first settlers [to America] enjoy. They possess, besides, a certain amplitude of benefits which great cultivated countries have lost. And if they carefully salt their cows at their doors, they are sure that every night they will punctually return home."

⁓

Across Appalachia, from the pioneer days, love of milk and dairy products was universal, a tradition that came straight from the British Isles. Early in the eighteenth century, William Byrd witnessed "seas of milk" in the

Piedmont foothills. And travelers to western Virginia just prior to the Revolution enjoyed a bountiful breakfast of "elegant milk, butter, pumpkin butter, corn bread, and venison."

And the Irish and Scottish and British peasants doted on buttermilk, the sourer the better. Author John Stevens called the Irish "the greatest lovers of milk I have ever met. They drink it about twenty different ways and what is strangest, they love it best when it's sourest."

It is no wonder that Appalachian households looked upon the milk cow as perhaps their most valuable possession.

"Absolutely!" grinned former Georgia State Senator William Hasty. "Those cows were the most important animal on every farm. We pampered them to assure that they would provide large amounts of rich, wholesome milk to feed our family."

The same was true in eastern Kentucky. Sidney Saylor Farr remembered that whole milk, skim milk, buttermilk, and clabbered milk were part of her family's daily diet. "Even 'blue John'—skim milk that turned sour—was used in breads and gravies when the whole milk had to be saved for churning," she said.

Most families sought to have two or three cows so that when one went dry, another would be coming "fresh." Or, as Mark Woody told me, "our family had a reciprocal understanding with the relatives and neighbors, in case our cow went dry."

Milking cows was not a preferred chore, but it ended up that in most cases it was a task handled mostly by the farm women. Even novelist-to-be Dori Sanders got the dreaded milking job when growing up on a Carolina farm.

But men often took on the assignment. My brothers Fred and Arthur

A family could not live decently without a cow... They were, however, nasty, brutish creatures. They had to be milked twice a day, which drastically limited the radius of social activity, especially for teenage milkers. Cows had nasty habits; their tails were annoying weapons when they swished at flies; they were prone to kick without warning; and none of them were housebroken.

—JOE GRAY TAYLOR, *EATING, DRINKING AND VISITING IN THE SOUTH*

worked their way through North Greenville College by helping milk the school's dairy herd. In earlier days, milkmaids and -men used cedar "piggins" to squirt the milk into during twice-a-day milkings. Later the galvanized bucket was the container of choice.

Hasty recalled the hazards of washing the cow's udder on a cold morning. "You'd leave the house with a bucket of warm water, but by the time you got to the cow, it was cold and the cow most likely would kick when that water hit. You had to watch out."

"Milking cows? No sir," declared ninety-year-old Ernest Parker who grew up in Gilmer County, Georgia. "That's somethin' I never done in my life. After my mother got where she couldn't milk the cows, though, my dad done all the milking.

Nina O'Kelly of the Upper Hominy district of Buncombe County, North Carolina, churns away as she makes fresh butter and buttermilk in this 1920s scene.

"They'd milk of a morning and again at night, strain the milk into the churn, except what we wanted to drink. If it was in the winter time, we'd set the churn up close to the fireplace to keep it warm. That would cause it to clabber. After it began to clabber, you'd turn the churn down sidewise and look down into it. If the gelatinlike clabber had turned loose from the side of the churn, it was ready to churn and make butter.

"You put that X-shaped dasher in there and churned the milk up and down until the butter came. If it was warm, it didn't take long, usually thirty to forty minutes. Then the 'butter would come,' as they would say...float to the top. Ma would take a spoon and dip the butter off and put it in a bowl and work the milk out of it, then put it in a mold. Or sometimes she'd leave it in a cup or a dish. At that point, she'd put the buttermilk and the butter in the springhouse."

Montaree Henderson Hasty could eyeball a churn of milk and determine if it was ready for churning. "She placed a white cloth covering on top of the churn, with a cloth string holding it in place," her son William recalled. "This kept the flies out and also the cats and small children."

Western North Carolina's favorite columnist, John Parris, now retired from the *Asheville Citizen-Times*, hated the "churning chore" when visiting his grandparents. When he dawdled at the tedious job, his grandmother would urge him to, "Keep churning, John! Keep churning!...the butter is going back!"

A. L. Tommie Bass believed that the weather figured in the speed of butter emergence. Cloudy weather always delayed the butter's arrival, he felt, and a stormy day meant a half-hour delay compared to a fair day.

Getting sweet milk to turn sour was another variable. In her delightful book *North Carolina and Old Salem Cookery*, Beth Tartan notes that cream soured quickly in summertime, "before you could get the dinner dishes washed, but in the winter…it took a long time." A common practice was to place the covered crock on the hearth in front of the dying fire before going to bed. Other times it might be pushed to the back of the wood stove."

*E*ven today, after having been out of the country two or three weeks, I ask Hazel to cook corn bread so that I can eat it with a glass of sweet milk. This makes me feel at home more than anything, while at the same time it seems to settle my troubled stomach.

—WILLIAM G. HASTY, CHEROKEE COUNTY, GEORGIA

Mrs. Azzie Waters recalled that "after we moved here within the city of East Ellijay (Georgia), we kept a cow for a number of years and I sold milk and butter. We kept a real good Jersey cow, kept her in the pasture down below the house and in that old barn that's about to fall down.

"Milk has to clabber," she explained to me, "and you churn it. Takes a day or so for milk to clabber. Then you 'pour up a churn,' as they called it, and then when it gets clabbered good, why you get your churn dasher out and you sit down and you churn and churn. Afterward you mold up the butter, make it real pretty. We had an oak leaf on top of our butter."

Clabber Cheese and Cakes

Clabbered or curdled milk was often used to make clabber cheese. The housewife made it by skimming off the cream and then putting the remaining milk in a container to sour, after which she would put the milk on the back of the stove to heat. Next she divided the whey from the curd and this became clabber. According to Beth Tartan, "the whole works was then poured into a cheesecloth bag or sugar bag and hung over the dishpan to drain. The bag held the cheese and the whey was fed to the hogs." This is a recipe for clabber cakes as published by Beth in her well-researched *North Carolina and Old Salem Cookery*:

Clabber Cakes

1 cup sifted flour
1 teaspoon baking soda
½ teaspoon salt

1 cup clabber (clabber cheese or soured milk)

Sift together flour, baking soda, and salt. Add clabber, and blend. The batter will be lumpy. Cook like pancakes on a hot griddle.

Yellow Cheese

Homemade yellow cheese was also a favorite on the frontier. I am indebted to Beth Tartan once again for the following cheese recipe which is attributed to Mrs. M. E. Reeves of the far northwest North Carolina community of Laurel Springs.

Homemade Yellow Cheese

Heat 1 gallon clabber milk, stirring occasionally until it is just comfortable to the finger. Strain through cloth, being sure to remove as much whey as possible. Heat curd over boiling water with 1 egg, dash of salt, and ¼ teaspoon baking soda, stirring occasionally until smooth. For softer cheese, add a little cream. For harder cheese, add egg yolk alone. Be sure the cheese is thoroughly melted and blended before pouring into mold. The cheese will not blend smoothly if there is too much whey left in the curd.

Speaking of dairy products, just about the most delightful derivative was what the late Bil Dwyer of Highlands, North Carolina, called "geranium butter," actually geranium-honey butter that came from the kitchen of his aunt Emma Weed.

Mrs. Weed mashed and minced geranium flower petals until she got about a tablespoonful. She mixed this into about a half pound of fresh, soft butter, along with a bit of honey. When served with a platter of hot biscuits, Bil declared, "It was something good!"

To end this chapter on milk and milk products, let me say that after the doctor prescribed buttermilk for me as a child, in 1932, I never returned to sweet milk until I was a college student in 1945 at Mount Berry, Georgia. By that time, at age sixteen, I was ready to "grow up," I suppose. Today, I grieve that my children and grandchildren shun delicious buttermilk. I tell them that it's an acquired taste, like learning to savor a good martini. Of course, they've never had the chance to know what real buttermilk tasted like, straight from the free-range cow and from the churn and springhouse. I would hope that some day they could find out.

Hog-Killing Day

Fresh Meat Frenzy

Hog killing was a festival as joyous as Christmas—and little less sacred.
—Martha McCullough-Williams, 1913

~

I longed for [hog-killing day] and dreaded it like death. To us all it was orgy
and holocaust, wild pleasure and terror that pounded the heart and dilated the
pupils of the eyes. But even so, on the perimeter somewhere…were visions of
platters of sausage and crisp spareribs and backbone.
—Lillian Smith, Memory of a Large Christmas

~

With the coming of cold weather, little streams of smoke may be seen during
early hours of the morning at country homes…Gathered around these little
fires are farmers killing hogs, and women tending lard…There is no depression
in the kitchen, for there is plenty to eat.
—Tennessee newspaper feature appearing January 14, 1932

When the chilly north winds of late November whipped through the Appalachian valleys, and frost's icy fingers circled the hillsides and curled into the deep coves and cabin chinks, mountain people pulled on their long johns and prepared for their most exciting food celebration of the year.

Rivaling family reunions, revival dinners, and all-day singings with dinner on the ground, "hog-killing day"—when mountain people killed a hog and "baconed hit up"— marked the long-awaited arrival of fresh meat. It was usually worth the wait.

At the foot of Whiskey Bill Mountain near Georgia's Blue Ridge Continental Divide, Mark Woody and his widowed mother, Laura Beaver Woody, longed for the day; it would bring a bounteous blessing to their meat box. Most important to Mark, his appetite soon would be joyously sated.

"Boy, we'd have us a general feast—back bones and ribs and plenty of liver…whoo-eeee!" Indeed, it was a jubilant and exciting day: And sometimes the working festivities would go on for a week. On a personal note, when I reached the age of remembering—around age four or five—I couldn't help but join in the festive hoopla. At that age, of course, I could only watch. What I remember best, though, was pausing at the end of the sausage grinding to savor the hickory sweet aroma wafting from Mother's kitchen. It was a joy to sit near her Home Comfort stove as the fresh sausage, laden with homegrown sage and red peppers, sizzled in the skillet, giving off such satisfying smells. Those sausages—along with the biscuits and milk gravy

I always had to stay out of school on hog-killing day to help out, of course. What I enjoyed most was getting the hog's bladder, inflating it with a homemade reed, and turning it into a kickball. You had to blow it up before it dried. It was like a leather ball almost. Some of the men turned bladders into tobacco pouches to keep their tobacco fresh and moist.
—SAM GATES, MOUNTAINTOWN DISTRICT, GILMER COUNTY, GEORGIA

and the coffee that Mama allowed me to taste with a biscuit dip even at that early age, left a memorable mark on my tender taste buds.

My father loved eating brains with his eggs at breakfast the morning after. It took me several years (by age ten) to reconcile myself to such on my plate, even if for only once a year. Many considered it a delicacy; some in the mountains pickled brains to give them longer life.

I grew to love tenderloin, a boneless pork chop, and backbones and liver. I can't recall if we had sauerkraut with the backbones—a mountain tradition—but knowing of Mother's love of kraut, I'm sure it must have been high on her hog-killing-day menu.

Hog-killing week had still more fresh pork delicacies to offer—the liver, the sausage, the ribs, yes, even the headcheese that my mother lovingly hand-crafted and called souse meat, a hand-me-down from Elizabethan England. Plus, of course, we felt mighty blessed that our smokehouse bulged with glorious hams and side meat middlings (bacon). Many mornings of gustatory pleasure lay ahead: biscuits and "muddy gravy," my father's description for red-eye gravy, the kind that would wink at you in the plate. (More about ham and other pork delicacies in the chapter to follow.)

The late Herbert Wilcox, my astute and articulate Elberton correspondent for the *Atlanta Journal* in the 1960s, described the delicious dividends for people who worked a hog killing:

By dinner time on hog-killing day—the midday meal is never lunch on a Southern farm—the family begins to satisfy that pent-up appetite for fresh meat. As a starter, there is a big dish of fresh liver seasoned with plenty of red pepper. Usually everybody makes a meal of this without bothering with side dishes. The spare ribs and backbones come later.

Ninety-two-year-old Nina Garrett, who was a neighbor of Mark Woody's in Gilmer County, Georgia, won her family's permanent assignment as hog-killing-day cook: "The boys (my brothers) wanted me in the kitchen; they said nary one of my sisters cooked the first mess and hit be fit to eat."

Then she leaned over and whispered with a wink, "My sisters never put in enough salt!"

$\sim$

Looking into the Appalachian dietary history, pork has been at the pinnacle of the region's food popularity from the beginning, along with corn. As soon as the foothills family got situated at their homestead, they planted a patch of corn and began raising hogs.

The first British swine reached America's Upper South in 1608, the first Jamestown arrivals being a boar and three sows. Within eighteen months, Virginia's pig population had quadrupled! Soon swine began multiplying mightily up and down the colony, including the interior.

The porkers bountifully met the newcomers' needs just as the wild game started declining. Thriving in the woods on nuts and wild berries and roots (providing flavorful flesh!), the pigs were efficient meat producers, dressing out to 75 percent edible meat, far more than beef.

Soon settlers were eating pork every day, along with

Cooking out pork fat, known as rendering lard, was carried out in big pots on hog-killing day. Such was the case here in Forsyth County, Georgia, during the early twentieth century.

their ever-present corn bread and garden vegetables. "Hogs and hominy" became the dietary cornerstone for an entire region for more than three centuries.

In 1900—when farmers across the South slaughtered twenty million hogs—the 1,714 farms in north Georgia's Fannin County, straddling the "Blue Ridge Divide," boasted 11,592 hogs, 2,107 milk cows, and only 359 head of beef cattle. The same was true across the Appalachians; mountain folks purely adored hog meat in virtually all of its forms...tenderloin, liver, sausage, ham, bacon, jowls, cracklin's, backbones, and souse meat. "The only thing we threw away was the squeal," said Curtis Underwood. Pork popularity stemmed from its traditional preference going way back to England and Europe and also the fact that hog meat could be easily preserved by salt and smoke-curing. Salt-curing of beef was not a favored option.

> *These [North Carolina] people live so much upon swine's flesh, that it...makes them likewise extremely hoggish in their temper and many of them seem to grunt rather than speak in their ordinary conversation.*
>
> —William Byrd of Westover, Virginia (1700s)

~

Killing a hog was a major undertaking. Despite eagerness for fresh meat, no mountaineer would dare attempt the ritual without first checking the "signs" as well as the thermometer. Mrs. Annabella Hill of LaGrange, Georgia, wrote in her 1820 cookbook that hogs "should be killed when the wind sets decidedly in the north."

In Georgia's Foxfire foothills, master hog-killer Garnet Lovell, legendary for his hog-killing skill with over two thousand hogs to his credit, always looked for a frosty 30- to 35-degree day when the moon was in the last quarter—a "waning moon." Killing a hog on a "growing moon," Garnet felt, would be an awful risk. "Even cracklin's will twist and curl up in the frying pan." Others said a new-moon killing would cause the meat to swell up and not keep well.

> *My parents lived to be 89 and I've seen the grease dripping off both of 'ems chins a many a time. Mary's father lived to be 93 and he ate pork most all the time, and lard. Pork meat was one of our main foods, for grease, for cooking, cured meat and fresh meat and we ate more pork than anything else except wild meat.*
>
> —Frank Pressley, a native of Cullowhee Mountain, North Carolina

Ernest Parker, now in his nineties, who grew up in Gilmer County's Bucktown district, helped his family with the slaughtering:

"Along in late November, when the weather got cool, was when you'd kill your hogs. We'd usually kill two if they were good-size hogs—enough to last us until the next hog killing. Back in them times, folks had free range, stock ran out in the mountains. Folks just fenced in their crops and gardens and let their stock run out in the woods. They'd notch their hogs' ears—splits of one, two or three in the ear; over bits and under bits, swallow forks...everyone had their own special identification.

"Along in late summer, we'd put two or three hogs in the pen and start feedin' 'em corn and scraps from the table and fatten 'em...get 'em good and fat. They really relished that stuff. All our neighbors would come in and help on hog-killing day. When we got through, my father would give each of them a good mess of meat. Then when the neighbor killed their hogs, we'd help them out and get us a fresh mess in return."

At the Gates Chapel community near the Cohutta Mountain range, Frances Gates Hill, scion of a legendary old

Tennessee farmer prepares to open up a fat hog held up by a singletree hitch.

mountain family, recalled that the techniques of her father Andy Gates followed those of her grandfather Samuel Gates and earlier ancestors who came to north Georgia from Buncombe County, North Carolina, in the 1800s.

As a community event, it was a day of joy and fellowship although also a day of hard work and greasy hands.

> We'd start the fire for the hog killing about daylight or before. By ten o'clock, with the first hogs slaughtered and processed, everybody was hungry. For lunch, we fried tenderloin, but the liver's what I liked. It was soooo good. We'd cook b-i-i-i-g skilletfuls.

> We killed a lot of hogs and salted them down. What we couldn't salt, Mama cooked 'em up and canned 'em in jars. We just fried our sausages like we was going to eat 'em right then. Instead, we put them in jars and poured in hot grease and turned each jar bottom side up. That grease sealed the meat in. We kept the jars in the smokehouse, along with our hams and shoulders and side meat.

Another Gilmer County old-timer, Bess Dover Pache, considered brains a hog-killing-day delicacy. But she also had a great love for fresh ham gravy. "Us kids liked gravy better than we did meat. The first meat we had—ribs and backbones—Mama would boil it and make dumplings with it. You know backbones had marrow, and we usta look for that. Mama always canned sausage in quart jars and put them in the smokehouse."

With the pots boiling with water, hill country farmers slice open a fat hog.

To get back to my own experience, after I reached about age twelve, my parents allowed me to take part in a few hog killings. The memories are clear...seeing Dad's roaring fire under the big black wash pots early on a frosty morn...watching the hog fall over at the crack of the .22 rifle shot...then watching as the men swung into action dipping the carcass into a metal drum dug into the ground and filled with boiling water…Then I watched as the men scraped the carcass clean of hair with sharp knives. Using a "singletree" hitch, they strung the animal up on a hickory pole, where Dad opened up the hog's chest and belly, allowing the removal of the intestines and vital organs… and started cutting up the major pieces of meat on a big table. Meanwhile, later in the day, Mother and her helpers took over at the wash pots, rendering the lard from the pile of fat meat and straining out the cracklin' morsels.

As a growing kid, my assignment was to help grind the sausage—good lean shoulder meat and other lean scraps cut into two-inch cubes—with a hand-crank sausage mill. My mother would then knead the meat with her hands, incorporating her homegrown sage and red pepper that she had dried over the kitchen stove. When the patties came off the fry pan, the taste was powerful and memorable.

Mountain folk met the challenge of getting an accurate reading of their hot water when dousing a hog to be cleaned. The objective was heating the water to around 150 degrees—hot enough so that the hog's hair would loosen up enough for "hair pulling" but not so hot as to cause the hair to "set." Their solution: a swish of an index finger around in the water three times. If the swisher suffered no scalding of his finger, the water was considered acceptable. In Gilmer County, Georgia, Frances Gates Hill recalled how her father heated the water:

"They would heat rocks on top of a cord of hardwood. Those rocks would turn red hot. My father would take a shovel and toss them right into the big vats. They heated the water fast. We'd take what we called then tow sacks, and pour the hot water onto the hog. You wanted the water hot but not boiling."

~

Neighbors came in to help Mark Woody and his widowed mother kill and cure their annual hog. One of the old-timers would do the shooting: "I can still see him settin' there with that gun barrel over the top of the pen taking aim at the hog; he'd aim for quite a while, trying to be sure to get the shot on the money (between the eyes). When the hog fell over, the men would grab their knives and slit the hog's throat, and let him bleed."

On Cullowhee Mountain, North Carolina, a strapping young Frank Pressley joined in to help his family scald their hogs:

There was a bunch of us there; we'd pull that hog out (of the pot) and
have a board at the end and slide him right onto it and start grabbing hair.

Hog-Killing Day ~ 181

If the water was not hot enough, the hair wouldn't slip. If it was too hot, over 150 degrees, it would set the hair, which was bad. When the hair started slipping, Daddy would shout, "Turn him over…he's ready to turn over!" We'd turn him around and slide him back down into the kettle. When we got him out, everybody would start grabbing hair.

After we got him clean as a whistle, we'd hook the hog's feet onto a gamlin stick, usually a well-seasoned hickory limb with the ends sharpened. People would reuse a good stick for years. We'd teakle that hog out of the pot. After getting the hog strung up, head down, we'd wash him thoroughly then cut the head off and put it in a pan of cold water.

Historian Joe Gray Taylor remembered that one's hands, wet and bruised from scraping the hog's bristles in scalding water, turned blue in the cold and lost their strength. "When the carcass was hung up and the belly opened to remove the edible organs and offal from the interior, it was a pleasure, almost sinful, to thrust one's frigid hands into the still-warm abdominal cavity."

The 1930s *WPA Guide to South Carolina*, a depression-era writer's project, told of how the meat was cut up:

"The method is not the orthodox one followed by meat packers. Instead of being split down the middle, the backbone is cut out. Then each side is cut into hams, middlings, and shoulders. Backbones and spare ribs are cooked immediately and generous portions of the fresh meat are given to neighbors. The heavily salted meat is packed into boxes or barrels for about two weeks. The middlings, now called bacon, are then washed and salted again, after which they will keep almost indefinitely. Hams and shoulders require further treatment."

*W*hen hogs were butchered…you could start eating at the Indiana end and eat every bite of it to the Tennessee end and still have the bristles left over for toothpicks.
—CHARLES PATTESON'S KENTUCKY COOKING

The lard that came from the hog fat gave families plenty of cooking grease for the months ahead, as well as the base for salve, soap and oil for their lamps. At the late Willie Davis farm east of Ellijay, lard was the primary object, with meat as a byproduct.

"That's all we had to cook with, lard was, except butter," recalled Willie's son Larry, a former Gilmer County commissioner. "We usually killed two hogs. We needed those two big old fifty-pound cans of lard. That took us over the winter. Mama would keep the fatback for cooking. But we never had meat all year. It went pretty fast with our big family."

While hog-killing day was demanding on all concerned, the food that came from the kitchen was a wonderful treat. As Ruth Swanson Hunter of Young Harris, Georgia, remembered it, "That night, when we got to eat, oh boy! We'd have tenderloin or fried ribs. And that cracklin' bread was oh, soooo delicious!"

Tenderloin

A favorite among mountain folk was old-fashioned tenderloin, a "high on the hog" delicacy—pork chops minus the backbone. Cooking tenderloin is fairly simple. Most cooks fry the slices in hot fat until brown on each side. Drippings from the loin are often used to make "sawmill gravy" mixing in flour and milk with the gravy to be poured over the slices or on biscuits.

Pork Backbones

One of Fannin County, Georgia's "adopted natives," my friend Carl Dodd, a Lockheed retiree, has moved right into the Appalachian lifestyle and is a great devotee of mountain foods and cooking. Here are Carl's directions for cooking pork backbones, a hog-killing-week favorite, with perhaps a few modern twists.

Carl Dodd's Backbones and Cabbage

3 pounds pork backbones   *½ cup all-purpose flour*
1 head of cabbage   *Salt and paprika to taste*

Preheat oven to 375°F. Place the backbones in a good-size boiler, and add water to cover. Add a small dash of salt. Simmer until tender, probably around 1 hour. Remove the meat, and brown in an oven at 375°F. Reserve broth. Chop up a cabbage into chunks, and place in the broth and cook, but not overly. To make a sauce, strain the broth, and put into a skillet. Add flour to thicken, along with paprika if desired. Heat and stir until thick and brown. Serve the meat in the center of the plate surrounded with cabbage. Pour the sauce on top of the meat.

Spareribs, Backbones, and Sauerkraut

A hog-killing-day favorite, spareribs and sauerkraut, came down from the German settlers of the Blue Ridge who combined their kraut with fresh pork. This is a casserole that also incorporates backbones and is much loved in Lick Skillet, Georgia. Located in Fannin County, the settlement of Lick Skillet got its name this way, according to students of West Fannin High School: During a tough time, people in the area would tell their kids, "now lick the skillet clean." Later a farmhouse restaurant in the Atlanta suburb of Roswell took a fancy to the phrase and took it as its name.

I know that being anti-lard is popular these days. For flavor mongers like me, this anti-lard trend is a pity. Tablespoon for tablespoon, lard has ½ the cholesterol and only a few more calories than butter...I only use lard occasionally, but I've used it often enough that my children know what lard is and how it tastes.

—MARK SOHN,
MOUNTAIN COUNTRY COOKING

Spareribs, Backbones, and Sauerkraut

3 pounds spareribs and backbones *1 onion, thinly sliced*
Pepper and salt to taste *1 quart sauerkraut*

Preheat oven to 350°F. Place ribs and backbones in pork fat with pepper and salt. Sear the meat, then place in a casserole dish in two layers, along with two layers of raw uncooked sauerkraut and onions. Add boiling water. Cover dish, and bake at 350°F for 2 hours or until done.

Sausage

Many mountain people fried their sausage into patties or balls immediately after a hog killing, packed them into earthen crocks, and poured fat on top that sealed in the sausage for the winter.

Another way, according to Ruth Swanson Hunter, was to use corn shucks. They called it shuck sausage. "Old folks would take an ear of corn and shuck it and take out all the silk and ear of corn, and pack the sausage down in that shuck and tie up the end of it and hang it up to let it cure." Some would smoke-cure their shuck sausage also.

Really good sausage depends on getting the right proportion of fat to lean meat...one part fat to two parts lean. And, of course, the addition of sage and pepper is also a key—said by some to be a hand-me-down from Elizabethan England. This dish, combining the sausage saltiness with the sweet tang of apples, is a favorite across the mountains, including people living in the Snowbird Mountains on the edge of the Great Smoky Mountains National Park near Cherokee, North Carolina.

Sausage with Apples

1 pound bulk sausage *Red pepper*
1 teaspoon garden sage *1 apple*
1 teaspoon salt *2 teaspoons brown sugar*

Mix pork, sage, salt, and red pepper, and fry until lightly brown. Take apple, core it, and slice into rings. Put in sausage drippings, and fry at low temperature for 6 minutes, turning as needed. Spread the brown sugar over apples, and keep frying until they are tender. Place apples on platter with sausage for serving.

Liver Mush

Liver mush was one of the delicious byproducts of a hog killing. A mountain delicacy, it was worked on a day or so later when the priority jobs had been taken care of. Chef and author Mark Sohn of Pikeville, Kentucky, puts liver mush in the same category with liverell, liver pudding, scrapple, and sausage scrapple, most of which combine pork liver and/or lean pork and are then thickened with cornmeal.

The following recipe is adapted from one that came from the kitchen of Mrs. J. D. Braswell Sr., of Newland, North Carolina, near Mount Mitchell. It was published originally by the Junior Service League of Johnson City, Tennessee, in its "Smoky Mountain Magic" recipe collection. Mrs. Braswell notes that on the final frying step, the mush can be fried with onion rings if desired. She also notes liver mush is great in a cold sandwich:

Newland Fried Liver Mush

Fresh pork liver   *Red pepper, salt, and sage*

1 cup cornmeal (approx.)

Scald pork liver to seal in blood. Cut liver into small pieces. Cook until tender. Remove from water; save water it was cooked in, a quart or more. Grind liver, and put back in pot with water. Bring to a boil. Stir in cornmeal, as much as it takes to make it very stiff. Cook well, stirring all the time. Remove from stove, and incorporate diced red pepper, salt, and sage. Check seasoning by tasting, adding more as required. Pack in covered container, and chill. When cold, slice and fry in bacon grease until brown on both sides.

Fried hog's feet were nearly the best of hog killing. After boiling tender, the feet were split lengthwise in half, rolled in sifted cornmeal, salted and peppered, and fried crisp in plenty of boiling hot fat. Served with hot biscuit, and stewed sun-dried peaches, along with strong coffee...made a supper or breakfast one could rejoice in.

Backbone stewed, and served with sweet potatoes, hot corn bread, and sparkling cider, was certainly not to be despised.

—Martha McCullough-Williams,
Dishes and Beverages of the Old South

Liver Pudding

Some of my friends in the mountains of north Georgia and North Carolina told of a different way of cooking liver—they called it liver pudding, and it is similar to the liver dishes made by the Palatine Germans who settled the Appalachians. It is differentiated from liver mush mainly by the increased proportion of liver used. They first drain all the blood from the liver, cook it until it is tender, then chop it up finely and season the dish with red peppers and sage. Some mountain people always put a whole onion in the liver mix being cooked.

This recipe comes from *Old Time Recipes* published by the famed Nu-Wray Inn in Burnsville, North Carolina:

Nu-Wray Liver Mush

1 pork liver	*Salt and pepper to taste*
Fresh pork	*Flour*
Cornmeal	

Boil liver and medium-size piece of pork together until done. Remove from vessel, and mash fine with a potato masher. Place the mashed liver/pork back in the same liquid in which it has cooked. Add enough cornmeal to make thick mush. Add salt and pepper. Allow to cook until the cornmeal is done.

Stir frequently after adding the meal to prevent burning. When done, pour into shallow dish and place in icebox. When ready to serve, cut into thick slices, and roll in flour. Fry in a greased skillet until it is golden brown.

Souse Meat (Hog's Headcheese)

Making souse meat, sometimes referred to as scrapple or headcheese, was a major job for the women of a household. When completed, though, it was a well-loved delicacy, and could be sliced off and eaten as desired in the weeks following a hog killing.

Azzie Waters, who grew up in Dawson County, Georgia, near the southern tip of the Appalachian Trail, remembered that her mother always cooked her hog head in the fireplace because it had to cook all day long. "She'd pull it out [of the fireplace] late of an evening when it got dark and take it out on the back porch. She'd put that head in a big old pan and work it up, pick out all the little bones and lay 'em over in a saucer. I just loved to suck them bones, because they had a good taste. She'd work them all up real good and then she'd put in black pepper. 'Course it was already salted. She'd put it in a big bowl and put a plate on top of it and put irons on top of that plate and let it set overnight. That would drain ever' bit of the grease out. Then it was pressed meat, or souse. That would keep well until people ate it."

This is an adaptation of a nineteenth-century recipe published by Duane Oliver in his Hazel Creek, North Carolina, recipe collection. Since it includes cornmeal, it could be termed something of a German-type scrapple:

Hazel Creek Souse Meat

Hog's head, plus related	*3 cups cornmeal*
pork items as listed below	*Flour*
Salt, pepper, sage, savory	

After removing the skin, brains, eyes, and ears, soak in salted water for a few hours. Drain off water. Slice head into sections and place in saucepan along with liver, heart, and pork scraps. Cover with water and boil until the meat falls from the bones. Remove the meat from bones, and chop fine. Reserve the stock, and throw the bones to the dogs. Heat 3 quarts of the stock and add salt, pepper, sage, and savory. Bring to a rolling boil, and gradually stir in 3 cups of cornmeal, stirring all the time. Cook an hour, stirring constantly all the time, to prevent lumps. When very thick like a mush, add the meat, and continue cooking over low heat about 20 minutes, stirring occasionally. Pour into loaf pans, and place in refrigerator. (Note, in the 1800s, this would be in a cold room of the house or smoke-house.) When congealed, slice as needed, dust with flour, and fry in hot grease.

While we were filming Fried Green Tomatoes, we were scouting locations for grocery stores when I wandered into a Piggly Wiggly with a Yankee member of our crew. I stopped by the meat section...They had pig's feet, pig ears, pig tails, pig snouts, all neatly wrapped in cellophane ready to be sold. My companion...was frozen in horror. Not knowing her terror of simple little pig parts, I proceeded to pick up a pair of ears and a snout and turned to her and jokingly made a snorting sound...She ran through Piggly Wiggly screaming like a crazy person and we haven't seen her since.

—*Fannie Flagg's Whistlestop Cafe Cookbook*

Rita Hall Bayett wrote a poignant remembrance in *Georgia Country Life* about hog-killing day:

"When the sun was dropping in the sky and the smokehouse was full with fresh meat, Uncle Frank and his family would head for home, carrying a big sack of the freshes with them.

"That night, sitting around the fireside, I would bask in the lingering excitement of the day's events, and start looking forward to next year's hog-killing day…Now hog killings are just a memory."

The wife was taking out the liver mush and souse meat and slicing it up and this old boy was sitting there; he'd come to invite us to a neighbor's corn shucking. It was real cold. I said, "Tom, get good'n warm 'fore you leave; you're going to

freeze going around inviting folks to the corn shuckin'."

He was just settin' there and looking at that souse meat like he wanted some; you could tell.

I said, "Sarah, give Tom a hunk of that."

"Which you'd rather have, Tom?" Sarah asked him.

"Both good," Tom said.

"Give Tom a chunk of both of 'em," I told Sarah.

So Sarah gave him a piece of souse meat and a piece of liver mush. We watched him walking down the hill from our house. He'd bite on one piece and then another.

—THE LATE OSCAR CANNON (AGE 98 WHEN INTERVIEWED BY THE AUTHOR) OF TURNER'S CORNER, GEORGIA

Smokehouse Ham

Ah, the Succulent Glory of It All!

A farmer who did not take high pride in his hams was likely to plow a crooked furrow.
> —*Joe Gray Taylor,* Eating, Drinking and Visiting in the South

~

Ham's substantial, ham is fat
Ham is firm and sound.
Ham's what God was getting at
When he made pigs so round.

> —*Roy Blount Jr.*

Nothing could be finer than to be in Carolina, or any other state in the Appalachian South, for a traditional mountain breakfast—a platter of smokehouse ham in all its splendid and succulent glory, accompanied, naturally, by hot biscuits, a shimmering bowl of red-eye gravy, and a steaming serving of hominy grits.

In earlier Appalachian years, and yet today, nothing could quicken a mountaineer's appetite like the aroma of ham sizzling in a skillet over fireplace coals or on top of a cast-iron stove. Such a bountiful breakfast gave the hill country householder a great sense of well-being, knowing that this was the mere tip of what his smokehouse held.

As Joni Miller has so eloquently written in *True Grits*, "The smokehouse supply of sausage, hams and slabs of bacon, was a delicious promise of plenty, a hedge against hunger and hard times."

The production of pork in colonial and frontier America developed into a high art, particularly in the upper South. This was due to the region's chilly winters, a slaughtering necessity, followed by hot, humid summers—the "July-August sweats"—perfect for curing smokehouse meats. Thus the states of Virginia and Maryland plus the Carolinas, Georgia, Tennessee, and Kentucky fit the pork-producing parameters perfectly. Thanks be to God, they fulfilled their swine meat potential in a splendid fashion.

Virginia's peanut-lush hams gained an early and widespread following, even in faraway England. During Queen Victoria's long reign as Britain's monarch—from 1837 until 1901—she had a standing order for six Smithfield hams a week. The records don't show whether her grocery order also included hard-crusted beaten biscuits, which Southern housewives loved to split open and fill with thin slices of ham. But Victoria's keen appetite for Virginia hams never waned. (This was all the more remarkable since her cousin and husband, Prince Albert, grew up on European Westphalia hams.)

Nancy Bell Dashiell, who grew up at Berry Hill Farms, recalls, "My mother was responsible for the smokehouse, the only building at Berry Hill that was always locked, and the big wrought iron key was never out of her possession. The last thing she did before going to bed at night was to put the key on the mantel in her room. If the key was missing, nobody went to sleep until it was located and safely in place."
—The Smithfield Cookbook

While mild-flavored pre-cooked honey-baked hams today are the most popular with American housewives, traditional "country hams"—cured in the old-fashioned ways—still command a premium price and are highly sought after. A mahogany-colored country ham, even though heavily salted, can, if properly cooked, give one a trophy of delicious texture and taste.

~

The smokehouse became one of the great symbolic buildings of the Appalachian frontier, second in importance only to the homestead residence itself. This was true whether smoking was part of the curing process or not.

Thanks to the generously instructive Indians, the early settlers received schooling in the smoke-curing art. This took place at first in "outdoor fireplaces" over which were built frameworks for the meat. In time, farmers enclosed the hearths, first in dirt-floor log smokehouses and later in clapboard buildings.

Englishman Nicholas Creswell sent home a vivid account in 1775:

> The bacon cured here (in Virginia) is not to be equaled in any part of the world, their hams in particular. They first rub them over with brown sugar and let them lie all night. This extracts the watery particles. They let them lie in salt for 10 days or a fortnight. Some rub them with hickory ashes instead of saltpetre, it makes them red as the saltpetre and gives them a pleasant taste. Then they are hung up in the smokehouse and a slow smoky fire kept under them for three or four weeks; nothing but hickory wood is burnt in these smokehouses. This gives them an agreeable flavour, far preferable to the Westphalia Hams; not only that, but it preserves them going rancid and will preserve them for several years by giving them a fresh smoking now and then.

The smokehouses continued to be called that, whether they were used to smoke meat or not. As I recall from my own childhood days in upper South Carolina, our smokehouse, located just off the back of the house near our kitchen, was a great meat storage building, but never was graced by smoke during our years living there. It was in this dark, windowless building that we salted down our hams, shoulders, and slabs of "middlin'" meat (bacon). Our smokehouse didn't have a chimney. Of course, true smokehouses were built without chimneys; smoke-cure devotees wanted the smoke to linger as long as possible so their hams would absorb the utmost in smoke flavor, much like today's Texas mesquite wood chips used for grilling.

Evie Shelton of Coffee Valley, Virginia, was famed for her country hams that she bought from neighboring farmers. She smoked them after a salt rubdown such as she performs here.

A typical first ham "rub down" included salt, usually followed—depending on the farmer's tastes—by sugar and saltpeter. After that came at least a month's burial in a deep layer of salt before the hams and shoulders were hung up on the smokehouse rafters.

Azzie Waters remembered, "We had a big old log smokehouse and a big old meat box up on a shelf. They'd put salt in the bottom of the box then put the middlin's in there, and put salt on one, then lay another one and put more salt. Then they'd lay the hams on top of that, salting each one as they laid them down."

Mary Randolph, in her 1824 book, *The Virginia Housewife*, wrote (in contrast to the on the next page) that readers should:

> Remember to hang the hams and shoulders with the hocks down, to
> preserve the juices. Make a good smoke every morning, and be careful not
> to have a blaze; the smoke-house should stand alone, for any additional

heat will spoil the meat. During the hot weather, beginning the first of April, it should be occasionally taken down, examined—rubbed with hickory ashes, and hung up again.

During hard times and among mountain folk in remote areas, salt was a precious commodity, and hardwood ashes became a superb substitute. Alex Stewart of Hancock County, Tennessee, told John Rice Irwin that his grandfather cured all his pork with ashes burned especially for the purpose from hickory, black oak, and blackjack. He recalled seeing a ham pulled from a seven-year ash burial. It was "as yellow as a pumpkin," had a perfect cure, and could be eaten without cooking.

A Southwest Virginia farmer keeps his smokehouse fires smoldering to provide plenty of hickory smoke for his hams in background.

The smoldering smokehouse fires across the Appalachian frontier featured not only hickory smoke but that from sourwood, sassafras, oak, apple trees, corncobs, and even peanut chaff!

One of the greatest old-time smokehouse ham practitioners was the late Rush Wray of Burnsville, North Carolina, who kept three hundred hams hanging from his rafters at one time. His grandfather built the smokehouse in 1850 when he bought the hotel that later and still today is called the Nu-Wray Inn. Current operators are Doug and Barb Brown.

Rush Wray continued his ancestors' traditions, using green hickory chips from small limbs to carry out a four-month smoking using a "low fire and slow smoke." Afterward he would pull down his hams, coat them with a paste of red pepper, water, molasses, and flour, and hang them back up for a cure of not much more than a year. He believed that a longer cure would cause his hams to get tough. Apparently his method was the correct one. Customers flocked to the Nu-Wray Inn for his great food, particularly the ham and red-eye gravy breakfasts.

After the turn of the century, salt became plentiful and inexpensive and many people—including my own father—abandoned the smoking part and depended almost entirely on the salt dry-curing method. Yet the meat house continued to be called the smokehouse.

> *In the 1800s, hogs roamed an open range...The sweetest meat was from hogs that fed on chestnuts, but did not produce good lard. Acorns made the meat bitter. So about a month before slaughter, hogs were rounded up and fattened on corn. Corn removed the bitterness and the fat was suitable for rendering lard.*
> —MERLE WEAVER, TICKANETLEY, GEORGIA,
> IN *THE HERITAGE OF GILMER COUNTY*

Bess Dover Pache of Ellijay, Georgia, remembered that when the weather turned warm, her father would bring the hams out of the salted meat box and hang them up "all up and down the rafters."

Not far away, in the mountains of east Gilmer County, Mark Woody had a similar experience. "By mid-February, most people would take the [salted hams] out and wash them off and coat them with boric acid; that kept out the flies."

In later years, after salting and smoking, many mountain people rubbed their hams with sugar and/or molasses, along with their individual recipes that included cloves, peppers, and ashes.

After the long curing—many old-timers insisted on at least two years for this final ham episode—the real test came when the ham was cut down from the smokehouse rafter and brought into the kitchen for the final and ultimate test. It reminded one of the poem by John Dryden,

> *He from the chimney took*
> *A flitch of bacon off the hook,*
> *And freely from the fattest side*
> *Cut out large slices to be fried.*

While sausage, liver, and tenderloin and chops were practically always fried, hams and shoulders could be boiled, baked, or fried. For the mountain home that was unable to commit a whole ham to be cooked at one time—and there were many—the housewife would merely slice off pieces and fry them as needed.

Mark Woody of Woodstock, Georgia, who grew up in the mountains of north Georgia near the Blue Ridge Divide, as a youth loved hog-killing day, mainly for the tasty pork dishes that followed.

Fried Ham and Gravy

An old Virginia cookbook declared that a ham should be "spicy as a woman's tongue, sweet as her kiss, and tender as her love." The following traditional recipe seeks to carry out this objective.

In frying ham, experts urge the cut be made crosswise, through the center of the ham, providing a good amount of fat meat along with the lean. Also, if you have the time, you may wish to soak your ham in water for a half hour or so to remove some of the ham's excess saltiness. Older saltier hams require even more soaking. (Mrs. Betty Talmadge, who formerly ran the famous Talmadge Ham operation at Lovejoy, Georgia, liked to soak her slices of ham for at least a half hour with a mixture containing a cup of buttermilk and three tablespoons of brown sugar.)

The late Mrs. Julia Wray, Rush's wife—one of the great cooks of the mountains—always used an iron skillet and got it piping hot and added a teaspoon of grease before plopping down her ham to fry.

Note that this recipe calls for coffee to supplement the red-eye gravy mix. Tennessee ham connoisseurs declare that coffee is superfluous and totally unnecessary for their luscious ham gravy. Tennessee ham, thank you, requires merely a cup of water added to the ham drippings. Also, if you make the gravy to go with your ham, be sure to bake a lot more biscuits! (All mountain housewives well know this).

Mountain-Style Fried Country Ham and Red-Eye Gravy

¼-inch thick slice ham, center cut	*¾ cup coffee*
½ teaspoon lard or oil	*Salt to taste*

Use heavy skillet, well heated. Add the lard or vegetable oil. Score the fat. Fry one side of the ham until it is brown. Flip, and brown second side quickly. Reduce heat to low, and cook covered for 8 minutes or until tender. Turn several times. Remove ham to warm plate. Pour coffee and salt into skillet drippings, and let boil for about 3 minutes. The red-eye gravy can be poured on the ham. It can also be mixed with sorghum syrup and sopped with biscuits.

Boiled Ham

Again I quote my beloved late friend from Elberton, Georgia, Herbert Wilcox—who was my *Atlanta Journal* correspondent in the 1960s—that a boiled or baked ham "is not only a thing of beauty on which to feast the eyes, it puts the busy housewife in a position to feed a family reunion at Christmastime or her share of guests at a Sunday school picnic or an all-day singing in the summertime." Herbert, with his usual wit, added that after the company has departed, the ham bone that remains "is the best thing there is to boil with a pot of frost-kissed collards."

The following recipe comes from Lettice Bryan's *Kentucky Housewife*. First published in 1839 and reissued by the University of South Carolina Press in 1991, it is a classic. Kentucky being the home of great hams, Mrs. Bryan's recipe is considered all the more authoritative. She points out that all smoked hams should be soaked in fresh water for at least twelve hours before being baked, boiled, or "toasted," and if very dry, for twenty-four hours. One addition I might add: Many modern-day cooks like to add a cup of brown sugar and a cup of vinegar to the water when the ham is around half done cooking.

Any winemaker worthy of the appellation knows instinctively that you can't rush a good wine. The principle also applies to hams...For nearly four centuries, farmers in the upper South have passed on and kept alive a traditional methodology of ham-curing that has made their product unsurpassed. Particularly in certain sub-regions of Virginia, North Carolina, Kentucky, Tennessee, and Arkansas.

But the very popularity of traditionally cured hams has prompted many meat-packing companies to simulate and speed up the process. Aided by scientists in the state colleges of agriculture, these firms now do in as little as six weeks what those devoted to the old ways insist can't be done right in less than nine months.

—JOHN EGERTON, *SIDE ORDERS*

Aging brings out the valued white flecks which appear in hams of superlative quality. The hostess who serves such a ham is proud of it, but the ignorant outlander shies from it in apprehension. A favorite story in Kentucky is that of the family who sent one of these hams to a Northern friend as a Christmas gift. They heard nothing from it for weeks and finally ventured to ask whether it had been received. Back came an apologetic letter. The recipients had been so embarrassed that they just didn't know what to write...When they cut into the ham, they found that it was spoiled; it had white spots in it—and so they had to consign it to the incinerator!

—Alvin F. Harlow, *Weep No More, My Lady*

Lettice Bryan's Kentucky-Style Boiled Ham

Put the ham in a large pot of cold water, and boil it slowly till it is done, which will take several hours, carefully removing the scum as it rises to the top. When it is sufficiently tender (which you may tell by trying it with a fork), draw off the skin carefully and smoothly, so as to preserve the skin whole, and not tear the ham. Trim the ham nicely, and spot it over at intervals with red pepper…Accompany it with stewed fruit and green vegetables.

(Here is a modern update: The ham should be boiled in a deep pan at the rate of l hour for each 3 pounds.

In other words, for a 12-pound ham, boil for 4 hours. When completed, let ham cool in the liquid until all heat has gone. Cut into thin slices using a very sharp knife.)

Baked Ham

Henrietta Stanley Dull—more familiarly known as Mrs. S. R. Dull—was the authority on Southern cooking as food editor at the *Atlanta Journal*, my old newspaper, in the 1920s and 1930s, long before my time there.

Women across the South—including the Appalachians—swore by her words. The following recipe comes from her *Southern Cooking* volume, which has been reissued in a hardback edition by Ken Boyd's Cherokee Press of Atlanta. Her baked ham recipe was a traditional one used by housewives across the Blue Ridge and up and down the Appalachians:

Henrietta Dull's Baked Ham

Select a ham of dependable make with skin. Scrub, and place in a baking pan with a rack. Place in hot oven for 15 to 20 minutes to sear outside. Reduce heat to 275°F and bake 20 minutes to the pound. When done, let cool, then remove skin and trim. Rub first with a bit of mustard, then rub all over with sugar as much as will soak in. Cover skin side with breadcrumbs. Brown in quick oven. If doubtful, soak ham in cold water overnight, wipe dry.

Ham Hocks and Dumplings

The following 1800s mountain recipe came to me from Professor Duane Oliver's compilation of recipes from Hazel Creek, North Carolina. The community along the creek in the Great Smokies was settled by his Proctor and Oliver ancestors. His only allowance for modern cooks is the use of self-rising cornmeal in the dumpling mix.

Hazel Creek Ham Hocks with Cornmeal Dumplings

Ham hocks   *Large stew pot*

Dumpling Mix

2 cups self-rising cornmeal   *¼ cup buttermilk*
¼ cup ham hock liquid   *1 tablespoon grease*
A pinch of baking soda

Wash and cover ham hocks with water in a large stew pot. Cook until well done. Remove hocks from juice but keep the broth hot. In a separate container, form the dumplings into soft balls. Bring the ham hock juice to a boil, and add water if needed to cook dumplings. Bring to hard boil, drop in dumplings. Reduce heat to medium, cover, and cook for 15 minutes or until done.

~

Connoisseurs will pay a premium for left (side) hams. They insist the left hams are tenderer than rights because hogs, all of whom enjoy scratching themselves against posts, invariably rub their right sides...This frequent rubbing makes the hog's right side calloused and tough.

—Herbert Wilcox of Elberton, Georgia

A Wild Hog Hunt in North Georgia

"Besides man," wrote Horace Kephart, "the razorback [wild hog] is the only mammal whose eyes will not shine by reflected light; they are too bold and crafty."

Author of the 1936 classic Our Southern Highlanders, *Kephart spent considerable time from his mountain base at Hazel Creek, North Carolina, observing the whys and the wherefores of the wily, tusked beast.*

"When he [the wild boar] is not rooting or sleeping, he is studying devilment. He bears grudges, broods over indignities, and plans revenge for tomorrow."

The late Arvil "Crockett" Wilson was a great storyteller as well as a superb hunter, and he loved to sit on his front porch, rocking away on hot summer afternoons, drinking his homemade scuppernong wines, and amusing his friends and visitors with tall tales about his forays into the wilds. I count it one of life's extras that I was able to visit him many times at his home in the Mountaintown District, Gilmer County, Georgia.

One of the tales he told me was about a time, decades ago, when he was visited by a man who wanted to get away from it all and had fallen in love with north Georgia's vast Cohutta Mountain range.

"So here he came," Crockett recalled. "Nice guy. He liked my stories about life in the woods and wilds. He came and said, 'I wanna go with you the next time you go deep into the mountains.'"

So a few months later, Crockett invited him to join him on a "sang hunt," looking for ginseng roots on a bald near Lake Conasauga.

After about a mile into the woods, Crockett noticed wild hog signs everywhere…dirt rooted up like it had been demolished by a double-bull turning plow pulled by two stout mules.

"What's that I smell?" the visitor asked.

"That's jest wild hogs," Crockett replied.

"Wild hogs? Good Lord, let's get out of here!"

"Calm down, friend," Crockett reassured him. "I ain't a'goin' nowhere. Them thangs can't do nothin' to you. Might run you up a bush, but don't you worry. I ain't a'lettin' no hogs bother you."

"All at once," Crockett recalled, "we saw what we'd been a'smellin'…the holler ahead of us was full of them Russian wild boars. Big, old black sow just standin' up there, you know. And they was about thirty or forty shoats with her, weighin' anywhere from forty to seventy pounds apiece.

"It was a sight to behold, a whole holler-full of hogs; no wonder we had smelled 'em. They came rootin' down that branch, flipping rocks, catching' crawfish, and spring lizards."

"Let's get out of here, Crockett!" the friend whispered, dancing backward all the while, his face twisted in torment.

Crockett put a reassuring arm around him and said, "Be real quiet now and don't say nothing. I won't let nothin' hurt you. Be real still."

"What're you going to do, Crockett?" the visitor whispered.

"I'm a'gonna climb up on top o' one of them boulders," he whispered, "and I'm gonna catch me one of them pigs."

Straight away, Crockett quietly mounted a six-foot-high rock where he could get a good view of the army of young shoats crossing in front. All at once, he took a flying leap into the middle of the herd and tackled a young forty-pound boar.

Arvil Wilson

"It was me and him!" Crockett laughed later as he told me the story. "Jest like a hound dog catchin' a coon. You talk about a tussle! Around and around we went while my friend was watching the action from atop the boulder.

"That shoat went to squealin' even fiercer," Crockett remembered. "Wheeeee!…Wheeeee! I grappled him with both hands by that long hair on his side and threw my knee on him again. Wheeeee! Wheeeee! His squeal was awful. I knew that with much more of that squealin', that old sow would turn and come up on us, and I'd have to beat that old sow up, too, the next time he went to squallin'."

Crockett clamped the shoat's mouth shut, but "he just kicked and he kept on raising hell. I could tell the pig was older than sixteen weeks since he'd already shed the stripes of youth, just like young fawns do."

Meanwhile, the rest of the herd took off. "You never heard such a racket in all your life," he remembered. "Sounded like a train roarin' down through thar. They all run like crazy."

Finally the little pig gave up, "and I helt its mouth so it wouldn't squeal. I tied him up with my shirt."

His friend breathed easier and handed Crockett a penknife.

"What's that for?" Crockett asked.

"I thought you'd want to stick him with it," the man said.

"Naw, friend," he replied. "I ain't gonna stick this little thang. I'm gonna take it home. We'll fatten it up."

Back at his farm in the Mountaintown District, Crockett placed the young boar in a pen and fed him generously with hog slop. It was obvious from the start, however, that the animal was too wild to tame. And under Crockett's care, the boar grew to a weight of 150 pounds.

Every day, just for the pure fun of it, Crockett would go down to the pen and catch the boar and wrestle him to the ground to show him who was boss. A few years later during one such wrestling lesson, the hog—always forever looking for revenge—saw his chance and used his tusks to slash a deep wound in Crockett's arm.

Crockett reluctantly decided it was time to let his pet go and sold him for four hundred dollars to a visitor eager to get a wild boar to service his sows.

After that, I often wondered whatever happened to Crockett Wilson's north Georgia razorback. I imagine the wild hog never did forget his old wrestling coach, and it's not difficult to imagine the razorback's joy at getting sweet revenge after years of humiliation and ending up in hog heaven (servicing sows).

Barbecue

As Old As Fire

*No one who has had the good fortune to attend a barbecue
will ever forget it. The smell of it all, the meat slowly roasting
to a delicious brown over smoking fires, the hungry and
happy crowds...*

—*John R. Watkins,* The Strand Magazine, *London, 1898*

~

*Get ten people together, and where the
Irish would start a fight, Georgians will
start a barbecue.*

—*Old Southern saying*

Carl Dodd of Blue Ridge, Georgia,
is a barbecue gourmet. Here, he holds
forth on his favorite subject at his
backyard grill.

Barbecue, my esteemed friend and Blue Ridge mountaineer Carl Dodd has informed me, "is the product of a piece of pork that has been carefully and lovingly juxtaposed to just the right amount of heat, just the right amount of smoke, for just the right amount of time. Then, sliced or chipped, enhanced with just the right amount of the just-right sauce and placed between two slices of perfectly toasted Piggly Wiggly white bread."

Brother Carl knows how to speak a mountain mouthful, doesn't he? But wait: He has more to declare on this delicate and delicious subject:

"In the South, and this is as Southern as I know how to be (at Blue Ridge, Georgia), barbecue is a 'noun,' even though many a good redneck cook doesn't know a noun from a dangling participle. You do not 'barbecue' (verb) a piece of pork. You either 'fix' or 'cook' the pork to get barbecue!

"There is no such thing as barbecued chicken, barbecued ribs, or barbecued burgers. You either smoke or grill chickens, beef, or ribs, and the like, with delightful results. But they ain't barbecue."

Okay, okay. Now that we have passed this test in the fundamentals of the barbecue art—and the definition of the term—did I say it right, Carl?—let's get on with the subject. How, for instance, did we get barbecue in the first place?

As someone has said, "Barbecue is as old as fire." And like many other famous mountain foods, we are the lucky beneficiaries, inheriting barbecue from the Indians.

A Depression-era scene from Lexington, North Carolina, shows pork shoulders being barbecued over hickory coals.

When Hernando de Soto and his troops marched through the southeastern U.S. in the 1540s, including part of the Blue Ridge, they encountered the Natives cooking venison and turkeys over hot pits of fire. Even before that, Spanish explorers in the Caribbean found the Haitian Arawaks doing the same thing, cooking meat outdoors on a frame of green saplings. Barbacoa was the name they gave it.

We are equally in debt to the Amerindians for Brunswick stew and burgoo—the region's two great stews that I will address in subsequent chapters.

While beef, mutton, and goat have made some barbecue inroads over time, most traditional Southern barbecue chefs are fairly unanimous that pork is the perfect meat. A North Carolina barbecue guru declared that a young shoat, even after being gutted, "is so full of blood and water and fat that it keeps him nice and moist through all the hours it takes to cook him."

But the key to great barbecue, as the old *Saturday Evening Post* reporter Rufus Jarman wrote four decades ago, is to approach the project unhurriedly, or, as he put it, with patience and more patience:

> Good barbecue cannot be hurried; it should be allowed to cook
> and drip for twelve hours over an outdoor fire of hardwood coals. Then
> it is done throughout. The excess grease has dripped off into the fire

after permeating the meat during the cooking. Every true barbecue chef—and every Georgia community has at least one locally celebrated amateur—agrees that no flame should be tolerated in the pit. Some say only half-burned-out coals, whitening with ash, produce heat delicate enough for fine barbecue.

One of the great repositories of the barbecue art (and Jarman found it) is the fertile Etowah River Valley in north Georgia's Blue Ridge foothills. There at Euharlee—near the old Cherokee town of Itawa (Etowah), later to be Anglicized to Hightower—the torch of traditional barbecue

> *If anything could be called the national dish of the South, perhaps barbecue, even more so than fried chicken, would be it. Southerners are passionate about it, almost to the point of being downright fanatical.*
> —DAMON FOWLER, *CLASSICAL SOUTHERN COOKING*

and Brunswick stew still burns brightly. The Euharlee Farmer's Club carries the flame, being the oldest continuously operated such club in the world. Descendants of distinguished old Bartow County families such as the Stiles, the Auchmuteys, the Nelsons, and the Fleetwoods carry forth the club's original charter—improving farming practices and carrying the cue 'n' stew art to its ultimate.

Farther north near the Blue Ridge Continental Divide, mountain- and Indian-style barbecue also are held in legendary reverence. There the Bailey family's annual cookout—with barbecue as the centerpiece—is a tribute to their deceased patriarch—Will Bailey, who died at age ninety-three at his Doublehead Gap home just up the hill from Bailey Creek.

One of the Bailey neighbors, Curtis Underwood, recalls the first such cookout in 1968 when the family pit-cooked a gargantuan barbecue "like the old Indians used to do."

> We dug a hole about six feet long, about four feet deep, and about three feet wide. We lined the bottom with rocks. We had barrels of barbecue. We had deer hams, and turkey and bear meat. And Homer Bailey, he throwed in a groundhog.
>
> We cut two big hickorynut trees and drug 'em down there with the tractor and sawed 'em up and built us a fire down in that pit. We piled all that hickory wood in and kept it going all that night. The next morning we shoveled all them fire coals out but we left the hot rocks down in the bottom. We put that sheet steel down in there.

We wrapped all the meat up in cheesecloth and battered them all over with Dan Bailey's special sauce he had fixed up—Worcestershire sauce, tomato juice, lemon juice, maybe a little vinegar. We soaked that meat in that sauce, laid it on that steel in there and put another piece of sheet steel on top of that, and covered it over with two inches of dirt. Then we piled them fire coals back over on it. And we kept that hickory fire going —it was a ferocious fire—on top of it all that day.

> *Rumor has it the Georgia State Patrol is under strict orders to intercept all Georgia barbecue sauce at the border, lest it make its way to the unenlightened masses in that Great Beyond, filling them with cravings and other paralyzing obsessions. It's a serious concern.*
> —STEVE HUDSON, *GEORGIA JOURNAL*, JULY/AUGUST, 1997

It was so hot you couldn't stand up to it. Made a Dutch oven of it. We did it the way the old Indians used to do—didn't turn the meat. All the steam stayed down in the hole, between the two pieces of steel, wrapped up and basted. We opened her up about seven o'clock in the evening. You could reach in there and get a bone and shake it and that meat would fall right off. It wasn't greasy in no way. It was juicy! And you talk about something good! Boy we had a feast. We had some rattlesnake, too, but it was char-broiled.

⌒

Barbecue has had its legendary figures. Among them was a part-Indian who lived near Athens, Georgia, several decades ago, Clayton Harris. He was, according to Dr. Sam Talmadge, unequaled in the barbecue art.

He was a veritable gentle giant, half Indian and half black. Clayton lived on a small farm near Athens with his wife, a small mulatto, and a large family, mostly boys. There they grew abundantly fresh vegetables, poultry, pigs, cattle and owned a pair of mules and a horse. Every other morning, Clayton toured a neighborhood with his horse and buggy, collecting kitchen scraps that he tossed in a wooden barrel on the back of his buggy. This was to supplement his hogs' diet. In the fall, with help from his older two sons, he would slaughter fattened hogs for a few families, including my grandfather's. His sausage was outstanding, along with hams and fresh pork loins that he processed.

Above all, however, cooking barbecue was Clayton's forte, which he carried out almost ceremoniously. A day or so before the picnic-type barbecue, Clayton and a son or two would visit the site for the 'cue.

There they would dig the pits, select with care green hickory wood and set up tables for the guests.

At noon on the day prior to the barbecue, Clayton would build hot fires in the one foot deep pit, and while it was warming up, he would secure the carcasses in 'spread-eagle' fashion, impaling each with a pair of slender iron rods which could be placed upon wood planks (2x6) longitudinally alongside the pit. The hot coals would next be spread evenly over the pit bottom.

Next, in a very clever innovation, he would continue to cook the meats 'from within' for several hours by heat conduction, by placing mounds of hot coals beneath the protruding ends of purposely exposed bones of each extremity. As the slow cooking continued, about every hour, two of his men with gloved hands would carefully turn the carcasses over.

> *Before their homes were built, the hardy settlers learned to cook their food in the same manner as the Indians. They dug holes in the ground and lined them with hot stones, placing in the meat and covering the entire thing in order to preserve the heat. In another method...the colonists built a rack above an open fire; the meat was placed on the rack and periodically rotated by hand...The racks were often large enough to hold up to six birds at a time.*
>
> —Colonial Cooking

After each turning, the exposed surfaces were liberally basted with a hot solution of salt water (a teaspoon full of salt to a quart of water), and throughout the long but enjoyable night, late in the morning, the basting with salt solution was replaced by barbecue sauce but at intervals based upon state of cooking to ensure that the viands would not become dry on the surfaces.

The sauce was kept hot in a small cast-iron pot, heated with coals at pit-side. Clayton's sauce was seasoned with ground black pepper and a small amount of red. When the meat was deemed done, each carcass would be placed upon an oil cloth on a table and the rods removed. After deboning, the meat was cut into slices which were placed into enamel-wear dishpans and then divided into two lots—one liberally basted with the mild sauce, the other seasoned strongly with red pepper for the 'men.'

The meals were then served to the drooling guests on the long tables. In addition to the individual barbecue servings, Clayton laid out platters filled with hash, sliced fresh tomatoes, corn on the cob, assorted pickles, and sliced fresh bakery white bread. He also made and served ice fresh lemonade from large dish pans. In the earlier days, a more potent drink was usually available alongside a nearby cool spring. Needless to say, the guests all departed over-stuffed but happy! Clayton was indeed a master, and we in Clarke County and surrounding area miss him most keenly.

~

Great barbecues, of course, depend on great sauces. The cook's big objective, as Carl Dodd will attest, is to balance the pork's rich and sweet succulence with a sauce of sharp tanginess, found in hot peppers, vinegar, and/or mustard.

In her 1860s book, Georgia's Annabelle Hill called for a basting sauce of vinegar, pepper, mustard, and butter. Today, as author John Martin Taylor points out, Southern sauces change their "hue and tone" when one crosses county lines. While vinegar, mustard, and red pepper-based sauces predominate in the Carolinas and Georgia, going farther west, into Texas, tomatoes reign king on the barbecue sauce circuit.

New York Times columnist Tom Wicker wrote over a decade ago that Tar Heel barbecue fans will have no truck with tomatoes. "North Carolinians are not taught, we are born knowing that barbecue consists of pork cooked over hickory coals and seasoned with vinegar and red pepper pods." Tom proceeded to pass on this sauce recipe for a sixty-five-pound pig that had been "handed down to me through generations of pig fanciers: One and one half quarts of vinegar seasoned to taste with red pepper."

After all this as preamble, here are a few representative barbecue sauce recipes, from Kentucky, Tennessee, and North Carolina.

North Carolina

This first recipe is adapted from one offered by the late great North Carolina restaurateur Bill Neal in his book *Bill Neal's Southern Cooking*. It's a classic vinegar-red pepper-based sauce that Bill claimed would give the roast "a crisp coat and cuts the fat."

Barbecue is the most Southern meat of all, long associated with political rallies and fire-department fund-raisers, and ideally served from a cinder-block building that says "BBQ." The word...can refer to a process, a dish, or an event; all three were well established by the eighteenth century (Washington barbecued at Mount Vernon). But Southerners disagree vehemently about how best to prepare 'cue. Texans and some Kentuckians even dissent from the regional consensus that barbecue means pork. In fact, Southern barbecue is like Europe's wines and cheeses—drive a hundred miles and the barbecue changes.

—JOHN SHELTON REED, *1001 THINGS EVERYONE SHOULD KNOW ABOUT THE SOUTH*

Tar Heel Barbecue Sauce

1 cup apple cider vinegar	1 teaspoon sugar
½ cup water	1 garlic clove, crushed
1 bay leaf	⅔ teaspoon thyme
2 tablespoons peanut oil	1 cup minced onion
½ teaspoon salt	2½ teaspoons dry mustard
1 teaspoon black pepper	5 teaspoons cold water
1½ teaspoons red pepper flakes	

Mix all ingredients except mustard and water in a saucepan. Bring to a quick boil, then simmer 5 minutes. Remove from heat. Dissolve the mustard in the cold water, then thin with some of the hot vinegar sauce. Mix the mustard into sauce. Let cool, and store in the refrigerator.

Tennessee

Martha McCullough-Williams wrote one of the wittiest books on Southern cooking in 1913, *Dishes and Beverages of the Old South.* The book fortuitously has been brought back to print by the University of Tennessee Press. Born in 1848 northwest of Clarksville near the Tennessee-Kentucky border, Martha was named Martha Ann Collins but she took on the more elegant name after moving to New York City, where she became a famed magazine writer. Here, in Martha's own words, is the recipe she obtained from her father, William Collins, of Tennessee's Montgomery County.

Tennessee Mopping Sauce

Daddy made it thus: Two pounds sweet lard, melted in a brass kettle, with one pound beaten, not ground, black pepper, a pint of small fiery red peppers, nubbed and stewed soft in water to barely cover, a spoonful of herbs in powder—he would never tell what they were—and a quart and a pint of the strongest apple vinegar, with a little salt. These were simmered together for half an hour, as the barbecue was getting done. Then a fresh, clean mop was dabbed slightly in the mixture, and was lightly smeared over the upper sides of the carcasses. Not a drop was permitted to fall on the coals—it would have sent up smoke, and films of light ashes. Then, tables being set, the meat was laid, hissing hot, within clean, tight wooden trays, deeply gashed upon the side that had been next the fire, and deluged with the sauce, which the mop-man smeared fully over it. Hot! After eating it one wanted to lie down at the spring-side and let the water of it flow down the mouth. But of a flavor, a savor, a tastiness, nothing else earthly approaches.

Butch Thompson of Kennesaw, Georgia, invented and fabricated his own special equipment that enables him to barbecue turkey breasts, ribs, and chicken in large quantities at a single cooking. His special on-site dinner events for employees, customers, and friends are legendary, sometimes attracting more than one thousand people.

Mountain Gravies

Soppin' Good

There is abundant life in ham gravy. It will put hair on the hairless chest of a man, or bloom into the pale cheeks of a woman.
— *Alan M. Trout,* Louisville Courier-Journal, *1948*

Ahhh, Grandma used to make that wonderful red-eye gravy. You remember that, Clarence?
— *Barbara Southern, Ellijay, Georgia*

A good gravy is like a good black dress," said Fannie Flagg. "It can hide a multitude of imperfections."

The famed *Whistlestop Cafe Cookbook* author had more to say on the subject: "You can put a really good cream gravy over cardboard and it would still make a delicious dinner. I'm sure I've had it a couple of times myself."

Truly. What I considered the most delicious Southern-fried chicken I've ever tasted (my mother's) was smothered with a soppin' great gravy. Was it the chicken or the gravy that conquered my taste buds?

Annabella P. Hill, in her pioneering 1867 book on Southern cookery, spotlighted what she considered the region's need to upgrade its gravies: "Upon many tables the only gravy which makes its appearance is the grease or drippings from the meat, thickened with a paste of water and flour, or the pure unadulterated grease minus the thickening."

Now wait just a Blue Ridge minute, Mrs. Hill; did you ever leave your LaGrange, Georgia, mansion long enough to get up into the hills of Tennessee and the Carolinas to check out the wonderful squirrel and rabbit gravies of yesteryear? And what about those delicious chocolate gravy breakfast desserts that housewives in Kentucky and West Virginia cooked up to top split biscuits? (And still do; I hear they taste even better than today's syrup-topped pancakes.)

And how about red-eye gravy: You missed a lot, Mrs. Hill, if you never tasted some of that winking ham byproduct mixed in with sorghum syrup and fresh cow butter! Such gravies were well acquainted with hungry folk across the upcountry of the Carolinas, Tennessee, Kentucky, Georgia, and Virginia.

Other than the usual admonitions to keep stirring, keep stirring, and be patient, there's another big secret to making good gravy; I'm not sure Mrs. Hill touched on it:

To avoid cooking up a lumpy gravy, mix in equal amounts of fat and flour before pouring in water or milk. Many mountain housewives mastered this technique and therefore produced superior gravies.

Here are some representative mountain gravy recipes that Mrs. Hill would have enjoyed had her travels taken her a little farther into the hills.

Red-Eye Gravy

It may be considered a bit redundant to zero in on red-eye gravy here since the subject was well covered in the ham chapter. Yet there is a lot more to be said about this most famous of all mountain gravies. The name, for instance, was said to have been coined by that great Scotch-Irish frontiersman, Tennessee's (Carolina-born) Andrew Jackson. Presumably the future president named it thus when he observed the eye winking in a bowl of gravy fresh out of the pan. But where did the color red get into the act? Mark Sohn theorizes the red eye is represented by the bone one cuts in slicing a large piece of ham. Another story credits a red-eyed drunkard who made a respectable ham sopping gravy under the watchful eye of Old Hickory himself.

But wait: This ham gravy has other names. Bird-eye gravy is what people on Sand Mountain, Alabama, call it. In upstate South Carolina, my father always bragged on "Miss Wincey's muddy gravy." So take your pick.

Whatever the name, red-eye is a simple yet classic gravy that depends only on the leftover drippings of fried ham, plus water, and/or perhaps coffee. Some mountain cooks prefer to use only coffee as the liquid. Olene Garland told the *Foxfire* students that she poured coffee over the ham while it was cooking. After it reached boiling, it was time for the gravy to be poured up (and the ham taken out) for serving.

This particular recipe adaptation comes from Bruce Whaley of Gatlinburg, Tennessee, with my thanks to Nancy Blanche Cooper, author of the *Gatlinburg Recipe Collection*. Bruce noted that "biscuits always go well with country ham, and when I was a kid, I liked to sop my biscuits in red-eye gravy." In preparing his ham for the frypan, he slices the ham about a quarter-inch thick and trims off most of the skin, leaving a bit of the fat. He adds a teaspoon of corn oil to his skillet to grease the bottom of the pan. After the gravy is made, Bruce pours his gravy on top of the ham. Other cooks of the region such as Rollins Justice of Hazel Creek, North Carolina, liked to spoon their gravy onto split-open biscuits.

Bruce Whaley's Red-Eye Gravy

Ham drippings   *½ cup water*
Small amount of ready-to-drink coffee

After frying your ham on both sides, remove to a warm platter. To make the gravy, add the water to the hot skillet and let sizzle. Add coffee if desired.

Even the name [sawmill gravy] suggests poverty. By some accounts, it derives from the fact that sawmill crews often subsisted on little more than coffee, biscuits, and gravy. In some parts of Kentucky, the dish was called poor-do—a little something on which the poor made do. Native Kentuckian Jane Brock Woodall recalls that her grandmother in Casey County made the gravy from sausage or chicken dregs, and when there was not enough food to go around, the men ate first and got whatever meat there was and the women and children got by on the poor-do. Elsewhere, people who would have shunned anything called poor-do or even sawmill gravy ate essentially the same thing and called it white gravy or cream gravy. By whatever name, it was and is a flavorful and familiar dish on many Southern tables.

—JOHN EGERTON, SOUTHERN FOOD

Sawmill Gravy (or Logging Gravy)

In the years following the turn of the century, logging camps sprang up all over the Smoky Mountains where timber companies had bought up tracts of virgin timber. Lumberjacks and sawmillers by the hundreds came in to snake out the logs to nearby streams, sawmills, and newly built railheads. Entire families moved in with the men to the camps. To feed the multitude was a big challenge. Breakfasts usually consisted of coffee and meat plus flour-based gravies and large "cathead" biscuits. One day, the story goes, the Tremont camp ran out of flour and had to substitute cornmeal in the gravy. Inquisitive loggers arriving for breakfast asked what kind of gravy was on the menu that day.

"This gravy's made out of sawdust!" the cooks replied. The name stuck. The cheap, easy-to-fix cornmeal gravy caught on. While "sawmill gravy" was the popular nickname, some called it "Logging Gravy." Others named it Poor Do or Life Everlasting, a reference to what many felt was its role in keeping them alive. This recipe adaptation comes from Janice Miracle of Middlesboro, Kentucky, located on the Tennessee line near the famed Cumberland Gap. My thanks to Katherine and Thomas Kirlin, authors of the *Smithsonian Folklife Cookbook*, from which the basic recipe comes. Some mountain cooks, I might mention, prefer to fry up four or five pieces of salted side meat rather than bacon for the grease base.

"Life Everlasting" Sawmill Gravy

3 heaping tablespoons	*½ teaspoon salt*
white cornmeal	*2¼ cups milk*
1 tablespoon bacon drippings	*A dash pepper*

In a frying pan, combine cornmeal, bacon drippings, and salt. Stir until brown. Add milk, and let boil until gravy thickens. Stir forcefully to keep gravy from lumping. Add pepper to taste.

White Sausage Gravy

A variation of sawmill gravy is white sausage gravy. Glenn Cardwell of Greenbrier, Tennessee, told author Rose Houk that "before God drove Adam and Eve out of the Garden of Eden, he gave Eve the recipe for this gravy, and it's been in the family ever since."

This particular recipe adaptation comes courtesy of *Fannie Flagg's Original Whistlestop Cafe Cookbook*, with personal thanks to that vivacious author. Ms. Flagg says, "This has a little kick to it, and is my favorite sauce over biscuits; this and a hot cup of coffee make a meal."

Fannie's Sausage Gravy

1 pound mild bulk pork sausage	*1 cup milk*
2¼ tablespoons all-purpose flour	*½ teaspoon pepper*

In large heavy skillet, fry sausage until brown, and stir to crumble. Remove from skillet with slotted spoon, and drain well. Leave 2 teaspoons drippings in skillet. Gradually add flour to drippings, stirring until smooth. Cook over medium heat for 1 minute, stirring constantly. Gradually add ⅔ cup of milk, stirring forcefully until mixture is smooth and thick. If you wish to have a thinner gravy, add the rest of the milk. Stir in pepper and sausage. Cook until hot, stirring all the while. Serve over split biscuits. Serves 4.

Chicken Gravy

John Egerton declares that "there may be no better gravy in the Western world than that made in a black skillet recently vacated by a piece of fried chicken."

Since fried chicken is a dish celebrated not only through the Southern Appalachians but throughout the South, chicken gravy is perhaps even more popular than ham red-eye gravy.

This adaptation comes from, and with my personal thanks to, the Junior Service League of Johnson City, Tennessee, and their wonderful recipe collection, *Smoky Mountain Magic*. Mrs. Lyman A. Fulton of Johnson City offered the gravy basics that appeared in the book's section on "East Tennessee Favorites."

East Tennessee Chicken Gravy

2 tablespoons all-purpose flour   *2 tablespoons chicken grease*

1 cup lukewarm water or milk   *Salt and pepper to taste*

After frying chicken, pour off all but 2 tablespoons of grease. Scrape brown crisp crumbs loose from bottom of skillet. Stir in the flour, making a paste with the grease, and stir until mixture becomes very dark, but don't allow to burn. Have medium-sized bowl filled with lukewarm water or milk and pour into skillet, stirring rapidly into smooth mixture. Reduce heat, cook gravy until it is as thick as desired. Season with salt and pepper. Stir to avoid sticking. Pour into bowl and serve with chicken over hot biscuits, mashed potatoes, or rice.

Tomato Gravy

Tomato gravy is a hill country favorite. This particular recipe adaptation comes from, and with my thanks to, Lynne Tolley and Pat Mitchamore, authors of Jack Daniel's *The Spirit of Tennessee Cookbook*. The tomato gravy can be cooked after frying salt pork, bacon, pork chops, or ham.

Tennessee Tomato Gravy

¼ cup finely chopped onion   *Chicken stock and water as required*

2 tablespoons all-purpose flour   *½ teaspoon powdered thyme*

2 cups tomatoes, peeled, seeded,   *1¼ teaspoons sugar*

and chopped   *Salt and pepper to taste*

In a fry pan containing around 2 tablespoons of drippings, sauté onion until tender. Mix in flour, and cook several minutes. Add tomatoes; stir well. Water or chicken stock may be required here, depending on the liquid available from the tomatoes. Season with the thyme, sugar, and salt and pepper. Cook over low heat, stirring periodically until gravy thickens. Yields 2 cups of gravy.

Rabbit Gravy

Rabbit meat is very similar to chicken, and can be rolled in flour and smother-fried. Squirrel, on the other hand, is softer and more like raccoon meat, and is excellent for making dumplings, a type of gravy. (See the squirrel dumpling recipe in the Wild Game chapter.)

After frying your pieces of rabbit (preferably in a black cast-iron skillet), make sure you scrape up and utilize the crispy leftover chunks.

The following recipe comes from *Cooking on Hazel Creek* and with my great appreciation to retired professor Duane Oliver. This tells you how to fry your rabbit. To make the rabbit gravy, follow the instructions for chicken gravy above.

Hazel Creek Fried Rabbit

1 rabbit

1 cup all-purpose flour

Salt and pepper to taste

Melted fat

¼ cup water

Chopped onion

1 teaspoon vinegar

Cut rabbit into serving pieces, roll in flour seasoned with salt and pepper, brown in fat, and then add water, onion, and vinegar. Lower heat, cover pan, and simmer until tender. Remove cover the last 10 minutes to tender.

Chocolate Gravy

Chocolate gravy in the Appalachians? Yes, says Mark Sohn of Pikeville, Kentucky, who says this recipe has been handed down over the years by mountain families in his region of eastern Kentucky and West Virginia. Mark loves the gravy so strongly he's spreading the word, seeking converts "as badly as an itinerant preacher." It's a milk-and-flour-based sauce that should be cooked thick enough to stick well on open biscuits. My thanks to Mark for permission to adapt this recipe from his book *Mountain Country Cooking*.

Kentucky Chocolate Gravy

1 cup European-style cocoa

¾ cup sugar

¼ cup all-purpose flour

2 cups milk

1½ teaspoons vanilla

In a saucepan, combine the dry ingredients: cocoa, sugar, and flour. Stir until well mixed and flour and cocoa lumps disappear. Pour in the milk gradually. Turn the heat up to bring mixture to boiling, simmer 1 minute, and stir in the vanilla. Remove from the heat. The yield is 6 servings.

I tell people right now, the way I used to eat a growin' up, that's the kind of groceries I'd like now.

I'd like to have me some fatback and fry the grease out, and turn around and make some white gravy outa that. They called it sawmill gravy.

—Jake Parris, a native of White County, Georgia, in a 1979 interview with Charles Salter of the *Atlanta Journal*

Brunswick Stew

It Began with the Indians

Brunswick stew is what happens when small mammals carrying ears of corn fall into barbecue pits.

—*Humorist Roy Blount*

~

I made a pot of [Brunswick] stew for some people in New York once. They kept picking at the meat, so I had to tell 'em to keep their damn hands off 'til I got it done.

—*Master stewmaker Bob Jackson of Euharlee, Georgia, as quoted by Jim Auchmutey*

I'll never forget my first encounter with Brunswick stew. It occurred in February of 1950 at a barbecue for state legislators in Cartersville, Georgia, located in the Blue Ridge foothills north of Atlanta.

When I tasted that first bowl of Bartow County Brunswick Stew there at the town's Legion post, my taste buds went into sublime bliss. When I recovered, I scrambled for a second helping, then a third. As the old saying goes, "I couldn't get enough of that wonderful stuff." It lived up to its reputation as "a highly seasoned rich conglomeration of meats, vegetables, and sauces simmered many hours in big iron pots over outdoor fires."

Being a fresh-out-of-college cub reporter for Cartersville's *Daily Tribune-News*, my curiosity was piqued. The stew and barbecue, I found out, came from farmers in the nearby Etowah River Valley. Later, my taste bud findings were confirmed by the *Saturday Evening Post*'s Claude Jarman who—after tasting the product and interviewing Robert Auchmutey and Roscoe Tatum—waxed eloquent about the wonderful stuff that came from the Etowah Valley pits and pots. 'Cue and stew have been a grand and glorious tradition over the years among members of Bartow's Euharlee Farmers Club, the oldest continuously operated such club in the world. It's located near the site of the Cherokee Nation's largest pre-removal settlement, Etowah or I-tawa ("muddy water" in English). Or, as the white pioneers pronounced and spelled it, High-tower.*

---

*It was in 1950 that the Etowah River was dammed up farther north by the U.S. Army Corps of Engineers to form Lake Allatoona, now an Atlanta suburban recreation lake.

When I was young (in Virginia), there were squirrels all over the place, usually raiding the corn field. Whenever we went to pick corn, my brother always took along his rifle so that he could get a few squirrels that were scampering in the fields. We would stew them plain or make Brunswick stew. Squirrels taste sweeter than rabbits because of the nuts they eat.

When we used to make Brunswick stew, I don't remember using as many vegetables as I do now...But the vegetables add good flavor and make the stew so filling you do not need anything else. Like other stews (Brunswick stew) gets better every day you warm it up.

—EDNA LEWIS, *IN PURSUIT OF FLAVOR*

I have been a Brunswick stew fanatic ever since that serendipitous Cartersville experience nearly a half century ago. Barbecue? I can take it or leave it. But never do I pass up a chance to check out Brunswick stew when I see a 'cue eatery sign, always trying to recapture that glorious Euharlee taste, circa 1950.

⌒

The origins of Brunswick stew—initially based on squirrel meat, then on chicken or rabbit or all three—are shrouded in mystery. Brunswick, Virginia; Brunswick County, North Carolina; and Brunswick, Georgia, all claim they were the birthplace, either in the 1700s or 1800s. Others credit Britain's Earl of Brunswick, who, visiting the South, discovered the derivative dish being served to Virginia workmen.

I am happy to report that the birthplace mystery has been solved, or at least reconciled. And by none other than the dean of Southern food critics and food arbiter supreme, Nashville's John Egerton: "It seems safe to say that Indians were making stews with wild game long before any Europeans arrived, and in that sense there was Brunswick stew before there was a Brunswick."

Now that we have that cleared up, let's go to some recipes. By the way, modern-day recipes often use chicken as the base, along with beef, bypassing squirrels. But purists insist on a squirrel representation of some sort if it can be obtained. (If anyone needs a few squirrels, I have a surplus supply at my home in Atlanta. My late brother Arthur had a big squirrel family living in his yard also, in Jackson, South Carolina. That is, until they crossed the line and grabbed off too many of his pecans. That was the day he pulled out his shotgun and brought down the whole bunch of 'em.)

⌒

The Euharlee Farmers' Club in Bartow County, Georgia, which celebrated its 125th anniversary in 2008 as the nation's longest running such farmers' club, stages an annual invitation-only barbecue celebration, pictured here. The event takes place at the Taylor farm, owned by the family of the late Glenn Taylor, a former member of the club. Middle photo shows club member Steve Southern serving dessert at the end of the serving line. See the club's original Brunswick Stew recipe on page 218.

Brunswick Stew

Euharlee Farmers Club BBQ 30 gal pot

8 to 10 gallons of Crushed tomatoes or

12 gallons of un-mashed tomatoes

20 lbs. Chuck or Round Ground Beef.

15 lbs lean Pork.

3 or 4 Bottles of Lee and Perrin Sauce.

1½ lbs Butter if eaten Immediately or

No butter if stew is Canned

For more red ~~color~~ Color Add up to 1 quart Calsup

if too Sweet — add Vinegar

if too Sour — Add Catsup

— Alvin B. Richards

Pictured is the "handed down" Brunswick Stew recipe of the 125-year-old Euharlee Farmers' Club in north Georgia, as presented to the author by club member Alvin B. Richards.

Crock-Pot Brunswick Stew

A modern-day "kitchen-friendly" Brunswick stew Crock-Pot recipe comes from the late Charles Auchmutey, a native of Bartow County, Georgia, and grandson of the founder of the Euharlee Farmers Club in the 1800s.

Euharlee Crock-Pot Brunswick Stew

1 pound coarse-ground
   round or sirloin

½-pound Boston butt pork
   (coarsely ground)

½-pound chicken pieces

1 28-ounce can tomatoes,
   coarsely chopped, with juice

1 (16½-ounce) can creamed corn

¼ cup ketchup

1 tablespoon butter (not
   margarine)

¼ cup cider vinegar

½ teaspoon salt (or to taste)

1 teaspoon black pepper

2 tablespoons sugar

1 teaspoon cayenne pepper

1½ cups water

Using a large skillet, cook the beef and pork very slowly and stir often. Do not overcook. Skim off excess grease.

Remove skin and excess fat from chicken. Place in a pan, cover chicken with water, bring to a boil, reduce heat, cover, and simmer until chicken falls off the bones, 20 to 30 minutes. Reserve broth for another use, if desired. Remove bones, and tear meat into tiny pieces with fingers.

Add chicken to beef/pork mixture in skillet. Mix well. Start cooking very slowly over medium-low heat and stir often with a wooden spoon until meats are thoroughly blended.

Place meat mixture in Crock-Pot. Add the tomatoes, corn, ketchup, butter, vinegar, salt, peppers, and water. Mix well. Cook at 300°F to 325°F for 5 to 6 hours. Set aside. Serves 8.

Smoky Mountain Brunswick Stew

Here, as the final recipe in this series, is a squirrel-based Brunswick stew offering from the pen of the late Horace Kephart. Author of the Smoky Mountain classic, *Our Southern Highlanders*, Kephart was a supreme camper. This recipe was included in his book *The Book of Camping and Woodcraft*. Both books are available in University of Tennessee Press reprints.

Horace Kephart's Brunswick Stew

Several squirrels	*6 potatoes, parboiled and sliced*
1 tablespoon salt	*1 teaspoon black pepper*
½-pound salt pork	*½ teaspoon cayenne*
1 onion, minced small	*2 tablespoons sugar*
1 pint butter beans or limas	*1 quart tomatoes*
1 pint green corn	*½ pound butter*

Soak the squirrels half an hour in cold salted water. Add the salt to one gallon of water, and boil five minutes. Then put in the squirrels, pork (cut into fine strips), onion, beans, corn, potatoes, and peppers. Cover and stew very slowly 2½ hours, stirring frequently. Add the tomatoes and sugar, and stew an hour longer. Then add the butter, cut into bits the size of a walnut, and roll in flour. Boil 10 minutes.

*T*he Southeastern Indians were fonder than we of soups and stews. After barbecuing fish, squirrel, or groundhog, they would make it into a stew, adding a little cracked hominy or hominy meal. They boiled meat and fish with vegetables to make a soup. Bear and deer meat, for example, were boiled along with squash and kernels cut from ears of green corn. They were especially fond of kidney beans, boiled with meat and seasoned with bear oil.

—CHARLES HUDSON, *THE SOUTHEASTERN INDIANS*

Vic Mulinix's Stew

Residents of Kingston, Georgia, and environs look forward to the annual Fourth of July Independence Day celebration put on by Vic and Marty Mulinix and Vic's parents, Rufus and Martha Mulinix. The big attraction is Vic's scrumptious 'cue and stew, which he cooks right on the premises near the homeplace on Mulinix Road.

While the Fourth of July tradition has been going on for several years, Vic has been conducting 'cue and stew parties at least once a year since 1970, including his parents' fiftieth wedding anniversary and his father's eightieth birthday.

"I guess the main thing that I have learned about cooking great tasting meat," Vic says, "is to cook it slow at a low heat." He added that when you cook in an open pit, "a good

cooking temperature is when you can hold your hand at the meat level of the fire for about seven seconds. If it's too hot to keep your hand there that long, you will burn the meat."

As to his stew, Vic prefers to call his creation "stew," not Brunswick stew. "I've seen some recipes for Brunswick stew that call for ingredients I do not like, such as lima beans, okra, and other things they use to thicken and extend the stew," he declares.

"I like for meat to be the primary ingredient—one pork

Master barbecue artist Vic Mulinix of Kingston, Georgia, cuts up barbecue at the annual July Fourth celebration.

shoulder, one turkey, about five pounds of grilled beef. I like to stew a couple of baking hens, a couple of rabbits, and maybe some venison. Needless to say, all this meat needs to be cooked before the party. Freezers are great to carry out this objective. I try to save one pork shoulder and some beef from the last time I cooked, to make the stew at the next party."

Vic grinds everything that goes into his stew. "Thus everything is fully precooked. It's just a matter of heating it up and flavoring it."

He heats the stew in a cast-iron pot that holds about twelve gallons. "And we start with some broth from the chicken and rabbit, adding tomato juice, some tomato ketchup, soy sauce, and Worchester sauce. Then we grind one or two gallons of whole cooked corn. When the corn goes through the grinder, some grains come out as whole corn, which will be okay, but most comes out as mush."

It takes a few hours to assemble the stew and getting it heated. "Someone has to keep it stirred so it doesn't stick," Vic said. "When all the liquid ingredients have been added, and the mixture is hot, we add the meat and stir it in. Because the meat is ground and dry, some additional liquid will be added, usually ten to twelve cans of beer. The brand doesn't matter."

At that point, Vic does a taste test and adds more tomato juice or Worchester sauce or soy as needed. Depending on the flavor, he may also add dark brown sugar and whiskey. "We also add about one-fourth cup of hot sauce. We limit the use of hot sauce, however, because some people will not eat stew if it is too hot. We reserve some hot sauce that we keep on the grill firebox for those who want it hot."

The result is a stew featuring a good overall flavor along with a strong meat taste, a wonderful combination in the opinion of his friends and neighbors.

Vic welcomes visitors, but he asks them to bring a covered dish that will feed eight people.

Western North Carolina's Great Craggy Mountains loom in the background as a herdsman salts his sheep in this early 1900s photo. Craggy Pinnacle is on left and Craggy Knob on right. Mutton was used in many mountain stews, including burgoo.

Burgoo

The Kentucky Wonder

An all-day political rally (in Kentucky) without burgoo and barbecue would be about as exciting as a wedding without the bride.
— *Thomas Clark*, The Kentucky

~

Kentucky burgout, or "burgoo," is a survivor of early times, when people assembled for some big political meeting or to hear some famed religious exhorter. Then they came long distances over the mountains…gun in hand, often killing some of the abundant game on the way. From the cultivated patches, corn ears and potatoes were brought and together these made a savory stew.
— The Boston Cooking-School Magazine *(1907)*

Some say burgoo originated in continental Europe and arrived on these shores in the nineteenth century with sailors from France and Belgium. They maintain that burgoo's name resulted from a mispronunciation of the French word *burgout*, or perhaps closely related to ragout, a red-hot vegetable/meat stew.

Old time "burgoomaster" Jim Looney of Lexington, Kentucky, claimed that his burgoo predecessor, Colonel Gus Jaubert, introduced the stew to Kentucky around 1810, and that it was indeed a version of a stew fed to French sailors at sea. Looney claimed the original version dictated 800 pounds of lean beef, a dozen squirrels (provided they were in season) for each hundred gallons, 240 pounds of fat hens, plus a bunch of vegetables.

Noted Kentucky historian Thomas Clark looked at burgoo's beginnings a bit differently:

(Burgoo) originated back in the days when hunters counted up their day's kill in the thousands of squirrels and when pigeons flew through the woods in veritable clouds, and bear, deer, buffalo, and hundreds of turkeys were available. The idea came from Virginia, where Brunswick stew was popular. Vegetables of all kinds were boiled along with the game meats, and the whole mass was highly seasoned with spices. This was a fine temptation with which to attract a crowd.

Some feel Clark's references perhaps relate also to what was known as Appalachian "hunter's stew" or "Daniel Boone stew."

In any event, modern-day Kentucky burgoo versions—still popular at political and sporting events such as the Kentucky Derby—are keyed to mutton, along with beef and chicken plus a great lineup of vegetables and red-hot peppers and cooked outdoors for hours in big kettles.

Kentucky burgoo's greatest promoter for years—a Gus Jaubert protégé—was *Louisville Courier-Journal* columnist and humorist Tandy Ellis. Here is Tandy's manageable (1½ gallon) recipe that has been spread all over Kentucky and the world. The following version is adapted from that published by Marion Flexner in her *Out of Kentucky Kitchens*. Tandy Ellis urged burgoo be served with cornpones and be followed up with a piece of pie.

Tandy's Burgoo

½ pound baby lamb	*2 cups fresh or frozen butter beans*
2 pounds beef cut from the shank (include soup bone)	*3 carrots, diced*
1 medium-sized chicken	*2 green peppers, diced (remove seeds)*
4 quarts water (use more if soup cooks too thick)	*3 cups green field corn, cut from cob*
Salt and black pepper to taste	*2½ cups okra, diced*
2 cups diced potatoes	*12 tomatoes or 1-quart can*
1 red pepper (or more to taste)	*1 "toe" of garlic*
2 cups diced onions	*1 cup minced parsley*

Place the lamb, beef, and dismembered chicken in soup kettle with tight-fitting lid along with water, salt, and black and red pepper. Bring to a hard boil, reduce the heat, and simmer around 2 hours with the lid on. Add potatoes, onions, and at intervals of 10 minutes, the butter beans, carrots, and green peppers. Then add corn, and simmer for 2 hours or until mixture seems very thick. Keep a watch so that mixture does not stick. If necessary add water, but only small amounts. Add okra and tomatoes and the garlic, and let simmer for another 1½ hours or until these last vegetables are also done and blended with the others. As soon as soup is taken from stove, stir the parsley in. Soup improves by standing and keeps for a long time in the refrigerator, being delicious when reheated.

Wild Game

Marvelous Meat of the Mountains

That wild taste is the taste I love.
—Will Bailey of Doublehead Gap, Georgia

~

One is sure to dream of a woman or the devil or both [after eating bear meat].
—William Byrd II of Virginia

~

If it hadn't been for rabbits and squirrels [during the Depression], I don't
know how we'd gone through the winter sometimes.
—Earl Dillard, of Rabun Gap, Georgia

~

Russle out, boys, we've got to git a soon start if you want bear brains an' liver
for supper.
—1920s Smoky Mountain bear hunt as remembered by
Horace Kephart in Our Southern Highlanders

Mountain people are plumb wild about the wild flavor in game meat. "I'd rather have that wild flavor than anything you can have in game," declared Curtis Underwood. A proud son of the north Georgia mountains, Curtis knows whereof he speaks. As a youngster he fished Noontootley Creek and climbed the "winding stairs" near the southern end of the Appalachian Trail and in later years helped make moonshine whiskey in the dark mountain coves of Lumpkin and Dawson Counties.

"You take tame rabbits, they don't have any flavor," Curtis declares with a raised eyebrow of disdain. "But you get out here and kill one off the woods; he's got the best flavor of all. Same with squirrels. The wild taste in meat comes from acorns, and from berries and nuts and persimmons. The deer is a big browser; he'll eat anything—tips of limbs, soybeans and nuts. You name it; and in the coolest of winter, he'll even eat mountain laurel, although some laurel is poisonous.

"Now you take wild hog meat; it tastes altogether different than that from a tame hog. I'd rather have it anytime to a tame hog. The wild hog has that wild taste and it's not got as much fat in it."

The wild taste of squirrels is another favorite of Curtis Underwood, who radiates a rounded, well-fed physique of one who knows and appreciates the nourishment one can extract from the mountain wilds. Now residing in semi-retirement in Resaca, Georgia, Curtis gets back to the mountains of Fannin County as often as possible and loves to hunt and fish and has not forgotten how to cook wild game.

Squirrels taste sweeter than rabbits because of the nuts they eat.
—EDNA LEWIS, *IN PURSUIT OF FLAVOR*

"The squirrel is good eating, got the best flavor. A young squirrel I like fried but an old squirrel—and that's what you get mostly—you have to boil him to get the meat tender. First you parboil him for ten minutes, pour off that water, then boil it until it's good and tender. Add a little pepper and salt. You leave the bones in the squirrel when you cook it. You get a little flour and milk, stir it up good, make a thin gruel and add a little black pepper...

"I get the old lady to make biscuits to go with the squirrel. You slice those hot biscuits and fork two or three pieces of that squirrel and pour on that gravy, it's delicious. You can't eat it with a fork; you have to sop it with the biscuits. Lot of people like to fix squirrel and dumplings but I prefer to eat 'em with biscuits. Awfully good eating."

Wild game has provided a savory and gamey continuity to the Appalachian diet from the days of the earliest pioneers. Indeed, one writer declared flatly that "game made the settlement of America possible." Waverly Root, the food historian, stated that for a long time after the arrival of the first settlers, game was not only the main meal of the colonists, it was often the main food.

"We eat just about everything in the mountains; we lived out of the woods," Curtis Underwood told me. And as Ruth Adams Bronz viewed it, "Appalachian poverty augmented by Appalachian ingenuity has produced a cookery that depends on an aggressive way with wild raw materials."

Davy Crockett was one of the aggressive hunters, going to great effort to pull a squirrel he had just shot from a hole in a tree. He would tell of the episode "only to show to what lengths a hungry man will go to get something to eat."

Squirrels, rabbits and deer, wild turkeys, doves, quail and passenger pigeons, plus the buffalo and black bear in the beginning—proved to be a godsend to people settling the mountain country. Even after homegrown pork and poultry became readily available, wild game warmed hearts and stomachs in many a

mountain cabin, taking an honored place in their bubbling black pots. During the winter, game animals could be eaten a long time after being killed. In fact, experts such as Horace Kephart urged people to leave their game hanging and eat later for the best taste. Mountain people were known to hang up their furred and feathered game in their chilly smokehouses and leave them there for some time before bringing them to the kitchen.

From their cabin doors the newcomers had only to walk out into the woods with their long rifles and bring some game home for dinner—a bear, perhaps, or a turkey, a squirrel, or rabbit, maybe even a deer. Rivers and creeks abounded in fish although they were nowhere near as popular and easy a target as wild game.

> *The boys learned to shoot accurately the long rifles of their times, with a log or a forked stick for a rest, and a moss pad under the barrel to keep it from jerking and spoiling the aim...*
>
> *It was part of their education to imitate the noises of every bird and beast of the forest. So they learned to lure the turkey within range, or by the bleat of a fawn to bring her dam to the rifle. This forest speech was...the language of diplomacy in the hunting season...*
>
> *The first light powdering called "hunting snows" fell in October, and then the men of the Back Country set out on the chase. Their object was meat—buffalo, deer, elk, bear—for the winter larder, and skins to send out in the spring by pack-horses to the coast in trade for iron, steel, and salt.*
>
> —CONSTANCE LINDSAY SKINNER,
> *PIONEERS OF THE OLD SOUTHWEST*

During the days of Daniel Boone, the vast Kentucky and Tennessee hunting grounds—well loved by the Indians from the Great Lakes to the Gulf—teemed with game. "A man can kill six or eight deer every day, which many do merely for their skins...," John Ferdinand Smyth wrote. "Wild turkeys, very large and fat are almost beyond number, sometimes five thousand in a flock, of which a man may kill as many as he likes." Herds of buffalo and elk were seen everywhere, from the South Carolina foothills north and west.

When pioneers crossed the mountain gaps from Buncombe County, North Carolina, into Gilmer County, Georgia, they found the country full of game. Ben Sitton told of the frontier in the early 1800s: "Deer wandering in droves through the woods, as many as you liked; wild pigeons blackening the sky as they flew over; wild geese descending on areas like Carter's Quarters (on the Coosawatte River) in such numbers as to gobble up whole crops of grain."

The game also lived on the wild fruits and nuts that grew profusely across the mountains, coves, and foothills—chestnuts, walnuts, and hickory nuts, and wild berries, headed by the peripatetic blackberry, plus the ever-present muscadine grape and the fruit loved most by possums, the wild persimmon.

Steve and Ethel Spruill show off their game following a January 1, 1947, hunt...quails, rabbits, and squirrels. The hunt took place on the Spruill farm on Atlanta's north side that is now covered by Perimeter Mall.

Finding the frontier wide open to all was a new and wonderful experience for the pioneers and settlers, a delightful contrast to their experiences in Britain where hunting preserves were reserved for royalty, and poor peons who poached were punished harshly. As on all matters of living in the wilderness, the settlers learned much about hunting wild game from the Indians.

During the period of Appalachian settlement came a booming market for rifles and guns. The great German gunsmiths of Pennsylvania were the undisputed champions in meeting this need, but gun-making multiplied across the region. John D. Nelson, a blacksmith living in the Boardtown District of Gilmer County, Georgia, had a great reputation for his long-barreled rifles that often measured three feet long. They were so accurate, it was claimed, a hunter "could knock the ear off a squirrel in the highest tree." Most mountain people confidently aimed for the head of a turkey, saving the meat of the bird for the family stew pot.

Typical of mountain men and their squirrel rifles, David A. Stanley, hunting on Jacks River near the Cohuttas in north Georgia, shot a squirrel out of a tree at a measured distance of 120 yards, according to his grandson, Lawrence Stanley.

Thanks to their rifles and muzzleloaders, Appalachian settlers had their run of game meat, beginning with buffalo beef.

"When the first settlers on Duncan's Creek arrived from Pennsylvania, and began to erect their cabins," stated John V. Logan in his 1859 history, *The Upper Country of South Carolina*, "they found its valleys and hills abounding in buffaloes."

Deeply rutted buffalo trails marked the country in all directions. Settlers named communities and creeks for the beast whose rump and hump were the favorite cuts. Logan quoted "the venerable Busby," then a ripe 110 years old, as having seen a vast herd of three thousand buffaloes grazing at a nearby meadow.

*S*hooting a bear out of a tree is just like cutting a tree down. I shore do love to hear that meat hit the ground. We killed a bear one night in a late November snowfall in Cocke County. We rolled the carcass down the side of the mountain, into a creek and on down into a deep hole of water. I had three dogs that didn't come out of the woods that night. Boy, they was guardin' that bear and wouldn't leave!

—RAYMOND LARGE, COSBY, TENNESSEE

But the bison didn't last long, falling victim to Indian and pioneer guns. The Native Americans of the Southeast were noted for killing buffalo solely for their tongues and skins. The frontier was so full of game in the early 1700s, however, that the disappearing buffalo were hardly missed. The ever-present black bear filled the need for food in a magnificent manner. Englishman James Adair observed that British traders and hunters in the late 1600s learned to relish the flesh of the lumbering beasts almost as much as the Cherokees:

> The traders commonly make bacon of the bears in winter; but the Indians mostly flay off a thick tier of fat which lies over the flesh and the latter they cut up into small pieces and thrust them on reeds or suckers of sweet tasted hiccory or sassafras, which they barbecue over a slow fire. The fat they fry into clear well-tasted oil, mixing plenty of sassafras and wild cinnamon with it over the fire, which keeps sweet from one winter to another, in large earthen jars, covered in the ground. It is of a light digestion and nutritive to hair.

North Carolina Indian women had an extra-special incentive to eat bear meat, according to William Byrd. To do so, they were taught, would assure them an easy baby delivery and would add to their vitality.

Bear meat, easily cooked and cured like pork, met many pioneer needs, producing cooking oil, grease for arthritic bones, oil for lamps, and even hair grease for the young man out to impress a lass on the other side of the mountain. Drops of hot bear grease eased the pain of many a mountain earache, while bearskins warmed cold cabin floors, provided wonderful blankets, and were used to make shoes.

But by the late 1800s, under relentless pressure from the tide of settlers rolling down the Shenandoah Valley and spreading through the Piedmont foothills and valleys, the Appalachian bear population began to thin out dramatically. This forced mountain people to turn more and more to the white-tailed deer, which for centuries had been an Indian food staple.

Accounts tell of huge deer herds roaming the region. In the Little Tennessee River Valley near Rabun Gap, Georgia, Andrew Ritchie's grandfather and friends killed seventy deer on one "long hunt." Following the Indian pattern, Ritchie hauled his surplus hides to the Augusta market, along with cured venison hams. This became a common practice across the eastern Blue Ridge and other sections of the Appalachians.

Venison kept mountain appetites satisfied through the nineteenth century and well past the Civil War. Roasting venison over a fire, Indian-style, was a popular way of cooking. But settlers learned also to throw chunks of deer meat into their big black pots, along with vegetables of the season, inventing a nourishing, slow-cooked "hunter's stew." This was a precursor to squirrel-based Brunswick stew that became famous across the foothills and flatlands, paralleling Burgoo in the Kentucky hills. Not only that, deer antlers found their way into every mountain cabin as racks for guns and clothes, while deerskins were turned into clothes and containers.

The frontier abounded in fowl that were seen in huge flocks—quail, doves, and wild turkey, and yes, millions of passenger pigeons on a single migration flyby to and from

How did an American bird [the turkey] get named for a Eurasian country? The answer is simple. Our country's early settlers had never even seen this American bird and they thought it looked a lot like a Turkish guinea fowl. So they referred to it as turkey fowl, or just plain turkey.

There are other good questions to ask in this type of discussion: Why is a live animal called a cow or calf, while we eat beef or veal? Answering this involves giving a bit of a history lesson.

The English language is a combination of several older languages. By the sixth century AD, Anglos, Saxons, and Jutes had set up shop in England. These folks spoke Germanic dialects. They supplied us with the old high German words that became cow, calf, pig, sheep, and ox.

In 1066, William the Conqueror crossed the English Channel and put a whipping on the Saxons at the Battle of Hastings. William and his gang, who

South America. Alfred Mynders, the noted *Chattanooga Times* writer, drew a sharp portrait of the wild birds in a July 17, 1946, column:

"The passenger pigeons would appear like swift moving clouds, with a terrific roar of feathered wings. Their flights would often darken the skies with such a great shadow as might be caused in daylight by an eclipse of the sun. The length of the flocks ran into miles and presented an inspiring spectacle. Settling in trees they would often break the limbs by their weight."

Amazingly, by 1914, passenger pigeons were extinct. While they lasted, they provided mountain people some of their favorite dishes—pigeon pie and pigeon barbecued on a spit.

Huge flocks of wild turkeys were to be seen everywhere through the mountains and foothills. So numerous were the giant thirty- to forty-pound birds—boasting purple and bronze feathers—that some frontiersmen salted and dried them. In Kentucky, turkey breast was used as a substitute for bread.

John Parris quoted the late Granville Calhoun, the "sage of the Smokies," that despite the abundance of

spoke Norman French, became the ruling class while the Saxons did the dirty work.

The Saxons continue to slop "pigs" and feed "cows." But if you were a member of the upper crust, it was only proper to refer to those critters by their proper French names at the table. Thus, our terms beef, veal, pork, and mutton are derived from Norman French. To this day, we use the language of the peasant to name the live animal and the language of the king to name the meat.

This is the reason you hunt deer (German origin) and eat venison (French origin). If you hunt raccoon, opossum, or moose, you get to eat the same thing; these are American words, borrowed from Native Americans by the early settlers. I guess they figured that when you are eating a possum, there is not much point in being pretentious about what you call it.

—Ronnie Silcox, University of Georgia Extension Service

the big birds in the 1800s, settlers ate them sparingly, only once every month or so, preferring instead their true love, the tasty squirrel, plus bear, coons, and venison, depending on the time of year.

Even so, over the years, the giant turkeys declined in population along with big game in the wild.

"They said my father killed the last wild turkey [in the Big Creek area of north Georgia] around 1910," eighty-two-year-old Mark Woody told me. A tall, well-spoken orphan who later left the mountains to attend Berry College, Woody was told his father brought down the area's "last wild turkey" with his thirty-six-inch-long twelve-gauge shotgun."They believed in those long barrels back then," Woody declared with a grin.

In the early 1900s, Mark Woody recalled, legendary north Georgia forestry official Arthur Woody—namesake for Woody's Gap and perhaps a distant kin of Mark Woody—began a program to replenish the area's wild game—particularly bear, deer, wild turkey, and other fowl that had been effectively thinned out by heavy hunting.

Hazel Farmer, seventy-five, of Blairsville, Georgia, who plays "Maybell" in the mountain musical *Reach of Song* poses with one of her three shotguns. When she takes a notion, she goes out in her fields and brings home a wild turkey or deer.

As wild turkeys declined in number, ingenuity was required—elaborate traps and special calls—for a hunter to bring home a turkey for supper. "Turkeys are accurate afoot," Gober Tipton would declare on a hunt in the mountains east of Cherrylog, Georgia. Not far away, near the Blue Ridge Divide in Fannin County, the late Will Bailey, who died at age ninety-three in the early 1970s, became a master hunter of the great birds in their diminishing days.

"You couldn't beat old man Will on wild turkey," Curtis Underwood told me. "He'd know where a bunch of 'em were and he'd walk up into the top of a mountain before daylight with an old single-barrel hog rifle or muzzleloader. Will'd hear a turkey gobbler and he'd set back and call one or two times, but none after that. Out across the mountain, an old gobbler would call back. Sometimes the turkey would circle around for two or three hours before coming close. Old Will was patient; and he'd always get his bird."

During frontier days and decades to follow, small game swarmed through the woods: squirrels, rabbits, possums, groundhogs, raccoons, all tasty and delicious when fattened up in the fall.

The possum, North America's only marsupial, became the common man's great game meat. A hunter didn't even need a firearm, just a dog to get the fat rascal treed at night. Of course it would help it you had a partner to hold your "tow sack" while you pulled or shook Mr. Possum from the tree. You never had to run one down, because even on the ground, he would go into his prone "playing possum" mode.

Daisy Hughes Hyde, who lived at the foot of north Georgia's Big John Dick Mountain, recalled fondly her mother's delicious possum suppers. Walking home from her one-room mountain schoolhouse, Daisy told her daughter Betty Jo Bailey in later years, "I could smell Mommie's possum cooking before I could see the house!"

While possums and sweet potatoes are still a favorite among the older generation, the late Jimmy Townsend of Jasper, Georgia, dissed young people "who call possums a white trash food, then go off to Atlanta to eat snails."

Coons were a favorite small game also. "They're awful good when you get a good cook on 'em," the late Gober Tipton told me at his cabin near the head of north Georgia's Noontootley Creek. "You can't hardly find nothin' to beat 'em. First you parboil 'em, put you a small onion in there and a pod of red pepper. Boil hit until you see the meat's gonna fall off the bone. Then pour the water off and take out the onion and pepper. Then you put your meat in the baker and black pepper it right good and salt it right good and put it in bear grease and bake it till it's sort of brown on the outside; it's good...mighty good."

Of all small game, squirrels and rabbits were probably the most populous and best-loved small game meat over the centuries, providing more meat over more years than all other game animals combined.

"Mother would make delicious dumplings out of squirrels," recalled Azzie Waters of East Ellijay, Georgia. "Now rabbits, Mother fried her rabbits and they were good too...made real good gravy."

Southern frontiersmen ate almost...any animal available to them. Opossum and raccoon were favorites from the beginning, the 'possum taking first place because, like a fall bear, he abounded in fat...

Records tell of a great feast on Christmas day, 1779, on the Kentucky side of the Ohio River on the tract that would become Louisville. Among the meats were venison and bear, wild turkey, rabbit, coon, and even buffalo, accompanied by three kinds of corn bread, milk, butter, and even homemade cheese. The main attraction, however, was a very large possum, baked whole, and hanging by its tail from a piece of wood in the center of the table. While it lasted, the marsupial was the preferred meat of the feasters.

—JOE GRAY TAYLOR, *EATING, DRINKING AND VISITING IN THE SOUTH*

In considering wild game, we should not forget the region's amazing wild hog population. While the beady-eyed "razorbacks" are not officially a "wild game" species, they are treated as such by many who love to hunt them in what is considered one of the most dangerous of sports. Rich in lean meat and low in fat, the gamy-tasting wild hog is considered by many to be a delicacy. During the "free-range" era up until the late 1800s, most hogs were turned loose to roam the woods, where, carrying the owner's special notches on their ears, they flourished on nuts and berries, fruits and grubs. Every fall, during "hog-killing weather," men and boys enjoyed rollicking hog roundups. Many times they would identify and slaughter the hogs on the spot, then sled them back to their smokehouses.

> Besides man, the razorback is the only mammal whose eyes will not shine by reflected light—they are too bold and crafty. The razorback has a mind of his own; not instinct, but mind—whatever psychologists say. He thinks. Anybody can see that; when he is not rooting or sleeping, he is studying devilment...he bears grudges, broods over indignities and plans revenge for tomorrow or the week after. If he cannot get even with you, he will lay wait for your unsuspecting friends.
>
> —HORACE KEPHART,
> *OUR SOUTHERN HIGHLANDERS*

Today more than two million "razorbacks" are said to be running wild in remote southern forests from North Carolina to Arkansas. Some of them are vicious long-tusked European wild boars introduced to the North Carolina mountains in 1912. Many of these have interbred with the more gentle "mountain rooter" wild hogs, creating quite a vicious animal.

The heart of the wild hog country is in east Tennessee southwest of the Great Smoky Mountains. Hunters enter state lotteries at Tellico Plains to win the right to get fall season hunt permits.

The tradition of wild game as the true meat of the mountains continues today across the Appalachians by people such as the Bailey clan of Doublehead Gap, Georgia—Will Bailey's descendants. They enjoy bringing home wild game and fowl and fish every chance they get—squirrel, venison, rabbit, and speckled trout, among others.

Every fall, carrying on a thirty-year tradition started by the family's late patriarch, Mr. Will's grandchildren throw a festive feed, complete with bluegrass music and religious songs at the old homeplace overlooking Bailey Creek near the Blue Ridge Continental Divide. The event—at which they share much of their wild game bounty, when available—brings over two hundred people, many natives now living in other states, who flock back to remember old times and to enjoy mountain foods of yesteryear.

Master chefs for the occasion are Mr. Will's grandsons, David, Dan, and Philip Bailey. The sounds of bluegrass fiddles and guitars and banjos and voices echo down the valley deep into the mountain night, way past midnight.

Wild Game Recipes

Most of these wild game recipes come courtesy of and with the author's personal thanks to the Cooperative Extension Service, University of Georgia College of Agriculture, Athens, Georgia.

A fine Extension Service booklet—*Wild Game, from Field to Table*—brings together many of the recipes in this chapter along with many more. Authored by Extension specialists Jeffrey Jackson and Catharine Sigman, the booklet, available free to the public, goes into great detail about preparing wild game and fish for cooking.

While most of the recipes and directions for preparation come from the Extension Service, (and are credited in each case), the comment related to each recipe is that of the author.

In a general way, experts advise people to

> *In this early period [1700s], the mountaineer had two important resources that have now almost passed away. One was in the wild game with which the whole region abounded. The other was the free and luxurious pasture for all kinds of livestock...As one who grew up in the last part of it, I look back upon it with a sigh of sadness in the thought of its having passed away, now that the wild game and free range are forever gone.*
>
> —Andrew Jackson Ritchie,
> *Sketches of Rabun County History*

delay eating freshly killed game meat for at least two days, otherwise it can be tough and lacking in taste. Horace Kephart, the sage of the Appalachians in the 1920s and 1930s, urged his readers as follows: "All mammals from the 'coon size down, as well as duck and grouse, unless young and tender or unless they have hung several days, should be par-boiled (gently simmered) from 10 to 30 minutes, according to size, before frying, broiling or roasting (baking)."

Black Bear

The bears roaming the Southern Appalachians are great browsers with individual ranges of fifteen to twenty miles. They consume all types of vegetation,

Tennessee hunter shows off his skins—bears and raccoons.

particularly wild berries and nuts, as well as ants and bugs. Mountain people prize the meat of a young bear, particularly in the fall when they are fat with chestnuts and other forest mast, plus berries.

The earliest mountain settlers, while waiting to get their swine established, found the bear a great meat resource. They cured bear hams just as they did hogs—if salt was available—and sometimes they smoked them. Virginia's William Byrd, a great traveler in the interior, found bear steak "a good relish, very savory," coming close in taste to that of pork. A Carolina cookbook, however, called for bear steaks to be cut one inch thick and to be cooked until well done, "otherwise the flavor may be too strong and gamy for the average taste."

While mountain people love the wild taste, there are those who seek to suppress the gamy flavor. Frances Gates Hill of the Mountaintown district of Gilmer County, Georgia, parboils her bear meat "to get the bear taste out of it." She chops up an onion and adds it to the meat when she's cooking, which helps remove even more of the wild taste.

Frances recalled the most recent bear they slaughtered. A neighbor came running to her front door: "Frances, I'm a-tellin' the truth if I'm a-standing hyar; they was a bear went through your yard just now bigger'n I am." Frances called her brother, Sam Gates, who tracked and quickly brought him down. Naturally the bear was slaughtered immediately; and most of the meat was frozen for later use.

While many people marinate mature bear to tenderize the meat and remove the gamy taste, Extension agents say marination is not necessary for younger animals. Before preparation, be sure to remove excess fat, sinews, and other undesirable parts.

Roast Bear

The shoulders, loin, and ham may be roasted in the oven the same as pork is roasted. Remove from the marinade, and wipe dry before putting in the oven. Like pork, these cuts of bear should be well done.

~

Bear Marinade

2 cups claret or other wine

2 cups vinegar (or 4 cups of either)

1 teaspoon Worcestershire sauce

1 bay leaf

2 whole cloves

Pinch of salt

1 tablespoon whole

black pepper

Combine all ingredients and pour over meat.

—*University of Georgia Extension Service*

(*Author's note*: Many prefer to soak bear meat in the marinade several hours or overnight.)

Broiled Bear Chops

Remove the chops from the marinade, and wipe dry; broil over the coals, and baste frequently with some of the marinade. Cooking time will depend on the thickness of the chops, but be sure they are well done. Serve with sautéed apples. Corn bread muffins should also be included for they are a staple with this food. To sauté apples, core but do not peel the apple and slice medium thick. Sauté in fry pan in butter. Sprinkle with sugar and any spices desired.

—*University of Georgia Extension Service*

Bear hunters near Hazel Creek, North Carolina, carry a bear out of the hills in this photo taken by author Horace Kephart.

In the 1800s, on Hazel Creek, my ancestors hunted and trapped bear. My great-great-grandfather, Moses Proctor, built a log bear pen or trap at the mouth of a little branch, from which its name Bear Pen Branch originated.

My great-grandfather, Joseph Welch, once went bear hunting and brought home a tiny baby bear that had not yet been weaned. At the time my great-grandmother was in the bed with a new baby. Not being able to stand seeing the cub starve, she let it suckle at her breast. In telling this as an old lady, she said her baby would suckle on one tit and the bear the other. I have no idea what happened to the bear; surely they didn't kill and eat it for that would have been like eating one of the family.

—Professor Duane Oliver, Hazelwood, North Carolina

Venison

In Elizabethan England, venison—the meat of antlered animals—was considered a delicacy, and choice bucks were set aside for the king. Most of the hunting was done by and for royalty, anyway, because the great game preserves were set aside for the royal family.

Thus Appalachian America settlers who came from Britain were well acquainted with venison and were overjoyed that the interior was so well stocked with deer, providing an abundant plenty for the common folk who had the run of the region's free range.

Traveling near the Toe River in western North Carolina in 1795, John Brown noted that after killing a bear, people hung up the carcass and sliced off pieces as needed until all was consumed.

The Cherokees ate a lot of deer meat, also, and sold tons of deerskins to traders who hauled the skins to Charleston on pack horses or mules. To preserve the deer meat, frontiersmen learned from the Indians to make deer jerky much like beef jerky, by drying thin strips and then smoking them. While the jerky lasted indefinitely, its consistency was that of a hickory stick, some said.

The texture of fresh venison is much finer and leaner than beef, but more watery. Liver, heart, and kidneys are best if eaten immediately while the rest of the meat is hanging. After the carcass has aged several days at 35°F to 40°F, you can easily cut the meat and remove it from the bones with only a sharp knife. Meat high on the upper hind legs and along the backbone is the most tender. For steaks and chops, slice the meat one-half to three-fourths inch thick.

This first venison recipe is considered a delicacy by long-term gourmet Dr. Sam Talmadge, a retired physician of Athens, Georgia. His guests over the years declare this dish is wonderful even when beef is substituted for the game meat.

Dr. Sam's Venison Sausage

4 pounds venison
4 pounds pork
1 cup brown sugar

½ tablespoon ground ginger
2 tablespoons finely ground red pepper
2 tablespoons black pepper

Coarsely grind equal portions of venison and pork. Perform a second (fine) grinding with a sausage plate, adding the sugar, ginger, and red and black pepper. Stuff into 1½-inch casings, and smoke with green hickory wood. Fry small patties, and serve with saltine crackers. The seasoned sausage will keep for about 3 months.

—*Dr. Sam Talmadge, Athens, Georgia*

Clarke Venison Roast

3- to 4-pound venison roast
Black pepper
1 package onion soup mix
2 cans water

1 clove garlic, slivered, or garlic salt to
taste (optional)
1 can cream of celery soup

Season roast to taste with pepper. Sprinkle onion soup mix and garlic (if desired) over meat. Spread celery soup over roast. Add water. Cover and cook in 250°F oven 2 to 2½ hours. Add more water if necessary. Yields 8 to 10 servings.

—*University of Georgia Extension Service, with credit*
to Jim and Linda Kundell, Clarke County, Georgia

Chops are another nice variation of the venison cooking art.

Venison Chops

6 venison chops, well trimmed
Salt and pepper to taste
¼ teaspoon onion or garlic salt

½ cup all-purpose flour
3 tablespoons shortening

Season chops with salt, pepper, and seasoned salt and dredge with flour. Cover and cook over low heat in shortening in a skillet for ½ hour. Turn occasionally, and add a small amount of water if necessary. Remove cover and brown the chops on both sides. Serves 6.

—*University of Georgia Extension Service, and credited to the*
Hancock County, Georgia, Extension Office

Wild Hog (Razorback)

Wild hogs—many prefer to call them feral hogs—have been a major source of meat in the mountains since colonial days. Every February, the Georgia State Legislature stages a "wild hog supper" in Atlanta as a social kickoff to the annual session.

The region's wild hogs came about by natural evolution plus unfortunate introduction of European boars in 1912. Some of the swine that came from Britain in the 1600s ended up in the interior wilds and grew up on forest mast, roots, and grubs. These domestic pigs may have interbred with earlier "javelina" boars left by the Spaniards. Early Appalachian settlers found the Indians barbecuing swine, possibly Spanish progeny. In any event, what resulted was a breed of wild "razorbacks" famous all the way from western Virginia to Arkansas. These animals have been described as "high in the shoulder, low in the rear, thin, with a long head and snout, and very swift of foot." The late Bil Dwyer said the wild boars could run like a deer and climb like a goat.

Wild hogs are still numerous in Appalachian wilds. One game biologist estimates they may number over two million, mainly in western North Carolina, east Tennessee, and north Georgia. The introduction in 1912 of sharp-tusked "Russian boars" into a western North Carolina game preserve—actually European boars from Germany's Harz Mountains—created an even more ornery animal.

The meaner boars began swarming into the Great Smoky Mountains National Park in the 1950s and are now considered a menace. They root up wildflowers and compete with bears and small game for mast and berries. In 1955, hunters in Gilmer County, Georgia, purchased several of the European boars in Robbinsville, North Carolina, interbred them with mountain rooter hogs, and released the offspring on the Aaron, Grassy, and Cowpen Mountains.

Tellico Plains in southeast Tennessee is considered the heart of the wild boar country. The territory includes the Cherokee National Forest, the Unicoi and Snowbird Mountains, and the Great Smokies. Would-be wild boar hunters register and await the luck of the draw. Those chosen to hunt must pay a license and guide fee.

Even though wild hogs are mean and menacing, the meat is considered delicious, with greater lean and less fat. One of the best ways to cook them is to roast them as you would a suckling pig:

Tellico Plains Wild Pig Roast

Small wild pig (15 to 18 pounds)	Currants
Vegetable oil	Butter
Salt and pepper to taste	4 cloves garlic, chopped
Apples, cored	

After killing the pig, remove all bristles and hair. Remove internal organs and intestines. Mix salt, pepper, and oil and thoroughly rub mixture on all of the pig's surfaces, inside and out. Insert in pig's cavity a quantity of cored apples filled with currants. Place pig on a spit, high enough from the flames so that skin does not blister. Place back of pig nearest the flames to begin with and turn over when back is thoroughly hot but not seared. Make a baste of butter and chopped garlic, and baste the skin often during cooking. Turn the spit frequently. Cooking will probably take about 3 hours. Test the meat; it should come easily off bones before inside parts are done.

Small Game

The early Appalachian settlers did not discriminate in selecting their small game animals to eat—they consumed everything available...possums, squirrels, rabbits, raccoons, quail, wild turkeys, passenger pigeons, and even robins.

While possums fattened on fall mast were an early frontier favorite, squirrels were eaten with relish, particularly from the stew pot and as a dumpling dish. Joe Gray Taylor noted that by killing squirrels and coons, the settler not only fed his family but helped to cut down primary predators of their corn patches.

~

Rabbit

During Great Depression years, a half dozen "rabbit boxes" could feed a family all winter. J. R. Coker and his brothers had thirty rabbit boxes, scattered all over fields and woods at Track Rock Gap, Georgia. "We'd run those traps every day. We had plenty of rabbit to eat. Mother would fry rabbits like chicken. We'd take our rabbit hides to Carl Jackson's Store. He'd pay you twenty cents for a rabbit skin, and write you a piece of paper, 'I owe you in trade 20 cents.' Yeah, done it many a time. Carl would hang his hides up all around that little ole store building. About once a week, he'd carry 'em to Atlanter and sell 'em."

My sister-in-law, Lib Dabney, recalls how her mother, Nannie Jones, of Greenville, South Carolina, cooked rabbits. "Nannie would boil the rabbit and boil it and boil it until it was good and tender. Then she would dry it off and roll it in flour and black pepper and salt and fry it until it was real brown. The broth made gravy that was soooooo good!"

Today, rabbit meat—tender and pink—is easily obtainable in supermarkets. Rabbit can be substituted for chicken in most recipes. To guard against tularemia, the Extension Service advises that one handle the meat with utensils or rubber gloves, and, of course, cook until well done.

Young boy with pop gun poses with rabbits that he supposedly brought home from a hunt near Hayesville, North Carolina.

UGA Rabbit Delight

1 rabbit	2 green peppers
1 tablespoon fat	½ cup mushrooms, chopped
¼ cup lemon juice	Pinch of ginger
¾ cup orange juice	1 tablespoon parsley, chopped
1 cup broth	Salt and pepper

Joint the rabbit, and brown pieces in fat. Add broth and other ingredients. Cover and cook slowly until tender. Season to taste.

—University of Georgia Extension Service

Squirrel

Squirrels have been the base of many great Appalachian eating treats. Hunter stews and Brunswick stews and Kentucky burgoo would never have been invented without squirrel meat. As one aficionado declared, "Squirrel pie has got soul in good measure." While smother-fried squirrels with gravy is the favored method of cooking by many, squirrel dumplings have been a mountain delicacy over the centuries and even yet today, as well as squirrel pie.

Gary and Dawn Davis, who reside in a wooded hillside off Aska Road in the rolling mountains of Fannin County, Georgia, are squirrel dumpling gourmets par excellence. Their neighbor, Carl Dodd, of self-described "Upper Hog Gut Road," loves Gary's squirrel feasts, calling them "the best (dumplings) in the world." Gary himself—a conservation ranger in the vast Chattahoochee National Forest—feels that "there's no better wild meat than good squirrel."

Gary invites friends from over the country to visit and hunt for squirrels around Doublehead Gap during the north Georgia squirrel season—mid-August through February. Sometimes the crowd reaches up to fifteen. Afterward, everyone congregates at the Davis home for the delicious dumpling feast.

Fixing squirrel dumplings, Gary Davis–style, is an art. First you should "grade" your squirrels into "fryers" and "boilers" in this manner: After you have skinned the squirrels, but before cutting them up, place a knife blade flat on the leg piece and see if the bone will bend. If so, keep it as a young "fryer" squirrel, and roll it in seasoned flour for "fried squirrel and gravy." Squirrels that fail the leg-bending test are "boiler" or dumpling squirrels.

To make dumplings for a large group, Gary figures on a squirrel and a half for each person he is going to feed. Here's his recipe for a small feed:

Gary and Dawn Davis

Gary and Dawn's Squirrel Dumplings

(In the words of Gary Davis)

4 "boiler" squirrels   *Large pot of lightly salted water*

Black pepper to taste

You skin and gut your squirrels, of course, and cut them up in quarters. You put 'em in a big boiler and boil 'em until they get tender. Season with salt and pepper.

For Dumplings

1½ cups self-rising flour   *Black pepper to taste*

½ cup lard

Make the dumplings like you would make biscuits only you use ice water instead of milk, enough to make a "heavy" dough. Use self-rising flour. Roll 'em out under a quarter-inch thick and cut into strips ¾ inch wide and 3 inches long. With your pot boiling you just drop the strips in gently one at a time into the boiling broth with the meat still in there. They cook pretty quickly, in 5 to 8 minutes. Put in a bit of black pepper near completion.

Gary and Dawn have this word of humorous advice when you are feeding squirrel meat to city people for the first time. "Tell them they are getting chicken and dumplings; they won't know the difference!"

~

Here is another way of cooking squirrel from the good folks at Athens, Georgia:

Baked Squirrel Pie

4 squirrels, cleaned and dressed   *Clove of garlic*

All-purpose flour   *Small bay leaf*

2 tablespoons onion juice   *2 tablespoons parsley, chopped*

1 can bouillon   *¼ cup Worcestershire sauce*

Preheat oven to 350°F. Season with salt and pepper to taste. Flour squirrels, and brown in roasting pan. Add remaining ingredients, and bake at 350°F for 45 minutes. Reduce temperature, and continue cooking until tender (about 45 minutes). Serves 4.

—*University of Georgia Extension Service*

Raccoon

Coon hunters of Union County, Georgia, say some of their best hunting takes place on Buck Snort Mountain, out from Blairsville. My friend George Houdeshel advises me that the mountain got its name from bucks who liked to snort and paw the ground on the mountain during rutting season. George lives on Buck Snort Mountain Road so he should know.

Raccoon meat is dark. The fat is strong flavored and some mountain cooks prefer to neutralize the gamy taste a bit by marinating the meat in vinegar or milk. And generally mountain people parboil the meat before roasting.

Buck Snort Mountain Raccoon Roast

Preheat oven to 275°F to 300°F. Leave a ⅓-inch layer of fat on raccoon. Cover carcass with cloth dipped in fat. Place on a roasting rack in a shallow pan. Do not cover or add water. Bake at 275°F to 300°F for 3 to 4 hours. Remove cloth the last half hour. Baste several times with drippings, and dust with flour after each basting for a crackly and crisp crust.

—*University of Georgia Extension Service*

Opossum

The late Horace Kephart, the Smoky Mountains' all-time great "writer in residence," had some important advice about hunting and cooking possums.

"He is not good until you have freezing weather; nor is he to be served without sweet potatoes, except in desperate extremity."

Possum hunting is a time-honored Southern sport during the chilly nights of late fall.

Curtis Underwood hunted possums for their hides in the 1930s, earning a quarter apiece. The fat ones ended up on the kitchen stove.

> We'd take the really fat possum home alive. Granny had a big cast-iron stove down on the creek. We'd throw that big old possum in that stove. He couldn't get out [of the oven], but he could breathe okay. We'd feed that bugger corn bread and water for two weeks, get him cleaned out.
>
> After skinning him, we'd cut up the possum meat and pare [*sic*] boil him twice, about 10 to 15 minutes each. We'd take him out, let him drip dry, then roll him in cornmeal and flour and put him in a big thick iron skillet and slow-fry him on an old wood stove, fry it good and brown. Take him out of there, put him in a big

*P*ossum hunting was a favorite [sport] because the slow possum could be caught and did not require the expense of guns or shells. Boys bought chestnuts from mountaineers and ate them on possum hunts. In the daylight they were too wormy to eat, but when a possum–hunter saw a friend eating wormy chestnuts, he liked them better himself.

—FLOYD WATKINS, *YESTERDAY IN THE HILLS*

bread pan with sweet potatoes around him and bake him for 35 to 40 minutes. And I guarantee you wouldn't turn him down, it would be awful good eatin'!

Mountain people consider the shy possum to be a superb game meat, with a wonderful wild taste, and is often served with sweet potatoes or with chestnuts. Some folks, however, to remove the gamey taste, either parboil or marinate the meat. Lucinda Ogle of Gatlinburg, Tennessee, remembered that her Grandfather Oakley gave his possums two par-boilings—the first to remove excess grease, and the second—injecting a handful of spice bushes in the boiling water—to smooth out the taste a bit more. This was followed by the traditional baking. People who marinate the meat usually do so overnight in a pot of cold water along with a cup of salt and a half cup of vinegar.

The possum is prized for its light colored, tender meat. Before cooking, remove the scent glands in small of back and under each foreleg between the shoulder and rib. Also remove excess fat before baking.

Possum and Sweet Potatoes

1 possum (about 2½ pounds)	½ cup water
2⅓ teaspoons salt	4 medium sweet potatoes
Black pepper to taste	2 tablespoons sugar
All-purpose flour	

Preheat oven to 350°F. Trim excess fat and discard. Wash quickly inside and out with warm water and drain thoroughly. Rub salt and pepper well into possum inside and out. Sprinkle inside and out with flour. Lay the possum on its back in a roasting pan. Add water, cover, and bake in 350°F oven until about half done (45 to 60 minutes). Split peeled potatoes in half lengthwise, and place in pan around possum. Add sugar and more water if needed. Cover sliced potatoes, and possum and cook 30 minutes more.

—*University of Georgia Extension Service*

(*Author's note*: A variation of this, "possum and chestnuts," calls for the possum to be stuffed with chestnuts, applesauce, and breadcrumbs in equal proportions, then covered with slices of sweet potato, a half cup of lemon juice, and one cup boiling water, and baked until tender, with frequent bastings.)

> We'd always carry our rifles with us going into the mountains, that and a stick, about a five-foot-long stick. We used it to kill snakes and to beat in the bushes. If you come to a place you wanted to go through, and you wanted to make sure there wasn't nothin' in there to harm you, you'd take that stick. We run up on a lot of snakes. I've eaten rattlesnakes. They're not bad eatin'.
>
> —Frank Pressley, native of Cullowhee Mountain, North Carolina

His First Possum Hunt

It was incumbent on the older boys [growing up on farms in Davidson County, North Carolina] to introduce the younger ones to the folly of hunting under the pretense we were about to experience our first glance at heaven.

Most boys were no more than five or six years old when the thrill of "possum hunting" was revealed. Possums were hunted at night, and by dusk, as the sun slid behind the horizon, the hunters—two cousins, a local hunter, an older brother, plus four hound dogs—were ready to go. I could sense the night would be different from anything I had ever done. How lucky could you get?

Down through the pasture we went in wet grass to my waist. The dogs and I trudged along the best we could, and by the time we reached the barbed-wire fence next to the woods, my shoes, socks, and pants were cold and wet.

Shortly Old Blue let out a prolonged yelp, and a cousin yelled, "Whoopee! I believe he's struck a hot trail." Almost in unison, the other dogs joined in the chorus with their noses to the leaf floor moving in small circles and barking. The dogs picked up their gait, and so did all five of us in a mad rush, tugging at bushes and tree limbs to stay abreast with the dogs.

Gene Younts, author of *We Are What We Were*

From my vantage point, the world was nothing more than dips and gullies on the ground that needed crossing, neither of which fit my short legs. "Come on," an older cousin yelled, carrying a kerosene lantern as he moved ahead, pushing limbs aside, and releasing them to hit me in the face and spray water from their leaves, which soaked every thread on my small body.

In a few minutes, one of the boys said he believed the dogs had treed a possum. Our pace quickened, but hard as I tried, my legs would move no faster. Not only was I cold and wet, but a tiredness hung over me like none I had ever known. Yet the older boys encouraged me on. Like a wind-up toy with a string too tight, my desire to go farther broke. My tears began to flow with a few sobs, but luck was on my side, because we neared a tree surrounded by four barking dogs.

The four older boys caucused in a small circle near the base of the tree. As they broke up from their meeting, one said, "You climb up and get him, Buster."

Off came Buster's shoes, and up the wet trunk of the tree he scampered as those on the ground shined flashlights into the limbs overhead.

"I see him," one cousin said, full of excitement, and when I gathered my emotions and looked up, all I could see were two beady eyes that sparkled like red reflectors on the rear fender of a bicycle. They belonged to the possum.

Buster reached the limb holding the possum and shook it vigorously until the catch let go. He hit the ground with a loud thud only to be suddenly grabbed by the jaws of the snarling pack. The possum made himself into a round ball for protection while the three older boys on the ground wrestled the dogs to free him.

Almost as if by magic, the tallest cousin proudly lifted the possum by the tail high in the air for all of us to get a good look. "Man, he's a nice one," they all agreed as I wondered, "How could such a frightened animal be worth a celebration?"

After admiring the catch of the evening for several minutes, they placed the possum in a burlap sack and gave the panting dogs a rest.

The older cousin decided it was time to return home, and he looked at me, remarking that I had had my lesson for the night. Indeed, I had, and the cousin led me by the hand for the trek home. Possum hunting and I were strangers no more.

—Excerpted from *We Are What We Were: Memories of Rural North Carolina*, by Gene Younts, Public Service Scholar and Vice President Emeritus, University of Georgia, Athens

Mountain Whistle Pig (Groundhog)

Many mountain folk call him a "whistle pig"—due to his penchant for whistling through his teeth as he heads to his burrow while being chased. In any event, groundhog (or whistle pig) meat is preferred by many over pork. Cling Webb of Big Ivy, North Carolina, was fond of saying he wouldn't trade a single mess of groundhog "for all the pork you could give me."

Well endowed with fat, the groundhog's dark, mild-flavored, and tender meat is highly prized. Curtis Underwood insists the time to kill a groundhog for the table is in the fall, otherwise you have an inferior "grass-gutted" meat: "In the fall of the year, when they get good and fat on acorns or whatever, is when I like to take 'em." The groundhog is a browser just like a squirrel. Curtis's instructions are as follows:

You skin him out, cut him up, and throw away the head. If he's extra fat, I pull all that fat off. Then you cut him up and put him in the pot and boil him until he's good and tender. Most of the time, it takes very little cooking. We pull him out of there and roll it in cornmeal and flour. We usually have cast-iron cooking skillets and slow-fry him in bacon grease until he's good and brown. Take it out of the frying pan grease, and let the grease drain out. Put the groundhog meat over in an old bread pan, and put Irish potatoes or sweet potatoes around him, and put him in to bake. We always liked sweet potatoes, but small round Irish potatoes are just as good put in a bread pan. I always put a little more pepper and salt that bake right into the meat.

*F*olks *called groundhogs whistle pigs. They'll just stand up on their hind feet and whistle at ye. And they're awful fat.*

—HAZEL FARMER, UPPER YOUNG CANE COMMUNITY, BLAIRSVILLE, GEORGIA

A traditional mountain way for eating groundhogs is with ramps, if in season, or an onion, along with corn bread, of course. Some people who wish to remove the gamy taste soak the meat overnight in salted water.

Whistle Pig Pie

Young groundhog, skinned and cleaned

1 cup onion

¼ cup green pepper

½ tablespoon minced parsley

1 tablespoon salt

⅛ teaspoon black pepper

4½ tablespoons all-purpose flour

3 cups broth

Cut groundhog into 2 or 3 pieces. Parboil for 1 hour. Remove meat from the bones in large pieces. Add onion, green pepper, parsley, salt, pepper, and flour to the broth and stir until it thickens. If the broth does not measure 3 cups, add water. Add the meat to the broth mixture and stir thoroughly. Pour into baking dish. Yields 6 to 8 servings.

—University of Georgia Extension Service

Biscuits for Pie

1 cup plain flour

2 teaspoons baking powder

¼ teaspoon salt

2 tablespoons fat

¼ cup milk

Preheat oven to 400°F. Sift the flour, baking powder, and salt together. Cut in the fat and add the liquid. Stir until the dry ingredients are moist. Roll only enough to make it fit the dish. Place dough on top of the meat; put it in a 400°F oven and bake 30 to 40 minutes or until dough is browned.

Game Fowl

While quail and dove were hunted and enjoyed by mountain people over the years, the meaty wild turkey rose quickly in the hearts of people in the mountains and beyond, becoming an honored guest in dining rooms across the land.

A U.S. original, wild turkey is synonymous with pioneer America. Fattened on chestnuts and acorns, the wild bird was a great sustainer for early settlers. While most turkeys today are domesticated, hunting wild turkeys is still enjoyed as a great fall tradition in the mountain country.

Game birds should be skinned or plucked. Skinning is easier, but plucking usually produces a tastier bird. The skin has an underlayer of fat that keeps the meat juicy while cooking. The skin is flavorful except in a few species. Plucking birds in a bucket of warm water with a little soap added will prevent feathers from floating about the kitchen.

Roasted Wild Turkey

1 turkey, 8 to 10 pounds, ready to cook	1 teaspoon salt
Salt black and pepper to taste	¼ teaspoon black pepper
8 cups partially dry bread cubes	2½ teaspoons sage
¼ cup chopped celery	1½ cups chopped onion
½ cup chopped walnuts	¼ cup butter or margarine
	¼ cup water

Preheat oven to 325°F. Sprinkle turkey inside and out with salt and pepper. Combine bread, celery, walnuts, and seasonings. Cook onion in butter or margarine until tender but not brown; pour over bread mixture. Add the water and toss lightly. Spoon stuffing lightly into body cavity. Put remaining dressing in a greased casserole dish. Cover and bake extra stuffing in oven with turkey during last 30 minutes of roasting time. Truss bird. Cover breast with bacon slices and cheesecloth soaked in melted butter fat.

Place turkey, breast up, on rack on roasting pan. Roast at 325°F 20 to 25 minutes per pound or until tender, basting frequently with bacon fat and drippings in pan. Remove cheesecloth, skewers, and string. Serves 8 to 10.

—*University of Georgia Extension Service*

Course all that wild meat had kind of a wild taste to it which we loved. My mama would cook that wild turkey, boil it tender, and she also would make chestnut dressing. She'd boil those chestnuts and peel 'em and put 'em in dressing. It had a sweet taste to it.

—Frank Pressley, recalling growing up on Cullowhee Mountain, North Carolina

Chestnut and Corn Bread Dressing

Mountain people would not think of serving turkey without a great dressing or stuffing. A dressing using chestnuts as a base was a real favorite over the years in the Appalachians, but equally loved was corn bread dressing, using crumbled corn bread, to which onions, celery, spices, and herbs are added.

Turkey and dressing time evokes wonderful memories such as those of John Egerton and his mother: "She returns to my memory every year at turkey and dressing time, simply because the corn bread dressing she made to accompany the big bird was a world-class side dish."

This recipe is based on a John Egerton favorite from Tennessee and Kentucky that is well over a century old:

Egerton's Corn Bread Dressing Favorite

Mix together 1 cup of white cornmeal, 1 cup of all-purpose flour, ¾ teaspoon of black pepper. Stir in 1 beaten egg and add up to 1½ cups of buttermilk—just enough to give the mixture a thick, pouring consistency. Mix 2 tablespoons of bacon grease in a large black skillet; when smoking hot, pour the batter in and set on the bottom rack of a preheated 350°F oven. Bake 5 minutes there, then move up to the middle rack for 15 or 20 minutes more, or until crispy brown. Turn out on a cake rack. When cold, crumble thoroughly in a large pan or bowl. Next, mince 1 medium-sized onion and 1 rib of celery, and sauté in 2 tablespoons of bacon grease. When the vegetables are soft, add them to the corn breadcrumbs, and sprinkle in 1 teaspoon of poultry seasoning or sage (according to taste). Moisten the mixture with broth from the roaster or giblets, making it just sticky enough to shape into patties. Taste and adjust seasonings if necessary. Spoon the dressing into the turkey's cavity to cook along with the bird. Serve hot with the turkey and giblet gravy. For 4 or more holiday diners, a double recipe may be advisable.

Chestnut Dressing

6 cups chestnuts, shelled and skinned	½ cup cream
	1 cup melted butter
2 cups dry bread, in small pieces	2 teaspoons salt
4 tablespoons chopped parsley	¼ teaspoon pepper
1 cup chopped celery	

Drop chestnuts into boiling salted water. Cook until soft. Put cooked chestnuts through potato ricer. Combine with remaining ingredients. This makes sufficient dressing for a small turkey.

—*University of Georgia Cooperative Extension Service*

Quail and Dove

It has been said that quail and pigeons were probably the most important small birds in the South, and quail still are, to a lessened degree. Walker Percy had a wonderful description of a quail breakfast—"half a dozen hot little heart-shaped morsels per plate, six tender-spicy, game-gladdening mouthfuls."

In the interior and mountain country, quail—known by many as bobwhite—became the great game bird. Plump and delicious, they were abundant and plentiful up until development and agricultural chemicals came onto the scene. Before then, quail had a great habitat—blackberry tangles and fence rows grown up in honeysuckle plus wide-open sedge-grass fields. In the years before and after the Civil War, quail hunting was a wide-open sport, the entire region was "open range" and hardly anyone ever posted land off-limits to hunters. In the old days, hunters would hang their game for several days after being killed—placed in the "meat house" that was often called a smoke house even though smoke never graced its walls.

In modern times, quail—produced on quail farms and featuring a taste only slightly stronger than chicken—are often served with grits at breakfast.

(From left to right) Hiram B. Wade, Guy Roberts, and Judge Newt Morris (R) show off the results of their two-day bird hunt in 1910 in front of the courthouse in Marietta, Georgia.

I wish I could recall all the tales I heard my Daddy and Uncle Phil tell of their early life...They spoke of the crops being so bad they had to depend on hunting, fishing and trapping for a lot of their food and some money...One way... [was] bird knocking. A group of the boys would take lighted pine knots and go out at night and surround cedar trees, roosting places, then scare the birds out and knock them down with small tree branches. These birds would be roasted before an open fire by hanging them by strings and letting the strings twist around and around until edible. This was a feast for the folks as meat was a very scarce item.

—JULIAN SAPP OF DALTON, GEORGIA, IN THE *WHITFIELD-MURRAY HISTORICAL SOCIETY QUARTERLY*, JULY 1989

Roasted Quail (Bobwhite) with Mushrooms

4 quail, dressed and cleaned

4 slices bacon

1 tablespoon butter

Juice of half a lemon

½ cup hot water

1 (3-ounce) can broiled mushrooms, drained

Preheat oven to 350°F. Wipe quail inside and out. Bind each bird with slice of bacon. Put birds into a buttered pan, and roast at 350°F, basting occasionally, about 30 minutes or until tender. Remove birds and add butter or margarine, water, and lemon juice to drippings in pan, stirring to make a gravy. Add mushrooms. Serve the birds on toast with gravy poured over them. Serves 4.

—*University of Georgia Extension Service*

Dove Delicious

8 doves, cleaned

1 onion, sliced ¼-inch thick

4 tablespoons butter

Salt and pepper to taste

Preheat oven to 400°F. Split doves down back, draw and clean. Boil doves for 15 minutes. Place inside each dove ½ tablespoon butter and ½ slice of onion. Add salt and pepper. Wrap each dove in foil. Cook for 30 to 45 minutes at 400°F, and serve in foil. Should you wish, you may go a step further and place the unwrapped doves in a saucepan with gravy and let simmer until gravy is thick enough to serve. Serves 4.

—*University of Georgia Extension Service*

We used to catch horneyhead fish. Best fish I ever ate. Also chubs, smaller than the horneys. We called 'em chelbs, some called 'em minnows. We caught white suckers. They had bones all through the meat; we would grind 'em up in the sausage mill.

My father-in-law, Booby Dave Seabolt, he'd set his hook overnight and go back the next morning and oft times he'd have an eel. They was awfully good to eat.

Booby Dave was also a turkey hunter. Out on a turkey hunt, he'd jerk off a briar leaf, tear it open, and make a turkey call and call turkeys. Usually they came.

—OSCAR CANNON OF TURNERS CORNER, GEORGIA

Fish

One of my fondest memories is taking our four sons on a fall outing in the 1960s to a trout farm in north Georgia. The boys caught fish so fast and furiously after dropping in their hooks—and I would have to pay per pound—that I had to reluctantly bring them to a fishing halt after a half hour. We brought our big catch home, filleted them, and enjoyed one of the greatest meals I have ever tasted. Only thing better would have been eating them on the spot where we caught them. Bill Neal has rhapsodized about how much better fried fish taste when you cook them right "in a mountain forest, by a limpid stream, at sunset, over an open fire." He adds that "fresh trout fried till crisp, ash-roasted baby potatoes, and, in the spring, perhaps a handful of freshly chopped ramps tossed into the sputtering fat…creates my idea of a great meal: strong, fresh flavors in equal combat, food that sustains, not just entertains."

Much of the native rainbow trout has been fished out of Appalachian streams. Ruby Mooney, who lives near Macedonia Church in the mountainous "Blue Ridge Divide" area in eastern Gilmer County, Georgia, remembered that "this creek down near here used to be full of rainbow trout, and all the natives just about all have been caught out. Nowadays there's just what [the state] puts in there."

The Pressley family of Cullowhee, North Carolina, caught mostly small speckled trout in years past, although one of the boys caught an eighteen-inch rainbow trout, a rarity. At Robinson's Creek, Frank Pressley and his brothers caught sixty "speckles" on one visit. "We loved to eat 'em for breakfast. Mama would skillet-fry those things in streak-of-lean grease. She fixed corn fritters to eat with them."

For most fish, the fresher the better. Small panfish, such as mountain trout, are easiest to eat when filleted. The following recipe comes from the famed Andy Cope Trout Farm in the Foxfire country north of Clayton, Georgia.

Mrs. Andy Cope's Fried Rainbow Trout

6 dressed rainbow trout

Salt and pepper to taste

Hot grease to cover (at least
½ inch in skillet)

Seasoned cornmeal (add salt and
pepper to meal and mix)

Season trout with salt and pepper and roll in cornmeal. Fry in hot grease until golden brown, turning only once. Allow about 7 minutes to each side. Serve with lemon slices and tartar sauce.

—*Courtesy Andy's Trout Farms, Rabun County, Georgia*

Catfish

Fried Mountain Catfish

6 fish, skinned, with heads cut off
(or 2 pounds catfish fillets)

½ teaspoon salt

¼ teaspoon freshly
ground pepper

¼ cup all-purpose flour

1 cup white cornmeal

2 eggs, beaten

5 tablespoons cooking oil

Sprinkle fish with salt and pepper. Combine flour and cornmeal, and roll fish in meal-flour mix, then dip into beaten eggs. Roll again in meal-flour mix and set aside. Add oil to heavy skillet and set on high (375°F). When fully heated, add fish. Lightly brown on each side. Serves 6.

Snapping Turtles and Softshells

Traditional old-time mountain people are fond of calling the four-footed reptiles found in the hills "turkles." Clarence Martin of Ellijay, Georgia, recalls that "turkles were a white man's food." Since turtles are eclectic in their dietary rambles, loving blackberries as well as rabbits, they produce a strange and wonderfully wild taste.

When cooking the snapping turtle, after removing the head, be very careful not to touch the head for at least twenty-four hours, as the nerves remain alive for at least that amount of time.

—*Native Indian Wild Game, Fish & Wild Foods Cookbook*

Mountain people called snapping turtles "mud turkles" and people loved to make a soup out of them. There's something about a snapping turtle, the reflexes stay there. To kill one you have to chop its head off and turn him on his back. He'd keep those legs moving. After hours, you could go back and touch one where his legs were sticking up and he'd move.

They had a saying in the mountains that if a mud turtle got ahold of you, he wouldn't turn loose of you until it thundered. They were pretty aggressive. Once we got one, we get him on a log, put a stick out for him to snap, and stretch his neck out and chop it. That head would lie there, holding on to that stick. If you left him where his legs were down, he'd crawl off. We'd leave him there for hours, on his back.

You found turtles in swampy areas. One of our chickens was down in the swamp at the bottom of Whiskey Bill Mountain and a turtle reached up and got him by the leg and was trying to pull him under. I took a hoe and flipped the turtle out.

In preparing a turtle to eat, you first cut the bottom plate off, then just cut around the shell; then you cut his tendrils next to the shell.

—MARK WOODY OF WOODSTOCK, GEORGIA

Mountain folklore is full of references to large snapping turtles that were often found along lower elevation creeks and branches. If you got bit by one, so the saying went, "he won't turn you loose till it thunders." Or, others said, "until the sun goes down." But once you got the turtle's head chopped off (still biting for hours), the meat was usually worth the trouble.

The soft-shell turtle is a delicacy, also, and cooked very much like the hard-shell. The way Edna Lewis's family did it, they would catch a turtle and put it in a small barrel of water. Then when ready to cook it, "you poke a stick into the barrel. The cooter will snap onto it and then you can pull him from the barrel…Next remove the head with a sharp ax."

~

Turtle Stew

2 pounds turtle meat	1 large onion, chopped
2 quarts water	1 cup potatoes, diced
4 tablespoons butter	1 can tomato soup
1 clove garlic	

Cut turtle meat into bite-size pieces, and boil in 2 quarts of boiling water for 20 minutes. Remove and save stock. In a Dutch oven, melt butter; add garlic and cook slowly until lightly browned. Add onion and lightly floured turtle meat, carefully turning until brown. Pour part of stock over this, and simmer for several hours until meat is tender. Add diced potatoes, tomato soup, and rest of stock and cook 30 minutes more.

—*University of Georgia Extension Service*

~

We caught a snapping turtle once; he was bigger than this steering wheel. We put him in the back of my truck and we were poking him. That thing rared back and struck and he hit the bed of my truck, a '72 model Ford, made out of real metal. He put a dent in the bed of that truck. He had a big old head on him. They're good eatin'. Everyone compares the meat to chicken. It's a white clean meat. I'd have to say it'd be more like frog legs than chicken, but it's good eatin', though.

—Anthony Llewellen of Athens, Alabama

FRESH, FRESH VEGETABLES
And the Tradition Continues

It is time to eat. Here is supper. Black-Eyed Peas with Ham Hock...Fried Okra...Country Corn Bread...Sweet Potato Pie...You talk of supping with the gods. You'd just done it, for who but a god could have come up with the divine fact of okra?

—James Dickey, Jericho

Nothing is more enjoyable on a bright summer day than a serving of nicely cooked vegetables fresh off the vine. Such was the great eating delight of southern mountain people during the sweaty hard months of the year. Hill country gardens, brimming over with the season's bounty and situated close to homesteads, enabled housewives to fill their aprons full of beans, tomatoes, okra, cucumbers and such for sumptuous midday repasts.

Insistence on fresh vegetables has been a time-honored tradition across the Appalachian hill country—indeed throughout the entire South. No less a nineteenth-century culinary personage than north Georgia's Mrs. Annabella Hill wrote of this freshness fetish in her 1820 treatise, *Mrs. Hill's Southern Practical Cookery and Receipt Book*:

> Vegetables intended for dinner should be gathered early in the morning. Only a few can be kept twelve hours without detriment. When fresh-gathered they are plump and firm and have a fragrant freshness no art can give them again when they have lost it by long keeping, though it will refresh them a little to put them in cold water before cooking.

During the Depression years in the Carolina Piedmont, my father, Wade Vertell Dabney, carried out this freshness tradition in a grand manner. Every April, using one of his favorite mules, he would personally lay off his quarter-acre sweet corn patch strictly for home consumption. The site always was near our home—usually just beyond Mother's garden. Beginning with his first planting of sweet corn (an ancestor of today's Silver Queens and supersweets), he followed up every two weeks by planting another few rows. That meant that we were assured of fresh corn from mid-June right on through the summer months.

I remember fondly Daddy's going out at daybreak when the dew was still glistening and bringing in an armload of fresh corn. Is there any wonder that the fried corn we had at the noontime dinner was at its wondrous and sugary sweet zenith? The same was true for vine-ripe tomatoes, crowder peas, okra, butter beans, and the like. When these resources were combined with Mother's kitchen wizardry, we were well on our way, as James Dickey rhapsodized, to supping with the gods.

And the tradition continues. Typical of many, my wife, Susanne, scion of the Southern old school (from Cheraw, South Carolina), makes a weekly produce pilgrimage to the fabulous Harry's Farmers Market in Alpharetta or to the closer-in Buford Highway Farmers Market, and usually succeeds in hauling home the freshest veggies obtainable. During the summer months, she will go down to the giant Georgia Farmers Market and pack her Honda hatchback with bushels of beans, corn, and the like plus a watermelon or two.

This tradition is confirmed by PBS cooking guru and friend Nathalie Dupree, who cites the region's persistent passion for fresh vegetables. Our ancestors took their vegetable cue from Thomas Jefferson who considered the products of his garden the focal point of a summertime meal. Jefferson even considered meat to be a mere "condiment" for vegetables!

Again to return to my youthful days: At our home and that of our neighbors, it was not unusual to see dinner tables laden with at least two or three green vegetables, plus a couple of yellow ones such as squash and yellow corn, plus, of course, sliced tomatoes. On this latter item, my mother always sprinkled a light dash of sugar to tone down the acidity. In any event, the tomatoes tasted just wonderful when combined with the butter beans, corn, squash, and the like that everyone consumed with great gusto.

Following the ever-present corn, the primary vegetables of the Appalachian farmstead over the years were beans, peas, turnips, cabbage, and sweet potatoes. For a time during colonial days, settlers feared the "poisonous nightshade plants"—tomatoes and white potatoes. Thomas Jefferson, in his usual fashion, took the lead on the matter, eating his tomatoes with great abandon and with no ill effect. His fellow Blue Ridge countrymen soon followed suit. As for white potatoes, the impasse was broken when word spread about a band of Scotch-Irish Virginia settlers who survived a winter on nothing but white potatoes. Thereafter, the "Irish Potato" became an Appalachian and American staple.

Joe Gray Taylor rated turnips high on the list of frontier vegetables, followed closely by sweet potatoes. And, of course, there were the invaluable wild vegetables such as the pokeweed, the base for "poke sallet," and wild cresses that mountain people loved and called "creases." Azzie Fouts Waters of East Ellijay, Georgia, recalled that creases grew wild on their Dawson County farm and that everyone cooked them in the early spring. One neighbor "would come and get big sackfuls across the creek in our bottom in the spring of the year."

By the 1800s, Appalachian mountain and foothill farms had a wide variety of home-grown vegetables in cultivation as well as fruits such as apples and peaches. These were supplemented by wild berries, nuts, and honey from the forests looming nearby. In addition to the old standards, no respectable farm would be found without its proud plots of sorghum cane, sweet potatoes, turnips, cabbages, onions, and the old standby, pumpkins. Professor Duane Oliver, who grew up on Hazel Creek at the eastern edge of the Great Smoky Mountains, recalled that the entire settlement raised pumpkins. They buried them under corn fodder in their barn lofts to keep them from freezing during winter. At harvesttime, they sliced them in rings and hung them up to dry in the sunshine. To reconstitute the dried pumpkin took only a good soaking and simmering in a fireplace pot. The result was a tempting dish that could be served with butter and honey.

There was a little ditty that gained fame perhaps a bit farther north that spotlighted the pumpkin's importance to every farm:

> *We have pumpkins at morning*
> *And pumpkins at noon*
> *If it was not for pumpkin*
> *We would be undoon.*

A family reunion is a great time to have a sumptuous and scrumptious spread of food, particularly fresh vegetables. That was no exception when the Roberts family held their reunion in the 1940s in Gwinnett County, Georgia.

Sweet potatoes were a favorite of the Indians, who taught the settlers a lot about how to cook them, particularly how to boil and mash them for puddings. But the tubers were a natural for baking right in the coals of a frontier fireplace or in a Dutch oven. Many families survived on sweet potatoes during tough times such as the Civil War and particularly during the rugged Reconstruction years.

The Appalachian vegetable bounty came as a result of hard and steady work by all members of a family. As Gladys Russell noted in her book, *Call Me Hillbilly*, "We were able to live because we worked—and we worked hard. Practically all of our food was grown on our place. The planting, hoeing, harvesting, and canning ran into long hours of work for us…" Indeed.

For a bit more vegetable folklore plus recipes, read on, dear reader…

Corn

From Soup to Dessert, an Appalachian Favorite

I know a valley green with corn
Where Nottely's waters roil and run
From the deep hills where first at morn
It takes the color of the sun.

—Byron Herbert Reece

~

[Fried corn] is fine for breakfast, and is sometimes introduced as a side dish
at dinner.

—*Lettice Bryan,* The Kentucky Housewife *(1839)*

One of my lasting childhood memories is the scrumptious stewed corn that came from my late mother's wood-burning stove. Actually, it was what we today call "fried corn," in that it was cooked in a fry pan—being stewed in its own milk. (My mother's cast-iron fry pan, by the way, was the same kind that I often use today in our home in north Atlanta; you can't beat 'em!)

I can't recall whether Mother used bacon drippings in her fried corn mix, a tradition across the upper South. But I do recall vividly the corn's taste—a sugary sweetness beyond parallel, more satisfying even than today's supersweet hybrids. In every respect, the 1940s era fried corn blended perfectly with the wonderful array of vegetables that she put on the table—crowder peas, tomatoes, butter beans, squash, and the like. It wasn't just a one-time or a Sunday occurrence. The big vegetable spread was routine throughout the summer for every noontime "dinner." And the lot of it so, so fresh.

As I mentioned before, throughout the summer at our upstate South Carolina farm, the veggies would be plucked off the stalk or vine the very morning that they went on our table at noon. That resulted—in the case of corn—from my father's splendid planting plan; he had new rows of fresh "roast'n'ears" coming onstream virtually every week throughout the summer.

Fried Corn

"Fried corn, that's the best," declared Ernest Parker. "Mother used just enough grease to season that fresh corn…that and a little salt and pepper."

"Nannie" Taylor Jones, who lived to be 103 years old and had a gorgeous lifetime view of Paris Mountain, South Carolina, was famed for her fried corn. "It was the country butter she put in it, that's what made it so good," said her daughter Lib Dabney, my sister-in-law and a superb cook in her own right.

For fried or creamed corn, mountain people insist on white corn. North Carolina's Beth Tartan quoted her chemistry professor, the late Charles Higgins, as saying yellow corn was good only for horses.

In my experience, there are two key elements necessary to producing a delicious dish of fried corn. First, make sure you buy a superior sweet corn variety such as the traditional Silver Queen or the new hybridized "super-sweet" varieties. Second—and almost as important—use precision when "milking" the ears of corn. If you use a "corn cutter," try to slice off only the tips of the grains, then use a table knife to scrape the milk into your bowl. A better way is to use a sharp knife to slice open the corn tips lengthwise on each row—called "cream-style cutting"—then use a spoon or the back of a knife to scrape out the corn milk. (Park Seed Company of Greenwood, South Carolina, sells a corn cutter by mail order that also does a good job; it slices open the grains vertically and scrapes out the milk.)

Using a gritter, Lula Conrad "grits" not-yet-hard corn in preparing to bake gritted corn bread. In earlier days, mountain families made their gritters by punching holes in a sheet of tin.

And what about sugar? Purists frown on adding any sugar to the mix since corn is loaded with its own sugar. Some mountain folk, however, have been known to add a dab of sugar when fixing a corn fry, particularly in modern days if the corn is not totally fresh or has been frozen.

Blue Ridge Fried Corn

8 ears of corn (medium size)   *6 tablespoons butter*

Small strip salt pork   *½ cup milk*

Salt and pepper to taste

Use fresh sweet corn. Shuck and silk corn. Then, using a large bowl and a sharp knife, slice down the rows of grain. Then, using a spoon, scrape the "milk" into the bowl. Cut the fatback into thin strips, and fry them first in an iron skillet until they are crisp. (Two teaspoons of bacon drippings can be substituted for the salt pork.) Pour the drippings into the bowl with the corn, and mix with melted butter, salt, and freshly ground pepper. Pour entire mixture into fry pan, and set on medium. Simmer for about a half hour, stirring periodically. Add milk or half-and-half if necessary to come up with a thick, sticky consistency. Add salt and pepper.

Roasted Corn

Country folk in earlier days loved to roast their corn, shuck and all, in a bed of hot hickory coals, achieving a superb nutty taste. Modern-day cooks favor grilling ears of corn, either in the shuck or in tinfoil, after first dipping them in warm water. Even better perhaps is to roast them in an oven.

Here's an oven-roast recipe adapted from one offered by Savannah's Damon Fowler in his masterful work, *Classical Southern Cooking*. As Damon points out, it's best to pull corn fresh from the field to get the most flavor:

Roasted Whole Ears of Corn

8 large ears of corn   *Unsalted butter*

Salt and black pepper

from a pepper mill

> *Roasted ears are certainly the greatest delicacy that ever came in contact with the palate of man...I defy all the arts of French cookery...to produce anything so delightful.*
>
> —WILLIAM COBBETT, EIGHTEENTH-CENTURY ENGLISHMAN

Preheat oven to 400°F. Soak corn in a basin of cold water for 10 minutes. Pull back shucks without breaking them. Rinse and remove silks under cold water. Trim out brown spots or worm holes. Return the husks up around ear and twist to seal. Place in oven and roast for about 20 minutes, just enough to make ears tender when gently pressed. Remove from oven (use kitchen mitts). Shuck the corn, cleaning off any remaining silks and place in a warm serving bowl. Serve promptly with fresh butter, salt, and pepper.

In preparation for cooking a corn dish, Mollie Running Wolf of Cherokee pounds corn the old-fashioned Indian way.

~

Corn, of course, reigned supreme almost from Day One in colonial times as the staple of Appalachian foods, being so nutritious, so easy to grow, and so versatile.

In the 1530s, Hernando de Soto, the Spanish explorer and the first European to set foot in the Blue Ridge country, watched with fascination as Indian tribes celebrated the arrival of the first ears of corn with their Green Corn Festival/ Dance. He noted also the importance of maize in the natives' diet. Earlier, Columbus had found maize in Cuba, being "most tasty boiled, roasted, or ground into flour."

It is no wonder that in Virginia's Jamestown colony, one of the first laws called for each settler to plant a set number of acres in maize. This guaranteed that people and horses could be properly fed and that there would be enough left over (hopefully) for their whiskey stills!

Indeed, had it not been for the role of corn and the help received from the Indians in the early 1600s, starvation would have wiped out even more of the early immigrants. White settler raids on Indian cornstocks caused some of the earliest disputes between the natives and the new Americans.

Thanks to the benevolent Indians, who showed the newcomers how to grow the fabulous maize, the settlers learned that green corn could be roasted, fried, or boiled. And that it took only a bit of salt to turn the dish into a gourmet treat.

The settlers soon learned that by allowing the ears of maize to dry on the stalk, nature would perfectly preserve each one for the winter. In this dried state, it was always available for use in baking bread, after being pounded by hand into meal. In later years, stone-mill grinding—in gristmills erected next to streams up and down the Appalachians—became universal. The resulting meal provided the base for the colonists' bread mainstays—ash cakes, cornpones, mush, spoon bread, and fritters as well as corn puddings and custards including hasty pudding. And dare we leave out popcorn and parched corn? (Many of the corn bread variations can be found in the Breads section).

> *Grandpa always said a man with a patch of corn could get along all right even if he didn't have a copper in his jeans.*
>
> —JOHN PARRIS,
> *THESE STORIED MOUNTAINS*

It is no wonder, therefore, that corn became the number one crop across the Appalachian/Blue Ridge region, and, indeed, zoomed ahead of "King Cotton" acreage in the entire South. By the 1840s, Tennessee led the nation in corn production. Up until 1935, the average Southern family consumed five hundred pounds of cornmeal a year, five times that of the rest of the U.S. This explains why—up until a couple of generations ago—mountain people ate corn in some form or fashion at all three meals, and in between as well.

> *Shelled corn could be parched. This is not done anymore, but the corn was fried until golden brown, and then, if desired, coarse-ground in the coffee mill or corn grinder.*
>
> —DUANE OLIVER, HAZELWOOD,
> NORTH CAROLINA

Thomas Jefferson delighted his guests in Paris in the late 1700s when he served them corn on the cob. The method that the early colonists used, that holds true yet today, is to drop shucked and silked green corn into a pot of salted boiling water for three or four minutes. The ears are served with plenty of butter and salt and pepper to taste.

Corn Pudding

Stewed corn and creamed corn were frequently taken a step further in the cooking of fresh corn pudding. Throughout the Appalachian and Blue Ridge country, people enjoyed eating what many called "a big bait" of corn pudding to celebrate the arrival of summer. For this recipe, we thank Linda Arnold, who with her husband, Stan, owns the Grandview Lodge in Waynesville, North Carolina. Their tables during the summer and fall reflect the season's bounty from neighboring gardens and local farmers' markets.

Linda's Corn Pudding

2 eggs	4 cups fresh sweet corn
½ cup granulated sugar	kernels (about 6 ears)
2 tablespoons all-purpose flour	½ cup milk
½ cup butter or margarine, melted	

Preheat oven to 350°F. In a medium mixing bowl, beat eggs with sugar and flour. Add corn and milk, and then stir in the melted butter or margarine. Pour into greased 1½-quart soufflé dish. Bake for 55 minutes or until pudding is set and browned on top.

A further refinement of this dish was one that mountain folk called "green corn pie," baked in a casserole dish and containing most of the ingredients listed in the pudding above. Some additions were a couple of tomatoes, 2 cups of crumbled corn bread, 1½ cups of grated sharp cheese, plus 5 slices of crisp bacon. The procedure was to line the casserole dish with the slices of bacon, sprinkle over with breadcrumbs, followed by slices of tomatoes plus the corn mix above, followed by another layer of crumbs and tomatoes and corn. The topping would consist of the grated cheese plus leftover crumbs.

Corn Fritters

Fritters, referred to as "flitters" by some, is a popular corn dish that goes well with ham, chicken, and/or most summer vegetables.

Corn Fritters

1½ cups corn pulp (6 ears)	*Black pepper to taste*
1 cup all-purpose flour	*2 teaspoons baking powder*
1 teaspoon sugar	*3 eggs, separated*
1 teaspoon salt	*Deep-fat-frying oil*

Milk the ears of shucked corn, scraping the cobs well to extract all the juicy pulp. Use a fork to mash the pulp thoroughly in the bowl. Mix the flour, sugar, salt, pepper, and baking powder.

Add the corn. Beat the egg whites, and fold them into the mixture. Add flour if necessary to form a thick batter. Drop the mixture into the skillet of frying oil or bacon drippings. Fry for 1 to 2 minutes on each side until browned. Pour in additional oil as needed for frying.

After a day at the grist mill, a mountain woman in western Virginia takes home a load of cornmeal in her oxen-drawn wagon.

Old man Will Bailey, he owned all this open property in here [near Doublehead Gap, Georgia]. He built a water wheel and ground meal. He made ever' piece of that mill, except for the rock, by hand, wooden spokes and all.

It was all made out of wood. Yeah, the wheels had spokes of wood. He figured it out how to build it. The only thing he didn't make was a steel rod and the rock. He dressed the millrock, sharpened it. He was a blacksmith, he could make anything around the farm.

He didn't have a dam. Bailey Creek where he had the mill, he run a trough from the top of the shoal, put it down in the mill. Old man Will, he'd start that mill up of a morning, put that corn in the hopper, and come back home and eat breakfast, and fool around for an hour or two and go back up there. If it was ground, he would cut it off and wait for the next batch.

When I lived on Whiskey Bill Mountain right through that gap right there, a mile and a half to it, I'd bring my corn down here and leave it at the mill.

Years ago he sold that mill to a historical society in Atlanta. They came up here and tore that mill down and set it up at Lakewood and they ground corn on it. I don't know what ever happened to that mill after that.

David Bailey (right), grandson of Will Bailey, patriarch of a large mountain family near north Georgia's Blue Ridge Divide, pauses at the annual Bailey family cookout to talk with friends. His grandfather was noted for building a water-powered grist mill without building a dam, using only gravity flow water.

—Curtis Underwood,
Resaca, Georgia

Greens

Plus Pot Likker and Corn Bread

I'll never go hungry again.
—Scarlett O'Hara, hoisting turnip greens in the movie Gone with the Wind

~

Back when I was a boy, it was a must that we eat at least one mess of poke sallet
or else we were sure to have pneumonia, or maybe it was typhoid fever.
                    —The late Jimmy Townsend of Jasper, Georgia

~

Greens without corn bread is like spring without violets, a fiddle without a bow.
                    —Celestine Sibley, Atlanta Journal-Constitution

While Popeye always popped open a can of spinach in time of need, Elvis Presley—if he were still alive—would surely opt for a mess of "poke sallet," the jolly wild springtime green that pleasures many a mountain palate.

After all, "Poke Sallet Annie," one of Elvis's early hits, glorified the springtime ritual that seemingly is almost as old as the ancient Appalachians—that of housewives going out with their baskets under their arms, gathering wild greens along the creeks and roadways, from poke to dock, from wild "creases" to crow's foot. And, oh yes, lamb's-quarter. And then serving the wonderful corollary—steaming dishes of glorious pot likker, with corn bread.

"After a winter of eating dried beans," Kentucky's Sidney Saylor Farr quoted her Granny Brock, "a body needed a good mess of greens to purify the blood and give vim and vigor for spring planting."

For many, getting a springtime poke-sallet fix was indeed a psychological if not necessarily a medicinal shot in the arm. Azzie Waters remembered a saying by "old Doc McClain" of Marble Hill, Georgia, who declared that "if you'll eat one good mess of poke sallet in the spring of the year, you won't have typhoid fever."

While poke may not have been a miracle drug some held it out to be, old-timers were on to something: Greens provide an amazing variety of vitamins, especially C, plus iron and other essential minerals.

The Ulster transplants to America brought the greens craving in their genes. In the 1600s, Lowland Scots and Ulstermen, progenitors of Appalachia's "Scotch-Irish," routinely ate greens and potherbs from their yards in the old country, along with their oatmeal and oatcakes.

Their Appalachian descendants continued the greens tradition, and transitioned from oatcakes to corn bread. Right off, they discovered that corn bread was (and is) a wonderful greens accompaniment, providing the perfect "pot likker" sopper. The newcomers were wowed by the greens they found in the American interior. Visiting the Carolinas in the early 1700s, Britisher John Lawson found "potherbs," wild and homegrown, all over...and lamb's-quarter (pigweed), plantain, nettles, rhubarb (dock), and comfrey...in "abundance more than I could name." It would have been easy for him to have added spinach, cabbage, sorrel, dandelion, lettuce, cresses, poke, and purslane. Even asparagus—"sparrow grass was thriving, to a miracle."

> *Turnip greens, turnip greens,*
> *Good old turnip greens,*
> *Cornbread and buttermilk*
> *And good old turnip greens.*
> —MOUNTAIN FOLK SONG

In the years following the Revolutionary War, John Brickell noticed that "Poke...grows in every Field, the tender Tops whereof may be boiled and made use of as other Greens...but the Roots are not to be meddled with, being in their Nature violent Purgers."

Indeed. Knowledgeable mountain folks have long known that while poke is an effective springtime pick-me-up, the nightshade plant has to be handled with care. Only the early first shoots should be used and even they must be parboiled before being fried and eaten. The poison fear caused Kentucky frontier wives to watch what the cows would eat before committing to do the same.

Frances Gates Hill—who lives in north Georgia's Cohutta Mountain area—recalled the story of the remote mountain mother who served her hungry family a mess of fully grown poke flavored with rabbit meat. The entire family got sick due to the poke's toxicity. Two mistakes were made—cooking mature poke weeds without adequate parboiling and second, according to Frances, not frying them in bacon grease.

Bil Dwyer of Highlands, North Carolina, gave friends a list of greens requiring parboiling. On his list were poke (boil three times); ramps (two times); broad-leaf plantain (twice); and field mustard (twice and add a dash of sugar).

Despite all the potential dangers, many mountain people still exhibit great enthusiasm and affection for the lowly weed and for greens in general, eating generous portions of greens smothered with hot pepper and sauce and, of course, plenty of hot corn bread, some onions, and maybe a piece of pork. They don't just buy a bunch of greens, they seek out a mess, denoting a generous amount that will leave no one at the table hungry.

Poke Sallet

Called "Cherokee Sallet" in some parts of east Tennessee—poke is described by many as a gourmet dish of majestic proportions. "Nothing sets off beans and 'taters like poke sallet," a Tennessean told me. "It's dee-licious; ain't nothin' better," says Arvil Wilson from his home near north Georgia's Holly Creek. "Absolutely extraordinary. But now you gotta fix it right. People comes up here in the spring of the year. They say, 'Arvil, I want you to cut me a mess of poke sallet.' They'd rather have it than turnip greens, collards, cabbage, or anything."

The word *poke* derives from the Algonquin Indian term *puc-cone*, while *sallet* comes from an ancient English expression referring to "a mess of greens." Actually the British version comes from Latin *sal*—a spread of salted greens.

Poke gets around. Its peripatetic nature is caused by its world record life-after-death seed longevity. Decades after being buried deep in the ground, poke seeds will spring back to life after a digging visit by a road-ditching machine! Every spring several poke plants pop up on the edge of my lot in Atlanta. Poke usually can be found growing on the edges of fields, in orchards, or near abandoned buildings. Frances Hill remembers the plant flourishing near where new roads were cut. "Back in the mountains, the sides of new roads would be just covered with pokeweeds." Nathalie Dupree looked forward every spring to poke's on-time arrival on her Mount Pleasant Village creek bank "about the time the dogwoods dropped their petals."

> *I* was first introduced to poke one very hot spring day when I set out to dig up my garden at Mt. Pleasant Village. My friend Grace Reeves...stood a ways away from me, watching with amusement as I amassed a knee-high pile of weeds.
>
> "Nathalie," she said, "what are you doing?" "Getting rid of these weeds," I answered. She nearly snorted. "That's poke," she said, "not a weed."
>
> —NATHALIE DUPREE, SOUTHERN MEMORIES

While most aficionados prefer their poke fresh off the stalk, some people, including Bessie Llewellyn of north Alabama, have had success in freezing poke and serving it year-round. And, of course, you can buy canned poke. Plain fried poke can be served with apple vinegar, pickle juice, or pepper sauce. Some fry poke as they would okra, after cutting it up and rolling it in cornmeal or flour.

*P*oke sallet? You bet I ate poke sallet, son, and it's good for you, got the iron in it your body needs. We broke it off when it got only three inches high. We'd make up a light batter of flour and salt and dip the poke in it and fry it just like fish. It's good that way; that's the best way to eat it.

—RUTH SWANSON HUNTER, YOUNG HARRIS, GEORGIA

⁓

Frank Pressley, a native of Cullowhee, North Carolina, near the Great Smoky Mountains, likes to cook up a mess of poke and eggs every spring to remind him of his childhood days in the mountains.

Frank Pressley's Poke and Eggs
(In Frank's own words)

Large bag of poke	*¼ cup bacon drippings*
4 eggs, boiled and chopped	*Salt and pepper to taste*
6 slices of bacon	*A few drops of vinegar*
A sprinkle of sugar	*A handful of dock (if available)*

I break off just the tender leaves on top and the buds. I leave it where it'll sucker out and make more. I take the tender shoots to the house, chop it up and put it in the pot, cover it with water, and parboil it 5 minutes. If dock is available, I put in a handful to cook with the poke. I pour that water off and parboil it again for 5 minutes with salt and pepper, and drain it off for the second time. Then I fry the bacon good and crisp and put the poke in the skillet and crumble the bacon up in it. I heat it good and fry it 'till it's sorta tender, put a lid on it and smother it a bit and then put a few drops of vinegar on it and sprinkle the chopped eggs on top. Sometimes I sprinkle a little sugar on it. Usually, though, I like it pretty natural.

⁓

After their first springtime greens fix, mountaineers loved to move on to a variety of "potherb" greens through the spring and early summer and then into the late fall…turnip greens (the most popular), followed by crow's foot, watercress (or creases), dock, lamb's-quarter (wild spinach), dandelion, and branch lettuce.

"We'd go get watercress out of the creek," recalled Betty Jo Hyde Bailey. "We'd wade in the creek and get it out. It's just like a palm, grows in the creek."

Dandelion

Nutritious dandelion was an early greens favorite also. Sidney Farr and her "Granny Brock" experienced good luck finding dandelion even when the leaves were as small as squirrel ears; that's when Granny thought they were at their height of taste.

Here is a recipe for a dandelion salad adapted from John LaRowe's recipe collection, *What's Cookin' in the Mountains*. For many years John operated the famed Mark of the Potter shop on north Georgia's picturesque Soquee River. He sold the shop to Jay Bucek who has reissued the cookbook. This recipe was offered by Debbie Koenig:

Debbie's Dandelion Salad

5 strips bacon	*2 tablespoons sugar*
1 egg	*Pinch of salt*
1 cup water	*Milk*
1 tablespoon flour	*2 quarts young tender dandelion*
Vinegar to taste	*picked before blossom appears*

Brown bacon and break up into short pieces. Mix egg with bacon drippings. Pour in the cup of water. Mix flour and water to thicken; add to bacon mixture. Add vinegar, sugar, and salt. Put in milk for desired thickness. Cut up dandelion greens and add just before eating.

Lamb's-Quarter, Dock, Crow's Foot

Most mountain cooks such as Mrs. Elvie Corn of Dodgin Creek near Cullowhee cooked their lamb's-quarter and speckled dock the same way they did poke sallet—that is, parboil the greens a few times, then fry them in bacon grease along with chopped onions. They had to be fast on their feet to harvest the dock, though, since groundhogs also had a special appetite for it.

Another early spring mountain favorite was crow's foot, or "Indian mustard," whose leaf pattern resembles the foot of a crow. A favorite cooking method was to scald the greens with hot grease, then serve the dish with a bit of vinegar on top.

"Branch lettuce," found growing in dark and damp hollows where water flows warm from the earth, was a favorite green. From these they made a wilted salad with a hot sauce of vinegar, bacon drippings, and a dash of sugar.

Many cooks like to mix up their greens—watercress, mustard, lamb's-quarter, and dock —and "wilt" them as Mrs. Corn did, sometimes serving them with crisp bacon and wild ramps and sometimes with a topping of sliced boiled eggs.

> *Speckled dock, lamb's tongue, and branch mustard provided a support of green food, especially necessary to prevent pellagra.*
>
> —DUANE OLIVER, HAZELWOOD, NORTH CAROLINA

"Mountain Creases" (Watercress)

The very first greens to appear—and a sign that spring was on its way—was wild watercress, more familiarly known as "creases," "creasy greens," "field cress," or "cressies." The wild creases exhibit a more full-bodied flavor than cultivated watercress.

While Frances Hill didn't remember creases when she was growing up, they are now abundant on her farm near the Cohuttas. "They grow on the east side of a hillside, in lowland, black bottomland."

My son-in-law, Anthony Llewellyn, a tall, high-cheeked part-Cherokee and a product of the Tennessee–north Alabama foothills, is enthusiastic about field creases also. He calls them "turnip greens gone wild. You'll see whole fields bloomed out with yellow blooms. They're good eatin'. Growing up, lots of time all we had to eat was corn bread and field peas and perch and creases. My mother, Muda, cooked the creases with fatback. 'Course back then you put fatback in everything. Nothing flavors greens better than fatback."

Turnips and Mustard

Without doubt the most popular greens that mountain folk depended on were turnips and mustard. By planting turnips in the spring and fall—supplemented by the early wild greens—families had virtually a year-round greens supply.

"Boy, did we love turnip greens," recalled Mark Woody. "Mother would cook the greens in a pot along with a piece of fatback. If we didn't have fatback, she'd put in a little lard." Traditional recipes call for parboiling then frying the greens in the grease of fatback or bacon.

Carolinian Martha Pearl Villas agrees to the parboiling and also adds a bit of sugar to reduce the bitterness. Here's a recipe adapted from one Mrs. Villas gave to her son James, a noted chef and food writer who wrote, with his mother's help, a sprightly and entertaining book, *My Mother's Southern Kitchen*.

Martha's Turnip and Mustard Greens

3 pounds mixed fresh turnip and mustard greens	*1 teaspoon salt*
	1 teaspoon sugar
1 lean chunk streak-o-lean pork, slice part way through	*Onions, finely chopped*
	Cider vinegar

Remove stems; rinse greens, then soak them in water 15 minutes to remove any trace of grit. Rinse again, place in a large pot, and add enough water to half cover. Add the meat, salt, and sugar, and bring to a boil. Reduce the heat to low, cover, and simmer the greens 1½ hours. Drain well in a colander, remove, and discard the meat. Serve the greens hot with the onions and vinegar to be spooned over each serving.

Pot Likker: The Wonderful Aphrodisiac*

One of the really delicious derivatives of greens is the delightful "pot likker"—some call it an aphrodisiac—the super-concentrated leftover liquid that combines the full nourishing taste of the greens, meat, and salt. While much has been written about this great mountain delicacy, pot likker is looked on as one of the South's great contributions to the culinary art.

Louisiana Governor Huey Long called pot likker "the noblest dish the mind of man has yet conceived," and entered a legendary verbal duel with *Atlanta Constitution* editor Julian Harris on the merits of dunking or crumbling corn bread into the dish.

In the modern era, beloved *Atlanta Constitution* columnist Celestine Sibley doesn't take sides on the dunking issue but comes down foursquare on the side of corn bread as a perfect side dish. "Greens without corn bread," Celestine loves to point out, "are like spring without violets, a fiddle without a bow."

While spring greens make great pot likker, traditional mountain-style pot likker calls for a combination of cabbage and pork shoulder. This recipe is adapted from one originated with Rubye Bumgarner of the Sylva, North Carolina, area:

Mountain Pot Likker

Portion of pork shoulder	*1⅛ teaspoons salt*
Head of cabbage	*2 small pods red pepper*
¼ teaspoon black pepper	

Place the pork shoulder in a pot with water, and simmer for 2 hours. Remove core from cabbage, quarter it, and place in pot. Add salt and peppers, and simmer the complete mixture for 2 hours. Add water to hold the initial amount. After the final water is added, continue cooking for another half hour. Serve the pot likker with corn bread.

Cornmeal Dumplings

Pot likker dumplings are another beautiful derivative. Mrs. Henry W. Lix of Oak Ridge, Tennessee, offered the following recipe to the Oak Ridge Junior Service League

---

*Author's note: Anyone who would like a periodic pot likker fix is advised to visit Atlanta's great "country" restaurant—Mary Mac's on Ponce de Leon Avenue—formerly owned and operated by the late, great Margaret Lupo. Mary Mac's offers turnip greens along with pot likker as a regular item, plus, of course, great corn bread pones and muffins.

*M*ama would boil poke and boil it and
boil it. Then when it was so mushy
she'd change the water then she'd put it in
hot bacon grease and fry it.

—Lib Dabney,
Jackson, South Carolina

for inclusion in the league's recipe collection. It originated in Tennessee and traveled to Alabama and Texas well over a century ago and was handed down to Mrs. Lix from her mother and grandmother:

Pot Likker (Cornmeal) Dumplings

You must have one large pot of turnip greens boiled with ham hocks. Start from scratch, with turnip greens fresh out of the patch and smoked ham bone or hocks. Or use chopped turnip greens canned, simmered an hour with the ham, which should already be boiled tender. Mix 2 tablespoons minced onion (fresh, young ones with part of the green tops are best), into 1½ cups unsifted cornmeal. Season with ½ teaspoon salt and ¼ teaspoon black pepper. Stir in enough boiling pot likker from the greens to make a dough. When slightly cooled, mix in 1 egg thoroughly. Take this by spoonfuls and shape into small patties about ½-inch thick. Lay them gently on top of the simmering greens. Cover and simmer 15 minutes until done.

~

Greens dumplings are similar to a "Turnip Greens and Corn Dodgers" dish that was one of the favorites at Oak Hill, Martha Berry's ancestral home on the Oostanaula River near Rome, Georgia, in northwest Georgia's Appalachian foothills. The late Miss Berry

*A*n otherwise charming and sensible New York friend of mine is fond of
recounting that Southerners throw out the only part of the turnip that is
edible and eat "the part that everybody else in the world throws away."
This is far from being true, however. To the contrary, all parts of the turnip
have always enjoyed a regular place on Southern tables.

—Damon Fowler, *Classical Southern Cooking*

was the founder of famed Berry College (my alma mater) which has the world's largest campus (28,000 acres) including its own mountain (Lavender). Dodgers are a form of cornmeal dumpling in ball form:

Turnip Greens and Corn Dodgers

3 pounds turnip greens	*Salt to taste*
4 cups water	*1 teaspoon sugar*
½ pound streak-of-lean meat	*1½ cups cornmeal*

Thoroughly wash the turnip greens. Place 1½ cups water and streak-of-lean meat in boiler and boil for 30 minutes. Place greens in separate boiler with 2 cups water, and parboil for 7 minutes. Pour off this liquid to remove bitterness. Add greens and salt to boiling meat and liquid. Cook for 45 minutes to 1 hour or until greens are tender. Add the teaspoon of sugar. Remove turnip greens from stock. Prepare corn dodgers by taking 1½ cups of cornmeal, adding 4 tablespoons of boiling water (more if needed so that meal will stick together), and shape by hand into small round balls so that they will not pull apart. Have the stock from the turnip greens at a rolling boil, drop the cornmeal balls in. Cook 15 minutes. When done, dodgers will be soft and pale green. Serve with the greens. Voilà! Or perhaps I should use a mountain expression for this: Sounds plumb scrumptious!

> *I have never tasted meat,*
> *Nor cabbage, corn nor beans,*
> *Nor fluid food one half as sweet*
> *As that first mess of greens.*
> —COTTON NOE,
> *THE LOOM OF LIFE*, 1912

Ramps
("Tennessee Truffles")
Wild Leek of the Mountains

A garlic is a wimp compared to ramps.

— *Carl Dodd, Blue Ridge, Georgia*

~

The only way the non-eater [of ramps] can protect himself [from the odor] is either to run or to eat some himself.

— *Former Georgia governor Zell Miller*

~

I love ramps; they'll shore keep people out of your face when you're trying to talk.

—*Claude Call, Ellijay, Georgia*

~

[Ramps are] the stinkenest vegetable known to man.

—*John Parris,* Mountain Cooking

Ramps reign royally in Cosby, Tennessee, every April. The Cocke County community, nestled in the shadow of the Great Smoky Mountains, goes wild over the odoriferous mountain leek, staging a Ramp Festival, crowning a Ramp Queen, and giving visitors the opportunity to fill up on ramps raw, ramps fried, ramps boiled, ramps sautéed, ramps jellied, and ramps pickled. Plus ramps and eggs, ramps and potatoes, ramp soups and ramp salads.

But Cosby isn't alone. Ramps are celebrated across the lofty, fertile, and shady coves in Southern Appalachia—those reaching above three thousand feet, that is—where the lowly leek finds near perfect growing conditions. The Appalachian "ramp country" ranges from West Virginia to north Georgia.

~

Wild ramps, a member of the lily family, and called "Tennessee Truffles" by some, flourish in buckeye flats in such places as Cruso (under Mount Pisgah in Haywood County, North Carolina); on Big Frog Mountain and Cohutta Mountain in north Georgia; in the Monongahela National Forest in West Virginia; across North Carolina's Nantahala Mountains; and, of course, in the deep coves of the Smoky Mountains in the vicinity of Cosby and Cleveland, Tennessee. Ramp Cove, located in Georgia's Rabun County, is "rampant with ramps" each springtime, along with moss-covered buckeyes. There's another Ramp Cove, in Swain County, North Carolina, near Hazel Creek.

Several West Virginia towns, among them Helvetica and Richmond, stage ramp cook-offs and festivals. In North Carolina, ramp conventions take place in Waynesville, Robbinsville, and Cherokee. Cleveland, Tennessee, honors the ramp with a festival of its own. The Mount Rogers, Virginia, Fire Department puts on an annual ramp cook-off.

And all this for a foul-smelling but wonderfully flavorful wild leek—*allium tricoccum*—that resembles the "lily of the valley" and that, some say, will ward off bad colds. Schoolmarms, faced with a cloud of ramp aroma, have called weeklong spring recesses until the strong smell has had time to blow over. Mountain wives have been known to bar their husbands from their beds until the strong-flavored ramp

The harvesting of ramps in the Great Smoky Mountains National Park has some people worried the wild onions will be picked into extinction. Known for their pungent flavor and strong odor, ramps are becoming increasingly popular.

Ramp festivals have brought new attention to the lowly leek, and now even trendy Northeastern restaurants are serving them up as exotic springtime delicacies. In May about 5,000 people attended the 64th annual ramp festival in Waynesville [North Carolina].

Possibly as a result, ramps apparently are becoming harder to find in the Smokies. A once–dense patch behind park headquarters is gone, and pickers report having to go higher into the mountains each year to find a good crop.

has been fully extruded from their spouses' skin. Then there's the story, perhaps apocryphal, about the Tennessee judge who was repulsed by a foul-smelling, ramp-eating chicken thief. Fearful of a jail riot, he held his nose and hurriedly passed sentence: "Three months, you stinko…and get as far away as you can go."

Despite all these seemingly repulsive ramp reverberations, old-time mountain people love the wild leek. Take Gary Davis, a retired conservation ranger from Fannin County, Georgia.

"If I don't get some ramps to eat in the spring, I may not make it to the fall. It slicks you off [as a tonic], makes you feel good and do good all summer. I especially love ramps in soufflés and with eggs."

Gary's wife, Dawn, spoke up: "There's a ramp casserole with potatoes that I like, and one with onions and sausage and cheese. It's wonderful."

Gary agreed. (Dawn's recipe is upcoming.)

Southern Appalachian folk are not the only ones to appreciate the flavorful ramp. Visitors travel long distances to check out the Appalachian wild leek. Four years ago, an English farm couple—Oliver and Anne Walson—flew from Cambridge to the U.S. to taste freshly dug West Virginia ramps. (Ramps grown in northern England and Scotland, by the way, were relished as far back as the Elizabethan era.)

Apparently the key to preparing and eating ramps without incurring the wrath of loved ones is to parboil them a bit and then use them in your dishes sparingly, as you would garlic.

Appalachian highlanders have been enjoying ramps for centuries, having gotten the idea— as we have for many of our basic foods—from the Amerindians. The Cherokees called them Wa-S-Di, "a smelly business but good." Frank Pressley grew up on ramps during his youth at Cullowhee, North Carolina. "We grew ramps every year when we were growing up. There was a place we named Ramp Cove, way back high on Cullowhee Mountain. To me, the ramp was a cross between garlic and onion. It has a taste and a smell that's delicious to me, but terrible to smell on people's breath. Mama would fry ramps in grease, but not too long a time. We enjoyed eating 'em with a sprinkling of vinegar. It's kinda like a vinegar and oil that you put on salads today."

Smokies Superintendent Karen Wade said the park service cannot officially permit the removal of native plants from the park. Unofficially, limited ramp harvesting has been allowed ever since the park was formed 62 years ago. "It's allowable to collect enough to do your scrambled eggs," park spokesman Bob Miller said.

A group of backcountry rangers wrote Smokies headquarters six years ago, concerned about a ramp decline. That prompted a five-year study that recently concluded the park's ramps are over-harvested.

The study doesn't make a recommendation, but it does cite the example of Canada's Gatineau Park, which has been protecting ramps since 1981.
—Associated Press dispatch from Gatlinburg, Tennessee, August 29, 1996

I was invited to go on a ramp dig early one May morning by Frank Elliott, the tax commissioner of Gilmer County, Georgia, and one of the world's greatest ramp devotees. Every year, Elliott leads a group of friends on a ramp excursion—usually to the Cohutta Mountains. After an early morning dig, he fries up some ramps for lunch right on the scene.

The wild mountain leek looks innocent enough. But bite into a raw one and you're sure to be a social outcast for a week.

I was unable to get up in time to join Frank's 6 A.M. excursion departure from Ellijay, two hours north of my home. But Frank saved and presented to me in his office on the Ellijay Square a gallon of the little rascals. They appeared, when shaken, to swim around in the jar like happy shrimp. But boy do they pack power.

Frank waxed eloquently about ramps, holding up the jarful and declaring that "Joe, after eatin' some of these, you find out exactly how many friends you got! The taste just gets all in your mouth, even after you've cooked 'em down."

Frank finds ramps growing on the north side of a mountain "where the dirt is real rich and is shaded. Best time to go diggin' is the first week in May. 'Course this early March hard freeze might set 'em back a bit. Seems like we always have to walk a long way to get to 'em. They're always way off and we're wore out by the time we get back home. But they're worth the effort. The green shoots look kinda like corn when they gets up about that high (five inches).

"You can cook 'em in eggs, but my favorite way with ramps is to chop some up with fried potatoes…just chop 'em up and cook 'em all together. Just put you some grease or oil in the fry pan. Mighty tasty. I ate some the other day. There's nothing better. I like to set down with some ramps and corn bread and get me a glass of buttermilk. 'Course my wife don't like me to be around for three or four days after I eat 'em."

"Aw, he just says that," Frank's wife, Sue Parker Elliott, quickly responded with a smile. "Now I like ramps, too. But I like 'em along with potatoes, and in hushpuppies. I like to put ramps in tuna salads instead of putting in onions."

Arvil (Crockett) Wilson, who lives near the Holly Creek prong of the Cohutta Mountain chain, is a natural-born lover of ramps.

My Ellijay friend Larry Davis took me out to meet Arvil at his place in Gilmer County's Mountaintown district. We sat around Arvil's homey kitchen talking about the merits of the wild mountain leek.

"Dardis Parks," said Larry. "Everybody knows Dardis. He came in to my shop one day after he'd visited the ramp patch. I'd done some work on his car that day and I'd always heard people talk about ramps. 'Well, bless God,' Dardis said, 'I got some out here right now.' He brought in a sack of 'em boogers. He pulled that onion-looking thing back and I chewed the back end of it; it was a tasty little morsel, I tell ye. And I didn't realize that ramp odor was just staying with me. When I got home, Alice said, 'What is that?' That's the only time I ever had to sleep by myself."

Crockett smiled. "Them ramps'll shore hang with you, Larry, mighty right. If you eat a bait of 'em, you might just as well stay in the mountains; you're going to have to sleep with yourself anyway. Larry, you can vouch for that. 'Course they're not so bad atter you cook 'em up; that breaks 'em down. I usually cut mine up and fry 'em with arsh potaters. Like an onion, with salt and pepper."

Frank Elliott of Ellijay, Georgia, loves ramps enough to go digging for them every spring. Here he shows off a little jarful he brought back. Before leaving a ramp patch, Frank and colleagues fry up a batch and "eat a bait" of them on the spot.

Ramps are adaptable to many types of dishes. They can be cooked with eggs, potatoes, venison, bear meat, ham—the sky's the limit. Some cooks, such as author Sarah Belk, make a ramp and potato soup with caraway. She also likes ramps sautéed and ramps added to omelettes and pasta. Ramps are an excellent substitute for onion, in moderation, of course, and are used in corn breads, soups, grits, and puddings. Here are a few recipes that may tickle your ramp taste bud fancy:

Ramp Casserole

This first one is offered by the aforementioned Dawn Davis, who lives with her husband, Gary, off Weaver Creek Road, a picturesque valley in Georgia's mountainous Fannin County. Dawn says this is a dish you can cook in advance and reheat when you're ready to eat. Serves about five.

Dawn's Ramp Casserole

Boil your potatoes in advance and parboil your cut-up ramps in advance. In a buttered casserole dish, place a layer of sliced potatoes followed by a layer of ramps, then a layer of crumbled-up sausage and a layer of minced cheese. You put about 2 layers of all that and then on top you sprinkle some cheese plus 2 or 3 tablespoons of butter or margarine and 2 cups of milk. Let it cook until it's brown on top.

Ramps, Bacon, and Eggs

The following recipe adaptation comes courtesy of and with my thanks to West Virginia's Barbara Beury McCallum. She is author of a wondrous ramp recipe collection, *Mom & Ramps Forever*, published by the Mountain State Press in Charleston, West Virginia.

Tennessee Truffles with Bacon and Eggs

1 quart diced ramps,	*5 large eggs*
including tops	*Salt to taste*
6 strips bacon	

Wash and clean ramps as you would onions. Dice medium-fine. Par-boil in salted water until tender, and drain off water. At the same time, fry the bacon crisp, dry with paper towels, and break into small bits. Pour off half the bacon drippings. Soft-scramble the eggs in the remaining bacon drippings, adding salt. Stir in bacon bits and ramps, and serve while hot. Serves 6.

Ramp Salad

This is another adapted recipe credited to the research of Barbara McCallum, but typical of ramp salads to be found across the region.

Ramp Cove Ramp Salad

2 cups ramps, chopped fine	*Salt to taste*
2 teaspoons bacon drippings	*2 hard-boiled eggs, sliced*
2 teaspoons vinegar	

Fry in bacon drippings until tender, but do not par-boil. Season with vinegar, salt, and sliced hard-boiled eggs. Serve warm.

Ramps and Grits

This is a fancy soufflé recipe utilizing hominy—an old mountain standby—and adapted from one that *Gourmet* magazine ran in April 1983. It was reprinted in Mrs. McCallum's ramps recipe collection.

Grits Soufflé à la Ramps

3½ cups water	½ cup minced ramps
1 cup hominy grits	3½ tablespoons freshly grated
Salt to taste	Parmesan cheese
6½ tablespoons unsalted butter	Cayenne pepper to taste
2 large eggs	Black pepper to taste
¼ pound grated Cheddar cheese	

Preheat oven to 350°F. Using a heavy saucepan bring the water to a boil. Mix in grits and salt. Simmer for 25 minutes, stirring occasionally. Remove pan from the heat, add 4 tablespoons of the butter cut into small chunks, and stir mixture until butter has melted. Add the eggs one at a time. Beat well after each addition and stir in the Cheddar. In a small fry pan, fry the ramps at moderately low heat using the remaining butter (2½ tablespoons), stirring until ramps are softened. Stir the ramps mixture into the grits mixture with the Parmesan, cayenne, and black pepper. Transfer mixture to a buttered 1½-quart soufflé dish. Place dish in a baking pan, add enough hot water to the pan to reach halfway up the sides of the dish. Bake the soufflé in the middle of oven at 350°F for 1 hour, or until it is puffed and golden. Serves 6.

Fried Ramps and Potatoes

This is a favorite in the Smoky Mountains around Robbinsville, North Carolina, which stages a Ramp Festival every spring. Ramps are rampant all around Robbinsville, particularly off the spectacular new "Cherohala Skyway" (NC route 141) that connects Robbinsville with Tellico Plains. My country music friends, Bill and Wilma Millsaps (both are great guitarists, and Wilma also sings a mean solo), declare that ramp and potatoes have

Every Easter, the Bryson family would go ramp hunting in the woods, and many times I would go with them. Ramps are similar to wild green onions, although leafier, and their smell can most charitably be described as horrible. You can fry them in lard or scramble them in eggs; and, after eating them, the smell stays on one's breath for days.

One of the quickest ways to become a social outcast is to go into a crowd after a meal of ramps. The only way the non-eater can protect himself is either to run or to eat some himself.

—Zell Miller of Towns County, Georgia, The Mountains Within Me

*I*n the early days of West Virginia, and other areas in the Southern Appalachian mountains, the winter diet consisted largely of cornpone, salt pork, molasses, and dried vegetables such as beans, supplemented...by wild game.

Lacking fresh fruit and vegetables, many mountain people in isolated areas suffered from scurvy, diseases of the mouth and gums (pyorrhea), and gastric disturbances caused by the lack of vitamins and minerals.

In the very early spring, often when snow still covered shaded glens, the deep green leaves of the ramp were seen as a welcome addition to the supper table. Probably not realizing it, here was the cure for their "winter complaints," for the ramp is chock full of vitamin C.

Many ramp devotees claim they possess other magical healing powers from prevention of colds...to cleansing of the blood. They may be right, for the ramp's European cousin, the ramson, has recently been identified as having antibiotic properties.

—BARBARA B. McCALLUM, *Mom & Ramps Forever*

been known to tickle many a Graham County taste bud over the years. "They ain't nothin' better," Bill declares with a drool in his voice. The springtime Robbinsville Ramp Festival also is noted for its ramp-based hushpuppies that organizers serve with fried fish.

Robbinsville Fried Ramps and Potatoes

1 quart ramps	*3 medium-size potatoes*
3 tablespoons bacon drippings	*3 eggs*

Clean the ramps, including the leaves, and cut into 1-inch-long pieces. Peel and slice the potatoes. Fry them together in bacon fat until done. Break the eggs over the ramps and potatoes and mix thoroughly. Allow the mixture to fry 2 minutes or until eggs are cooked on bottom. Turn and fry on other side for several additional minutes. Serve hot with biscuits and fresh butter. Serves 5 to 6.

Pickled Ramps

Ramps weren't part of the diet at the home of Frances Gates Hill when she was growing up. But two years ago, someone presented some Cohutta Mountain ramps to her and asked her to pickle them.

"I'd heard of people picklin' 'em before but nobody would ever tell me how to pickle ramps," she said. But Frances decided to pickle them in her own way. She served them at her annual "crawfish boil" at her home in the Gates Chapel community near Fort Mountain, Georgia. Apparently she did everything right, because "everybody just had a fit over 'em."

Frances's Pickled Ramps
(In Frances Gates Hill's own words)

I cleaned and chopped the ramps and put them in a saucepan. Then I boiled some vinegar along with a little bit of sugar. I poured that hot vinegar mixture over the ramps, just scalded 'em. Then I sealed the mixture up the jar and put it up with my other jars of canned fruits and vegetables.

Ramp Pudding

This meat pudding featuring a strong flavoring of ramps is a favorite in the Smoky Mountains and up and down the Blue Ridge.

Blue Ridge Ramp Pudding

2½ pints ramps	6 eggs
1 cup ground beef	1 teaspoon Worcestershire sauce
1 can tomato soup	2 tablespoons butter
Salt and pepper to taste	

Preheat oven to 350°F. Clean and finely chop the ramps and parboil them. Drain off water. Set aside. Sauté the ground beef. Mix all the ingredients except for the butter and place in a buttered casserole. Top with pecan-sized chunks of butter. Bake at 350°F for 1 hour and 10 minutes or until done.

Irish Potatoes

A Slow Start But Soon a Hero

Anyone can get tired of family, husband, or friends, but who gets tired of a good, luscious baked potato, stuffed, twice baked, or plain?
—Cissy Gregg, Louisville, Kentucky, Courier-Journal

~

Along with white beans and cabbage and yams, garden potatoes were a symbol of survival in the Depression-era South.
—John Egerton, Southern Food

~

In the mountains today, baked potatoes are more popular than apple pie or hot dogs.
—TV host Mark Sohn of Pikeville, Kentucky

The potato—one of the all-time great basic foods of the Appalachians, indeed, one of its best loved and most nutritious—got off to a rocky start in pioneer America.

Dubbed "the Irish potato," in contrast to the sweet potato, the white tuber was shunned by colonial Americans right up to the mid- to late 1700s. The primary reason was fear of its poisonous nightshade family connection along with the equally feared tomato. Fears were confirmed when it was pointed out that the potato was not mentioned in the Bible. Another rumor in France linked leprosy to the lowly spud.

It is ironic that although the potato was a South American native, Europe and the British Isles embraced the vegetable in the mid-1500s, long before England's American colony at Jamestown. Indeed it became a popular dietary mainstay, first in Ireland and later in England.

Finally, in the early 1800s, Appalachian settlers joined the "Arsh 'Tater" bandwagon after learning of a pioneer Scotch-Irish settlement that survived a harsh winter on nothing but the potassium-rich white potatoes.

Being a cool-season plant, the potato was a natural for the high-altitude Appalachian valleys and coves. When acceptance finally came, mountain people became Irish potato fanatics, giving the potato near equal status to corn and beans. Potatoes were added to the region's early spring vegetable lineup that included onions, mustard, turnip greens,

Curtis Belcher, eighty-two, of Black Ridge in Floyd County, Virginia, still plants the same "taters" that his father planted, Irish potato seed that came from a Civil War veteran.

and beets. Popularity became so strong that an old saying was that "dinner is hardly worth coming home to if there are no potatoes on the table."

During the last days of February or certainly in March, mountain people slice up and plant their seed potatoes, with one or two eyes per slice. Rose Houk told of an old saying that on steep land, potatoes could be planted in up and down rows, enabling a smooth harvest by just letting the potatoes roll down the hill.

At one time, bottomland pockets across the Blue Ridge were primary areas for potato production. North Georgia farmers hauled their potatoes into Atlanta, Gainesville, and Athens for good prices. In time, big potato states like Maine and Idaho pushed the Appalachian farmer out of the big commercial market. But garden potatoes are still grown on many farms and gardens in the region.

Roast Potatoes Dutch-Oven Style

A favorite method was roasting potatoes in hot fireplace embers where they would receive a special smoky flavor, particularly with hickory or oak firewood.

"Mountain-style" potatoes called for the potatoes to be chopped and roasted in a fireplace Dutch oven. Old-timers in Sylva, picturesque county seat of Jackson County, North Carolina, and home of western North Carolina's chronicler emeritus John Parris, were partial to the Dutch-oven style of roasting. While this recipe calls for the use of a Dutch oven, the recipe works almost as well with modern-day ovens.

Sylva-Style Potatoes

5 medium-size baking
   potatoes
½ teaspoon salt

½ teaspoon black pepper
5 strips of fatback

Scrub the potatoes well with a brush. Cut them into quarters and place in Dutch oven. Sprinkle salt and pepper on top, then place the strips of fatback. Close the Dutch oven lid and place on top of hot embers. Place hot embers on top of the lid also. The length of cooking will depend on the heat. Periodically open the lid and use a long fork to check for tenderness. When tender and brown, pull them out and serve. A similar result can be obtained with a modern oven and with the use of bacon as a substitute for the fatback. Set oven at 450° and cook for about 1 hour. Check to make sure potatoes are tender and brown.

Boiled Potatoes

Winters that were not too harsh allowed mountain people to set out potatoes as early as March 1. A favorite tradition after digging up the early potatoes was to toss them into the pot, skin and all, for boiling until tender. This is still done today in many mountain kitchens.

"Next to greens, potatoes were the first vegetable to reach our table," Bill Hasty recalled. "We'd go out to our garden, take an old table fork and 'scratch' the dirt around the plants until we could locate a potato. After grappling one, we'd cover the roots so the plant could continue growing more potatoes."

Around the year 1500, the Irish were a pastoral people who kept enough goats, cows, and sheep so they could practically live on the milk (called "white meat") gathered from their flocks. Years later, when the potato arrived and the English forced the Irish to live on smaller plots, the potato replaced much of the white meat.

Still the Irish cared about milk. They drank fresh milk, sour milk, clotted milk, and buttermilk, and they used milk to make cream, curds, cheese, and butter...

The Irish boiled potatoes in their skins in a giant cast-iron pot...To stay warm they sat on the large hearth that fronted a walk-in fireplace, eating potatoes and passing mugs of buttermilk. This synergy of milk and potatoes has influenced our cooking, from scalloped potatoes to mashed potatoes and many more.

—MARK SOHN, MOUNTAIN COUNTRY COOKING

Boiled young potatoes were well loved in Waleska, Georgia, where the Hasty and Henderson families resided. The name Waleska, incidentally, derives from the Cherokee Indians. Indeed, Waleska is located in Cherokee County.

Waleska Boiled Potatoes

4 pounds spring potatoes   *3 tablespoons butter*

Salt and butter to taste

Give the potatoes a good scrubbing, then peel and cut them into 1-inch cubes. Place them in a large cooking container. Cover with water, and turn on high long enough to bring to a boil. Simmer for a half hour. When well cooked through center, place in serving dish, and cover with butter. Sprinkle salt and butter. Another boiled potato serving option is to sprinkle finely chopped spring onions over buttered and seasoned potatoes.

Mashed Potatoes

As expected, mashed potatoes quickly became a favorite across the region. Residents around the Skeena Gap area in far north Georgia have a great fondness for this dish. Skeena Gap got its name from an Indian saying that means black bear. According to the aforementioned West Fannin High School student-produced history, *Touching Home*, Skeena Gap had many black bears in the Cherokee era.

Skeena Gap Mashed Potatoes

6 potatoes (medium size)   *1 cup milk*

¼ cup butter or margarine   *2 teaspoons salt*

½ teaspoon pepper

Peel and dice potatoes. Boil them in salted water until tender. Drain. Mash potatoes with a masher, adding the butter and pepper. Add ½ cup of milk. Whip (beat) thoroughly, adding milk as necessary to achieve the desired smoothness and fluffiness. Add salt.

Because potatoes grew underground, the Irish could keep them from the hands of the landlord's tax collector, who would not deign to dig in the ground to seize them. Potatoes were good, filling fare, and people soon added them to their diet. The Irish, however, paid dearly for their almost exclusive reliance on potatoes. When blight struck the crop in the 1840s, at least a million Irish died in the resulting famine.

—Rose Houk, *Food and Recipes of the Smokies*

Potato Dumplings

Potato dumplings, introduced by the Palatine German immigrants who came south into North Carolina's Piedmont country from Pennsylvania, achieved great popularity among settlers of all immigrant extractions as well as the Native Americans who remained. Montaree Henderson Hasty, who resided near the aforementioned Waleska, turned out what her family called "the most delicious dumplings that man has ever eaten," a scrumptious early spring dish. Mrs. Hasty used fresh milk and butter along with the same type of dough strips that she used in making her highly sought-after deep-pan fruit pies. She boiled her potatoes until tender, then added the milk, butter, and thin dough strips.

Making superior dumplings is an art, and one that Mrs. Hasty well mastered, that of using the proper amounts of flour, shortening, and milk to produce a "light and bubbly" mix, avoiding a heavy grease soaking that would cause the dumplings to harden.

Potato dumplings also were considered an early spring delicacy in Hazel Creek, North Carolina, on the eastern edge of the Great Smoky Mountains. Their dumplings weren't dough strips, but balls made of dry bread. Hazel Creek native Duane Oliver recalled people "grabbed" potatoes out of the ground and boiled them in their jackets until tender. The following is from Duane's encyclopedic *Cooking on Hazel Creek* collection:

Hazel Creek Potato Dumplings

8 medium-size potatoes	*1½ teaspoons salt*
½ cup flour	*Black pepper to taste*
2 eggs, slightly beaten	*1 tablespoon minced onion*
¼ cup milk	*2 tablespoons butter*
3 slices dry bread, cut into small cubes	

Peel, slice, and cook potatoes until tender. Mash and let stand overnight. Add flour, eggs, milk, salt, and pepper, and mix well. Brown onions in butter. Add bread cubes and brown. Flatten a spoonful of potato mixture in your hand, and press a few breadcrumbs into dumpling. Roll into a ball. Repeat till mixture is used. Drop into a kettle of boiling water, and boil uncovered 20 minutes. Drain and serve at once.

Potato Cakes

According to chef, author, and public television host Mark Sohn of Pikeville, Kentucky, a traditional supper in mountain areas of western Virginia and eastern Kentucky calls for fried potato cakes to be served with soup beans, a thick slice of sweet onion, and a glass of buttermilk. Here follows a typical recipe. It calls for the use of cold mashed potatoes fresh out of the refrigerator:

Mountain Potato Cakes

2 eggs

4 cups cold mashed potatoes

1 onion, finely chopped

¼ cup flour

8 tablespoons butter

Beat the eggs and mix thoroughly into the mashed potatoes along with the onion and flour. Form into biscuit-size patties about 1-inch thick. Spread butter on each side of patty, and fry at medium temperature until golden brown on each side.

Mrs. Bill Crookshanks of Jonesboro, Tennessee, offered the following recipe for German potato cakes to the Johnson City, Tennessee, Junior Service League for its delightful *Smoky Mountain Magic* collection.

German Potato Cakes

4 medium-size raw potatoes

2 eggs, separated

1½ tablespoons flour

Salt to taste

½ teaspoon baking powder

2 teaspoons grated onion

2 tablespoons diced fried bacon

Pare and grate raw potatoes (use blender if you wish). Add beaten egg yolks, flour, salt, baking powder, onion, and bacon. Fold stiffly beaten egg whites into the mixture. Into a skillet of hot fat, drop spoonfuls of the potato cake mixture. Lightly brown on each side. Serve with applesauce. Nutmeg and cinnamon may be substituted for onion and bacon. Serves 6.

Indian Squash

A Summer Delight

Squash…is perhaps the best way to seduce a Southern man if you believe the way to a man's heart is his stomach.
— *Nathalie Dupree,* Southern Memories

Squash reach fruition right smack-dab in the middle of the Appalachian summer. And no finer dish could hill country folk enjoy, be they crookneck (yellow), acorn, cushaw (a green-and-white-striped beauty) or the fairly modern zucchini.

Several varieties of squash were on the scene as Indian favorites when the Europeans arrived and started moving down Virginia's Great Valley to populate the Appalachian interior.

Actually, American Indians were cultivating over twenty squash varieties long before the birth of Christ, some say even before native maize. As the newcomers quickly learned, the dish goes well with most meats, particularly ham and chicken.

Baking is one of the favored ways of cooking squash, using a baking pan or casserole. However, in her 1836 cookbook, *The Virginia Housewife*, Mary Randolph suggested that squash could be boiled and stewed for "the most delicate way of preparing squashes." She noted that since the squash amount could vary, "use enough cream to cover the squash in the pan."

Squash or Cimlin

Gather young squashes, peel and cut them in two; take out the seeds, and boil them till tender; put them into a colander, drain off the water, and rub them with a wooden spoon through the colander; then put them into a stew pan, with a cup full of cream, a small piece of butter, some pepper and salt —stew them, stirring very frequently until dry.

Baked Squash

Typical of the old-time baked squash dishes is the following recipe that utilizes a half pint of honey. Actually, squash, particularly cushaws, can readily absorb honey or sorghum as well as butter, giving it, in the words of Mark Sohn, a "rich and sweet" flavor. This recipe is much revered in the far north Georgia mountainous community of Hiawassee, hard by Lake Chatuge, formed by the waters of the Hiawassee River, and site of the Georgia Mountain Fair every August.

Honey-Baked Squash

4 medium squash   8 tablespoons butter
  (preferably acorn)   Black pepper
½ pint honey

Preheat oven to 350°F. Cut open the squash and clean out the seeds and pulp. Place honey in the hollow of each squash (2 teaspoons) along with a tablespoon of butter and a sprinkling of fresh pepper. In a 2-inch deep baking pan, lay squash and bake at 350°F for just over 2 hours or until the squash are soft and tender. Serves 6.

⌣

To the south of Hiawassee, in Sautee, Georgia, near the resort town of Helen, my friends John and Emily Anthony once operated a wonderful guest house and buffet-style restaurant, the Sautee Inn. Originally, in the early 1900s, it was a summer hotel, catering to people from the Georgia and Carolina coast escaping the heat. John and Emily are now retired. One of their prize recipes is this squash casserole:

Sautee Inn Squash Casserole

3 cups summer squash, chopped   1 cup breadcrumbs
1 cup onion, sliced or chopped   Salt and pepper to taste
¼ cup butter, melted   Paprika
¼ cup almonds, finely chopped   1 cup Cheddar cheese, shredded

Preheat oven to 350°F. Cook squash and onion together in small amount of water until tender. Drain well. Mix with other ingredients. Place in baking dish, and top with additional crumbs and paprika. Bake at 350°F until slightly browned, about 45 minutes.

Crookneck Squash Casserole

This second casserole is also typical of those found in the Appalachians. It demonstrates that squash can be amenable to many additional ingredients—onions, peppers, tomatoes, bacon, cheese—which blend in beautifully.

This particular colorful casserole recipe goes well with chicken or roasts. It is adapted from the *Gatlinburg Recipe Collection* published in 1986 by Nancy Blanche Cooper, and credited to Fay Hoffman who lives on Gatlinburg's Soak Ashe Creek.

Gatlinburg, I might mention, is where Susanne and I spent our honeymoon in June of 1954. Back then, Gatlinburg was a quiet, laid-back little village where gurgling mountain streams coming out of the Smoky Mountain foothills ran under rustic cabins. Ah, fond memories.

⌣

Gatlinburg Squash Casserole

8 yellow crookneck squash	1 large red or green pepper,
2 ripe tomatoes, chopped	finely chopped
½ teaspoon black pepper	2 medium onions, chopped
Buttered breadcrumbs	8 ounces Cheddar cheese, chopped
1 teaspoon salt	½ teaspoon pepper

Preheat oven at 350°F. Slice squash and parboil them for about 2 minutes. Drain well and place in a buttered casserole. Add all the other ingredients (except for buttered crumbs) and gently mix. Top with the crumbs and bake at 350°F for 30 minutes, or until bubbly and crumbs are toasty brown.

Squash Pudding

A pudding is a delightful way to utilize summer squash. Such a recipe is used often in one of north Georgia's few surviving antebellum plantation homes, Bulloch Hall. A Greek Revival masterpiece, Bulloch Hall, located in Roswell, was built in 1840 by James Stephens Bullock, son of Archibald Bulloch, Georgia's Revolutionary War–era governor. The home was the site of the marriage in 1853 of President Theodore Roosevelt's parents, Mittie Bulloch and Theodore Roosevelt. The home's original basement kitchen and its grand open hearth are still used on special occasions. The following recipe adaptation was designed initially for Dutch oven cooking in such a fireplace. This recipe, however, as well as others still used in Bulloch Hall, is adaptable to modern oven cooking.

Bulloch Hall Summer Squash Pudding

10 to 12 summer squash, sliced	½ cup cream or condensed milk
2 medium onions, chopped	4 eggs
½ cup butter	Generous amount of pepper
1 teaspoon salt	

Preheat oven at 400°F. Boil squash and onion in water until tender; drain. Place in casserole dish. Add other ingredients, mix well. Bake in 400°F oven for 35 to 40 minutes until puffy and slightly browned on top.

Cushaws ("Indian Pumpkin")

Hattie Cochran, who lives off Aska Road in north Georgia's Fannin County, loves to cook cushaw squash ("Indian Pumpkin"). Her friend Carl Dodd, who introduced me to Mrs. Cochran, says the yellow-and-green-striped cushaw looks like a "crooked neck pumpkin." In any event, here is how Hattie fixes her baked and fried cushaw:

The way I do, I just halve it and put it in the oven on a sheet…set at about 350°F. After a little while, when it gets soft, you dig all the meat out and put it in a bowl. If you want to make a pie, you put eggs in it. But usually I like to fry it up in a skillet.

Cabbages, Chestnuts, and High-Proof Moonshine

Bile them cabbage down, boys,
Turn the hoecake brown
The only song that I can sing is,
Bile them cabbage down.

—1850s minstrel song

~

My grandmother said cabbage boiled less than four hours would kill you.
—Ben Robertson, Red Hills and Cotton

Wagon trains rolling out of the Appalachian hill country at the turn of the century, many pulled by sure-footed oxen, brought lush loads of country bounty—cabbage, turnips, apples, sorghum syrup, honey, chestnuts, and the like, plus an even more valuable commodity at the bottom of the pile: kegs of high-proof, double and twisted corn whiskey.

Their destinations were cities in the downstream population centers such as Asheville, Knoxville, Chattanooga, and Atlanta, and smaller towns like Sevierville, Johnson City, Dalton, Morganton, and Gainesville. Such fall forays earned mountain farmers enough money to buy a few necessities that they were unable to produce on their own—sugar, salt, and coffee—with enough cash left over to pay their county taxes.

As Floyd Watkins and his father, Charles Hubert, chronicled in their nostalgic and masterful reminiscence, *Yesterday in the Hills,* such wagons were welcomed visitors as they stopped off for the night at Cherokee County's Sharp Mountain settlement on their way to Atlanta.

"The long horns of the oxen had tips and bands of shining and glistening brass. The homemade yokes and hickory neck bows used on the oxen were like those described in the Bible."

The trips to Atlanta, at a rate of only twelve miles a day, sometimes took a week going and a week returning. The Messrs. Watkins reported the wagons carried two men each and they often camped out overnight in a grove of oaks near the Sharp Mountain church. Early mornings, youngsters enjoyed walking out and savoring the delicious aroma that wafted from the camp as the mountaineers fried up their cabbage and corn bread in their breakfast skillets.

Southern mountain folk have been growing and eating cabbages for over three centuries now, and mostly loving every minute of it. Contrary to the minstrel song that would indicate boiling was the only way of cooking cabbages, mountain people over the years have enjoyed shredding and salting them (sauerkraut), as well as frying,

steaming, and stewing them, and, of course, serving them raw (coleslaw).

The Jamestown colonists were cultivating and consuming cabbage as early as 1625 along with corn and beans. Like maize, cabbage was relatively easy to grow and could be easily stored for winter consumption.

The valleys and coves of the Appalachians—black rich bottomlands—are ideal for growing cabbage and other truck crops. Thus in addition to family garden plots, you often find quite a bit of commercial cabbage acreage

Mrs. Jewell Jones shows off two heads of cabbage that she grows in a fertile bottomland next to her home in Gilmer County, Georgia.

yet today in the foothills of north Georgia, western North Carolina, east Tennessee, and Virginia. Typical of small farmer cabbage growers is Jewell Jones in north Georgia's Cartecay community, whose farm boasts glistening green fields of cabbage every spring and summer.

Several people told me how they preserved their crop over winter by burying the cabbage heads upside down. They brought them in for eating one at a time, having to discard only an outer leaf or two. For those people who had root cellars, the cabbage could be stored alongside their potatoes and apples.

Boiled Cabbage

While most cabbages in the region traditionally were green, the red variety was in evidence back to Thomas Jefferson's day. In 1796, Hannah Glasse, writing to the American colony from London, offered the following interesting recipe:

*O*n almost any day in October, travelers driving past Milepost 192 on the Blue Ridge Parkway in southwest Virginia will find encamped there a mountain farmer by the name of Donald Brady. He'll be easy to spot. His mode of transportation is a covered wagon drawn by a team of oxen, and his principal cargo is cabbage—hundreds of heads of it, freshly harvested.

This stretch of the Virginia mountains southwest of Roanoke...is known as "the cabbage capital of the world." With allowances for some slight exaggeration, the title seems to fit. They grow about 3,000 acres of cabbage in Carroll County each summer—and at 34,000 heads to the acre, that's a gross yield of just over 100 million heads.

"Yep, this is the place," says Donald Brady. "The soil is just right and the climate's perfect in these mountains..." Brady remembers from his childhood the sight of ox-drawn wagons hauling cabbages to Hillsville, the Carroll County seat, and to the little ridgetop communities of Fancy Gap and Meadows of Dan. Cabbage growing is much more of a scientific and technological undertaking than it used to be. The hybrid seeds, developed especially for the "no till" method of farming now used in these mountains, were produced in upstate New York; they yield "supermarket cabbages" of uniform size, color, firmness, and weight.

—JOHN EGERTON, *SIDE ORDERS*

Red Cabbage Dressed After the Dutch Way, Good for a Cold in the Breast

Take the cabbage, cut it small, and boil it soft, then drain it and put it in a stew-pan with a sufficient quantity of oil and butter, a little water and vinegar, and an onion cut small. Season it with pepper and salt, and let it simmer on a slow fire till all the liquor is wasted.

~

What a shame that Hannah would "waste" the wonderful cabbage liquor. But apparently the word had not reached her about the leftover "pot likker" that American mountain folk grew to relish. This is now considered a standard delicacy to save and savor. (More about pot likker in the Greens chapter.) Many old-timers (and even moderns) like to crumble up corn bread into their cup of pot likker and eat it as a soup. The corn bread was always available at the table in any self-respecting Appalachian household. Which means practically every one of them.

From the time the first settlers arrived, the typical mountain way of cooking green cabbage was that of boiling, with the obligatory piece of fatback thrown in to provide the down-home flavor.

Savannah's Damon Lee Fowler, a flamboyant yet careful food and cooking historian (*Classical Southern Cooking*), maintains that, contrary to popular misconceptions that Southerners cooked cabbage "until it was a watery mush," his research indicated otherwise. He noted that nearly all early cookbooks warned people to avoid overcooking.

Along Hazel Creek, North Carolina, made famous by the late and legendary writer Horace Kephart (*Our Southern Highlanders*), boiled cabbage, properly prepared, is still appreciated. Here is a recipe offered by Anne Ballew and Myrell Ballew Moore and published in Duane Oliver's recipe collection, *Cooking on Hazel Creek*. But as you will note, the recipe writer urges that the cabbage should be cooked only until tender.

Myrell and Zenia's Boiled Cabbage

Quarter and slice an average head of cabbage. Add a medium-size hunk of salt pork. Salt to taste and boil in enough water to cover. Boil until tender but do not overcook.

Baked Cabbage Pie

Another popular mountain dish is cabbage pie. This "two-crust" recipe comes from the highly acclaimed John C. Campbell Folk School at Brasstown, North Carolina. This one has a fairly modern touch with the inclusion of cream of mushroom soup and cream cheese ingredients, virtually unknown in the hill country until this century.

Campbell Cabbage Pie

2 pie crusts	*8 ounces mushrooms*
8 ounces cream cheese	*Butter*
4 hard-boiled eggs	*1 teaspoon dill*
½ head of cabbage, shredded	*Salt and pepper to taste*
2 onions	*1 (10 ounce) can cream of mushroom soup*

Preheat oven to 350°F. Place bottom layer of crust in pie pan and spread with cream cheese. Slice hard-boiled eggs over the cream cheese. Saute cabbage, onions, and mushrooms in butter. Add dill, salt, pepper, and mushroom soup. Spread over eggs. Cover pie with top crust. Punch steam vents. Bake at 350°F for 45 minutes.

Baked Cabbage with Apples

Another delightful variation is to bake cabbage with fruit added. Dottie Woody of Woodstock, Georgia, who tested this and other cabbage recipes in this chapter, noted

*T*here was a woman in our community who kept food on her table all the time. If you went by, she'd invite you in to eat, just pull back the extra table cloth she had the food covered with. We'd be walking down the road; they'd be settin' on the porch. We'd talk a little while and then they'd say, "Come on in an' eat." If you didn't go in there and eat, they'd be insulted and get mad.

—LARRY DAVIS OF GILMER COUNTY, GEORGIA

that she likes, and often cooks, the cabbage/apples combination. Her husband, Mark, was especially fond of the recipe below that came from my friends Emily and John Anthony. As noted earlier, the Anthonys ran the popular Sautee Inn Restaurant in north Georgia's beautiful Nacoochee Valley. Legends say Nacoochee (Evening Star) was a beautiful and bewitching Indian princess.

Nacoochee Baked Cabbage with Apples

1 medium head cabbage, coarsely chopped	⅓ cup sugar
	1 cup fine breadcrumbs
2 cups apples, sliced and cooked	6 tablespoons butter, melted

Preheat oven to 350°F. Drop chopped cabbage in boiling water, and cook 3 to 5 minutes until slightly tender but still crunchy. Drain well. Layer cabbage and apples in 2-quart casserole dish, sprinkling sugar and breadcrumbs on each layer. Pat top layer flat before adding last crumbs. Pour melted butter over top of casserole. Cover and bake at 350°F for 45 minutes until hot throughout. Remove cover during last 15 minutes. Serves 4 to 6.

Fried Cabbage

Fried cabbage is an old Appalachian dish. An excellent example is this recipe that has been handed down over the years and is served at the Nu-Wray Inn, a great mountain hotel in Burnsville, North Carolina.

The inn is situated in the high mountains of western North Carolina not far from Mount Mitchell, at 6,684 feet the tallest mountain east of the Rockies. Run for over a hundred years by the Ray and Wray families, the Nu-Wray Inn is now operated by Doug and Barbara Brown.

Mount Mitchell Fried Cabbage

Chop cabbage coarsely. Place in hot skillet in which 1 tablespoon of grease has been poured. Fill the pan to the top with the cabbage, and pour over this ½ cup of water. Salt to taste, and cover with lid. Allow to cook slowly for about 30 minutes. When done, sprinkle 1 tablespoon of sugar on top. Serve while hot.

Coleslaw

Today coleslaw is a daily menu item across many mountain households. Easy to prepare—shredded cabbage with the addition of mayonnaise and other dressings of choice—coleslaw is a perfect side dish for family reunions and other social occasions. It can be served cold or hot. Coleslaw got its name from *koolsla*, a Dutch word introduced into England in the late eighteenth century that means "cold cabbage salad."

The following recipe is adapted from one offered by Kathy Sohn of Pikeville, Kentucky, wife of the aforementioned author and TV personality Mark Sohn. Kathy serves slaw as a salad and as a side dish for chicken and fried fish. It's also great for use on hot dogs.

Kathy's Coleslaw

4 to 5 cups shredded cabbage　　*½ teaspoon dill weed*

¼ cup mayonnaise　　*½ teaspoon salt*

¼ cup Italian dressing　　*Green olives*

Mix the cabbage, mayonnaise, dressing, dill, and salt in a large bowl. Pour and scrape into serving bowl. Garnish with green olives and dill weed. Serves 6.

Sweet Potatoes

The October Delight

It was a good meal they had together that night…fried chicken…mashed rootabeggars [sic], collard greens and hot, pale golden sweet potatoes. Miss Amelia ate slowly, and with the relish of a farm hand.
—Carson McCullars, The Ballad of the Sad Cafe

~

Right now [October] is the time when golden potatoes are being baked in their jackets, brought hot to the table, there to be opened and crowned with big lumps of butter. It is food fit for the gods, yet it is a regular dish on the menu of the humblest Georgia homes.
—Herbert Wilcox, Georgia Scribe

Sweet potato pies…sweet potato soufflés…casseroles…pones…puddings…puffs: What a glorious fall-time panoply, enough to sate the appetite and warm the cockles of any mountain heart. And all the result of an earthy, humble tuber, which, when placed in a Dutch oven, as one Tennessee writer rhapsodized, would release its sweet juices, "covering the soft potato in a thick syrup as rich and tasty as maple syrup."

Mountain housewives wouldn't think of celebrating the cooler year-end months, particularly the Thanksgiving and Christmas seasons, without whipping up some luscious sweet potato dishes to go along with the salty meats of the fall—country cured hams, fresh winged fowl, and yes, possums.

As my erudite *Atlanta Journal* correspondent, the late Herbert Wilcox, wrote to me over three decades ago, "The sweet potato season and the possum-hunting season arrive at about the same time…Possums and taters go together like ham and eggs."

Herbert was a wonderful storyteller. He liked to recount a tale about the Elbert County possum hunter who vowed his two possum dogs knew precisely when the sweet potatoes were coming into season.

"The minute one of the dogs strikes a possum trail the other hightails it to the nearest sweet potato patch and begins to scratch out potatoes to go with the possum he knows his pal will tree!"

Harvested during the "R months" of September, October, and November, and stored usually in small pyramidlike "hills" (cocooning the potatoes in a nest of pine needles), sweet potatoes were available for cooking all through the fall months, and into the winter and the following spring—as long as they lasted.

Well-off mountain folk erected "potato houses"—almost as big as their smokehouses—for storing their crop. And a small percentage built cellars, particularly those whose cabins had a convenient hillside drop in the back.

Sweet potatoes are to the...country cooking of the South what beans are to Boston: a signature dish of symbolic importance and great public favor.
—John Egerton, *Southern Food*

Near Waleska, in north Georgia's Appalachian foothills, the late Henry Grady Hasty hired his brother-in-law, George Cline, to build him a potato storage house. Measuring twenty by thirty feet, the house was insulated with sawdust between the weatherboard exterior and the inside pine walls, providing a snug interior. After Grady plowed up his potatoes and got them cured and stored, his wife, Montaree, would start baking them up to the delight of all members of the Hasty clan.

"We ate 'em hot and with plenty of butter," Bill Hasty recalled.

It was a universal experience throughout the Piedmont and mountain country. Youngsters packed baked sweet potatoes in their lard buckets to take to school. The kids didn't realize it at the time but, along with their biscuits, ham, and sausage, they were getting superbly nutritious meals. The sweet potatoes alone included carotene and fifteen essential vitamins. According to the Georgia Sweet Potato Commission, sweet potato vitamins include generous amounts of thiamine, riboflavin, iron, and dietary fiber. Besides that, the tubers are low in sodium and free of cholesterol!

America's yellow tubers came with two names, sweet potatoes and yams. Although a bit different in appearance—sweet potatoes (*Ipomoea batatas*), a morning glory offshoot with a pale yellow appearance, originated in America. Yams (a member of the *Dioscorea genus*) came from Africa—and have a lighter flesh color.

The first settlers arriving at Jamestown in 1607 found sweet potatoes being grown and eaten by the native tribes. Britishers were already familiar with the root plant, named the "batata" by the Spaniards who shipped boatloads to England during the reign of Henry the VIII. The good king, it seems, had a lusty appetite for the batata since it was generally believed to be loaded with aphrodisiac properties. King Henry's favorite dish was sweet potato pie laced heavily with sugar and spices.

For Appalachia's pioneer settlers, fireplace-roasting was a favorite cooking method, following the Indian style. Some of the cookbooks of the 1800s promoted the low-heat baking of sweet potatoes including twice-baking them for certain pies, pones, and puddings. From the Indians, settlers learned they could slice the tubers and dry them in the same manner as apples.

In north Georgia, the first settlers in what became Fannin County, on the North Carolina line, named one of their communities "Tater Hill" in honor of the spot where the Cherokees were said to have gathered wild potatoes. Across the region sweet potatoes became a big hit, due to their ease of cultivation and their culinary versatility. As North Carolina's Lyn Kenner noted, "the sweet potato was one vegetable that could be boiled, baked, whipped, or souffléd and always come out a winner."

> *In the lean years of the War between the States and the period of Reconstruction that followed, sweet potatoes were the only thing that kept many impoverished Southerners alive...They have remained a staple in our diet and are still a distinguishing feature on most Southern tables. Most of the traditional recipes have survived right along with the potatoes, virtually unchanged by modern ranges.*
> —DAMON FOWLER IN
> *CLASSICAL SOUTHERN COOKING*

My north Georgia buddy Curtis Underwood—who became a chef and restaurateur as the culmination of a multifaceted and colorful career—launched a new twist to the sweet potato cooking art in the 1950s when he got into moonshining. The site was Lumpkin County, near the site of America's first gold rush. An imaginative cook among his other talents, Curtis earlier made waves in the mountain country when he substituted whiskey mash for buttermilk in his corn bread mix, giving corn pone a spunkier taste. He approached the sweet potato challenge with the same inventiveness.

I helped the Crawford family farm for a year. Marion Crawford was a super blacksmith and cooper and still-maker. Very skilled. I helped him make many a whiskey still. And I helped 'em farm for a year or two. One spring we set out a thousand sweet potato slips (plants) in an old cotton field near Marion's home. Those red hills would grow the best sweet potatoes.

We'd go out there and dig them sweet potatoes in September and October. About the same time, we were making whiskey back in the mountains. We couldn't get white sugar for mashing our corn; we had only brown sugar. When we'd make a run, I'd pull out about ten or fifteen pounds of that brown sugar and take it home to Mrs. Crawford. The first time I asked her to try it out with her next sweet potato pie, it turned out wonderfully.

She would take a big old dish pan, about eight inches deep and twenty-four inches long. She'd slice them sweet potatoes, and put down a layer of potatoes and a layer of dough, a layer of potatoes and so forth. She'd lace each layer of the pie with that brown sugar.

She placed that sweet potato pie in the oven when she put in the biscuits for breakfast. She kept that fire going in the stove until dinner (noontime). That's how long it took to bake the pie. You talk about second helpings; we didn't just go for seconds, we went for thirds and fourths.

In my own sweet potato cooking experience, I find that adding a bit of honey provides an additional sweet touch to the potato flavor, particularly in pies and casseroles such as the following recipe.

Sweet Potato Bake

Honey and brown sugar are nice elements of this sweet potato pie recipe offered by Ozella Jordan of Whitfield County, Georgia. This appeared in the recipe collection published by the ladies of Gates Chapel United Methodist Church in nearby Gilmer County. It's named for the gorgeous mountain range that juts into north Georgia covering portions of Murray and Gilmer Counties. *Cohutta* is a Cherokee word that means, "A shed roof supported on poles."

Cohutta Sweet Potato Bake

8 medium sweet potatoes	½ teaspoon cinnamon
¼ cup brown sugar	¼ teaspoon nutmeg
¼ cup honey	2 teaspoons orange rind
1 teaspoon cornstarch	2 teaspoons margarine
½ cup pineapple juice	¼ cup chopped walnuts

Cook sweet potatoes until tender. Poke with fork to check. Peel and cut into ½-inch slices. Arrange slices in a lightly greased 12 x 8 x 2-inch baking dish. Set aside. Combine brown sugar and next seven ingredients in a saucepan. Cook over medium heat, stirring constantly until mixture begins to boil. Boil 1 minute, stirring constantly until mixture is thick and bubbly. Pour over sweet potatoes, sprinkle with nuts. Cover and refrigerate 8 hours. Preheat oven to 350°F. Remove dish from refrigerator, and let stand 30 minutes. Uncover and bake at 350°F for 30 minutes or until thoroughly heated. Serves 8.

Sweet Potato Pudding

I am indebted to *Marion Brown's Southern Cookbook* for the following grated sweet potato pudding recipe that came out of Tennessee. The recipe is attributed to Mrs. George Osborn of Murfreesboro, situated on the Cumberland plateau "Highland Rim"—an Appalachian offshoot. Mrs. Osborn urges cooks to follow instructions carefully to assure a crunchy, candied, coconut-flavored crust.

Grated Sweet Potato Pudding

1½ cups butter	4 cups grated raw sweet potatoes
½ cup sugar	1 cup raisins
1 cup Georgia cane syrup, or substitute	1 tablespoon allspice and cinnamon (mixed)
½ teaspoon cloves	3 eggs, beaten
1 cup sweet rich milk	

In a heavy iron skillet, melt the butter. Mix all ingredients, adding the beaten eggs last. Pour into the hot pan with butter; stir until heated. Put in moderate oven to bake in skillet at 375°. As a crust forms around the edge and bottom, stir. Do this several times while baking. Bake 40 minutes. Serve with sweet flavored cream or lemon sauce.

Sweet Potato Pone

Another testimony to the sweet potato's amazing versatility was the pone. This one is a typical traditional Appalachian dish, well loved in mountain communities such as Suches in North Georgia. Suches, by the way, was said to have been named for a Cherokee tribal chief.

Suches Sweet Potato Pone

2 tablespoons butter, melted	2½ cups grated raw sweet potatoes
1 cup sugar	Grated rind of half an orange
⅔ cup milk	½ teaspoon powdered ginger

Preheat oven to 400°. Mix butter and sugar. Blend in the milk and grated sweet potatoes and beat well. Add orange rind and ginger. Pour into a 1-inch-deep baking dish and bake until medium brown.

~

There are dozens of ways to make the sweet potato a treat instead of a mass of goo. But there's at least one currently chic thing I wouldn't do with them: They don't crisp up properly when they're deep-fried, so I pass on that; but they mash as nicely as white potatoes, and unlike mashed white potatoes can be reheated nicely or transformed next day into a casserole.

—RUTH ADAMS BRONZ, *MISS RUBY'S AMERICAN COOKING*

Fried Sweet Potatoes

Frying sweet potatoes is a wonderful option. Martha McCullough-Williams declared that sliced sweet potatoes "deserve frying in ham fat." That's how western North Carolina's grand old Nu-Wray Inn does it. Located in the high mountain country at Burnsville, and now operated by Doug and Barbara Brown, the inn has a recipe handed down by the Wray family that calls for one to peel and slice the potatoes and fry them in deep fat until golden brown.

Here is a similar but much earlier recipe for fried sweet potatoes that called for butter. It was published in an 1847 cookbook, *Miss Leslie, Directions for Cookery*:

Fried Sweet Potatoes

Choose them of the largest size. Half boil them and then having taken off the skins, cut the potatoes in slices, and fry them in butter or in nice drippings.

Sweet Potato Soufflé

Cooks at the famed Dillard House in far northeast Georgia have turned mountain cooking into a beautiful art form. Situated on the southeastern side of the picturesque Rabun Gap—made famous by the series of Foxfire books on mountain living—the Dillard House Restaurant has been pleasing visitors since Carrie Dillard opened her first boarding house in 1916.

The first Dillard to come to the valley was Revolutionary War officer John Dillard who galloped in on his horse in the late 1790s. He bought acreage from the Cherokees for a jug of apple brandy, a muzzleloading rifle, and three dollars in cash. One of his descendants, John Dillard, is the present operator of the inn and restaurant complex that overlooks the Dillard-owned valley and its great spread of truck crops—vegetables grown for use in the motel restaurant. One of the restaurant's favorite dishes—of which this is an adaptation—is its sweet potato soufflé. This recipe calls for old-time basics with a few modern twists such as marshmallows and margarine.

Dillard House Sweet Potato Soufflé

2 cups mashed sweet potatoes	1 cup heavy cream
6 tablespoons sugar	2 eggs
¾ teaspoon cinnamon	2 teaspoons vanilla
2 tablespoons margarine	Marshmallows to cover top of dish

Preheat oven to 325°F. Boil sweet potatoes with skins on until tender. Peel and mash. Add sugar, cinnamon, margarine, and cream. Beat eggs well, and add to mixture. Add vanilla. Pour into buttered 2-quart casserole dish, and top with marshmallows. Bake at 325°F for 30 minutes. Serves 6.

Sweet Potato Puffs

In 1839, Kentucky's Lettice Bryan brought out an encyclopedic cookbook, *The Kentucky Housewife*, which luckily is back in print in a University of South Carolina clothbound volume with a foreword by Bill Neal. This is an adaptation of Mrs. Bryan's recipe for puffs that she noted were good for breakfast as well as for afternoon tea.

Lettice's Sweet Potato Puffs

4 medium-size potatoes	*¼ cup sugar, or to taste*
¼ teaspoon powdered cinnamon	*1 tablespoon butter*
¼ teaspoon freshly grated nutmeg	

Put enough water in a large kettle, and bring to a boil. Add the potatoes (thoroughly scrubbed), and bring back to a boil, then reduce to a simmer. Cook about 45 minutes until potatoes are soft. Rub through a colander, adding the butter, sugar, nutmeg, and cinnamon to the pulp. Work the mixture well together. Cover and refrigerate. Later, form the pulp into small balls, placing them on a buttered cookie sheet. Preheat oven to 400°F, and place the puffs in oven and bake for about 25 minutes or until golden brown. Use a spatula to place them on a warm plate for immediate serving. Makes 2 dozen puffs.

Sweet Potato Pie

This potato pie recipe is adapted from Lyn Kellner's *Taste of Appalachia* collection. As Lyn points out, sweet potato recipes are about as numerous in the mountains as cooks, but this one seems to stand out.

Grandma's Sweet Potatoes

2 to 3 pounds sweet potatoes,	*1 teaspoon vanilla*
fresh cooked or canned	*6 tablespoons butter*
½ cup brown sugar	*6 tablespoons butter, melted*
1 teaspoon cinnamon	*⅓ cup honey or pancake syrup*

Preheat oven to 350°F. If using canned potatoes, drain well. Slice potatoes ½-inch thick, and lay in bottom of a 9 x 13-inch baking pan. Mix rest of ingredients, and pour over potatoes. Bake for 30 minutes, turning once or twice. If a thicker syrup is desired, bake longer. Serves 6 to 8.

⁓

There is one more sweet potato dish that was well loved across the Appalachian foothills, sweet potato custard. You can find the recipe for that dish in the Desserts section.

Mountain Favorites

Leather-Britches and Other Delectable Beans

My suburban-Baltimore-reared husband to this day swears that the reason he married me is because I introduced him to his favorite food, shuck beans.
—*Kentucky native Ronni Lundy*

~

Beans, beans, the musical fruit,
The more you eat, the more you toot,
The more you toot, the better you feel,
So eat some beans at every meal!

—*"The Brilliant Bean," 1988*

I just love leather-britches!" declares Rilla Chastain Nelson. And after checking out a mess of her beans, I love 'em too. Rilla lives on the banks of north Georgia's scenic Cartecay River. Across the road from her house stand the ruins of the old gristmill operated by her late father, Harley Chastain, and her Baptist preacher grandfather, "Blue Mountain Joe" Chastain. The Chastains had to abandon the mill some years ago after a heavy rain destroyed the dam that provided the water power.

Rilla was good enough to offer a mess of the reconstituted beans to me on a visit I paid to her home in 1995 with our mutual friend Larry Davis. Larry and I found Rilla's leather-britches outstanding, full of wholesome virtual reality, a taste that you never experience with canned beans.

Rilla's cooking method is typical of that used by folk across the Appalachian mountain country with one exception. Instead of an overnight cold water soak, she gives her leather-britches a one-hour soak in boiling water:

"I break 'em up and try to get all the strings off of 'em and I sop 'em in boiling water for an hour and then put them in (a pot) and cook them. Usually you put meat with them, either fatback or ham bone. You have to cook 'em a long time, though, to make 'em good."

In earlier days, old-timers loved to boil their dried green beans in a Dutch oven or a pot right in their fireplaces. And some people, such as Dora Tipton Underwood (wife of the aforementioned Curtis Underwood) parboiled their beans with a bit of baking soda and later added soup beans for the long cooking period. Declares Dora: "You talk about eatin' some'n good!…oh, my goodness!"

One of the great attributes of the runner (string/snap) beans is that they are ideal for the drying method of preservation. Leather-britches originated with the Indians as a wonderful way to preserve the beans over winter. They are also called "shuck beans" or "shucky beans." One Tennessee name is "fodder beans." I must say that the "shuck beans" definition runs a little counter to that given by Horace Kephart in his *Our Southern Highlanders*. He noted that shuck beans were those that you had to shell, or "shuck," to get the beans out of the pods.

> *In the coldest part of winter we were fortified by broth-rich pots of full-bodied, bronze-hued shuck beans—green beans my aunts strung on threads and hung up to dry every summer, just as their pioneer forebears had done...There is nothing in the world so addictively satisfying in winter as the earthy robust flavor of shuck beans. The shuck beans were served with real corn bread: no sugar, no flour, but covered in a crust turned glistening brown by a well-greased and scorching hot cast-iron skillet...For people like me with mountain roots, a pot of shuck beans and a skillet of corn bread is the best part of winter eating.*
> —RONNI LUNDY, *SHUCK BEANS, STACK CAKES AND HONEST FRIED CHICKEN*

In any event, to preserve green beans the leather-britches way, you use a number forty thread and a large needle to string the snapped or full pod beans, then hang them up in the sunshine or over a stove in a warm kitchen. Once dried, the lightweight beans can be packed in a storage bag (or modern-day refrigerator) until needed, usually in the dead of winter. Incidentally, the Cherokees called them "leather-britches" because that's what the beans looked like when strung up on a line after a bit of drying and shriveling.

To resurrect them, as Rilla and Dora noted, you have only to soak them overnight. The following morning they are ready for the pot.

～

The Cherokees and other Indians of the "five civilized tribes" of the Southeast had been cultivating beans long before the arrival of the European setters in the early 1700s. Like maize, beans were greatly nutritious and fairly easy to grow, particularly in the rich valley bottomlands across the Piedmont and mountain water courses.

So when the newcomers from across the Atlantic arrived and began to consider food crops, they quickly picked up lessons taught by the Indians. Along with squash, beans were found to be natural companions to maize, particularly runner beans that could be planted alongside corn, nature's own jolly green lattice to the sun. They also were well suited to uncleared land filled with stumps.

Probably the twentieth century's most popular pole bean variety (also known as "string beans" or "snap beans") was, and

> *Our slow-cooked, drab, olive-green beans have flavor and character. They are vastly different from the bright-green, just-blanched, almost-raw, restaurant-style green beans.*
> —MARK SOHN, *MOUNTAIN COUNTRY COOKING*

is, Kentucky Wonders. However, the white "half-runners"—growing half vertically and half on the ground—also proved to be in great demand.

The summertime maturity of green beans—usually in mid-June—marked a time of Appalachian celebration. Many families staged "bean-stringings," inviting in neighboring wives. As country music personality Dwight Yokum told Ronni Lundy, "My granny (Tibbs) would come to the back porch with a big laundry basket full of beans. We would sit down and we would snap 'em, and string 'em and crack 'em, and throw 'em in the pan. We would sit there snapping and stringing for the whole afternoon."

Almost as much fun as a quilting bee, bean-stringing was a necessary process whether the beans were being prepared for immediate consumption or whether they were being strung up for drying or for canning. My mother pressed me into bean-stringing several times during my teen years. Although it was not one of my more happy pursuits, the idea in stringing beans is to snap off each end of a long bean and rip out the string from both sides. Then you break each bean into one-inch-long sections.

The next step, of course, if you want to eat a mess of fresh beans in the old mountain style, is to toss the beans into the pot with a little water and the obligatory piece of salted fatback.

In Fannin County, Georgia, Gus Hallum told students of the West Fannin High School that "when everybody was at home she would cook a bushel of beans for dinner." His mother cooked the beans in a fireplace pot.

Green Beans

The way you cook beans today is not much different from the way of the pioneer era except that you perhaps substitute a bit of beef or chicken boullion in the place of fatback, and, of course you cook the beans much more quickly. In earlier times, what gave beans their full-bodied flavor was the long, slow cooking at a relatively low temperature in the cast-iron fireplace pot.

Rilla Chastain Nelson shows Larry Davis a bowl of leather-britches (dried beans) she has just taken out of the pot at her home on the Cartecay River, Gilmer County, Georgia.

Here's a typical mountain recipe from earlier times around Cullowhee, a beautiful area of western North Carolina and home of Western Carolina University. My friends Doug Reed, assistant to the chancellor at WCU, and Duane Oliver, a former WCU professor, informed me that the name Cullowhee is the Cherokee word for Valley of the Lilies. Duane informed me a Cherokee town was located in the area now occupied by the university's campus. "It had a nice little mound which, until the school had it bulldozed for a parking lot, sat just outside my office window." The lily referred to is a rare plant that grew in the swampy area along a creek now filled in and used as a ball field. The Cherokees are believed to have eaten the lilies in the winter, perhaps to prevent scurvy.

Cullowhee Green Beans

8 cups green beans, strung and broken
¼ pound salt pork

1 small red pepper, dried
Salt to taste

Wash whole beans. String and break into sections. Rinse broken beans. Place in large pot with a lid. Add the pork, which should be about ½-inch thick, along with the pepper pod. Cover with water. Bring to a boil, then reduce heat and cover. Simmer rapidly for an hour. Stir beans occasionally. Add small amount of water if beans begin to dry out. After first hour, take a sip of the broth and add salt. Amount of salt required will vary with the salt in pork. Simmer for 1 more hour. If there is excess water in bottom of pot, remove lid and let excess boil off. Before serving, add salt again if necessary.

Pickled Green Beans

Pickled green beans are also a popular mountain dish, being salted down either in a barrel or a large churn. They are cooked much like shuck beans, except that after soaking them overnight, you drain off the water with two rinsings to remove the excess salt, then boil them with a piece of meat.

As Rose Houk noted in her *Food and Recipes of the Smokies*, "In late fall, cooked beans, corn or both mixed together were covered in a salty brine and stored in crocks, barrels or canned in jars to be eaten throughout the winter. If a wooden barrel was the vessel, the seams were sealed with beeswax."

Butter Beans

For my Atlanta writer friend Sibley Fleming, butter beans have been one of her favorite dishes over the years, being "salty and smooth to the tongue, soothing to the soul." Her love has extended to the writing of a children's book, *The Adventures of Butter Bean*.

Butter beans are also a favorite of my older brother Connie—the Reverend Dr. Connie A. Dabney, if you please. Connie—whose Appalachian past includes having pastored the Brainerd Baptist Church outside Chattanooga—loves to eat butter beans in combination with tomatoes, corn, and, of course, accompanied by a hot slice of steaming corn bread. (So do I!)

A brownish-gray cousin of the lima bean and a native of Peru, butter beans weren't popular in the Blue Ridge in earlier days, except at Monticello, the home of Thomas Jefferson. But butter beans were grown in Virginia fairly early and became a great bean for cooking and drying. Their only drawback is that they require a lot of intensive hand labor in shelling, unless you are fortunate to have access to a shelling machine.

Connie's Butter Beans

2 cups butter-beans	2 tablespoons sweet cream
2½ cups cold water	½ teaspoon salt
1 teaspoon butter	

Shell beans, and cull out inferior beans. Put in pot along with water, butter, sweet cream, and salt. Boil gently until tender and water has almost evaporated. Taste broth periodically and add salt if necessary.

Soup Beans

Soup beans, or "shelly beans," as some of the mountain folks called them—a type of navy bean or pinto bean—were well loved in the mountains nearly from the beginning, and were great beans for drying, either shelled or inside their leathery pods.

Soup beans cover a variety of varieties—Great Northern, pinto, October (also called the cranberry bean), and yellow eye. European immigrants were familiar with a similar bean grown overseas called the broad bean.

Here is a typical recipe for cooking dried shell beans. Incidentally, all country aficionados insist that to fully appreciate dried beans, or any vegetable for that matter, you must accompany them with a big pone of steaming corn bread, properly buttered, of course.

Mountain Dried Beans

2 cups dried beans	6 cups water
Piece of salt pork	¾ teaspoon salt
1 pod dried red pepper	

Using a 3-quart saucepan, place beans and other ingredients in the pan. Cut the pork into 6 pieces. Bring pot to a boil, then reduce to simmer for 1 to 2 hours, depending on the type of bean. Simmer until beans reach tenderness.

Bean Cakes

Cooking up dried beans into cakes was an Indian favorite—sort of a type of ash cake except that beans were used along with cornmeal. This was a typical Cherokee recipe:

Cherokee Bean Cakes

1½ cups dried beans	1½ teaspoons salt
¾ cup milk	1 cup cornmeal
2 eggs, beaten	2½ tablespoons bacon drippings

Beans should be soaked 12 hours in cold water. Rinse and place in cooking pot, along with enough water to cover. Boil for 1½ hours until tender. Drain off water and set aside. Mix together the milk, eggs, salt, and cornmeal. Add the beans, and form into palm-size patties. Place bacon drippings or oil substitute in skillet, and fry at medium temperature until light brown.

Field Peas

In this area of shell beans we could add field peas, one of the South's great vegetables that were grown extensively across the Piedmont and Blue Ridge foothills. They were a good legume to grow either in a field by themselves or with corn.

Field peas arrived in the Southeast (Charleston) in 1750 from the Caribbean and eventually reached the Appalachians, taking their place with other shelly peas such as Whippoorwills, cream, purple hull, crowder, and of course black-eyes. At our home in South Carolina, our favorite was crowder peas, much more plump than the field pea or the black-eyed pea that is traditionally eaten by Southerners on New Year's Day—

along with (you guessed it) a piece of ham hock. It's supposed to bring you luck during the new year.

The aforementioned Frank Pressley, a Cullowhee, North Carolina, native, has a favorite recipe that he likes to share. Actually this one—a fairly modern recipe that calls for canned peas—reached the finals of a cooking contest in Valdosta, Georgia, near where Frank formerly lived and worked as one of the town's most popular barbers.

The traditional Appalachian method for the cooking of peas is the same as with dried beans, with the piece of fatback or bacon drippings as the additional flavoring agent.

Pressley's Peas, Country-Style

8 slices bacon

½ cup chopped onion

½ cup chopped green pepper

2 12-ounce cans green peas

¼ cup parsley, chopped

Salt and pepper to taste

1 teaspoon sugar

Fry bacon, crumble, and set aside. Reserve 2 tablespoons bacon drippings. Sauté onions and green pepper in drippings until soft. Add remaining ingredients except bacon; cover and cook over low heat 5 minutes, stirring occasionally. Crumble bacon on top. Serves 6.

Bean Bread

This is one of the great foods handed down by the Cherokee people. This particular recipe is adapted from one offered by the late Aggie Ross Lossiah, granddaughter of Cherokee Chief John Ross who went west on the 1838 Trail of Tears. The recipe, along with many others, has been lovingly preserved by Mary Ulmer Chiltoskey, the grand dame of the Cherokee Nation East. At age ninety, Mary resides along the majestic Oconoluftee River in Cherokee, North Carolina, with her beloved husband, Goingback "GB" Chiltoskey, also ninety. Mary's excellent book is *Cherokee Cooklore*.

Mary says this bean bread is the way Aggie's "old Cherokee Granny made it" when they lived in a cave on the Tennessee River prior to the days of water-run gristmills. Basic components are beans and corn, the primary foods eaten by the Cherokees and other Amerindians. Mrs. Chiltoskey says Aggie's bean bread goes well with venison or other game meat.

Aggie's Cherokee Bean Bread
(Tsu-Ya-Ga Du)

Shell beans and place in pot separately. Cover with water, and begin a slow boil. In a separate pot place grained corn along with a sprinkling of wood ashes that will cause the grain husks to peel off and form hominy. Wash these grains of corn in a basket sieve to remove the skins. Then take this hominy corn and beat in a beater until fine. Add the hot corn into the boiling beans. Do not add salt; it will cause bean bread to crumble. While mixture is still hot, work into round patties. These can be fried or can be wrapped into blades of corn, tied with strong grass, and dropped into the boiling water as dumplings. These "broadsword" dumplings will need to be cooked for one hour. The bean bread can be eaten plain, or with game grease or butter. If you wish, you can bypass the hominy-cooking part by purchasing precooked canned hominy in a grocery store. This hominy would then need to be beaten thoroughly to be added to the bean mixture.

~

No account of food habits in East Tennessee would be complete without a discussion of the role of dried beans. If there was a single staple when I was growing up, it was dried beans. They might be white, pinto, or mixed, but they were always there. Every two of three days beans would be cooked, usually seasoned with fat salt pork; they were much better if cooked with a country ham (or shoulder) shank.

Then they were reheated each day until they were gone and a new batch was started...Given this heritage, is it any wonder that I still must occasionally find a pinto (or Great Northern) bean fix to make it through a hard week?

Even though East Tennessee humor tends to be a little strange, I ought to give you one bean story. It seems that a farmer came home after a hard day's work to see that supper consisted of pinto beans and corn bread. He turned to his wife and asked, "Why are we having beans again tonight?" She thought for a moment and said, "I just don't understand you. You liked beans on Monday, Tuesday, Wednesday, Thursday, and Friday. Now suddenly on Saturday you don't like them anymore. I just don't understand you."

—WALTER LAMBERT, *KINFOLKS AND CUSTARD PIE*

Big Hominy, Little Hominy (Grits), and Mush

My mother made hominy in an old black pot in the yard. I thought it tasted better than candy.

—Betty Jo Bailey, Adairsville, Georgia

~

When my mind's unsettled,
When I don't feel spruce,
When my nerves get frazzled,
When my flesh gets loose—
What knits
Me back together's grits.

Grits with gravy, grits with cheese.
Grits with bacon, Grits with peas…

Grits, grits, it's grits I sing—
Grits fits in with anything

—Roy Blount Jr., One Fell Soup

Grits?" Eighty-five-year-old Ruth Swanson Hunter of Towns County, Georgia, said, with a look of disbelief on her face. "I never knew about that."

"Grits weren't eaten all that much around Mountain View, South Carolina, when I was growing up," my sister-in-law Lib Dabney, told me recently. "Now my mother, Nannie Jones (who lived to the ripe old age of 104), would cook grits for someone who was sick, it was sort of a soup…"

Cullowhee, North Carolina, native Frank Pressley, also had an opinion about grits. "I didn't get into grits until I left home. We didn't have grits in the mountains; we ate corn-meal mush. If we'd a had grits we'd a used sugar and butter on it, you know, as a cereal."

Mark Woody, who was raised in the high mountains near the Blue Ridge Divide, agreed. "Grits is a little coarser than meal. That would have taken some extra-fine grinding at the gristmills, so most folks just used the coarse meal and made corn mush."

Tennessean and north Alabaman Anthony Llewellyn made it unanimous. "Families back then would fix mush. They'd take a pot of boiling water and throw in a handful of meal. Sometimes we'd put a little butter and sorghum syrup on top of it, or anything sweet to give it some extra flavor." (In this regard, mush was similar to "hasty pudding" that was popular in colonial New England.)

~

Indeed, grits as we know them (or *it*; there's a dispute about the proper use), were a little late coming to the hill country. And while grits are celebrated as the South's flagship down-home dish, and subject of jolly jokes by Yankees and poetic adoration by Southerners such as Roy Blount, mountain people gave them short shrift in earlier days. They called grits "small hominy" in contrast to what they had eaten down through the years—whole-grain "big hominy," "whole hominy," or, the really traditional name, "lye hominy."

The latter name came from the pioneers' practice of boiling the whole grains of corn in their washpots after leaching off the bran with lye. Indeed, the Algonquin term, *rockahominie*, means "hulled corn."

Sarah Belk explained it all in her authoritative *Around the Southern Table*: "Hominy is made by soaking whole, dried field corn kernels in a caustic alkali solution (such as lye or ground limestone), which loosens the tough outer hull (the bran) from the softer edible center. It is this lye that changes the flavor of the corn and gives hominy and grits their unique taste."

As with so many foods, mountain people learned how to make lye hominy from the Amerindians. And the lessons came down through succeeding generations. Ruth Swanson Hunter of Young Harris, Georgia, remembered it well:

> *T*he thing that most northerners don't understand is that grits require a lot of preparing after they are on your plate. First, you add plenty of salt, and then you start with the black pepper. When you put so much pepper on your grits that you can hardly tell they were ever white, they are just about ready to eat.
>
> Then you put a large dob of cow butter right in the middle of your hot grits. As the cow butter starts to melt, mix the salted and peppered grits with the melted butter, and then get ready for something good to eat.
>
> Now I don't believe in making brash statements, but I just bet when my northern friends try grits this way, they'll be sorry they won that war.
>
> —LUDLOW PORCH, *THE CORN BREAD CHRONICLES*

Old folks built wooden ash hoppers. They poured their ashes in that over a period of time. Now and then, they'd sprinkle in some water.

Come time to make hominy, they'd pour more water in there and it'd seep down through and would drip out the lye. You put your lye in your pot with a bunch of water and your shelled corn and you let it boil 'til the husks begin to slippin' off the grains. Then you'd take it out and wash it through four or five waters. Then you put her back in the pot, pour your good clear water in there and you'd boil it 'til it got tender. We would fry our hominy in bacon grease and pork grease. Sometimes a potful would last over a week.

⁓

Hominy got the attention of William Bartram when he supped with an Indian chief in 1776. He found it to be "a refreshing repast" and "a pleasant cooling liquor made of homony well boiled, mixed up with milk…served up…in a large bowl, with a very large ladle to sup it with."

What Bartram ate was what mountain people came to call, as mentioned earlier, "mush," a quick fix of coarsely pounded cornmeal and hot water and served almost as a hasty pudding or a porridge, often topped off with butter, plus sorghum or honey.

> *M*ost mountain folk would not consider making hominy with anything but Hickory King [corn]. Hominy—cooked whole corn with the hulls off the kernels—was a culinary staple for both the Cherokees and Euro-American settlers in the Smokies.
> —ROSE HOUK, *FOOD AND RECIPES OF THE SMOKIES*

But honest-to-God hominy—the first truly American food—was on the scene at Jamestown, Virginia, when the first London Company Englishmen stepped ashore in 1607. The sea-weary newcomers were welcomed by hospitable Powatans bearing steaming bowls of "rockahominie"—boiled and pounded hearts of maize flavored with bear grease.

The colonists quickly Anglicized the name to "hominy" and set up their own hominy blocks by hollowing out tree stumps, and bending down green saplings on which their wooden pestles cracked their corn.

"Hominy blocks were as much a part of the pioneer American scene as fireplaces and rain barrels," wrote Nicholas P. Hardeman in his *Shucks, Shocks and Hominy Blocks.* "By the eighteenth century, every cabin and clearing had one or two of them. Sailors could sometimes tell when they were nearing the East Coast in a fog because of the thump, thump, thump of samp mills. And pioneers used these thudding contraptions like signal drums to communicate with each other."

Big Hominy, Little Hominy (Grits), and Mush ⁓ 325

Soon the settlers started figuring ways to speed up the tedious "hominy block" process. In time, particularly through the Appalachians where fast-rushing streams coursed down every hillside, little turbine-powered "tub mills" and later overshot-water-wheel "grist-mills" began popping up in every settlement, such as John's Mill at Talking Rock, Georgia. In 1772, at the first session of court in Buncombe County, North Carolina, the judge gave William Davidson authority "to build a gristmill on Swannanoa."

In 1845, Gilmer County, Georgia, had twenty-two gristmills and four whiskey distilleries to process the county's corn crops.

"We had two mills within a mile of us," Ernest Parker told me. "Some people called it Ticanetley River, some called it Bucktown River. It came out of Bucktown and down through Tickanetley. We shelled our corn at home and took it to the mill on our shoulder, usually a half bushel at a time. I took many a sack of corn that a way, on my shoulder, and poured it up in that hopper. Out of a half bushel of corn, you'd get about a peck of meal, atter the miller took out his grinding."

Mark Woody had a similar experience. "Hard Wilson's gristmill was a country mile from our home (at the foot of Whiskey Bill Mountain). I started out when I was younger carrying a peck of corn on my back. That would last me and my mother a couple of weeks of meal. Later I got to where I could carry a half bushel. Hard had two millstones on his tub mill. He'd built a dam to get water into the raceway. After I got up in my teens, Hard would tell me to go ahead and grind the meal myself and just leave the toll; he'd be working on the farm."

Here are some recipes for traditional hominy, for hominy grits, and for mush—the cornmeal dish that has been popular down through the centuries across the Southern Appalachians.

Grits are not difficult to cook. All it takes is water and salt, perhaps a little butter, and a bit of patience. John Egerton suggests that should you buy supermarket grits and are undecided between "quick" and "instant," that a more flavorful dish will result from the "quick" (five-minute boil) option than from the instant.

Some people like to slow-cook their grits for extended periods, sometimes well over an hour. Such lengthy boiling results in a more creamy dish. But it is possible to cook grits in much less time provided you give them a good stirring every few minutes. And, of course, grits can be enriched with an egg or two while cooking. Many people love to add Cheddar cheese to their grits pot.

Many of these recipes are old-timey and have the taste that your grandparents were familiar with.

~

Homemade "Lye Hominy"

Making authentic "lye hominy grits" in the old way takes a lot of time and effort. But the end product is quite tasty. You can take Red Devil Lye to make the dish but lye made from wood ashes is the best. On Cullowhee Mountain, North Carolina, Iva Ashe Pressley made her lye by leaching it from fireplace ashes. She would soak her shelled corn in the lye water overnight. The next day, she would find the corn grains had "slipped" their husks and floated to the top of the water. With a few boilings and many rinses, including removal of all the husks and lye, Iva was ready to cook the "defrocked" corn in her big wash pot. When the grains had cooked enough, they puffed up and became "lye hominy." This could be eaten as whole hominy or could be pounded or ground up to make hominy dishes.

Here is a recipe adaptation for homemade hominy by Martha Whaley of Gatlinburg, Tennessee, with my thanks to Nancy Blanche Cooper, author of the *Gatlinburg Recipe Collection*.

Gatlinburg Lye Hominy

1 gallon large kernel corn　　　　*1 quart hardwood ashes*

Cover corn with water. Tie ashes in muslin, and cook with corn until skin will slip off when pressed between thumb and forefinger. Remove ashes, and wash corn through 3 waters. Boil for 1 hour, then wash again. Repeat this 3 times, or until all lye is removed. Cook until corn is soft, about 6 hours in all.

Cherokee Hominy

Rose Houk obtained this authentic old Cherokee recipe from the Museum of Cherokee archives in Cherokee, North Carolina. It came from Bessie Jumper. Walnuts and pinto beans give this adapted recipe an unusual richness.

Cherokee Hominy

½ gallon flour corn	*1 cup walnuts*
1 can pinto beans	*⅓ cup cornmeal*
Lye water	*6 cups oak or hickory ashes*

Mix ashes with cold water, but not too thick, and set on high heat. When it begins to boil, pour in the corn. While it boils, stir with whisk. As you stir, the skin comes off the corn. After the bran has been poured off, wash the corn real well, wash off all the ashes, and boil the corn again for 2 to 3 hours. Just before it's done, put in pinto beans. When both are cooked, pour in the walnuts and cornmeal, mix together and beat fine. Serves 4.

Hominy and Cracklin's

At hog-killing time, usually around Thanksgiving or Christmas, mountain people loved to combine their hominy and cracklin's, the juicy morsels left over from the wash-pot rendering (or cookout) of lard. This recipe comes from Frank Pressley, a native of Cullowhee, who says the dish was good by itself or with any meat. "I want to tell you, you ain't never eat nothin' in your life any better than hominy and cracklin's." Here, in Frank's own words, is how his mother, Iva Ashe Pressley, made the dish:

> We loved hominy and cracklin's. Mama would put equal parts hominy and cracklin's in a large skillet. The cracklin's usually had enough grease in them but if not we would add a little. You didn't want it too greasy. Since the cracklin's and the hominy were both already cooked, all you had to do was heat them up with salt and pepper. Stir constantly to avoid overfrying.

Basic Boiled Grits

If possible, try to obtain stone-ground grits from one of the authentic gristmills still to be found throughout the Appalachian South, particularly Tennessee, the Carolinas, and Georgia. Such a one is Nora Mills in Helen, Georgia, which ships out its various types of grits, cornmeal and spoon bread meal all over the country. Another is the two-hundred-year-old "Old Mill" of Oak Ridge, North Carolina, operated by Charles Parnell. Of course, store-bought grits—enriched with vitamins—can provide a respectable dish, provided you give enough cook-time to bring the grits to a nice creaminess. As a supplement to this dish, you can add a half cup of diced Cheddar cheese. That would turn it into "cheese grits."

Old Timey Boiled Hominy Grits

1 cup hominy grits	4 cups water
2 tablespoons butter	Salt to taste

Into a saucepan, place the salt and water, and bring to a rolling boil. While stirring the water with a whisk, gradually sprinkle in the grits. Reduce the heat to low, and let the grits simmer until you notice only a sporadic bubble on the mixture surface. The boiling should continue for an additional 35 minutes, during which time you can add the butter. To ensure against scorching, continue to stir periodically until you remove the pot from the heat. Use gloves to protect from splattering grits.

Fried Grits

Slicing up and frying leftover solidified grits is one of the favorite dishes in the Southern mountains, particularly for a light supper. They go well with meat and gravies.

This recipe is adapted from one published by the late North Carolina restaurateur and author Bill Neal in his *Bill Neal's Southern Cooking*:

Bill Neal's Fried Grits

1 pot of boiled grits (basic	*1 egg, beaten*
boiled grits recipe above)	*3½ tablespoons bacon fat*
5 tablespoons butter	

While the pot of grits is still hot, place 4¾ tablespoons of butter into the mixture and beat well. Also add the beaten egg to the mixture. Use the other half teaspoon of the butter to grease the loaf pan. Pour the grits into the loaf pan and allow mixture to cool at room temperature for just under an hour. At that point, grits can be turned out and sliced into half-inch slices. Heat the bacon fat in skillet and fry at medium heat on each side for about 11 minutes or until golden brown. If you wish, the cooled grits mixture can be refrigerated for later use. Serves 6.

Hominy Casserole

This is a fairly modern Appalachian dish, the basic recipe of which was published by Phila Hach of Clarksville, Tennessee, in her *Official Cookbook of the 1982 World's Fair* (held in Knoxville, Tennessee). The reason I call it "fairly modern" is that it calls for canned hominy. Of course, there's nothing wrong with that. It's difficult to find authentic freshly made hominy unless you can go where it's being made. One place is the Georgia Mountain Fair held every August in Hiawassee, Georgia.

Appalachian Hominy Casserole

1 pound sausage	*1 can hominy (#2½ can)*
2 cloves garlic	*1 can tomatoes (#2½ can)*
1 green pepper, chopped	*1 teaspoon sugar*
1 onion	*Salt and pepper to taste*
3 stalks celery, chopped	

Preheat oven to 350°F. Into a skillet, crumble and fry sausage until done but not brown. Add garlic, green pepper, onion, and celery. Sauté until vegetables are about half done. Run the hominy through a food chopper. In a large bowl, mix the vegetable mixture with the hominy. Add tomatoes, sugar, and salt and pepper. Place in a buttered and preheated casserole dish, and bake at 350°F for 30 to 40 minutes. Serves 6.

∽

*U*sing a stone pestle, [Cherokees] beat their corn in a mortar till it was reduced to a coarse meal, of which they made a thick soup or mush called connehaney, relished everywhere. With this, a family would fill a large wooden bowl. Then all the individual members, spoons in their hands, gathered around and helped themselves.

—George Gordon Ward, *The Annals of Upper Georgia Centered in Gilmer County*

Cornmeal Mush

Mush, fried mush, and whole-grained hominy have been more popular in the Southern Appalachians over the years than grits. In 1824, Mary Randolph, in her pioneering Southern cookbook, *The Virginia Housewife*, gave recipes for polenta, mush, and other corn-based dishes. Mush is similar to grits except made with finer-ground cornmeal. It becomes a type of porridge or what the Italians call polenta. All it takes to make mush is to add boiling water or milk, and stir it constantly while the meal is being added.

And making fried mush is very similar to frying grits. You put the mush mixture in a buttered loaf pan and let it congeal overnight. The next day, drop the mush out and slice for frying with butter.

Here is a typical mush recipe. The dish can be served hot with butter and honey, syrup, or sugar.

Mountain Mush

5 cups boiling water   1 teaspoon salt
1 cup freshly ground cornmeal

Into a saucepan place the water and salt. Bring to a quick boil and slowly pour in the cornmeal in a thin trickle. Stir constantly with a wire whisk to avoid lumpiness, and let cook for around 18 to 20 minutes. Serves 6.

Soup

The Everlasting Meal

Soups are probably closer to the heart of any…region than any other item of its food.

—*Lillian Marshall,* Cooking Across the South

Ah, splendid soups! Could the hardy settlers of the Appalachian and Piedmont hill country—and the Indians before them—have survived the cold mountain winters without the soups, stews, and succotashes simmering away in frontier fireplaces?

Possibly. But they would have been greatly diminished, in soul, spirit, and stomach. Fortunately, most were not deprived. From the earliest pioneers who penetrated the mountain gaps, coves, and valleys, soups were great sustainers, being a fusion of the Appalachian frontier's bountiful vegetation and ever-present wildlife.

The pioneers took their cue from the Algonquian and Iroquoian Amerindians, who always kept a friendly pot of soup or stew simmering, not only for family members, but just in case someone stopped by.

In those early days, soups and stews served many families as their dietary mainstay—along with corn bread. Early American housewives—with no cookbooks to guide them, only the Indian example—began by plunking hunks of flesh or fowl into hot, salted water. That is, anything that could be brought down in the wild—pigeon, deer, rabbit, raccoon, turkey. Or perhaps an old hen for those who had established homesteads. These were combined with available vegetables such as beans, corn, and tomatoes. This followed down to recent generations.

"If my mother had a [ham] bone, she used it," said Ernest Parker of the Bucktown district of Gilmer County, Georgia, who grew up in the early 1900s. "That along with our garden vegetables—beans, corn, tomatoes, onions, okra, and the like."

In the winter, soup- and stew-makers were constrained to stored or dried vegetables, such as beans and pumpkins.

The earliest cookbooks to reach the interior called for hanging the pot "high and to the side" (referring to the fireplace). Instructions to "draw the pot back" referred to wood stoves that came along in the 1800s.

In any event, slow-cooking over wood fires, sometimes for days, was standard practice, assuring a fulsome flavor. This lengthy process was reflected in the colonial-era nursery rhyme:

Pease porridge hot
Pease porridge cold
Pease porridge in the pot
Nine days old.

Some like it hot
Some like it cold
Some like it in the pot
Nine days old.

Whatever the cooking length, housewives then, as today, loved to give the broth a little verbal encouragement periodically along with a few stirs and a taste or two.

~

Soup-making, while subject to much experimentation, is something of an art, albeit a simple and expansive art. As Sarah Belk has stated, "In the truest form of this art, there is probably no such thing as a 'little soup'—at least in the South."

Vegetable Soup

The best time for enjoying the most delicious of soups—those involving vegetables—is in the late summer and early fall. During this "putting-up season," fresh vegetables are plentiful and appetites are hearty.

Such was the case during my own early 1930s childhood in South Carolina's upcountry. My late mother would offer up for her family a glorious vegetable soup. It was a meal unto itself, so smooth and satisfying. During late summer "wheat threshing time," when crews and machines would descend on our farm trailing a cloud of dust, Mother would provide plenteous vegetables for the workers. But for our household, she added the real bonus—her magnificent vegetable soup. Her method was similar to that of Sidney Saylor Farr's mother who had "an instinctive knowledge of portions of vegetables to be used with each other."

Mother usually would start off with a piece of meat—leftover chicken, a ham bone, or a piece of side meat. To this she added many of the summer vegetables—onions, field peas, tomatoes, okra, and corn.

But there was something that gave it an extra smooth and tasty punch and my brother Connie recently revealed to me Mama's secret: She added, he said, a pinch or two of sugar!

I know, I know. Some say this is a sacrilege, severely frowned upon by purists in the Piedmont and Cumberland country. So I state it as a matter of fact for what it is worth. Lately, in my own soups, I have been putting in a dash of sugar or Sweet 'n Low just to check their effect. And, indeed, sugar does give soup a nice leveling taste, particularly if you have an acidic base such as fresh tomatoes. (The catsup-makers discovered this long ago.)

Here is a typical mountain vegetable soup:

Mountain Vegetable Soup

Soup bone	*1 cup onions, chopped*
2½ quarts water	*2 cups corn*
1 cup cabbage, chopped	*1 cup turnips, chopped*
1½ cups tomatoes	*Salt and pepper to taste*
2 cups lima beans	*2 teaspoons flour*

Place soup bone in saucepan with water, and boil 3 hours. Pour off fat, and add seasoning and vegetables. Combine flour with the salt and pepper, and combine with soup. Boil for 45 minutes and serve. Serves 10.

Bean Soup

A great Appalachian favorite is bean soup. The following recipe originated in the Shake Rag community in western Gilmer County, Georgia. The recipe comes from Martha Hopkins, wife of "mountain man" Paschal Hopkins, a former colleague of mine from Lockheed.

Shake Rag, by the way, got its name in the following manner: Earlier in this century, there resided in the community a moonshiner. His home sat on a hillside at the end of a remote narrow road off of the old "CC Road." Patrons who arrived in search of a jug of spirits would holler to announce their arrival. The bootlegger's wife usually would yell from her porch, "How much whiskey you want, boys?" If she merely waved her dishrag, it meant, "Sorry, boys, we're out of the recipe today."

Shelley beans, of course, are soup beans that require shelling, such as limas, butter beans, or the like.

Shake Rag Shelley Bean Soup

1 medium onion, chopped	*1 pint stewed tomatoes*
1 clove garlic, minced	*¾ tablespoon chili powder*
1 pound ground beef	*Juice of 1 lemon*
1 pound shelley beans	*½ teaspoon brown sugar*
2 pickled banana peppers, chopped	*Salt and pepper to taste*

In a skillet, sauté onion and garlic with ground beef until meat is browned or grayed. Place beans, peppers, tomatoes, and spice in a kettle. Bring to a boil. Add meat and onion mixture to bean pot. Simmer 2½ to 3 hours, at which time they're ready for serving. Serves 10. Yee-hah!

Colonial travelers, who need a long time to cover even short distances, actually filled their pockets with soup before they left on a trip. This Portable Soup...was prepared in the usual way and could contain practically any ingredients. The only difference was that no water was added to replace that which boiled away during cooking, so that the soup became thicker and thicker as it shrank in volume. Then it was poured into dishes, given several days to dry out completely, and at last cut into little cakes that were kept in a tin. When the travelers felt hungry he simply boiled some water and dropped in a cake of Portable Soup...and in no time had a delicious meal.

—LUCILLE RECHT PENNER, *THE COLONIAL COOKBOOK*

Corn Soup

It is understandable that corn soup would have been a favorite with mountain people. In her wondrous 1839 *Kentucky Housewife*, Lettice Bryan called for combining poultry or veal broth with the milk of green corn along with butter and seasoning and boiling it 'til done. She called for the addition of sweet cream before serving.

Here is a typical mountain corn soup recipe, named for the beautiful Conasauga River, a Cherokee-named stream that spills out of northwest Georgia and joins with a Creek-named waterway, the Coosawattee, to form the beautiful Oostanaula River, still another Native American namesake. To continue this rumination a bit further, the Oostanaula then joins with the Etowah to form the Coosa, which flows into Alabama!

Conasauga, by the way, comes from the Cherokee word *kahnasaguh* which means "grass."

Conasauga Cream of Corn Soup

1 cup chicken broth	1 cup cut green corn
2½ tablespoons flour	1 cup hot water
1½ cups sweet cream	Celery salt and pepper to taste
2 tablespoons butter	

Mix chicken broth with flour, cream, and butter and simmer over 250°F heat. Add the corn, water, and seasoning, and cook over low heat for 8 to 10 minutes. Keep stirring as soup thickens.

Tomato/Corn Soup

This tomato-corn soup is equally delicious. This recipe is adapted from one offered by Sidney Saylor Farr of Berea, Kentucky, in her delightful and autobiographical *More*

Than Moonshine. She notes that this soup is best served piping hot, garnished with bits of parsley.

Sidney's Tomato-Corn Soup

4 cups milk	*Parsley, chopped*
2¼ cups cooked tomatoes	*2 tablespoons butter*
1½ cups cooked corn	*Salt and pepper to taste*

Heat milk separately, but do not bring to boil. Bring tomatoes and corn to a boil, and add scalded milk slowly, stirring constantly to prevent curdling. Add seasonings and serve.

Potato Soup

Potato soup is one of those perennial favorites. As my friend John Parris of Sylva, North Carolina, testifies, "My folks, like many others here in the mountains, have always been partial to potato soup." This recipe is adapted from one published by the late Ferne Shelton of North Carolina in her *Pioneer Comforts* collection:

Pioneer Potato Soup

5 large potatoes, diced	*Dash of pepper*
2 large onions, diced	*2 tablespoons butter*
1 teaspoon salt	*1 quart milk*
1 quart water	

Cook potatoes and salted onions in water until tender. Add pepper, butter, and milk, and bring to a boil. Serve hot. (Add celery to recipe, if desired.) Makes 2 quarts.

Yellow Jacket Soup

Let me end this soup unit on an exotic note with directions for cooking Cherokee yellow-jacket soup. This recipe originated with the late Aggie Ross Lossiah, of Cherokee, North Carolina, granddaughter of Cherokee Chief John Ross. Mrs. Lossiah was one of the stalwart scions of the Cherokee Quala Reservation. She died in 1966 at the age of eighty-five.

> Corn, beans, and squash were unusually well suited to each other. When grown in the same field they complemented each other...The Iroquois called them the "three sisters." Corn and beans are particularly suited to each other, because while corn removes nitrogen from the soil, beans replace nitrogen, and the soil is therefore exhausted more slowly.
>
> —CHARLES HUDSON, *THE SOUTHEASTERN INDIANS*

Aggie reportedly once served a bowl of clear soup to a white friend visiting in her home in Cherokee. When the visitor—obviously enjoying the soup—could no longer contain her curiosity, she asked its base and was told it was yellow jackets. The friend sputtered in shock, got up, and left without taking another mouthful.

Many of Aggie Lossiah's traditional Cherokee recipes, handed down from her ancestors, were lovingly published by my friends Mary and Goingback Chiltoskey in their booklet *Cherokee Cooklore*. Actually Mary is the author and Goingback was her backup adviser. Goingback, now ninety years old, is one of Cherokee's most colorful personalities and a nationally renowned wood carver. Mary, also ninety, is a former teacher at Cherokee, which is located near the eastern side of Great Smoky Mountains National Park. The yield of this soup, an adaptation of Mrs. Lossiah's recipe, depends, of course, on the number of yellow jackets you can capture.

Goingback and Mary Chiltoskey

Cherokee Yellow-Jacket Soup
(OO-GA-MA)

Hunt for ground-dwelling yellow jackets in the early morning or in the late afternoon. Gather the whole comb. Place the comb over the fire or on the stove with the right side up to loosen the grubs that are not covered. Remove all the uncovered grubs. Place the comb over the fire or on the stove upside down until the paperlike covering parches. Remove the comb from the heat, pick out the yellow jackets, and place in the oven to brown. Make the soup by boiling the browned yellow jackets in a pot of water with salt. Add grease if desired.

Tangy Mountain Magic

Relishes, Pickles, Krauts, Chutneys, and Chow-Chows

Mountain women and girls learn early how to make a variety of pickles and relishes.
> —Sidney Saylor Farr, Berea, Kentucky, in More Than Moonshine

Making relishes, chutneys, preserves, and marmalades may come close to a science; it is also an art—a row of these preserved fruits is a beautiful thing.
> —Camille Glenn, Louisville, Kentucky, in
> The Heritage of Southern Cooking

Pickles are one of the joys of life.
> —Grace Hartley, Atlanta Journal

Granny Tipton had a big fifty-five-gallon wood castor-oil barrel; it come from Italy. We cleaned that booger out, and we made kraut in it. We'd chop that barrel full of kraut every fall. Not early cabbage but late cabbage. I still got Granny's old kraut cutter. It's an old wooden hoe…the hoe's straightened out. We'd chop that thing, forty-five to fifty gallons for the winter. Put cabbage down in there, salt and cabbage and salt and cabbage. Cabbage ferments, you know, makes its own juice. We had a big wooden lid made to fit down inside that barrel with a big rock laid on top of that lid to keep that kraut down in the juice. It'd take a week to ferment. I'd go in there in the wintertime, take a cup, and get a cup full of that ice-cold kraut juice. OOOoooo, it was good. Lot better than this canned kraut that you buy today. We kept us a cup on the barrel where we drank the juice off the kraut.

My friend Curtis Underwood was reminiscing about his days as a young man growing up in the north Georgia mountains near the southern tip of the Appalachian Trail. Mrs. Tipton also pickled beans by the barrel.

The kraut art, brought to the Southern Appalachians by the Palatinate and Moravian Germans, was just one of the great pickled foods that sustained the settlers as they swarmed into the interior.

It is from the Germans and Scotch-Irish and English and Scots from colonial days that we have inherited our love for "the sour and the sweet" of our foods.

On the sour side, salt and vinegar-preserved pickles and relishes and chutneys and chow-chows have put tangy pizzazz into the palates of many a mountain mouth over the years.

Azzie Waters of East Ellijay, Georgia, told me that her folks pickled beans the same way they pickled kraut—in a large crock. "This big old glass thing I have here holds about two gallons. I make a jar of pickled beans for my daughter every year, and I go boil corn and cut it off and put corn and pickled beans together, you know. Put in a layer of beans and some salt and a layer of corn 'til it gets the jar full."

Crocks and barrels were the way of preserving vegetables and fruits before the invention of the glass Mason jar in 1858.

> *A feller said he had an ulcer and thought he would die. He took cans of kraut juice and swore it made him better. Mother always had some juice around. I've drunk a lot of kraut juice for a sick stomach or a sore throat. It's good for "herniary." We used to grow a lot of cabbage. We'd generally make six to ten gallons of kraut...*
>
> *It was the idea years ago that if you made kraut in the middle of October, it would be bitter. But that's a superstition. Some ate sauerkraut with everything. When hamburgers came in, they had sauerkraut on them. I reckon it made them healthier than they are now.*
> —A. L. TOMMIE BASS OF SAND MOUNTAIN, ALABAMA,
> IN *PLAIN SOUTHERN EATING*

~

A daughter-in-law at the turn of the century was sized up largely by the volume of food she preserved during the first summer of her marriage.

"Those who flitted around doing things other than filling fruit jars [with fruits and vegetables]," wrote author Beth Tartan, "were regarded in the same way as the lazy grasshopper compared to the busy little ant."

But those who packed their pantries with pickles and relishes and chutneys and chow-chows along with the other fruits and vegetables of the season, say a few hundred jars, were held in great esteem, as well they might have been.

Pickling and preserving by salt-brine and vinegars are ancient arts. In colonial Virginia, Helen Bullock has written that pickles, preserves, jellies, sweetmeats, conserves, and relishes were "staple table delicacies." Estate records are replete with listings of stoneware and earthen jars used to put up such pickled preserves.

This was duplicated across the Appalachian interior. As Joni Miller has noted, in earlier days, "no Southern larder was complete unless it was stocked with comforting rows of hand-canned relishes and pickles. Cherished family recipes…were used to preserve the bounty of the summer harvest as a hedge against the dreary winter

> *The real recipe for pickling is a cup of vinegar, a cup of water, and a cup of sugar.*
>
> —LUCINDA OGLE,
> GATLINBURG, TENNESSEE

months ahead." Mrs. S. R. Dull, in her 1928 book, *Southern Cooking*, had fifty-six recipes for pickles and relishes!

In my research for this book, I found this tradition is still alive.

It is amazing how many pantries in the hill country are packed with a rainbow of jars of all the sweet and sour fruits and vegetables. Here are a few recipes that may whet your appetite for the way they did things in an earlier era with a few modern-day recipes to make it easier for you.

Pickles

As one of my fellow coworkers at the *Atlanta Journal*, Grace Hartley, wrote twenty years ago, "Pickles…add that extra special something to food at picnics, family reunions, church suppers, family gatherings, and to meals in general."

How true. Down through the past four centuries, mountain people have put great store in and have stored up millions of tons of pickles. Pickled beans and corn—often through the brine salt method by the barrel—were favorite pickling objects in early pioneer days. Today, cucumbers are at the top of the list, followed by the whole gamut of vegetables and fruits—beans, corn, peaches, tomatoes, and watermelons among them, even ramps.

Pickled Cucumbers

"The cucumber," says John Egerton, "seems made to be a pickle." The story is that Christopher Columbus brought cucumbers in his boat when he discovered America in 1492. In any event, the settlers arriving from England a century later were familiar with the vined vegetable; the native of northwest India had already become well known in kitchens on the Continent and the British Isles.

Early writers such as Amelia Simmons, in her 1796 *American Cookery*, promoted the pickling of "small, fresh-gathered [cucumbers] free from spots." For salt-brined cucumbers, Mrs. Lettice Bryan, author of *The Kentucky Housewife*

(1839), called for the use of young, long green cucumbers. My thanks go to Phyllis Connor of Bluefield, West Virginia, the source of this "cucumber and onion" recipe that originated with Mrs. Glen Davis of Bluefield.

West Virginia Bread and Butter Pickles

4 quarts medium-size cucumbers	5 cups sugar
6 medium-size white onions	1½ teaspoons turmeric
2 green peppers, chopped	1½ teaspoons celery seed
3 whole garlic cloves	2 teaspoons mustard seed
⅓ cup salt	3 cups vinegar

Make sure cucumbers are not seedy. Slice thin but do not peel the cucumbers. Add the onions, sliced thin; the green peppers, garlic cloves, and salt. Mix thoroughly. Place in covered container with cracked ice and let stand 4 hours. Drain well. Combine sugar, turmeric, celery seed, mustard seed, and vinegar. Pour this over the cucumber mixture. Heat just to boiling point. Seal at once in hot, sterilized jars.

~

Sidney Saylor Farr of Berea, Kentucky, says her mother and grandmother put up pickles this quick way, enabling them to rapidly process a bushel of cucumbers at one time. This is an adaptation of her technique, with my thanks to Sidney.

Mother Saylor's Fast Pickles

Water	Sugar
Vinegar	Cucumbers

In a large saucepan, put equal parts water, vinegar, and sugar. When heat reaches boiling, drop in young cucumbers, either whole or cut into quarters lengthwise. Cook for 8 minutes. Pack in hot, sterilized jars and seal.

~

My new friend Beuna Winchester of Bryson City, North Carolina, who is a retired interpretative commentator at the Great Smoky Mountains Park's Oconoluftee Visitors Center, is fond of this "universal pickle" recipe. It embraces a wide range of vegetables—peppers, onion, horseradish, cucumbers, cabbage, green tomatoes, and/or other vegetables.

Beuna's Universal Pickles

1 gallon vinegar	1 dozen sticks ginger
5 pounds brown sugar	½ cup cloves
1 box ground mustard	2 dozen green peppers, chopped

| ½ cup salt | 2 dozen small onions, chopped |
| Few pieces horseradish | ½ cup whole black pepper. |

Mix all the above together, and let stand in jars for 1 week, stirring each day. After that, add the following:

| Chopped cucumbers | Chopped green tomatoes |
| Chopped cabbage | |

Add or substitute other vegetables as desired. Seal in individual jars.

Pickled Beans

Willia Mae Hall Smathers, of the Haywood County side of Balsam, North Carolina, remembers her mother, Fannie Payne Hall, pickling barrels of beans as well as barrels of whole ears of roast'n'ear corn. This was when they resided on Hazel Creek before the 1945 completion of Fontana Dam that forced them to move out. Willia Mae advises that before starting out to brine-pickle beans such as this, one should consult the almanac: "Do not make pickled beans when the signs are in the feet, bowels, or secrets."

Willia Mae says that on this recipe, as an option, you can add corn cut off the cob to the beans at the beginning of pickling preparations.

Willia Mae's Brine-Pickled Beans

1 dishpan of snap beans	1 ½ cups salt
(about 2 gallons)	Several large grape leaves
Large churn crock	Large flint rock

String and snap beans. In a very large saucepan, place beans in water, and cook until beans will mash between your fingers and thumb. Cover with cold water, and drain several times until water ceases to be warm. Pack in crock or large container (large enough to have space left for weight on beans). Add plain or pickling salt. Mix well and cover with several large well-washed grape leaves. Weigh down with a plate and a good-size flint rock. Cover with a clean white cloth big enough to fold once then tie around top of container.

The importance of pickling on frontiers is obvious from the frequent mention of it in old writings. At the end of winter or on the trail, when diets consisted largely of salted meat and fish, pickles offered a vibrant note, and it was noted that "children and menfolk could get through a barrel of pickles faster than a hog through clover!"

—GERTRUDE HARRIS, *FOODS OF THE FRONTIER*

Place in cool place for 6 days or until sour. After the sixth day, rinse once in cold water then put in container with just enough of the pickling brine so that you can see it. Heat until it beads and comes to a boil. Put in clean, hot quart jars and seal.

~

From her Bakersville home in the high mountains of Mitchell County, North Carolina, Mrs. Bessie McKinney offered the following dilly beans recipe to the Johnson City, Tennessee, Junior Service League. The recipe was included in the league's comprehensive recipe collection, *Smoky Mountain Magic*.

Bakersville Dilly Beans

1 gallon green beans	*1 head fresh dill*
2 cups vinegar	*1 clove garlic*
6 cups water	*Salt to taste*
½ teaspoon red pepper	

String and wash tender green beans until you have 1 gallon. Leave whole. Scald beans in hot water until tender enough to stick with a toothpick—about 10 minutes. Pack beans into sterile jars. In saucepan, mix remaining ingredients, heat, and pour over beans. Seal jars and store. Yields 6 pints.

~

This recipe adaptation comes from Pat Mitchamore's *Miss Mary Bobo's Boarding House Cookbook*. The legendary "Miss Mary" ran her down-home boarding house in Lynchburg, Tennessee, not far from the Jack Daniels Distillery. While this recipe calls for freshly picked string, snap, or wax beans, another option is one pound freshly hulled pink beans or one pound pinto or dried white beans, cooked.

Old-Fashioned Tennessee Pickled Beans

2 pounds green beans	*¾ cup sugar*
5 cups apple cider vinegar	*1 teaspoon salt*

When I was a child, we lived in the north Georgia mountains. Mother would make a barrel of pickled beans with pickling salt. She put them in the springhouse but never canned them. Mother made pickles by the signs of the zodiac, never during Virgo or Scorpio. She only used white half-runner or cornfield beans. But that was long ago. I think any fresh tender bean would do.
—LUCINDA MCCLURE CHASTAIN, CHEROKEE COUNTY, GEORGIA

Fresh beans should be cooked to the tender-but-firm stage. Place beans in a glass dish under cover. In a large pan combine the vinegar, sugar, and salt, and bring to a boil. Pour the vinegar mixture over the beans, and stir well. Cover the dish, and leave for 2 hours before serving to allow the flavors to meld. Can be served either hot or cold. Serves 6 to 8.

Pickled Corn

Decades ago, families throughout the Southern Appalachians would salt-pickle barrels of corn on the cob. Ernest Parker of Gilmer County, Georgia, remembered that "they started doing that somewhere around the early thirties, when the Great Depression came on. They'd brine-pickle barrels of whole ears of corn just like they pickled kraut and beans."

In Swain County, North Carolina, the aforementioned Beuna Winchester's family salt-pickled corn in sixty-gallon barrels. On their place near Bryson City, it was not uncommon for them to also pickle a barrel of corn and beans mixed.

This recipe comes from Bonnie Myers of Townsend in east Tennessee, who gave details to Rose Houk for her book on mountain foods published by the Great Smoky Mountains Natural History Association.

Bonnie's Pickled Corn

Armload of fresh corn   *1 cup salt*
(12 to 15 ears)

In fall pull armload of corn from stalk. Shuck the ears, removing damaged ends and silks. In a large pot, cook until done. Cut corn off cob into a large pan. Add the salt, and stir well. Put into clean, sterile quart jars. Fill jars with boiling water. Seal and store in cool place or put into crock and store in cool place.

Pickled Cabbage (Kraut)

The Palatinate and Moravian Germans brought the kraut art to the Southern Appalachians. Since cabbage grows well in the Piedmont and high-elevation mountain valleys, it was common during the past century for families to salt-pickle their cabbage by the barrelful (and in large stone crocks) as well as beans and corn. On "kraut day," they used straightened hoes (with razor-sharp blades) to chop the cabbage in the barrels. At our home in upstate South Carolina, my mother usually made a churn (crock) of kraut every fall. And what a delicious and tasty taste! I loved to eat Mama's kraut as a stand-alone dish, but I'm told it's a great side dish to fresh pork and other meats (and for hamburgers and hot dogs!).

The key to making deliciously crispy kraut is to get the right salt-cabbage combination—around 2½ percent salt. This comes to about three and a half tablespoons of salt for every five pounds of cabbage. Wide-mouth crocks were commonly used so that a stone or brick weight could be placed on top during fermentation.

The old-fashioned method called for salting the cabbage down into a crock with the weight on top—sometimes a plate topped by a stone or brick. This would keep the cabbage submerged during the fermenting process. Typically a housewife would shred ten heads of cabbage and use a half cup of coarse salt. Fermentation would usually take just over a month.

Fast and Simple Sauerkraut

Today, many cooks in the region—such as Frances Gates Hill—have resorted to a fast, yet simple, modern-day kraut-making method. It calls for dissolving a cup of salt into a gallon of water and a cup of white vinegar. The cabbage is then chopped or shredded and packed into quart- or half-gallon jars. (Frances opts for the quart size). Two inches of head space is left in each jar. Into this the water/salt/vinegar mixture is poured over the cabbage. The jar should be sealed and placed in a cool, dark corner of the house. In about four weeks, the kraut should be ready to eat.

Pickled Peaches

In Carrboro, North Carolina, pickled peaches won the children's popularity contest in the Neal household. Author and restaurateur Bill Neal recalled "how we loved its sweet and sour tang!" Such peaches have been a dinner table treasure in the region since pioneer days. This recipe is adapted from one published by Betsy Tice White of Marble Hill, Georgia, in her book, *Mountain Folk, Mountain Food*.

Betty's Pickled Peaches

1 gallon ripe peaches	*6 cinnamon sticks*
3 pounds white sugar	*Whole cloves*
3 cups cider vinegar	

Select unbruised, firm, and ripe peaches. In a large saucepan, bring water to a boil, and dip the whole peaches in, a few at a time, for a half minute or so, to make the skins slip off easily. Immediately plunge peaches into cold water, and slip off skins. In a large enamel kettle, combine the sugar, vinegar, and cinnamon, and bring to a boil. Simmer for 30 minutes. Dip 6 peaches at a time into the hot syrup, and cook to the tender stage, but not enough to turn them mushy. Lift out with slotted spoon, and pack peaches into hot, sterilized jars, sticking a few cloves into each peach on the way. Fill jars with hot syrup and seal.

Green Tomato Pickles

This recipe comes from Virginia Underwood of Cherrylog, Georgia, who in 1981 put out a nice collection of recipes and reminiscences, *Georgia Mountain Heritage*, and followed it up with a second printing in 1990.

Cherrylog Green Tomato Pickles

½ peck tomatoes	*Salt*
3 green peppers	*2 cups vinegar*
3 onions	

Chop the tomatoes, peppers, and onions, put in a sieve, and drain dry. Salt in layers, and let stand overnight. Scald the vinegar, and pour over mixture. Let stand 2 days. Drain again. Then separately mix the following ingredients:

1 quart vinegar	*3 ounces ground cloves*
3 ounces mustard	*1 tablespoon black pepper*
¼ pint mustard seed	*1 tablespoon allspice*

Bring to boil, and pour over pickles in hot quart jars. Seal and store.

Relishes, Chow-Chows, and Chutneys

This is a great field unto itself. Mountain folk love to make these as a tangy pizzazz for their fall and winter tables to accompany fresh pork and wild meats, indeed for the entire year as garnishes and condiments. Mountain people love relishes to go with springtime greens.

This first recipe for corn relish comes from John D. Webb of Townsend, Tennessee, just to the west of the Great Smoky Mountains Park. While some mountain cooks such as Louise Woodruff of Walland, Tennessee, like to "hotten up" their corn relish with a few pods of red hot peppers or hot sauce, Mr. Webb's recipe opts for green (sweet) peppers only.

Townsend Corn Relish

4 cups fresh corn	4 cups vinegar
2 cups sliced, unpeeled	2 cups sugar
cucumbers	¼ cup salt
4 cups chopped ripe tomatoes	1 tablespoon turmeric
5 cups chopped green peppers	1 tablespoon mustard seed
2 cups chopped onions	

In large bowl or container, mix the vegetables. Add vinegar, sugar, salt, turmeric, and mustard seed. Heat to boiling, then simmer 25 minutes or until the vegetables are tender. Seal in hot, sterilized jars. Yields 6 pints.

Squash Relish

This recipe comes from my friends John and Emily Anthony, who ran a wonderful mountain restaurant, The Sautee Inn, from 1972 until they retired in recent years. The Inn is located in the beautiful Nacoochee Valley near Helen, Georgia. Much of the valley, including a historic Indian mound, is soon to become a Georgia state park, a gift from the descendants of former Governor Lamartine G. Hardman.

Sautee Squash Relish

16 cups squash, finely chopped	4 cups vinegar
4 cups onions, finely chopped	2 tablespoons celery seed
6 green peppers, chopped	4 cups sugar
4-ounce jar pimentos, diced	4 tablespoons mustard seed
½ cup salt	

Grind or finely chop the squash, onions, and peppers, and combine in large plastic container with pimientos, and sprinkle with salt. Cover with ice, and allow to set at least 3 hours. Then, in a large pan, combine the vegetable mix with the vinegar, celery seed, sugar, and mustard seed, and bring to a boil. Can mixture in hot, sterilized jars. Seal and process in water bath 10 minutes.

Chow-Chow

Chow-chow has been a fixture in the Southern Appalachians since the early 1800s. The word apparently derives from the Chinese word *cha* (mixed). Chow-chow can be served as a vegetable, a garnish, or as a condiment. Most chow-chows contain green tomatoes, cucumbers, cabbage, and onions, and, as an option, apples and corn. An 1879 Virginia recipe by Marion Cabell Tyree called for only cabbage and onions.

Kentuckian Mark Sohn, author of *Mountain Country Cooking*, developed this authentic chow-chow recipe for the present day. Easy to fix, it is a small-sized recipe and one that the cook can serve immediately, without aging.

Mark Sohn's Kentucky Chow-Chow

1 red bell pepper	½ cup sugar
1 medium onion	1 teaspoon ground mustard
1 cucumber	½ teaspoon turmeric
2 cups cabbage or a	⅓ cup white vinegar
large green tomato	⅓ cup water
2 tablespoons salt	

Chop, grate, dice, or julienne the pepper, onion, cucumber, and cabbage (or tomato). Reduce to 4 cups of tiny pieces, and stir in salt. Cover and let stand overnight. Drain the vegetables. Stir in the sugar, mustard, turmeric, and vinegar. In a large saucepan over medium heat, simmer with the water for 15 minutes. Yields 3 cups.

Chutney

Chutneys are kin to the other sour relishes in that they are made of fresh vegetables and fruits and are preserved for use during the winter and spring.

This chutney recipe adaptation comes from Mrs. Gunther Reid of Chattanooga, Tennessee, and was published originally in *Marion Brown's Southern Cookbook*. Peach chutney can be made from the same formula but slightly unripe fruit is suggested.

Mrs. Reid's Pear Chutney

4 large onions	2 teaspoons celery seed
1 dozen green peppers	2 tablespoons powdered turmeric
3 hot red peppers	2 teaspoons white mustard seed
½ cup salt	4 cups sugar
8 whole allspice	2 quarts good cider vinegar
6 whole cloves	½ peck pears, unpeeled and ground

Grind onions and peppers together; mix well with the salt. Place in large cloth bag, and let drain for 12 hours. Then pour cold water over mixture, and squeeze out as much liquid as possible. Make a bouquet of the spices by tying in a cloth. Mix sugar and vinegar, and put on to boil with the spice bouquet. When it comes to a boil, add the ground pear, onions, and peppers. Let simmer slowly until tender, from 30 to 40 minutes. Pour into sterilized pint jars and seal either with a top or paraffin. Yields 10 pints.

A "Witch's Brew" of Beets

I grew up at Iron Station in western North Carolina, and one of my favorite childhood memories, the highlight of our summers, came when my parents allowed me to pitch in and help them cook beets for later pickling. My parents still harvest and boil beets today in the same manner there in Lincoln County.

We would cook the beets outside in an iron pot. Mama said it was always so messy, but it was a thrill to me as a child of seven or eight to help out.

Sometimes the dark water would bubble up and appear much like a witch's brew. One day, a grandchild visiting our neighbors came over to our yard and asked my mother if she were a witch. It looked that way, with Mama dipping into the pot with a spoon and stirring the beet cauldron as the dark "brew" frothed up, sending vapors into the morning air.

I loved taking part in the ritual, along with my sister. When the water cooled down enough, our job would be to peel off the beets' outer skins that were easy to sluff off. Thus we got to put our hands down into the warm wine-colored water—up to our elbows—and laughed at the wonderful experience. We particularly enjoyed grappling around the bottom of the pot, trying to pluck out the few little beets that we had missed in the first round.

Eventually, the beets would end up in my mother's kitchen, where she and my grandmother would turn them into delicious pickles. The key added ingredient in preserving the pickles was sugar. I remember my grandmother, Estelle Keever Robinson, cautioning us that, "They won't be sweet if you don't add enough sugar!"

As I grew older, my father allowed me to use a big knife to chop off the beet tops, which I scattered in the garden as compost.

—*Arty Schronce, Director of Public Affairs,*
Georgia Department of Agriculture, Atlanta

Arty Schronce

Gordon Schronce of Lincoln County, North Carolina, dips out beets that have been boiled in his black pot in preparation for pickling.

A Table Constantly Spread

The fields and the hills are a table constantly spread.
　　　　　　　　　　　　　　　　—Henry David Thoreau

～

Peaches in the Summertime,
Apples in the fall,
If I can't get the girl I love,
I won't have none at all.

　　　　　　　　　　　　—Shady Grove mountain tune

～

To gather any wild fruit is to be most happily busy.
　　　　　　　　　　　　　　　　　—Charles Abbot

The sixteenth-century Europeans who wagoned down Virginia's Great Valley and moved through the Cumberland Gap into "America's Great Southwest" found that God had blessed them with an abundance of wild fruits and nuts—from persimmons to pawpaws, from chestnuts to chinquapins. And seemingly climbing every tree, heavily laden vines of muscadine grapes, including that bronze prince of the forest fruit kingdom, the almighty scuppernong.

Earlier pioneers on the seaboard were joyous at what they encountered on the fruited plain: "The Peach-Trees are much broken down with the weight of Fruit this Year," Quaker preacher James Harrison exuded in 1686, "...Raspberries, Goosberries, Currans, Quinces, Roses, Walnuts and Figs grow well...Our Barn, Porch and Shed are full of Corn..."

Jamestown's John Smith wrote back home to England in 1612 to tell of tasting an American maypop, "a fruit the inhabitants call maracocks...a pleasant wholesome fruit much like a lemon." (Soon to be called "field apricot.")

With the exception of citrus fruits, bananas, and pineapples, the mountain pioneers found virtually all of America's wild fruits and nuts had been deposited by the Almighty almost at their cabin doorsteps. In a short time, apple seed and cuttings came from England. Soon the interior hillsides were ablaze with apple blossoms; apple trees adapted well to the hill country climate and elevation. The forests abounded in chestnuts, walnuts, hickory nuts, beechnuts, and hazel nuts.

A home orchard was found near every farm house. Apples, pears, peaches...furnished fruit for preserving and drying (and after glass jars became cheap, for canning). A few grape vines and the ever-present scuppernong arbor supplied juice for jelly and wine.

—Martha A. Kenimer, Watkinsville, Georgia

Frontier housewives became adept at converting the cornucopia of fruit and nuts to tasty dishes, many of which carry down to this day: scrumptious pies, puddings, preserves, puffs, tarts, butters, jellies, jams, and the pickled varieties such as chutneys, relishes, pickles, marmalades, and the like. For a while, a classic dish from England called a "fruit fool" caught on; it called for combining and puréeing several fruits, boiling them briefly, then serving the dish with sugar and whipped cream.

And then, of course, there were the luscious liquid derivatives—wines, ciders, beers, and brandies to say nothing of the bracing "bounces." One of the grand all-time mountain favorites was the "cherry bounce."

Settlers reaching the Blue Ridge and Cumberland foothills not only rejoiced in being able to eat wild fruits in season fresh from the vine, they quickly learned the Indian ways of preserving their bounty so that they would carry over through the winter months. One of the simple techniques was that of drying. This worked well with apples, peaches, and grapes just as it had with pumpkins and beans ("leather-britches"). The drying technique (described in detail in the Art of Preserving chapter) extended to persimmons, blackberries, and huckleberries. Amazingly, the sweet taste was preserved while the sun removed the fruit moisture and weight so that the dried harvest could be packed up in bags and stored away to be used when needed.

Early in this century, on Cullowhee Mountain, North Carolina, the late Iva Ashe Pressley had her husband, Robert, build her a five-foot-long shelf to dry her apples on. The platform featured a two by two-inch lip on it to keep the slices of fruit from falling off.

"She'd peel and core the apples and slice them and spread them on that shelf," Iva's son Frank remembered. "We'd set it up on the top of the kitchen roof to dry.

Would take a few days. Then in the wintertime she'd pull those dried apples out of the sack and stew 'em for our breakfast. We'd eat 'em with butter and sugar to taste. That was one of our main breakfasts."

Another way of preserving fruits, of course, was to cook them up and can them. Eighty-five-year-old Azzie Waters of East Ellijay, Georgia, loved to help her parents cook apple butter on their Dawson County farm. "I still make it. You take real tender apples—ones that cook real good. Best'uns you can buy now are these Detroit Reds that get ripe along in August. I wash the apples real good and put the peelings in one cooker to make jelly out of. Then I slice the apples real thin and pour some water over 'em and cook 'em in another pan. Doesn't take 'em very long to cook.

> *Southerners know how to seize the moment to turn these fleeting gems of perfect ripeness [fruit] into preserves and jams. How else would it be possible to serve a wedge of Heritage Jam Cake with Kentucky Fruit Filling or a generous square of Fig Preserves Cake with Buttermilk Candy Frosting on a chilly January Day?*
>
> —SOUTHERN HERITAGE CAKES COOKBOOK

"Then I take a potato masher and mash 'em up real good in the pot. Then I dip them out and run them through a colander…makes a real fine applesauce. Then I take that sauce and make my apple butter in a deep pressure cooker–canner.

"I put three cups of applesauce and two cups of sugar and some cinnamon and let it cook 'til it cooks down and gets all the water out. I have a long-handle spoon and I stir it till it's as thick as you think it should be, then take it out and put it in jars."

And, of course, some folks saved apple cores and peelings, converting them into vinegar which they used to pickle other fruit!

The fact was that in early America, fruits and nuts represented a big portion of the settlers' diets, headed by blackberries as the most prolific and equally as popular, followed by the ever-present foxgrapes and muscadines and wild plums that volunteered and spread quickly when the forests were cleared for planting corn.

Orchards became a point of pride for mountain farms, and young people enjoyed getting out among the blooming fruit trees. In Tennessee's Sevier County, author Florence Cope Bush, in her classic *Dorie: Woman of the Mountains*, recalled her grandfather John Watson's orchard that included damson plums, black cherries, Indian peaches, and several apple varieties including Winter John, June apples, Early Harvest, Summer Rambo, and a small yellow, red-striped variety they called the "stinkbug apple."

"Granny Jane, Aunt Rintha and Ma processed and preserved fruit with methods handed down by earlier generations," Mrs. Bush wrote. "Cider, vinegar, applesauce, apple butter, dried apples, bleached apples, and jelly kept us well fed all year…"

One of the crowning glories of fruits and nuts utilization on the frontier—and down through the centuries to follow—came with the fruitcakes that housewives fixed for the holiday season.

My mother's favorite (and mine as well) was one she called the Japanese fruitcake. It included a myriad of fruits and nuts and was topped with shredded coconut. That cake would be the centerpiece of our Christmas table and oh, so delicious it was.

More about that in the Desserts section. Now we want to take up some of the individual fruits found in the mountain country.

When our work confined us to the area on the east side of the Chickamauga [river]...we spread our dinners beneath the wild cherry trees...It was my father's habit to lie down and take a half hour's nap after eating dinner under the trees. He urged us to do the same, and we found this easy to practice except when the black cherries were ripe. While he was sleeping, we would climb the trees and gorge ourselves on the cherries that were blackest. They were far more tasty than the cultivated cherries.

—ROBERT SPARKS WALKER,
AS THE INDIANS LEFT IT

Apple Time in Appalachia

I'm sure God made little green apples just so my mother could cut them into brown sugar and make the most delicious side dish for pork, ham, or breakfast that a child ever tasted.

—*Ronni Lundy*

~

The Lord is good to me,
And so I thank the Lord:
For giving me the things I need.
The sun and the grain and the apple seed,
The Lord is good to me.

—*Anonymous Grace*

The people who settled the Shenandoah, Blue Ridge, and Cumberland interior had strong links to Elizabethan England. It showed up in their speech, mores, and manners. Even their love of apples and apple pies came directly from the Queen Elizabeth era.

Check your history books: When Elizabeth I was Britain's monarch in the late sixteenth century, apple pies became a vital part of the English cuisine. No less a literary figure than Jane Austen wrote that "good apple pies are a considerable part of our domestic happiness."

Apple cuttings and seeds that reached the colonies from England soon spread to the Southern Appalachians. Before long, no respectable hill country homestead was without its apple orchard. The orchards along Virginia's rolling Blue Ridge, in particular, became one of America's premier and prolific producers of apples. In time, western North Carolina and northern Georgia also became big in apples.

"We had a pretty good orchard," remembers ninety-year-old Nina Garrett. Nina still lives near where she grew up, on north Georgia's Blue Ridge (Continental) Divide. Precipitation descending on the east side of the divide flows into the Atlantic Ocean. That coming down on the west side flows to the Gulf of Mexico. Apples from orchards on this lofty Appalachian plateau find their way into ciders and apple butters and cobblers all over the area.

"We never did have to spray our apples to keep the worms out," Nina Garrett recalled about her turn-of-the-century experiences. "Once in a while you'd find a worm in one…just cut that piece out and put it in the hog feed."

As Johnny Appleseed proclaimed, the apple is just about the most adaptable fruit of all, being amenable to slicing, dicing, drying, leathering, combining, saucing, smoking, steaming, buttering, baking, stewing, puffing, frying, canning, fermenting, distilling, and what have you! And the early Southern mountain folks, and later ones, too, took advantage of every potential of the versatile fruit.

Housewives peel apples in preparation for a run of apple butter.

As was true with most mountain families, the Garretts made good use of their apple harvest each year. In addition to drying bushels of apples and making a few barrels of apple cider every fall, they produced dozens of gallons of apple butter, enough to tide the big family through the cold months. Nina's recollections were sharp.

"Apple butter, it was mighty good back then. The way we made it, we'd cook our apples and make applesauce, then mash 'em until they were cooked real good. Then we put about the same amount of white sugar in as we had applesauce and boil it until it got thick. You'd have to stir it constant; it'd stick if you didn't. And it'd boil over if you cooked it too fast and too hot. The secret was to cook it real slow."

One of the earliest American eating places to take advantage of the apple potential was Hanover Tavern in Virginia—where Scotch-Irishman "Give me liberty" Patrick Henry tended bar. Founded in 1723, the tavern became famous for its apple dishes, among others. Even today, stewed apples are on the menu. This recipe is reproduced from colonial days:

Hanover Tavern's Stewed Apples

2 cups apples, cooked	1 teaspoon lemon juice
and smashed	½ teaspoon salt
½ cup brown sugar	½ teaspoon nutmeg
4 tablespoons cornstarch	1 teaspoon cinnamon
1 teaspoon vanilla	3 tablespoons butter

Preheat oven to 350°F. Place apples in medium-size bowl; mix sugar and cornstarch and add apples, mixing well. Add remaining ingredients, except butter, and mix thoroughly. Pour mixture into an 8-inch square, greased baking dish, and dot with butter. Bake at 350°F for 30 to 45 minutes. Serves 6.

Although the Hanover recipe doesn't state it, sun-dried apples are essential to authentic apple recipes. And while sun drying removes all the apple's moisture, amazingly, dried apples retain a remarkable sweetness. Drying apples was a summertime chore for many people such as the late Bil Dwyer of Highlands, North Carolina, who remembered that a bushel of apples would dry out at about four pounds. He put his peeled and sliced apples on his shed roof, covered then with curtain netting, and dried them in the hot sun. "If a rain came up, I had quite a scramble," Dwyer recalled. (The apple-drying technique is described in detail in the Art of Preserving chapter of this book.)

Fried Apples

A delightful springtime dish, plain pan-fried apples came with the arrival of the first green apples in early May—usually sour ones. Housewives didn't do any canning that early in the year; their families were starved for fresh fruit. Thus the green apples were fried for instant use! Fried apples also were handy to serve with wild meat and pork.

Even springtime breakfasts in the mountains often called for fried apples. On Cullowhee Mountain, North Carolina, Iva Ashe Pressley fixed a delicious fried apple breakfast dish that she called "larp." Fried apples also came in handy to serve with pork or wild meat.

The usual fried apple technique called for slicing ten to twelve small green apples, then dropping them into a heated iron skillet covered with butter or margarine (or bacon grease as suggested by some early chefs including Mrs. S. R. Dull). They would be cooked on low heat, being stirred until they became soft. Then a cup of sugar was added, and the heat turned up until the batch began to turn brown.

As noted previously, experts say that if you want to obtain the optimum in fried apple deliciousness, you need to obtain firm, tart, possibly even sour early apples and cook them "just so," leaving in as much flavor as possible.

The late Mrs. Dull, for many years the South's grand dame of cooking, advised that a tart apple cooks quicker and smoother than a sweet one. But if you have to cook sweet apples, she advised a dash of lemon juice or cream of tartar will help induce tenderness.

Here is a fried apple recipe from Glenn Cardwell of Greenbrier, Tennessee. Glenn told Rose Houk that "if corn was the staff of life for the mountaineers, then apples were the spice of life." Glenn urged using sweet apples such as Limbertwig, Jonathan, McIntosh, or Delicious. These apples stay chunkier and don't cook up as much as tart apples.

Glenn's "Spice of Life" Fried Apples

Four apples, quartered   *½ stick of butter*
Vegetable oil   *¾ cup sugar*

Remove core from quartered apples, and slice into thin pieces. Fry in oil. Stir to brown. Add butter and sugar, and keep cooking until the butter melts, at which time they are ready for serving.

⁓

Kentucky's Ronni Lundy, author of the wondrous book, *Shuck Beans, Stack Cakes, and Honest Fried Chicken*, uses butter to soften her apples then she tops them with just enough brown sugar to give them a caramel glaze. "Once in a spirit of real decadence," Ronni wrote, "my sister Pat and I put dollops of sour cream on ours. If you're feeling in a wicked mood, I recommend you try it. It's a taste worth sinning for." The following recipe, a side dish for six, is adapted from the one Ronni published in *Shuck Beans*. She urges before starting to cook that you taste a slice of the apple to check its sweetness. If it's exceptionally sweet, use a lesser amount of sugar. If tart, add more sugar.

Ronni's Fried Apples

2 tablespoons butter   *⅓ to ½ cup brown sugar*
4 medium apples

Melt butter in skillet over low heat. Quarter and core apples. Cut each quarter into 3 slices lengthwise. Place sliced apples in the butter, cover, and cook on medium-low heat for about 5 minutes, turning a couple of times. Spread sugar over the apples and let it melt just a bit, then gently turn the apples so all the slices get coated with the sugar. Some of the apples will mush up a bit while others will stay in slices; that's the desired effect. Cook over medium-low heat for another 10 minutes until the sugar begins to thicken just a bit into syrup, then serve hot.

Apple Cobblers

And, of course, there are the apple cobblers. As my Baptist minister brother Connie (now retired in Augusta, Georgia) would exclaim, "My, oh my, Mother, you really know how to fix a cobbler!"

Most mountain cobbler recipes called for dumplings to be made from biscuit dough and rolled out in thin strips. A layer of strips would go in the pan, followed by a layer of stewed dried apples and sugar, followed by another layer of dumpling strips stretched crosswise. This would be followed by another layer of fruit and on top, a layer of rolled-out batter. All that was then required was to put the cobbler in the oven for about 30 minutes or so.

Michie Tavern in the Virginia Blue Ridge near Monticello, started in the 1770s by Scot immigrant and religious freedom seeker John Michie, serves yet today a cobbler recipe faithfully reproduced from colonial days. This is the tavern's recipe for a big fifteen-person cobbler:

Michie Tavern's Apple Cobbler

¾ cup sugar

2 tablespoons flour
   if fruit is juicy

1 teaspoon nutmeg

½ teaspoon cinnamon

⅛ teaspoon salt

½ teaspoon grated lemon peel

6 to 7 cooking apples peeled, cored and
   thinly sliced

Pie crust

1 tablespoon butter

Preheat oven to 450°F. In a mixing bowl, combine all ingredients except apples, pie crust, and butter. Prepare pie crust and line either large ovenproof square or rectangular dish; add half of apples and sprinkle with half of sugar mixture. Top with remaining apples and remaining sugar mixture. Dot with butter. Add top crust, rolled to desired thickness. Make slits for steam to escape, and dot with more butter. Bake pie at 450°F for 45 to 50 minutes.

Apple Dumpling

Close kin to the cobblers were apple dumplings, those oh-so-delicious deep-pan pies that date back a long way in our colonial history. In her 1747 cookbook, *Art of*

The idea that apples have curative...powers arises in part from Celtic and Greek legends. In Greek mythology, the apple was the sacred fruit of Apollo. Aside from being the sun god, Apollo had the power to heal...Even now, in the north Georgia mountains, people attest to the power apple cider has in curing an illness called the shengers. Shengers are bed sores and rashes which are suffered mainly by elderly people. One drinks apple cider to combat them.
—Steve Oney, *Atlanta Journal-Constitution Magazine* (1977)

Fried Apple Pies

Of all the mountain dishes calling for dried apples, luscious fried apple pies—introduced to the Appalachian South in the 1830s—were at the top of the list. Most southerners remember fried pies "from when they were about eye-level with an iron skillet," the late legendary Chapel Hill restaurateur Bill Neal declared. Stewed dried apples made up the fillings, sometimes jam or jelly. The dough would be either biscuit or pie dough, depending on your grandma's preference. Most cooks would slow-stew the apples along with brown sugar.

Cooking Made Plain and Simple, Hannah Glasse offered the following recipe to early American housewives:

Hannah's Apple Dumplings

To make a good puff-paste, pare some large apples, cut them in quarters, and take out the cores very nicely; take a piece of crust, and roll it round enough for one apple; if they are big, they will not look pretty; so roll the crust round each apple, and make them round like a ball, with a little flour in your hand. Have a pot of water boiling, take a clean cloth, dip it in the water, and shake flour over it; tie each dumpling by itself, and put them in the water boiling, which keep boiling all the time; and if your crust is light and good, and the apples not too large, half an hour will boil them; but if the apples be large, they will take an hour's boiling; when they are enough, take them up and lay them in a dish; throw fine sugar all over them, and send them to table; have good fresh butter melted in a cup, and fine beaten sugar in a saucer.

According to Kay Moss and Kathryn Hoffman of Gastonia, North Carolina, who did a fascinating study of eighteenth-century foods in *The Backcountry Housewife*, a fancier dumpling results from the recipe just listed if the cored apple is filled with sugar and cinnamon.

Apple Fritters

Over the years, apple fritters have been a great mountain dish. My friend John LaRowe, who for many years ran the famed Mark of the Potter shop on north Georgia's picturesque Soque River, obtained this recipe for fritters in a collection he published and that is still being published by the pottery's present owner, Jay Bucek. The recipe was offered by Sue Tharpe of Glenmeadow:

Sue's Apple Fritters

1 cup plain flour
Pinch of salt
2 egg yolks, plus 1 egg white
1 tablespoon cooking oil
5 ounces milk

1 pound north Georgia cooking apples
Juice from 1 lemon
Sugar
½ cup butter or cooking oil

Sift flour and salt into medium-sized mixing bowl. Make a well in the center and add eggs and oil. With wooden spoon, mix eggs and oil slowly into flour, gradually adding milk. Beat well, then cover and keep in cool place for 30 minutes. Peel and core apples; slice into rings ¼-inch thick. Sprinkle with lemon juice and sugar. Dip apples into batter and fry in the hot butter. Drain and serve immediately.

Of course, apple cakes are not to be forgotten. Barbara Southern's mother in Gilmer County, Georgia, used "Streaked June" apples—now about nonexistent—to make an applesauce stack cake.

"Mother canned them to make applesauce cake. Little thin layers of cake, put apples between them. Then when they'd soak up [the juice] like in a couple of days, oh, they were so good!"

(I'm not going into apple cake recipes here. Look for them in the Desserts chapter.)

Apple Bread

One of the most popular apple products in the mountains today is apple bread. People visiting Gilmer County in the autumn for the big Apple Festival usually come home with several loaves of Ellijay Apple Bread, a wonderful concoction of apples, sugar, dough, and cinnamon—a recipe developed and patented by Bernice Branch. While Bernice's recipe is not available, this one is adapted from one offered by North Carolina's Lyn Kellner in her *Taste of Appalachia*.

When a mountaineer's raucous voice announcing, "Ap-ples! Ap-ples!" sounded on the crisp November air, the Obed and Riley children always left their places...They ran up the hill to wait for the Apple man. His wagon, decorated with shiny red apples on the end of sticks was, to their childish fancy, the result of some good fairy's magic wand...The children didn't know that those big red apples were covering up...jugs of blockade liquor.

—FROM THE NOVEL A LITTLE LEAVEN, BY FRANCES ADAIR

Annie's Apple Bread

2 eggs, beaten	2⅛ cups all-purpose flour
⅔ cup sugar	1 teaspoon baking powder
½ cup butter or margarine	2 cups chopped apples
1 tablespoon lemon juice	1 cup chopped black walnuts
½ teaspoon salt	

Preheat oven to 350°F. Cream the eggs, sugar, butter, and lemon juice. Stir in the salt, flour, and baking powder. Stir in the apples and nuts. Bake in a greased, floured loaf pan for 45 minutes to an hour. Makes 1 loaf of apple bread.

∼

While modern-day apple farmers (the ones that I'm most familiar with are in north Georgia's Gilmer County) grow quite an array of apple varieties all the way from Red Delicious to Ozark Gold, Stayman, Rome, Gala, and Detroit Reds, Appalachian apple orchards at the turn of the century and before had a few old standbys that today are about gone with the wind.

On Cullowhee Mountain, the Robert Daniel Pressley farm that came down from several generations of Pressleys had an orchard of forty trees.

"We had one called a buff apple," recalled Robert's son Frank Pressley. "It was similar to this Red Delicious apple today. It was pretty good and meller to eat right off the tree. In my mind I can remember right where it stood. Then we had what they called the Garden apple. It looked more like the Green (Golden) Delicious apple today. We had a small sweet apple, yellowish…about the size of a large hen egg. It was sweet. That was what we'd make our sweet apple cider out of."

Pressley remembered another apple they called the Limbertwig. "The Limbertwig was the best keeper we had. We'd put it in the cellar. You could go in there and dig that thing out at Christmas and it was about the size of a big hen-egg and kindy of a rusty-looking color, greenish on the bottom and rusty looking on top. It was a delicious apple. Those we'd keep to eat through the winter.

"Those old apple varieties are all gone," Frank Pressley said wistfully. "Folks have all hybrids now."

Peaches

A Joyous Time When They Hit

*When the peach orchard "hit," it meant joy…Peaches had so many charms—
and there were so many ways of stretching the charms on through winter
scarcity…a six-gallon crock of peach butter was no mean household asset—
indeed it ranked next to the crock of black-berry jam.*
> —Martha McCullough-Williams of Tennessee,
> Dishes and Beverages of the Old South

~

*Few fruits are as wontonly luscious [as the peach]. The fuzz stings your
tongue, the flavor explodes in your mouth, the juice dribbles sensuously down
your chin…*
> —Steven Raichlen, Celebration of Seasons

The Cherokees were big into peaches before the first settlers came into their territory. Indeed, the British explorer John Lawson found that the Indians claimed the red-blushing cling fruit as their own, "and affirm they had it growing amongst them before any Europeans came to America."

> The tree grows very large, most commonly as big as a handsom apple tree; the flowers are of reddish, murrey color, the fruit is rather more downy than the yellow peach, and commonly large and soft, being full of juice. They part freely from the stone and the stone is much thicker than all the other stones we have, which seems to me that it is a spontaneous fruit of America…Of this sort, we make vinegar; wherefore we call them vinegar peaches, and sometimes Indian peaches.

Despite all this beautiful description, the U.S. Bureau of Ethnology writer—who quoted Lawson—felt that the "Indian peach" as Lawson described it, actually had reached American shores in the 1500s with the Spaniards. He reasoned that the Indians likely got the seeds from the conquistadors who came to Florida or perhaps from the de Soto troops who marched through the Carolinas before heading west.

Whatever the American peach's ancestry, it is acknowledged as having been one of the pioneers' staple fruits, providing the base for pies, cobblers, preserves, butters, "leathers," and for the best of brandies. Even today dried peaches are fantastic for pies and fruit dishes, being perfectly preserved and wholesomely delicious. And, of course, there are the peach pickles, conserves, and marmalades.

Old-timers considered August yellow stone cling peaches good for drying; early September peaches, the Heaths, best for preserves and brandied fruit; and clear seed October peaches best for peach butter.

Lots of folks have a peach tree but they're short-lived. Now the pear tree is different; it lasts a long time, like a Supreme Court judge.
—A. L. TOMMIE BASS, SAND MOUNTAIN, ALABAMA, IN *PLAIN SOUTHERN EATING*

On North Carolina's Cullowhee Mountain, there was a wild peach known as the "open stone." Frank Pressley remembered that "they didn't get but about the size of a big hen egg, and were light yellow. You could just pull that thing open and the seed would just drop out and it would melt in your mouth.

"Then we had a yellowish-looking peach we called the cling peach. That meant the meat grew to the seed, clung to it. We also had an Indian peach there, a cling, and it was almost bloodred on the inside. That was a gen-u-wine good peach."

Peach Cobbler

In Dillsboro, North Carolina, not too far from Cullowhee, stands the one-hundred-year-old Jarrett House, known across the country for its outstanding traditional Appalachian cuisine. Frank and "Miss Sallie" Jarrett operated the hotel until Frank's death in 1950. It is operated today by Jim and Jean Hartbarger. One of the favorite dishes carried down through the years is their peach cobbler. Here is the Jarrett recipe with my thanks to the Hartbargers who include this in their *Jarrett House Potpourri* recipe collection.

Jarrett House Peach Cobbler

3 tablespoons cornstarch
1 quart sweetened peaches
1 cup all-purpose flour
½ cup shortening
Butter or margarine

Preheat oven to 350°F. Mix cornstarch with ice water, enough to moisten. Mix peaches and cornstarch, and put in an oblong pan. Heat until cornstarch is dissolved. Make a dough using flour and shortening with enough ice water to mix. Roll out very thin, cut into strips, and crisscross on top of fruit. Dot with butter, and bake at 350°F for about 30 minutes or until brown.

The arrival of the peach season provided a time of fun and festivity at many a mountain household, second only perhaps to apple butter parties. While plantations farther east had their own special kilns for peach-drying, most mountain farmers put their peaches out on a convenient roof or ledge to dry, just as they dried their apples and green bean "leather-britches" or "shuck beans."

But there were some individual kilns in the mountains. John Parris's grandfather, Rufus Parris, at his farm at Burning Hills, North Carolina, made his own kiln of stone with pieces of iron laid across the top. Before putting the peaches into the kiln, however, family and friends would have a lively "peach peeling/ paring party" rivaling in fun a community corn-shucking. Rufus Parris told his grandson "sometimes there'd be a pile of peaches as high as your head." It took eight bushels of ripe fruit to make a bushel of dried peaches. After the peaches were kiln-dried, workmen pulled them out and spread them on blankets for a final drying by the sun.

*P*eaches spread through Indian America faster than the white man did.
—WAVERLY ROOT, FOOD HISTORIAN

Peter Kalm, the observant Swedish visitor to America in the eighteenth century, had this to say about an old-fashioned peach-drying:

> The fruit is cut into four parts, the stone thrown away, and the fruit put upon a thread, on which they are exposed to the sunshine in the open air, till they are sufficiently dry. They are then put into a vessel for the winter. Or, having lost their juice by this means—they are put into an oven, out of which bread has been just taken…soon taken out and brought into the fresh air…repeates several times.

Peach Fried Pies ("Mule Ears")

Tennessee's Martha McCullough-Williams asserted that "very bright and sweet" sun-dried peaches were required for making superior fried peach pies. She quoted an unnamed "famous doctor" as saying, "You would be only the better for eating an acre of (fried pies)." This was Mrs. Williams's fried pie recipe from her early 1900s tome, *Dishes and Beverages of the Old South*, republished in recent years by and with my thanks to the University of Tennessee Press. In some areas of the Carolinas fried pies were nicknamed "mule ears."

In the fall of the year, many mountain people hauled their farm products—including apples, peaches, and berries—to nearest towns requiring several days of travel. The late Oscar Cannon and his mule team are pictured hauling a load over north Georgia's Logan Turnpike in 1917.

Tennessee Peach Fried Pie

Soak (dried peaches) overnight after washing in three waters, simmer five hours in the soaking water. With a plate to hold the fruit under, mash and sweeten while hot, adding spices to taste—cinnamon, nutmeg and ginger. Roll out short paste into rounds the size of a small plate, cover one-half with the fruit, fold over the empty half, pinch well together around the edges and fry in deep fat, blazing hot, to a rich quick brown on both sides. Drain on paper napkins, sprinkling lightly with sugar. Serve hot or cold.

Peach Leather

One of the distinctive Appalachian peach derivatives was "peach leather." Production of this unusual dish was achieved by running the peeled peaches through a course sieve, then cooking them up with brown sugar. The final step was spreading the sauce out on plates and drying it in the sun over several days. When the mixture was thoroughly dry, the housewife would cut the leather into strips and hang them from a string in the kitchen where they remained until needed.

Although drying peaches in the old manner is nearly extinct, back in earlier decades, up through the 1940s, home-dried peaches were a great item for bartering. In the late fall, mountain folk would haul loads of dried peaches to nearby towns where there was always a ready market.

Whatever leftover peaches the farmer had oftentimes went to brandy distilleries, which operated legally—with no taxation—up until the Civil War and with government sanction (and taxes) afterward except during the era of state and national Prohibition. "Brandy peaches" usually brought fifty to sixty cents a bushel, about one-third the value of the better quality fruit. Stillhouses shipped out their brandy by the wagonloads to markets across the Southeast.

Peach Butter

Peach butter, like apple butter, will give biscuits a tasty pizzazz in the morning. Here's a recipe offered by Mrs. Bessie Whisman of Johnson City, Tennessee, in a substantial recipe collection, *Smoky Mountain Magic*, put out by the Johnson City Junior Service League:

Bessie's Peach Butter

Wash a bushel of ripe peaches thoroughly; remove seeds and slice into thin slices without peeling. Use a brass kettle over an open fire, keeping the fire good and steady

The peach (Prunus persica) persists around old orchard sites, or is sparingly found along roadsides, where birds or school children scattered the pits. These are usually like the well known horticultural peach, although fruit may be smaller in size. There are also wild-looking scraggly, small trees known as Indian peaches and said to be relics of Creek and Cherokee orchards. The Amerindian tribes got the peach from the Spaniards at an early date and had flourishing orchards when the first Scotch and English settlers came...Lawson mentions the Cherokees having "barbecued [spiced] peaches and peach bread."

The fruit is usually small, very sweet, and white meated, with a red heart... Fragrant pink flowers appear on the bar boughs in early spring.
—MARIE MELLINGER OF RABUN COUNTY, GEORGIA, *ROADSIDE RAMBLES*

throughout the cooking time. Put 1 gallon of water in the kettle, and then add peaches. Cook and stir about 2½ hours, using a long handle. Then add 16 pounds sugar and cook until mixture turns dark red and has a nice glaze, about 1½ to 2 hours more cooking. To test mixture, spoon a little on a dish and let it set a few minutes. If it has a glaze and no water stands around it, it is ready to can. Seal in sterilized jars.

~

I regret having to end this chapter on a down note but I cannot overlook one other important peach derivative: Switches for mothers to use to discipline their children! In my case, Mother seemed always to have on hand a nice supply of peach switches; they were keen and sharp and quickly got your attention when applied to your bare legs. Truth be told, doubtless many American youngsters recognized the error of their ways at the end of their mothers' authoritative little peach limbs.

Berries

A-berryin' on the Blue Ridge

Honey, how'd ye like ter take a leetle walk?
Ye like to go a-berryin' on the mountain?
　　　　　—From the novel, Give Us This Valley *by the late Tom Ham*

~

Children learned early about nature's wonders by gathering berries
and fruits.
　　　　　—Former Georgia governor Zell Miller, in The Mountains Within Me

Blackberry Winter was the springtime talisman, the last gasp of cold weather. Winter-weary hill people knew that wild blackberry bushes soon would be blooming out in all their white glory, giving the roadsides and ditch banks the look of a light snowdusting. By summertime, the thorny plants would yield bountiful bucketloads of the luscious black fruit.

One of the joys of growing up in the Appalachians in earlier decades—indeed across most of the South—was going berry picking with your lard bucket in hand.

Zell Miller, who grew up on north Georgia's Blue Ridge plateau and later became governor, as a young lad enjoyed joining his friends on blackberry jaunts. Even the stinging briars and the heat seemed only minor irritants, "when everyone was joking and singing while they picked."

During the colonial and pioneer era, wild fruits—elderberries, strawberries, service-berries, dewberries, blackberries, huckleberries, wild cherries, plums, and crab apples—represented a vital part of the mountaineer's diet, particularly in the early years until he could get his farm and orchard up and going. Even in after years, to Appalachian families, the fresh fruit of early summer was a welcome relief from the winter food limitations.

The first Britishers to settle Virginia in the early 1600s found blackberries growing abundantly. For three centuries, the wild berries became a dietary staple for seacoast and interior settlers, providing families with delicious pies, cobblers, fritters, jams, and jellies. The blackberry was also used for medicinal purposes. One doctor had a concoction that called for making up a syrup by boiling a pound of sugar with a pint of water. To this he added a pint of fruit juice for each pound of syrup. After boiling this mixture for a quarter hour, the good doctor added a half pint of brandy to each quart of the syrup. Usual dose was a half glass for an adult and a tablespoon for a child.

Late June usually marked the beginning of the berry-picking season. Dewberries, as the first to ripen, were an early delight to mountain taste buds, long denied fresh fruit. These usually went into pan pies. Next up were huckleberries, followed in early July by the big, juicy blackberries.

In the 1700s prior to the Revolution—with the Cherokees still on the warpath defending their ancient homeland—settlers on the frontier had a challenge getting the wealth of wild fruit picked and preserved for the winter. The women and children did most of the plucking while the men kept watch with their muzzleloaders and long Pennsylvania German rifles.

> *O*ddly enough, blackberries, considering how many there were later, did not arrive on Hazel Creek [North Carolina] until about 1840...According to Inez Ewich, the first blackberries [on Hazel Creek] were discovered by Moses Proctor on the edge of one of his fields in Possum Hollow.
>
> Delighted with his discovery, he took his family to them and they picked over a gallon in...a bucket he made out of bark. Blackberries will grow only in open, cleared ground which, by that time, was there. Birds must have carried the seeds, and they spread everywhere.
>
> —DUANE OLIVER, *HAZEL CREEK FROM THEN 'TIL NOW*

In the years since, greatest dangers have been briars, chiggers, berry-loving bears, and ever-present snakes. Bessie Llewellyn, of near Pulaski, Tennessee—known as "Muda" to her children and grandchildren—boasts a nose that can smell out copperheads or rattlesnakes as she approaches a bank of blackberries. She always takes along a hoe to clear the path, and, if the snake doesn't promptly clear out, she proceeds to dispatch him.

And then there were the thorns. In her younger days, Elree B. Worley would get excited coming upon a blackberry patch.

"We'd dive in with a bunch of gusto 'til those briared vines would reach out and grab your sleeves or pants legs," Elree recalled in her book of reminiscence, *We Made It.* "When you'd dislodge one sleeve, the idiot would grab you in the back, while another would reach over and snatch off your hat!"

Despite the difficulties, berry-pickers have prevailed. Beuna Winchester told of going berrying on the eastern edge of the Great Smoky Mountains with her three brothers. Their annual goal was to pick enough blackberries to enable their mother to can upward of two hundred quart jars of the fruit for the winter. The canning started when they returned home with two bucketfuls apiece. As their mother got busy canning, the kids returned to the berry fields for additional loads.

In the Cullowhee mountains, Frank Pressley and his siblings would be pressed into serious duty during the berrying season.

"Ma wouldn't let us quit picking blackberries until we gathered at least fifty half-gallon buckets. That would be enough to last us through the winter."

In our modern age, pesticide sprays, bulldozers, and developers have eradicated wild blackberry growth from many

Blackberries are not so abundant in the Appalachian countryside today, but the roadsides of Clay County, North Carolina, are filled with blackberry vines such as these that are allowed to grow wild to the delight of blackberry lovers.

roadsides, ditch banks, and vacant fields where blackberries could be found in earlier days. Yet my Cohutta Mountain wine-maker friend Arvil Wilson says that if you know where to look, there still are wild berries out there in the foothills. His own secret blackberry haven is near Holly Creek on the western edge of the Cohutta chain.

"One year I picked six bushels up there. They cut the timber off that land and it come back in blackberries...big old briars, big old berries," Arvil said, then whispered: "And nobody don't know exactly where they're at except me...I go up there for two weeks in a straight run. Ever mornin' I go and in about two hours, get about eight to ten one-gallon buckets full, and then I have blackberry wine just a runnin' everywhere. Usually have even more wine in August and September."

Among the range of berries, blackberries traditionally have been the most popular for eating, since they can easily be converted into pies, tarts, cobblers, dumplings, jams, and jellies. Some mountain people loved a blackberry dish called "larp." Frank Pressley remembered "larp" well: "We'd have a half-gallon jar of larp for breakfast, along with biscuits and fried meat and sawmill gravy. The way Mother made larp, she'd take one of those half-gallon jars of blackberries and put it in the dish, along with a bit of flour and a sprinkling of sugar. It really hit the spot at breakfast along with a strong cup of black coffee and biscuits. Those blackberries kept us going 'til the springtime."

Blackberry Dumplings

Blackberry dumplings figured high among dishes across Appalachia and much of the South. Here's a recipe adapted from one offered by Bessie Mae Eldreth of Boone, North Carolina, as quoted in the *Smithsonian Folklife Cook Book*:

Bessie's Blackberry Dumplings

1 quart blackberries	*1¼ cups sugar*
	2 cups water

Dumpling Dough

3 to 4 cups self-rising flour	*½ cup milk*
½ cup buttermilk	*1 cup shortening*

To make dumplings, fill a large mixing bowl almost full with sifted flour, and make a hole in the middle. Mix in buttermilk, milk, and shortening. Knead dough, then tear off pieces. Bring blackberries, sugar, and water to a boil. Drop in dumpling dough. Cover and simmer until dough is done.

Blackberry Cobbler

One of the first results of a berry picking jaunt was a good blackberry cobbler. This no-mix cobbler recipe is adapted from one published by Lyn Kellner of Asheville, North Carolina, in her delightful book, *The Taste of Appalachia*.

Lyn's No-Mix Blackberry Cobbler

1½ cups sugar	*2 teaspoons baking powder*
2 cups fresh blackberries	*½ teaspoon salt*
5½ tablespoons butter	*¾ cup milk*
⅔ cup all-purpose flour	

Preheat oven to 350°F. Stir ½ cup sugar into fruit and set aside. Melt butter in baking pan. Sift together the flour, 1 cup sugar, baking powder, and salt, then add the milk. Pour batter into the pan of melted butter, but do not mix. Pour fruit over batter, but do not mix. Bake for 50 minutes. Serves 6.

Huckleberries and Buckberries

Next to blackberries, huckleberries probably have been the most popular and useful berry in the Appalachians. Long before the arrival in the mountains of the first Europeans, huckleberries—called by some "wild blueberries" or "whortleberries"—were being eaten by the Cherokees. In the eighteenth and nineteenth centuries, Appalachian folk loved to dry the huckleberries by putting them out on a tin roof much like they dried apples, peaches, and beans.

Frank Pressley remembered that, "up there high on the mountains (of Cullowhee), we had a place where buckberries and huckleberries grew. The buckberries were named after the buck deer, I'm sure, because they loved to eat them. We didn't have that many deer in those mountains then, a few. You'd see bear tracks and deer tracks.

Back in grandpa's day, when it was huckleberryin' time in the hills, you could tell the ages of the children by the blue rings around their legs.

—John Parris, Mountain Cooking

"Anyway, we'd go up there and gather those buckberries and they made real good jelly. You didn't get many of them, maybe two or three gallons was all you could get. Now the huckleberries, they were kinda like blueberries today. They were blue and sweet as sugar. My mom'd use those to make pies. Buckberries were sour, tart sorta, and they were a different color, reddish black, and didn't have the blue to them. They were about twice as big as huckleberries. We'd eat those in season."

During the 1930s, Appalachian young folks loved to go berrying on "huckleberry balds." The berry-picking excursions, in July and August, were considered by many to be a great opportunity for "sparking" (that's courting in modern-day lingo).

Another favorite mountain berry was the elderberry. Found on mountainsides and next to small streams, elderberries produce in nice clusters. A picker within a short time can gather enough for several pies. My friend the late Maude Thacker of Pickens County, Georgia—who grew up in a rollicking moonshining family at the foot of Hendricks Mountain—loved to hunt elderberries on nearby mountains, and she turned hers into as elegant a wine as I've ever tasted.

It's ironic that the wine is so smooth; in contrast, the fresh, raw elderberry picked straight off the vine has a strange odor and an equally odd taste. Even birds tend to shy away. The reason may be because the berry is so bereft of acid. But once you either cook elderberries in a pie or ferment them into wine, the results can be shockingly stupendous. Even my wife, after taking a taste of "Miss Maude's" elderberry wine, decided that being an alcohol "teetotaler" perhaps was not a good idea after all.

Elderberry Pie

For my friend John Parris of Sylva, North Carolina, the elderberry pie became one of his all-time favorite mountain dishes, with or without a cream topping. He enjoyed eating them either hot or cold. Yet John, the distinguished folklore laureate of the Blue Ridge mountain country, admitted that elderberry pie even decades ago had become practically unknown in the mountains, apparently lost in the sands of time.

But not totally. In Laurel Cove, Parris found a ninety-seven-year-old lady, one Dorothy by name, who made an old-fashioned "two-crust elderberry pie—one with a roof on it," and that got his attention right off. Here's an adaptation of the recipe John obtained with thanks again to my friend, the peripatetic Mr. Parris, who now lives in retirement in the idyllic town of Sylva, North Carolina.

Dorothy's Elderberry Pie

Pastry for 2 (9-inch) pie crusts	4 tablespoons all-purpose flour
2½ cups fresh elderberries	4 teaspoons vinegar or lemon
3 cups sugar	juice or half and half
¼ teaspoon salt	2½ tablespoons butter or margarine

Preheat oven to 450°F. Line 9-inch pie pan with pastry. Wash elderberries thoroughly. In a bowl, mix berries, sugar, salt, flour, and vinegar and/or lemon juice. Mix gently with a fork. Pour berry mixture into pastry-lined pie plate. Dot the top with butter. Wet rim of pie shell lightly. Cover with top pastry, which should have 6 to 8 slits ½-inch long in it. Trim off edge. Seal by pressing the 2 rims together with thumbs or with fork tines. Place on cookie sheet in oven at 450°F for 10 minutes. Reduce heat to 350°F and bake 40 to 45 minutes until crust is golden brown. Serve slightly warm.

Wild Strawberries

Wild strawberries have been highly regarded as a flavorful mountain delicacy and a great dish to revive someone suffering from depression. As a writer said, "Drink strawberry juice for the passions of the heart, alone, or in wine. It makes the heart merry!"

Loaded with calcium, niacin, iron, thiamin, riboflavin, and phosphorous, the small tart berries can be found volunteering on the cool north sides of hills and on abandoned farmland coves and mountain balds. Many pioneers, following in the steps of the Indians, burned off their strawberry meadows in February, paving the way for a perfect crop. Lilly Wikle of Jackson County, North Carolina, told Warren Moore, author of *Mountain Voices*, that her grandfather burned off his strawberry fields every February to kill off the weeds, resulting in a field thick with strawberry plants and luscious red strawberries "big as the end of your thumb, as sweet as they could be." As a young lady, Lilly toted her berries, three gallons at a time, to Dillsboro where she got paid a dollar a gallon, enough to buy her clothes for the year.

The Cherokees made a type of wild strawberry bread using the berry juice and cornmeal. But the best use of wild strawberries, say many mountain people, is to bake a shortcake using wild strawberries.

Wild Strawberry Shortcake

In making the wild strawberry shortcake—a type of stack cake—you roll out the biscuit dough—fixing up as many as four or five stacks. First off you bake the stacks. Then, take the stacks out, cover each with butter and berries, and stack them up, with the cooked berries generously poured between (on top of) each stack. On the top layer, you make a filling that should spill down the sides. Afterward, pop the entire shortcake stack cake back into the oven for a few minutes, then put it on the table in all of its tasty doneness. Some folks like to add a bit of cream or whipped cream on top.

~

The era of family mountain berryin' is about to become one for the history books.

Back in the mid-1950s, when U.S. Army bulldozers were clearing out the Chattahoochee River valley for the Lake Lanier reservoir with its 550-mile shoreline, my wife, Susanne, then pregnant with our first child, would go berrying with her friends Susie Duke and Verdell Wofford Clark. They would come home with pails loaded and faces aglow. That night we would always enjoy a luscious blackberry pie. Little did we

Cherokee oral history tells how strawberries came to the people. A woman, angry at her husband, left her home one day. Her husband prayed to the Great One, who tried to stop the woman by putting berry bushes in her path. First he put serviceberry, then huckleberry, but she ignored them both. Then he put a small plant at ground level, its leaves hiding a sweet-smelling fruit. When the wife stumbled upon these...she forgot her anger and picked the biggest ripest red berries to take back to her husband. When they met she put one in his mouth, and then they both started picking the berries. The husband decided that to keep his wife forever he would plant a patch of strawberries near their home. She wondered how she could have ever left her home, and determined always to keep a jar of preserved strawberries as a reminder how fragile home is and how powerful anger can be.

—ROSE HOUK, *FOOD AND RECIPES OF THE SMOKIES*

know that those would be the last berry-picking fun days that our family would probably ever experience. Today, you don't find many such berry-picking oppor-

tunities, even in the Blue Ridge. A nice tradition, unfortunately, that has succumbed to the modern age.

So has the nice tradition of mountain families toting their berries into towns and villages to sell the fruits of their labors.

In the crossroad community of Cherrylog, Georgia, in the mountainous Chattahoochee National Forest region, Virginia Key Underwood remembered picking berries during the thirties to make money for school supplies: "I sold blackberries for 15 cents per gallon. I remember one year I made a total of $3.65

Mountain couple pick a new harvest of strawberries.

for the berries I sold. It was enough to buy all of my books except one!"

That era of picking and selling berries house-to-house has just about come to an end. But with the old-timey recipes from the past, the taste of long ago will continue to live, along with memories of the gallant mountain people whose close-to-the-earth lives were an inspiration to all.

Persimmons
The Sugarplum of the Mountains

If it be not ripe, it will draw one's mouth awrie with much torment.
—*Early visitor to America*

~

Once ripe, persimmons are very good to eat, and go well with squirrel.
—*Former Georgia governor Zell Miller*

~

Raccoon up a 'simmon tree
Possum on the ground
Raccoon said to the possum,
Shake them 'simmons down

—*1850s minstrel tune*

During my growing-up years in upcountry South Carolina, I never would have imagined giant orange-size persimmons such as those I harvest each December from my oriental persimmon tree in Atlanta. And from which, last Christmas, I pulled down over ninety persimmons—enough for more than a dozen persimmon puddings!

The plum-size wild persimmon we enjoyed out in the country in the 1930s and 1940s—called in Latin *Diospyros virginiana* in contrast to the fat modern-day Japanese cousin, *Diospyros kaki*—was one of the most delightful fruits you could find in the Appalachian countryside. But it was also known for its ability to give you a "wrongside-outards" pucker-mouth if you bit into one before its time. Growing up in Towns County, Georgia, the state's future governor, Zell Miller, joined friends in daring one another to bite into a green persimmon hanging from a tree in Carter Berry's pasture. As a testimony to the fruit's astringent authority, a stream in Cherokee County, North Carolina, was dubbed early on by the Cherokees as Tsa-La-Lui, meaning, literally, "pucker mouth!" (Today the water course is called Persimmon Creek.)

A native of China, persimmons got their first serious cultivation in Japan. But our word for the fruit is a derivative of the Algonquin *pessemin*. Actually, the Cherokees had plenty of persimmons and were obviously enamored of the fruit when the first European explorers came to visit. Some of the Cherokee bread incorporated the prunelike fruit.

The wild persimmon at first develops hard and green and very, very "puckery." As soon as the first frost hits, the fruit begins to turn orange, softens up, and, in time, becomes edible. That's when you harvest it. But you must be swift to beat out the night-time animals.

In the case of my own tree, fruit maturity comes in early December. At that time, all the leaves fall off and the tree takes on a skeletonized Christmas tree look, complete with orange-size (persimmon) ornaments. I try to pick them when they're soft and juicy, and just as they're ready to fall. My usual harvest date is the day after Christmas.

Alex Chappel of Salacauga, Alabama (I interviewed him in 1975 when he was well past one hundred), recalled going persimmon hunting "where I got into it the worst of anywhar.

"It was in the fall of the year. A crowd of us chilluns, gals and boys, went down there where the persimmons had got ripe and I beat 'em and I was checking out a tree. I got up there and bent the tree over. Maw had made me a pair of white Aldenbergs. She didn't have enough cloth to make galluses to hold 'em up. She took a rubber band off the loom wheel and made me galluses out of that rubber band.

The news in the country is that wild persimmons are ripe. When I get out of my car in the driveway, I check out the tall grass in front of the storage shed. There is almost always a feast there—beautiful soft, orange, luscious fruit off the big persimmon tree.

The fruit nestles in the grass, clean enough to eat out of hand...and it is cool and very sweet.

Some comedian who bragged about his country upbringing used to say his folks were so poor he had to beat the possums to the

"Well, I got up there and bent the tree over. The other kids reached up and got me by the britches and pulled me down. The wheel-band gallus popped and my britches came down. They all ran and left me hanging there with my pants down." That was the same year that Alex caught nine possums in his box and treated his family to a feast of possums and baked sweet potatoes, the traditional combination.

In a separate chapter, you will find recipes and folklore about persimmon beer—one of the South's all-time great fruit beverages. In some households during the difficult Civil War and Reconstruction years, folk used persimmons to make a coffee substitute by boiling the seeds.

Also during those times, home folks used persimmons to make syrup and even vinegar. There's the story that when mountain soldiers came home from the Civil War, they were shocked to find that the recipe for making persimmon vinegar called for three gallons of corn liquor. They immediately halted the practice because of what they felt was a terrible waste of good corn whiskey.

In times past, mountain moonshiners liked to make a bit of persimmon brandy in between runs of corn liquor. North Carolina mountain man Zeb Vance—who became governor and U.S. senator—promoted persimmon brandy as a fine way to cut down on long political speeches.

The fruit was also revered by many for its medicinal value. A type of persimmon tea was used to treat thrash, diarrhea, sore mouth, fungus-infected athlete's foot, and was touted as a tonic to help retain one's hair!

Then some folk cut open persimmon seeds to predict the weather. If the seed showed the leaf embryo image of a knife, it meant the weather would be so cold the winds would slice through you. If you saw a fork, you could expect warm weather.

> persimmon tree to get any breakfast at all. I never saw a possum in a persimmon tree, and I'm glad, because I might figure they got there first and needed the glorious repast worse than I did.
>
> I miss the days before the subdivisions came, when persimmon trees abounded in our woods. Now I can't find some trees that used to be ornamented like Christmas trees, with what Euell Gibbons...called sugar plums. Maybe road-widening crews got them.
>
> —Celestine Sibley,
> Atlanta Journal-Constitution

If the image of a spoon showed up, look out—that meant you would have such a heavy snowfall that you would have to shovel your way out!

Persimmon Pudding

Back to reality: Two years after I set out my persimmon tree—and when I was preparing for a nice harvest—I nosed around a bit trying to find a good recipe to make use of this magnificent fruit. I found a great one—for persimmon pudding—in the *Clemson House Cook Book*. Offered by Robert Spangenburg , it is one I have adapted and used many times and always to the delight of guests. As Tennessee native Betsy Tice White has written, "A persimmon pudding is worth waiting a whole year to enjoy." I like to serve this pudding with vanilla yogurt.

If you've ever wondered what tanin is (wine buffs use the term), take a bite of an unripe persimmon. Your lips will pucker, your throat will constrict, and your tongue will feel like a chalk-covered blackboard. No wonder the first Europeans...didn't rush to bring the tree back to Europe.

But when a persimmon is ripe (squishy soft), it is downright delectable; its texture is as creamy as custard, its flavor reminiscent of dates (indeed, it is sometimes called the date plum).

—STEVEN RAICHLEN, *CELEBRATION OF SEASONS*

Clemson Persimmon Pudding

2 cups sifted flour	1½ cups sugar
½ teaspoon baking soda	1½ cups muscadine wine
1 teaspoon salt	3 eggs
½ teaspoon cinnamon	¼ cup milk
½ teaspoon nutmeg	3 tablespoons butter, melted
2 cups persimmon pulp	Whipped cream or lemon sauce

Preheat oven to 300°F. Sift the dry ingredients together. Mix the persimmon pulp, wine, eggs, milk, and butter with the mixture. Pour into buttered pan (8x8 inch). Bake at 300°F. When cool, cut into squares and serve with whipped cream or lemon sauce. Serves 8.

~

There are many variations of this, including the insertion of a half teaspoon of vanilla extract, and perhaps a quarter cup of cream or buttermilk rather than sweet milk. And lemon juice. Mountain people love to substitute honey for sugar. Atlanta's own Edna Lewis, the famed culinary expert and writer, has her own version that, among other ingredients, calls for rum, suet, breadcrumbs, hot milk, and brown sugar. She serves her persimmon pudding with a clear sauce that has a brandy base. Sounds delicious! Mountain people served persimmon with wild game and pork.

There are many other persimmon-based recipes for cakes, custards, salads, breads, whips, soufflés, sherbets, custards, and jellies. Persimmon pie is a nice variation. This following recipe adaptation comes from the seasonal *Appalachian Livin'* booklets published in 1987 by the Children's Museum of Oak Ridge, Tennessee.

East Tennessee Persimmon Pie

1 teaspoon baking soda

1 heaping cup of
    persimmon pulp

½ cup butter or margarine

2 cups sugar

3 eggs

1 cup all-purpose flour

1 teaspoon nutmeg

1 teaspoon cinnamon

½ teaspoon cloves

3 cups milk

Preheat oven to 350°F. Mix baking soda with persimmon pulp and let stand. Cream the butter or margarine and sugar. Add the eggs and beat. Sift together flour, cinnamon, nutmeg, and cloves. Mix the milk with flour and creamed mixture. Add pulp, and bake in a shallow greased pan for 30 minutes at 350°F. Serves 6.

Persimmon Loaf Cake

Unfortunately, the recipe the Cherokees used for persimmon bread—the one they treated Hernando de Soto to when he traveled through western North Carolina in the 1500s—apparently has vanished into the pages of antiquity. But Marie Mellinger, the Euell Gibbons of the Appalachians (in Rabun County, Georgia), published a wonderful recipe for persimmon loaf cake in her authoritative book, *Roadside Rambles*. Here is an adaptation of that recipe, with my thanks to Marie.

Rabun County Persimmon Loaf Cake

2 cups all-purpose flour

½ cup milk

⅔ cup sugar

1 egg

4 tablespoons shortening

1 cup persimmons (finely
    chopped)

1 cup nuts or sunflower seeds

1 tablespoon vanilla

1 teaspoon cinnamon

Preheat oven to 350°F. Mix well. Bake in a greased tube pan for 50 minutes at 350°F.

*P*ersimmon beer appears in many mid-nineteenth century Christmas dinner accounts, including one in frontier Georgia described as a "feast of 'possum (or squirrel) sop and tater, oven pone corn bread, Georgia collards, smoked bacon with a 'streak of lean and a streak of fat,' fresh butter, fritters, buttermilk, ginger cake, apple cider and [per]'simmon beer."

—EMYL JENKINS, *SOUTHERN CHRISTMAS*

Last, but not least, we should not forget dried persimmons. Here's how many mountaineers processed their persimmons to come up with a prunelike fruit:

Rinse ripe persimmons and spread out on a wire or cloth sheet, with each persimmon about a quarter inch apart. Put in the sun. When they take on a datelike texture, you know they are fully dried. Put the fruit in sterilized glass jars. Seal and store in a cool, dry place.

This Japanese persimmon tree located in the author's front yard in Atlanta yields upwards of 100 orange-size persimmons every December. He turns them into persimmon puddings.

Wild Grapes, Plums, Pawpaws, and "Mountain Apricots"

*The land [North Carolina]...is so full of grapes, as the very beating
and surge of the Sea overflowed them...I think in all the world the like
abundance is not to be found; and my selfe having seene those parts of
Europe that most abound...*

—*Sir Walter Raleigh's report to the
queen of England, 1590s*

The entire Appalachian country—the Alleghenies, the Shenandoah Valley, the Blue
Ridge, Kentucky, and the Cumberlands—once abounded in wild muscadine vines
that climbed trees and spread along fences. For youngsters growing up in earlier times—
up to the 1940s—the amber-bronze "scuppernongs" and black-blue muscadine "bullaces"
were tempting targets along with other wild fruits and nuts.

"In those warm, early fall days, we went muscadine hunting, seeking out the big old
large grapes that hung in great clusters on vines that climbed trees or bushes near a field
or pasture land."

Thus spoke former Cherokee County state senator and school superintendent
William G. Hasty. "When the grapes got ripe, we'd climb the vined trees and shake the
limbs; the muscadines would come tumbling down like hail."

Naturally the end result—other than filling young bellies—was a bunch of buckets
of grapes their mothers could turn into pan pies.

"But pies were just the beginning," Bill Hasty declared. "Mother made preserves and
jelly out of the hulls, and other people made muscadine wine."

Muscadine grapes have been around in the Appalachians, indeed across the
Southeastern seaboard states, since before the days of the earliest European explorers.

In later years, muscadine/scuppernong grape arbors became commonplace on backcountry farms, usually not far from a homestead. People rarely pruned the vines as vintners
do today. Even so, the yields were tremendous. In the early summer, arbors would fill up
with clusters of muscadines. The thick canopy was a favorite nesting place for blue jays and
other birds, to say nothing of being a delightful "play house" for children. I remember

I'll meet you under the scuppernong vine" is about the most welcome promise a Georgian can offer to a friend, and it is a promise that seldom goes unfulfilled... A distaste for scuppernongs is unheard of, and no one has been known to get sick from eating too many, whether he practices the efficient Georgia technique of leaving the seeds within the hulls or whether he prefers the plumb–all method of eating the pulp, seeds, and even the hulls...

Summer cannot slip by without Georgia housewives putting up jar upon jar of scuppernong and muscadine jelly and preserves, and a favorite old–fashioned dessert is a hot buttered biscuit with an ample helping of tangy muscadine preserves.

—JANNELLE JONES MCREE, DOWN COOTER
CREEK AND OTHER STORIES

fondly the canopied arbor as being our own little folks' house, one that attracted my little neighbors and visiting cousins who came to stay for a few days with their folks.

I remember the scuppernong taste from those childhood days. What a delicious memory: popping those fat grapes in your mouth on a hot day and spitting out the seeds and hulls. In recent years, I have tried to re-create that luscious childhood remembrance. With the encouragement of my old *Atlanta Journal* cohort Bob Harrell, now a gentleman grape farmer, I planted my own Ison Dixieland muscadine vine. The failure was almost total; yields reached only about a dozen little grapes each fall. The diagnosis was simple: too much shade, too little sun. Even though I've trimmed out the nearby low-hanging poplar limbs, I'm about reconciled to giving my vine to someone with some sunshine. Will one more year (with a lot of fertilizer) turn the trick? I doubt it. Maybe I need a shade-tolerant antique wild grape species to run up one of my poplar trees.

Scuppernong Pie

Scuppernong pie was a favorite among mountain families. Among those were Clete and Virginia Underwood of Cherrylog, Georgia.

This is Virginia's scuppernong pie recipe, one of scores of recipes and reminiscences she lovingly compiled and published under the title *Georgia Mountain Heritage* to help support the Fannin Regional Hospital. Virginia produced the booklet without personal remuneration, under encouragement of her employer at the time, the Levi pants factory. The recipe is named for Virginia's home community, Cherrylog, also home to the famous Pink Pig barbecue eatery. Cherrylog got its name years ago, local folk say, when a cherry tree fell across a stream and became a handy and well-used foot log.

Cherrylog Scuppernong Pie

1 cup sugar	3 cups scuppernong juice
8 tablespoons all-purpose flour	4 tablespoons butter
Dash of salt	3 egg yolks, beaten

Mix sugar, flour, and salt together. Add juice and butter. Stir constantly over medium heat until mixture begins to thicken. Remove from heat, and slowly add egg yolks, one at a time. Let thickened mixture cool for several minutes. Pour into baked pie shell, and cover with meringue. Put under broiler for a minute or two, or until lightly browned. Watch carefully. Serves 6.

The Fox Grape (Winter Grape)

The tiny fox grape was another Appalachian favorite. William Hasty remembered their sharp and acidic taste, which was a plus because they could be turned into "the best jelly ever." On occasions, though, the vines climbed trees so high the fruit went beyond the reach of the grape hunters. After such a futile climb, Hasty recalled that "we would just hang there on a tree for a while, looking up at all those grapes, realizing that the coons and possums would be enjoying a good supper that night."

Arvil Wilson calls them winter grapes. "They're small grapes, about the size of the end of your finger. They hang in bunches." Wilson's favorite fox grape haunt came as a gift of nature…a 1973 tornado that swept across Cohutta Mountain and down its eastern slope. "After the tornado blowed all that timber down around Holly Creek, the Forest Service made a clear-cut, so the trees would come back like before. Well, they come back, did they ever, and some; that wind brought us some wild winter grapes."

Fox Grape Bonanza on the Blue Ridge Divide

In 1947, we moved into the Steer Creek area near the Blue Ridge Divide. The following year the fox grapes hit. All the grape vines up and down that creek were hanging big, full of wild fox grapes. The old lady and all of 'em we picked grapes up and down that creek. We made jelly out of 'em. I fooled around one day and picked eleven bushels! I made thirty-six gallons of wine out of it…

Back then, the fox grapes—out in the field of alders—could be counted on to produce a big grape haul every four or five years. But today, all the wild fox grapes are gone from that territory [in north Georgia]. The muscadines are still there, but the fox grapes have disappeared.

—Curtis Underwood, Resaca, Georgia

Nina Garrett also remembered them as winter grapes, but more specifically as "possum grapes," a fox grape variant. "People would get those possum grapes and can the juice and also make pies out of 'em, or jelly," she recalled.

Wild Grapes and Molasses

One of the uniquely Appalachian wild grape dishes was one derived from the Cherokees—wild grapes and molasses. The interaction of the sweet and sour elements produce a flavor that mountain folk say is one of a kind. Nina Garrett recalled that fox grapes were the usual wild grape used for the unique concoction.

"Atter it frost, we used to get them fox grapes from the trees and make up our grapes and molasses treat. We'd either use sorghum syrup or sometimes we'd use sugar and water to boil up a thick candy-like syrup. Then we'd pour that syrup over them grapes. It set there a few days and drawed that juice out of them grapes. You'd drain the water

Arvil Wilson of the Mountaintown district of Gilmer County, Georgia is a wild grape fancier. He loves to pick winter grapes from a formerly wooded area near Holly Creek that was opened up by a tornado.

out, put it on and boil it again, and that kept 'em preserved. They were just delicious."

A derivative of the grape-syrup dish called for the use of a large crock into which was placed a gallon of wild grapes and a gallon of syrup. A layer of grapes was placed on the bottom of the crock, followed by a layer of syrup, followed by successive layers of grapes and syrup, with the grand finale being a generous dollop of syrup to top it off. At this point, the crock would be sealed up and set aside in a cool place to be opened around Christmastime. At that time, the two flavors would have intermixed. "When you opened a crock," an old-timer recalled, "it would never last long."

Wild Plums

Wild plums have had a hallowed place in mountain foodlore—from the northern Blue ridge, right on down to north Florida. There the late Marjorie Kinnan Rawlings, best known for *The Yearling*, wrote of the delightful tart jellies that came from their wild "hog plums." Just like Appalachian folk who go plum-hunting at the right time of fruit maturity, Mrs. Rawlings would go out plum-pickin' and bring home slightly green plums to beat the raccoons, possums, and jaybirds.

Dried Mountain Plums

Like apples and peaches, plums can and are often dried, making for a datelike taste, and delicious pies. Appalachian people traditionally sun-dried their plums just as they dried their apples and peaches, over a period of one to three weeks. Some people strung their plums the same as green bean "leather-britches," with apparent great success.

Nature writer Billy Joe Tatum's favorite method of preserving plums is to dry them in an oven. After washing and stoning the plums, she cuts them in half. Then she pours boiling water over them and lets them stand for twenty minutes, then drains them in a colander for half an hour. At this point, she covers a baking sheet with waxed paper and spreads out the plums in a single layer and dries them in an oven set at 150°F until the pieces are dry but still flexible. Then she stores them in an airtight container.

Pawpaws

Speaking of interesting old-time fruits with interesting flavors, whatever happened to all the Appalachian pawpaw trees? In days past, pawpaws were found everywhere in the country—on wooded slopes, under bluffs, and along streams. Poet James Whitcomb Riley

Her face lit up as the idea struck her. If the huckleberries were turning in the valley, chances were they'd be full ripe up on the mountain...And if she could pick a mess of them, she could cook them with some of the sweetening Mr. Stonecypher had got out of that bee tree and make him a pie for his dinner.
—Lizzie, in the novel *Give Us This Valley*,
by the late Tom Ham of Atlanta

once described pawpaws as custard pie without a crust. Others have linked their taste to a combination banana, pear, and sweet potato custard or to "custard apples." They were used to make puddings, pies, jellies, and pawpaw brandy.

Largest in size of native North American fruits—about like a cucumber—the pawpaw was one of the staunch dietary standbys of Appalachian and Amerindian folk in times past. Pawpaws kept Lewis and Clark alive when returning from their trailblazing exploration across western America. Almost three hundred years earlier, in the 1540s, Hernando de Soto and his army were starving as they reached the Mississippi Valley. Presto!…Pawpaws to the rescue!

In Sylva, North Carolina, one Roland Parker planted his own pawpaw patch after finding that the wild fruit trees had just about disappeared. Once his pawpaws were producing, his wife found she could peel and slice and freeze them and bring them out year-round as a dessert.

Pawpaw pudding is a fairly easy dish to prepare. For this adapted recipe, my thanks go again to Marie Mellinger, author of *Roadside Rambles* and probably the most knowledgeable wild food expert in the Southeast.

> *Where, oh where, oh where is little Sally?*
> *Where, oh where, oh where is little Sally?*
> *Where, oh where, oh where is little Sally?*
> *Way down yonder in the pawpaw patch.*
>
> *Pickin up pawpaws, putn'em in her pocket.*
> *Pickin up pawpaws, putn'em in her pocket.*
> *Pickin up pawpaws, putn'em in her pocket.*
> *Way down yonder in the pawpaw patch.*
>
> —FROM PLAY PARTY GAME, "PAWPAW PATCH"

Marie's Pawpaw Pudding

1 cup pawpaw pulp	3 eggs
1¼ cups sugar	½ teaspoon salt
1 teaspoon baking powder	1 teaspoon baking soda
½ cup melted butter	2½ teaspoons cinnamon
1 teaspoon ginger	½ teaspoon nutmeg

Strain out the pawpaw pulp. Mix with all ingredients, and bake in a greased pan for approximately 1 hour or until firm.

~

Passionflowers ("Mountain Apricots")

Blue-blooming maypop passionflowers—known as "wild apricots," "field apricots," or "mountain apricots"—were a special treat to the people living on Hazel Creek, North

Carolina, according to Professor Duane Oliver, unofficial historian of the legendary community near the Great Smoky Mountain Park. The peripatetic plant—*Passiflora incarnata*—can be found growing everywhere in the Appalachians—on roadsides, in old fields, and on rocky slopes.

"The delicately flavored yellow fruit," Oliver says, "was best eaten after the first frost." Most people ate them raw when they matured and turned yellow in October or November. They used them to make puddings, preserves, and jellies. And the Amerindians, including the Cherokees, made a delicious drink of the fruit.

Legend says the name passionflower came from the imagined resemblance of the fruit's corona to Christ's crown of thorns. According to the legend, the other parts of the flower resemble Jesus' wounds on the cross and the nails in his body. The petals and sepals are said to symbolize ten of Christ's apostles (subtracting Judas the betrayer and Peter the denier).

If you'd like to make a passion fruit drink as the Cherokees did, here's how, according to Marie Mellinger:

Slice open some of the maypops, and simmer them in water for a few minutes. Strain and add lemon juice and sugar or sweetener. Serve over ice with lemon slices or mint. White wine can be added if desired.

Chestnuts, Chinquapins, Walnuts, and Hicker Nuts

Where there be mountains, there be chestnuts.
—A member of de Soto's expedition
crossing the Blue Ridge in 1520

~

After the red haws and the wild grapes comes the nutting season,
raining down blessings.
—James Norman Hall

~

When I was a boy in the North Carolina mountains, we roasted
chestnuts in the fireplace. But we had to cut the ends off to keep
them from exploding.
—Frank Pressley, Lakeland, Georgia

The very best taste of all…was to crack out a handful of black walnuts and eat them with a piece of cold corn bread, first a bite of nut and then a bite of bread. That's the best eating in the world!"

Thus spoke Kentucky's Jean Ritchie, a member of The Singing Family of the Cumberlands, who authored a delightful book by the same name.

Indeed, from the days of the Amerindians, black walnuts have been a mountain mainstay and have provided much nutcracking fun and food. Not only black walnuts but the rest of Appalachia's richly prolific "forest mast"—hickory nuts, beechnuts, chinquapins, hazelnuts, and, until the trees were struck down by a tragic blight in the 1920s, chestnuts.

~

The hardy Europeans arriving in the Southern Appalachian frontier felt that God had blessed them beyond measure with a beautiful promised land of milk and honey and nuts. They were reminded of the Almighty's generosity in the fall of the year when their cabin shingles would clatter with the staccato of nuts raining down from the magnificent hardwoods they found on the frontier.

Not only did the nutmeats provide a wonderful base for soups and dressings and breads and desserts, the fresh mast every fall meant that the wild game out in the wilds would become fat and delicious just in time for holiday feasting and the long cold winter to come.

Recent generations have never seen the like of the American chestnut tree, which towered over the forests of the Appalachians...until it was virtually wiped out by a mysterious fungus nearly a century ago.

There were whole groves of these majestic trees in Pickens County until the late 1930s, and by the 1940s they were all dead. Now, for those willing to tramp deep into the woods, new American chestnuts can be seen rising from the old root systems that never died.

But these new trees are doomed, just like their forebears, for they will live only a few years before they are attacked and killed by a deadly blight, the spores of which are spread by the wind, birds, and insects.

—JACK STILLMAN, PICKENS COUNTY PROGRESS, JASPER, GEORGIA

"Chestnut meat was sweet, and it sweetened up the hog meat," mountain man Harry Brown told Atlanta reporter Charles Seabrook. "You didn't have to grain-feed the hogs before butchering, because their meat was already sweet."

As English surveyor Nicholas Cresswell wrote from Virginia in 1770, "When there is a plentiful Mast...the Hogs will get fat in the woods with little, or no acorns."

The vital role of nuts in the mountains was reflected by the action taken early on by settlers who put down roots on the southeast edge of the Great Smoky Mountains. They named their settlement "Hazel Creek" for the hazelnut bushes they found growing luxuriously along the stream. But the chestnut led the name game: Scores of mountain communities named gaps, streams, mountains and settlements for the celebrated but now departed native chestnut. In *Foxfire*-famous Rabun County alone, there are Chestnut Mountain, Chestnut Bald, Chestnut Ridge, Chestnut Top, Chestnut Gap, Chestnut Creek, Chestnut Cove, and Chestnut Road.

~

The first explorers reaching Appalachia's mountain interior were impressed by the nut-fruited forests and the inventive bent of the Indians in harvesting and consuming the mast. They found that the natives, in addition to eating the nuts raw and drying them for long storage, were fond of hickory nut oil, called by the British "hickory milk."

Used for cooking and seasoning, "hickory milk" gave "a particularly delicious flavor" to venison, corn bread, and Indian corn cakes. The Indians also used finely-cracked hickory meats to thicken stews and to make a seasoning the Indians called "sof-ky." For the hickory-milk oil, the Indians pounded several nuts simultaneously on multiple-depression "nut stones," then followed by dropping the broken shells and meats in a pot of cold water. After a bit of stirring, the milky oil floated to the top, to be skimmed off and preserved. It was a laborious task; to make a gallon of oil required pounding and processing a hundred pounds of hickory nuts!

The Indians also made a "sof-ky" stew thickener and seasoning from finely ground hickory nut meats. The settlers liked it, also, and called it "Tom Fuller." Why, the author was unable to learn.

Thomas Hariot found walnut trees covering a third of the forests. "Besides their eating of them after our ordinaire manner, they breake

Eighty-two-year-old Curtis Belcher from Floyd County, Virginia, cracks black walnuts on a favorite stump.

them with stones and pound them in morters with water to make a milk which they use to put into some sorts of their spoonmete."

But it was the fun of harvesting, cracking, and eating the walnuts that attracted the attention of the settlers, particularly the young people.

In the fall, mountain youth loved to get together for "nuttin' parties," riding wagons to favored spots in the woods. There they picked up walnuts, beechnuts, and hazelnuts by the bagload. Often they would use small rocks to crack some right on the spot. But everyone was expected to take a bag or two home for a family nut-cracking by the fireside. Jean Ritchie remembered that her family enjoyed cooking up nut fudge on winter nights, particularly using black walnuts and long walnuts.

Like many housewives, Phoebe Burgess cracked nuts on a flatiron held between her knees. As her grandson Bil Dwyer recalled, her apron caught all the shells and stray nut-meats. "The other nutmeats she picked out of the shells with a hairpin."

Black Walnuts

Of all the nuts of the Appalachian forest, from then 'til now, none have been more universally loved than black walnuts, for their strong, oily flavor, their contribution to cakes and cookies, and as a dietary lubricant. As the "champion walnut-cracker" of Dutch Cove, North Carolina—George Smathers—told columnist John Parris, "I'll tell you one thing right now. When you eat a cake of them walnuts, they'll sure work you the same as...castor oil. But oh, how I love 'em."

The first German immigrants to settle in Pennsylvania and down the Shenandoah Valley sought to find acreage containing black walnut trees. That meant the land boasted fertile limestone-based soil that would guarantee bounteous yields of fruits and crops.

Native walnut trees—often standing a hundred feet high—most often are found in cool coves and valleys, but also thrive on fertile hillsides. But on the frontier, the job of hulling and cracking walnuts was laborious. Maurice Brooks detailed the walnut-processing job in his book, *The Appalachians*:

> On a warm Saturday, the children in a family were equipped with small wooden clubs, one end rounded for easier holding, the other left square. Piles of walnuts, still in their sticky hulls, were assembled, the hullers went to work with their clubs, used their fingers as supplementary tools, and by hand and staining but fragrant toil, finally produced a pile of nuts in the shell. These were...spread out and dried for winter consumption. A school child who didn't have walnut stain on his fingers would have been an autumn curiosity.

A dramatic walnut-hulling improvement came when the early T-model Fords reached the hill country. It is said that mountain people learned they could spread out their green walnuts on a shed floor or in a burlap bag and drive the car wheels over them—whoever said that has never cracked a walnut! After cracking, housewives used hairpins, nails or nutpicks to extract the meat.

Marie Mellinger says walnuts and butternuts can be mixed in recipes or used interchangeably, both being rich in protein, carbohydrates, and minerals. Mrs. Mellinger, the aforementioned "Euell Gibbons of the Appalachians," leads a group of wild-food enthusiasts called "The Incredible Edibles." They gather periodically to check out various "living-off-the-land" recipes. Here's an Indian-originated recipe that Marie published in her *Roadside Rambles* that is an easy-to-fix snack:

Cherokee Corn and Walnuts

1 cup broken walnut meats   2 cups corn off cob, cooked

2 tablespoons butter or margarine

Heat the precooked corn with the walnut meats and butter, and serve hot.

~

Recipes for a scrumptious Appalachian black walnut cake will be found in the Desserts section. But here is one of Marie's recipes for walnut bread.

Se-Di Bread

(*Se-di* is the Cherokee word for walnut)

2 cups all-purpose flour   ½ teaspoon salt

½ cup broken nutmeats   1 egg

½ cup sugar   1 cup milk

3 tablespoons baking power

Mix flour, nutmeats, sugar, baking power, and salt. Stir in the egg and milk. Place in a greased baking dish, and bake in a moderate oven for 45 minutes.

Hickory Nuts

When our house was being built in northside Atlanta in 1967, Susanne and I rescued from a pile of bulldozer dirt a grand old hickory tree and an oak. They became the center-pieces of our wraparound backyard deck. A number of other big hickory trees on our lot joyfully produce a shower of nuts that are the delight of squirrels and chipmunks. The squirrels pepper us with the shells when we picnic on the deck.

The hickory has been one of the most productive trees in the Appalachians, providing not only abundant fruit, but a strong wood known for its enduring qualities such as for making hog hangers, ax handles, rifle butts, barbecue chips, and you-name-it. President Andrew Jackson, Appalachia's contribution to the White House, was known as "Old Hickory," a testimony to his toughness.

The Cherokee Nation had a settlement known as Hickory Log. But it was the sweet-meated hickory nut—known as "hicker nut" through the Southern Appalachians—that has brought the hickory its greatest fame. Billy Joe Tatum says, "This nut is the most flavorful, the nuttiest of any kind growing wild." William Bartram had this to say after traveling through North Carolina and Georgia in 1770:

> I have seen above an hundred bushels of these [hickory] nuts belonging to one
> family. They pound them to pieces, and then cast them into boiling water, which,
> after passing through fine strainers, preserves the most oily part of the liquid: this they
> call by a name which signifies hiccory (sic) milk; it is as sweet and rich as fresh cream,
> and is an ingredient in most of their cookery, especially homony and corn cakes.

Hickories belong to the walnut family and are called by some "yellow walnuts." They flourish on mountain slopes and along streams. Bill Hasty told me the nuts come in three sizes—a small nut with a thin shell, easy to crack; a "pig hickory nut" with a hull extension making it look like the snout of a pig; and the third, the large "shellbark" nut. While hard to crack, the shellbark's meat is delicious. Other designations are shagbarks, mockernuts, and nutmeg hickories. Hickory nuts are prized for use in breads, cakes, cookies, candy, and as a pudding and casserole supplement. Here are some recipes utilizing this sweet and versatile nut. This first one comes from the aforementioned Marie Mellinger, guru of the "Incredible Edibles" wild-food enthusiasts.

Sugared Hickory Nutmeats

1 cup sugar	*½ cup hickory nutmeats*
1 cup maple syrup	*Granulated sugar to taste*

Combine sugar and syrup, and bring to a boil. Pull from heat, and allow to cool. Spread the nutmeats on a greased pie tin. Dribble the sugar mixture over them and stir. Then separate, and coat nutmeats with granulated sugar.

Chestnuts

Seventy years ago, hundred-foot-tall native chestnuts ruled over Appalachian forests. It was said that in 1900, a squirrel could hop aboard a chestnut tree in Maine and travel all the way to Georgia without ever having to leave Chestnut branches. Today, the majestic chestnut forests are no more, victim of what has been called the nation's worst ever ecological disaster. It was caused by a parasitic Asian fungus that came to the U.S. with Chinese chestnut trees.

"Up on the face of Buck Knob there, a big mountain, it looked like someone went in there and deadened it…the mountainside just turned brown," Herschel Everett of north Georgia's Coosa community told me. "Our hogs had been eating those chestnuts. We fattened them on chestnuts. It was the soundest timber in the country, trunks four and five foot through, big heavy timber."

While the chestnut trees lasted, they provided mountain people a wonderful resource of nourishing golf ball–size nuts, solid timber for fence rails and fence posts, plus a nice blossom from which bees extracted a delightfully flavorful honey.

Atlanta Journal-Constitution reporter Charles Seabrook quoted Andy Cope from north Georgia's Foxfire country as saying that "the chestnut made a living for us; it put food on the table and shoes on our feet." In other words, the trees provided food for the wild game of the forest—bears, passenger pigeons (now extinct), turkeys, squirrels, deer, and raccoon to name a few, and these provided food for the mountain table and hide to shod the family's feet.

Chestnut hunts were a great recreation for mountain youngsters. "Sunday afternoons in the fall, we children thrilled to chestnut hunts," recalled Gladys Trentham Russell in her book, *Call Me Hillbilly.*

"For those [hunts] we usually put on shoes because of the sticky chestnut burrs. However, my brothers often opened the chestnut burrs by stomping them with their bare heels, just to prove that they could."

Chestnuts also provided a great medium of exchange. Mountain people would haul wagon loads of nuts and produce to population centers where they earned money for necessities and to pay their farm property taxes. Early in this century, ninety-nine-year-old Chris Boatwright and his father would take wagonloads of chestnuts and apples over the Cohutta Mountain to Dalton and sell them for twenty cents a quart. "It would take us all day," Chris told me. "We'd camp out going and coming. Sometimes it would take us three or four days to sell out. I done sich as that."

Frank Pressley praised chestnuts that he said gave breads and dressings a sweet flavor.

Mountain people called the departed chestnut their best friend in the forest. They ate its fruit with relish. So did wildlife. Here five people line up at the trunk of a giant tree. An Asiatic fungus brought down the chestnut forests. About the only remnants of the majestic trees are split rail fences on Appalachian farms.

"When I was a growing up [at Cullowhee Mountain], us boys would get up on fall mornings; we'd grab on our brogan shoes and head to the chestnut trees before the squirrels could get 'em, the ones that fell that night. We'd take 'em home and my Mama would boil 'em and peel 'em and put 'em in dressings and different things."

Chestnuts, Chinquapins, Walnuts, and Hicker Nuts ⌒ 395

*C*hestnut wood was awful bad too. Made a cracket in the fireplace. An old feller said if he died he wanted his coffin made out of chestnut so he could go through hell a poppin'.

—Chris Boatwright, 99,
Holly Creek Road,
Murray County, Georgia

I am indebted to retired Western Carolina University professor Duane Oliver for this Cherokee dumpling-type recipe, using imported chestnuts, of course. Oliver's ancestors were the original settlers of both Cades Cove, Tennessee, and Hazel Creek, North Carolina, and were well acquainted with Cherokees in both states, on both sides of the Smoky Mountains.

Cherokee Chestnut Bread

1 quart hulled chestnuts	*½ teaspoon salt*
2 cups water	*½ teaspoon baking soda*
1 cup sugar	*Large hickory leaves*
1 quart cornmeal	

Boil nuts 3 minutes, then peel. Boil peeled nuts 15 minutes in 2 cups water along with the sugar. Drain. Pound or grind chestnuts. Mix chestnut mixture with meal, salt, and baking soda. Add just enough water to make a very stiff dough. Knead well. Place walnut-sized balls of dough in the center of each hickory leaf. Wrap up and tie with a string. Drop in boiling water and simmer 1 hour or until done.

～

Here is a recipe for a nice chestnut dish. It is adapted from one offered by Mrs. Henry Church of Chattanooga, Tennessee. I have substituted ¼ cup of brandy plus ¼ cup of water for the ½ cup of rum that her recipe called for.

Chattanooga Chestnut Purée

1¾ pounds chestnuts	*¼ cup water*
1¼ cups sugar	*½ pint heavy cream, whipped*
¼ cup apple brandy	*Nutmeg*

Place shelled and skinned chestnuts in a saucepan and cover with boiling water. Add the sugar, and cook until chestnuts are soft. Drain and mash. Mix brandy with water, and add to the purée. Top with whipped cream, and sprinkle with nutmeg. Serves 6.

The story of the chestnut demise is a sad one. As seventy-year old William Hasty told me, "As a young boy in Cherokee County [Georgia], I recall picking up gallons of chestnuts from under some of the last native chestnut trees in America. Even then, the limbs were dying. Each year, a number of limbs would die, while others stayed and produced nuts. Finally, after four or five years, the tree would give up the ghost and die."

But there is some encouragement on the horizon. Scientists, with support from private sources, have founded the American Chestnut Foundation. Its aim is to transfer the resistance of the Chinese species genetically to American chestnuts. Some leading scientists have founded the American Chestnut Foundation "to put the American chestnut, king of the Eastern forests, back on its throne."

Chinquapins

Former Georgia governor Zell Miller recalls spending many early fall afternoons harvesting chinquapin nuts, a diminutive relative of the chestnut. While the dark little nuts were prickly on the outside like chestnuts, and possessed a meat difficult to dig out, the result was a tasty treat. Mountain people loved to eat chinquapins either raw, roasted, or boiled. Chinquapin meats can be substituted for chestnuts and hickory nuts in dressings, desserts, and other dishes.

Hazelnuts

Hazel Creek, North Carolina, got its name from the hazelnut bushes that grew along its banks. Usually growing in dense thickets around twelve feet high, they can be found along streams, on fence rows or along woods edges. Marie Mellinger says the nuts—considered good for one's digestive system—are small, with sweet kernels enclosed in a hard brown shell. "To gather them, you have to get ahead of the squirrels, chipmunks, and blue jays—all avid nut eaters." Here with my thanks is Marie's recipe for a nice hazelnut appetizer that goes well with sweet drinks. It's named for Warwoman Mountain in Rabun County, Georgia, which took its name from a famed Cherokee.

An old fellow from the backwoods used to bring us a poke of chinquapins every fall, but I haven't seen a chinquapin in forty years. Little brown nuts, like baby acorns that have lost their hats, chinquapins are the best things to eat. We parched them in the oven, then cracked the shells and devoured handfuls of the sweet round kernels inside...I would love a pokeful of chinquapins, right this minute.

—BETSY TICE WHITE, MOUNTAIN FOLK, MOUNTAIN FOOD

Warwoman Spiced Hazelnuts

*2 tablespoons butter
or margarine*

1 cup nuts

Salt to taste

1 teaspoon curry or chili powder

In a skillet, place butter or margarine and nuts. Brown the nuts, stirring constantly. Remove skillet from heat. Turn nuts on a paper towel to drain. Sprinkle with salt and curry or chili powder.

Beechnuts

I have a wonderful old beech tree perched on the banks of our little branch out back that drains into Atlanta's Nancy Creek. Beech trees have a beautiful complexion, and it was said that Amerindians loved to carve hieroglyphics on them. In this century, young people have left their love valentines on the bark of many a beech. (I'm happy to say that my tree is free of such scars.)

Beech trees bear a crop of nuts only every two or three years, yielding three-sided kernel nuts enclosed in a tough husk. Marie Mellinger tells us that the kernels can be roasted or ground into flour, cooking oil, or boiled as a coffee substitute. Here is her modern-day recipe for a beechnut pie.

Marie's Quick-Fix Beechnut Pie

1 cup chopped beechnuts

*1 package instant butterscotch
pudding (make as directed)*

Graham cracker pie shell

Allspice, cinnamon, and/or ginger

Mix the beechnuts with the butterscotch pudding mix. Pour into pie shell. Sprinkle allspice, cinnamon or ginger on top. You have an instant beechnut pie, ready to eat!

White Oak Acorns

I end this "nutty chapter" with a brief report on the acorns of white oak trees that are abundant across the Appalachians. The Swedish visitor to colonial America, Peter Kalm, found that the oil from boiled acorns was "the best remedy yet found against the dysentery." The Indians also taught settlers how to boil and eat the large white oil acorns. They touted the oil skimmings as a great liniment to soothe the aches and pains of bones plagued by rheumatism.

And, oh yes, the Indians loved to eat the acorns, after boiling.

They taught settlers how to grind up the acorns as thickeners with hominy and wild rice. Of course, the newcomers from the old world were finding out what their newly introduced swine were learning—that acorns were quite nourishing, if you had the boldness to try them out!

Jellies

Sweet Sustenance for the Mountain Winter

*During apple season, my mother seems to keep a little saucepan of
peelings perpetually stewing on the stove, thus increasing with no apparent
effort, her shelf of jellies.*

—Marion Brown, Burlington,
North Carolina, Pickles and Preserves

~

*The quince tree is the clown of the orchard, growing twisted and writhing,
as if hating a straight line. Notwithstanding, its fruit, and the uses thereof,
set the hall mark of housewifery. Especially in the matter of jelly-making
and marmalade.*

—Martha McCullough-Williams,
Dishes and Beverages of the Old South

Jellies, jams, marmalades, and preserves gave the Southern Appalachian family sweet
sustenance to carry them through hard mountain winters.

In addition to providing a nice spread for breakfast biscuits, the jellies were (and are)
wonderful condiments for wild meats, including venison, bear, groundhog, possums,
and squirrels.

The old standbys—apples, peaches, berries, and grapes—were abundantly used for
making jellies and jams. But some offbeat jellies emerged, using such fruits as maypops,
pawpaws, wild strawberries, and even corncobs! Jellies, of course, are made from fruit
juices; jam from fruit pulp; and preserves from fruit whole or in chunks.

In the pioneer years, housewives had no packaged fruit pectin to help them out, and
depended on the natural pectin in the fruits themselves. As a result, the making of jellies
required patience and skill, two traits of good mountain wives.

The wild blackberry, a fruit high in natural pectin, was and still is a mountain jelly
favorite. Apples, grapes, and plums also are high in natural pectin. In making jellies, wives
seek to cook the fruit as quickly as possible after picking while the pectin is high and the
fruit not overripe. In some cases, they might even throw in a few pieces of green fruit to
give the finished product an extra little tad of tartness and to make it jell.

Mrs. Hattie Cochran of the Aska Road area of Fannin County, Georgia, makes her jellies the old-fashioned way, particularly when she "puts up" wild blackberry jelly, one of her favorites.

"After cooking the berries, I mash them and get a real thin cloth and strain it through. It makes pure clear jelly…squeeze it through there. After that I measure it out—a cup of the blackberries to a cup of sugar, and then it jells quick. I don't use any SureJell or anything, just the pectin in the fruit. Then I can it [in a jar]."

As Hattie points out, good jelly is nice and clear, even shimmering, and should be strong enough to stand alone after being sliced.

Apple Jelly

One of the big byproducts of the Appalachian apple orchards, naturally, is apple jelly. When the University of Tennessee's Walter Lambert was growing up near Knoxville, apple jelly was made by boiling apple peelings with water, then straining the juice through a jelly cloth. He remembered another way. Walter described the process in his book, *Kinfolks and Custard Pie*. "The apples were cut up and placed in a pot with about half as much water as fruit, and cooked until very tender. Then the juice was drained off and strained through a jelly cloth to make the jelly; the pulp was run through a colander for apple butter. Waste not, want not!"

Apple jelly is used by many cooks as a base for other jellies such as wine, mint, rose petal, and the like. This recipe was collected by the Northwest Home Health Agency, head-quartered in Jasper, Georgia, and published in its *North Georgia Apple Recipes* booklet.

Apple Jelly

2½ pounds tart apples, ripe

3 cups sugar

¾ pounds under-ripe apples

2 tablespoons lemon juice, if apples are not tart enough

Wash and cut apples in small pieces, unpeeled or cored. Put apples and water in heavy kettle, cover, bring to boil. Reduce heat, and simmer until apples are soft. Pour cooked apples in jelly bag; collect juice, return 4 cups of juice to kettle; add sugar and lemon juice. Place over high heat—boil rapidly—until temperature is 8°F to 10°F above water boiling point. Remove immediately; skim and pour in hot, sterile jelly jars. Seal and store. Yields 4 to 5 pints.

Corncob Jelly

This is one of the more unusual Appalachian jellies. Corncob jelly comes out with a surprisingly red color and tastes a lot like apple jelly. Hickory Cane or Tennessee Red

Although you can buy jelly bags, they are easy things to improvise. I always use the washed and bleached out bags that Virginia hams come in, and you can also use the bags that hold popcorn rice. Just wash them well, and hang them in the sun to dry and bleach. If you want to make one, sew up the sides of a piece of pure white cotton so that it does not have a bottom seam, just side ones. When you are making jelly, hang the bag on a hook and let the juice...drip into a large glass jar or bowl. Some of the store–bought bags come with a frame for hanging the bag.

—EDNA LEWIS, *IN PURSUIT OF FLAVOR*

corn varieties are said to yield the prettiest jellies. Of course, you must use fresh corncobs, preferably from roast'n'ears.

For this recipe adaptation, I am indebted to the late Rubye Alley Bumgarner, of Sylva, North Carolina, author of *Sunset Farms, Spring Fryers Caused It All*. An intriguing title. For many years Rubye operated Sunset Farms, near Sylva.

Cherokee Corncob Jelly

12 ears fresh corn	*4 cups sugar*
4½ cups water	*1.2 ounces liquid fruit pectin*

Slice grains from corncob, and set aside for other use. Place cobs in water, and bring to a boil. Cover and cook around 15 minutes. Remove cobs, and strain liquid through cheesecloth. If necessary, add enough water to make 3 cups. In saucepan, place liquid, and mix in sugar. Bring to a boil, and cook until sugar is dissolved. Stir in pectin, and cook 1 minute longer. Remove from heat, skim, and spoon into sterilized jars. Seal and store. Yields 3 cups.

~

Wild grapes and plums have provided megatons of jellies for mountain families over the past three centuries. Blue Ridge settlers had experiences similar to that of author Marjorie Kinnan Rawlings who moved to the Florida scrub in the 1920s and reveled in the "finest tart jellies" that local people made from a wild Florida grape. It was an obvious version of the muscadine.

Beloved cook and author Edna Lewis, one of Atlanta's distinguished newer residents, loved the wild fox grape jellies made by her mother when she was growing up in Virginia. Walking through nearby woods, she could sniff out maturing fox grapes. In her fascinating book, *In Pursuit of Flavor*, Ms. Lewis wrote that "fox grapes revealed their presence

> When Ben Hutcherson was growing up in a tenant-farming family around Jingo, Tennessee, in the 1920s, he watched and learned as his mother made jams and jellies from the fruits and berries that grew wild around them. Jingo has become Fairview in the modern age, and Hutcherson's jelly making also includes a modern touch with the addition of packaged fruit pectin. "It's quicker," he says, "and it takes the guesswork out of cooking the fruit."
>
> But he still uses the same methods...that his mother favored, and he also gets the same good results. From sumac bushes, for example, he gathers deep red berries that stand up in a tightly bunched cone (another variety, of gray metallic color and drooping, is said to be poisonous) and boils them to extract a sour liquid. Mixed with sugar, lime juice, and pectin, it makes a tart and distinctively flavored jelly. "Sumac—or shoemake, as we always called it—is an old, old jelly," says Hutcherson. "The Indians used to make it."
>
> —John Egerton, *Southern Food*

by giving off a strong aroma of grape that permeated the woods and along the streams where they grew. The aroma was especially strong at twilight. We knew from the aroma that they were ready for gathering."

Scuppernong Jelly

That most prolific of wild grapes, the bronze scuppernong (a Muscadine cousin with an unmistakable musky smell), provided jelly meat to people all through the mountains and foothills. The sunset-colored jelly gives off a delicious fragrance.

North Carolinians Norma Jean and Carole Darden had a nice scuppernong jelly recipe in their engaging book of reminiscences, *Spoonbread and Strawberry Wine*. Their recipe calls for "red scuppernongs." In my country-boy South Carolina past, I always considered the blue-black wild grapes to be the "bullace" muscadine version and the amber-bronze version to be "scuppernongs." In any event, for this recipe, you can substitute any wild grape or even Concords. My thanks to the Dardens from which this adapted recipe comes.

Mrs. Sheridan's Scuppernong Jelly

5 pounds scuppernongs   *Sugar*

Wash grapes well. Place them in a large saucepan, and cook over medium heat for 10 to 15 minutes or until the skins burst (do not add water). Strain through a cheesecloth bag, and squeeze out all of the juice. To every 2 cups juice add 1 cup sugar. (For Concord grapes, use ¾ cup sugar for each cup juice). Boil the mixture for about 25 minutes, stirring frequently. The mixture is ready when it drips heavily from a spoon. Pour immediately into hot sterile jelly jars and seal. Yields 8 6-ounce jelly jars.

Wine Jellies

"Vedy English" in origin, wine jellies were very popular in the colonies. Sharon Williams (Kitty Caperton) shared the following 1800s recipe with the Atlanta Historical Society's *Tullie's Receipts* collectors. It had been originally owned by Mrs. Jane Bouie Caperton of Rome, Georgia.

Sherry Wine Jelly

2 sticks cinnamon	¼ cup cold water
Juice and rind of two lemons	1 cup sherry wine
2¾ cups boiling water	1 cup sugar
2 tablespoons gelatin	

Add cinnamon, lemon juice, and rind to boiling water for 5 minutes. Strain and add gelatin, softened in ¼ cup water, to hot mixture. Stir well. Add sherry wine and sugar, and strain through cheesecloth. Pour into mold, and place in icebox until set. Serve with whipped cream, if desired.

~

Jams, Preserves, and Oh, Glorious Apple Butter

*We often make apple-butter; this in the winter is a most excellent food,
particularly where there are many children.*
            —*J. Hector St. John de Crèvecoeur,* Letters from an
       American Farmer and Sketches of 18th Century America

~

Apple butter! That's what I loved, with hot biscuits and butter.
                   —*Curtis Underwood, Resaca, Georgia*

Ah, heavenly apple butter! The very thought brings a tingle to my taste buds! As I may have mentioned earlier, my introduction to this magnificent mountain epitome of the apple art came somewhat late in my young life. I was only sixteen—"going on seventeen," as they say in the country—when my mother and father put me on a train in Hamlet, North Carolina, and sent me off to college at "far off" Mount Berry, Georgia, but fortuitously right near north Georgia's great apple country.

There, just beyond Berry's Gate of Opportunity, in the college's elegant old Blackstone Hall, a shiny gallon can of apple butter was popped open at our table one bright morning, and a bowlful of the delicacy came to me along with a platter of Vernie Nabors's great "cathead" biscuits plus a plate of fresh butter from the college's dairy farm. Such a combination was one to warm the cockles of any homesick young lad's heart, particularly so when the rich cinnamon and apple flavors wafted up from the table along with the aroma of steaming hot coffee.

I realized right off that obviously I had been deprived in my earlier youth in the Carolina Piedmont. For some inexplicable reason, my sweet Scotch-Irish mother, one of the world's greatest cooks, had never served apple butter in our home! But all that was made up for when the Berry chefs got hold of me. Vernie and her husband, Fred, saw to it that I would no longer be denied God's apple/cinnamon creation, at least not for the four years immediately ahead of me. Nor since. That first encounter hooked me, and I've been an apple butter aficionado ever since. Maybe apple butter junkie would be more descriptive.

~

Since starting the research on this volume, I have learned even more about apple butter's ancestry. In my humble opinion, it's the greatest culinary contribution our

German migrants brought to the Southern Appalachians. And that's saying a lot, since the Germans were responsible for so many wonderful dishes—dumplings, sauerkraut, and great meats, plus magnificent puddings and pies and Moravian love feast delicacies.

> *Homemade mountain apple butter is still spoken of in soft reverent tones by some of the old-timers.*
>
> —THE LATE BIL DWYER,
> HIGHLANDS, NORTH CAROLINA

And while apples came from England, there's no doubt that the German Rhinelanders (and Moravians) who came south into the Blue Ridge and Cumberland country in the 1700s really honed apple butter–making to a deliciously fine art.

So much so that the apple harvesting season became a glorious event up and down the Great Valley and across the Appalachian foothills. The *Genesee Farmer* of 1839 gave a nice account of a rural farmstead during the autumn days when the apples hit:

> The host should in the autumn invite his neighbors, particularly the young men and maidens, to make up an apple butter party. Being assembled, let three bushels of fair sweet apples be pared, quartered, and the cores removed. Meanwhile, let two barrels of new cider be boiled down to one half. When this is done, commit the prepared apples to the cider, and henceforth let the boiling go on briskly and systematically. But to accomplish the main design, the party must take turns at stirring the contents without cessation, that they do not become attached to the side of the kettle and be burned. Let this stirring go on till the liquid becomes concrete—in other words, till the amalgamated cider and apples become as thick as hasty pudding.

Appalachian Apple Butter

In western North Carolina's great apple country—embracing the counties of Alleghany, Avery, Buncombe, Henderson, and Watauga—folks loved to cook up their apple butter in big outdoor pots.

The late Jim Hall of Asheville, North Carolina, was one to carry on the old-time tradition. Every autumn, Jim and his wife, Eleanor, would, as the *Genesee Farmer* suggested, get together a party of friends to spend a day and a night cooking up apple butter.

"Due to the amount of stirring required," Jim told his friends, "the more people you can find to help with the party, the better off you are—except when it comes time to divide the product."

And that's what Jim would do—invite a passel of folks from all around that end of North Carolina. His colleagues at Carolina Power and Light Company would compete for the opportunity to join in the fun. The catalyst for the annual frolic was the Jim Hall Olde Time, Sure-Fired (you have to be there to believe it) Apple Butter Recipe.

Thanks to an introduction by my Asheville cousin Tom Dabney, Jim's widow, Eleanor Hall, graciously shared this recipe with the hope that it would help perpetuate the tradition.

Jim Hall's Olde Time Apple Butter
(You have to be there to believe it)

*1 12-gallon cooking pot
(copper if possible)
2 gallons apple cider (soft variety)
4 or 5 bushels Stayman Winesap
apples (picked within hollerin'
distance of Hendersonville, NC)*

*1 quart sorghum syrup
20 pounds sugar
Nutmeg to taste
Cinnamon to taste*

Peel and slice all the apples in sight. Bring apple cider to full boil over an open fire. Cook apples down to a sauce. (Add apples slowly so that they might be stirred.) Add syrup and sugar. Cook mixture from 8:30 on a cool morning until 5:30 that night, stirring vigorously all the time. During the last two hours of cooking, add nutmeg and cinnamon to suit your spouse's taste. Yields approximately 8 gallons.

~

It is necessary to constantly stir the applesauce while it is cooking to keep it from scorching. Long handled paddles riddled with holes are used for the tedious task.

The late Reed Stanley, who grew up with the great Stanley clan in the Big Creek area straddling north Georgia's Fannin and Gilmer Counties at the Blue Ridge Divide, gave me an interview in the kitchen of his Cartecay Highway home. He declared that it takes a good sour apple to make good apple butter. "Golden Delicious will cook up but a Red Delicious won't. They got the best taste and the loudest smell of anything but you got to grind 'em up, otherwise they won't cook up. The Detroit Red will cook all to pieces as quick as it gets hot. These old-fashioned Dan'iel apples,

A western Virginia housewife dips up apple butter directly from the copper pot in which it was cooked.

lots of people calls 'em sugar apples, they'll cook. And they make the best and most apple brandy."

Mrs. Stanley declared that she liked to cook apple butter in a dishpan on the stove. Reed still preferred the black iron wash outdoors but said you had to keep an eagle eye on the apples in the pot. "They'll stick on ye; they'll scorch. You've got to stir 'em continuously."

Farther west toward the Cohutta Mountains, Frances Gates Hill confirmed that keeping the fire hot enough but not too hot is the secret to making great apple butter. That and plenty of continuous stirring.

"Mama cooked her apple butter in a wash pot outside. She didn't want a roaring fire, you know, just enough to keep it good and hot. She'd let it cook at least a couple hours after she had the applesauce ready.

"If you put a little sugar in it, it'll thicken better. Back then, Mama cooked her spices with it all the time—nutmeg and cinnamon. That's what gave it the flavor. I really don't care for a lot of spices myself."

Nowadays, many people such as Hazel Farmer of Union County, Georgia, use Surejell, including its recipe. "But I can remember Mama making apple butter the old way. She used to put the apples in a dishpan in the bread oven."

This recipe is named for Ellijay, county seat of Gilmer County, Georgia's premier apple-growing county and scene of its well-attended autumn Apple Festival sponsored by the Chamber of Commerce.

Ellijay Easy Apple Butter

1 quart unsweetened applesauce　　*1 teaspoon cinnamon*
2 cups sugar　　*⅛ teaspoon ground cloves*

In a saucepan, combine applesauce, sugar, and spices. Bring to a boil, reduce heat, and simmer about 15 minutes, stirring frequently to prevent sticking. Pour into hot canning jars; leave ¼ inch headspace. Seal and process in boiling water bath for 10 minutes. Yields 4 cups, 30 calories per tablespoon.

Peach Butter

The apple wasn't the only fruit that was "butter" material; mountain folk also made luscious butters of persimmons, plums, quinces, pears, peaches, grapes, and apricots. The advantages of the butters was that they took only about half the sugar that jams did. Frances and her mother, Tamer Sumner Gates, also loved to fix peach butter at their home on the Cohutta Mountain side of Gilmer County.

A wonderful peach butter recipe came to me from Atlanta friend and public TV cooking guru Nathalie Dupree. Nathalie and her husband, Jack Bass, the noted author and historian, like to serve this peach butter as a spread on toast and croissants at their new home at Social Circle, Georgia. The basic recipe from which this is adapted came from Nathalie's 1986 book, *New Southern Cooking*.

Nathalie's Peach Butter

4 pounds peaches (about 14)	*2 tablespoons peach brandy*
1 cup water	*1 tablespoon candied ginger (optional)*
3½ cups sugar	

Simmer the peaches in the water until the skin is easy to remove. Peel and pit the peaches, saving the cooking liquid. Purée the peaches (about 8 cups), and place with the liquid and the sugar in a pot and cook over low heat, stirring occasionally until thick. This will take about 3 hours. Taste and add brandy (or orange liqueur), and cook a few minutes more. Add the ginger if desired. Remove from heat, and allow to cool. Store in the refrigerator in a container, and keep refrigerated or frozen until ready to use. Yields 4 pints.

Jams and Preserves

Jams, of course, have been and continue to be extremely popular throughout the Southern Appalachians. Like preserves, jams are made by combining a fruit and sugar, or several fruits and sugar.

In contrast to making preserves, to produce jam, you must crush the fruit. The product ends up much thicker than with preserves. For instance, in making peach jam, you cut the peaches up into tiny pieces and simmer them in a saucepan until tender. Then you crush the fruit, usually with a potato masher. At this point, most recipes call for adding the same amount of sugar (in cups) as your peach pulp—for instance, two cups of cooked pulp to two cups of sugar. You turn up the heat again and cook it slowly—stirring it all the while to prevent scorching—until it is thick and the fruit looks transparent. At that point you have a jam that is ready to be poured into jars and sealed.

Melvin and Ruth Swanson Hunter of Young Harris, Georgia, recall that home grown vegetables and fruits a half century ago—including those made into jams and jellies—were much tastier.

Wide-mouth Mason or Ball jars with metal dome lids and screw-on bands are the handiest jars to use in jelly- and jam-making. They can be frozen or they can be sterilized after filling. Other boilable glasses need to be sterilized before filling, and the hot jams poured into them immediately. After cooling, two thin layers of paraffin are required. Refrigeration is not necessary but it's advisable to keep them in a cool, dark, and well-ventilated storage place.

Blackberry Jam

The famed Jarrett House in Dillsboro, North Carolina—in the heart of the Blue Ridge mountain country on the edge of the Smokies—is noted for its bountiful tables of traditional mountain food. This is the Jarrett House recipe for blackberry jam, with thanks to Jean and Jim Hartbarger, operators of the venerable hundred-year-old inn.

Jarrett House Old-Fashioned Blackberry Jam

1 cup sugar   *1 cup blackberry pulp*
1 cup water

Wash and clean berries. Add a small amount of water, just enough to start berries cooking. Cook until berries are soft. Press through a sieve to remove seeds. Combine berry pulp and sugar. Bring to a boil and simmer for 20 to 25 minutes, or until mixture reaches a soft ball stage. Pour into hot, sterilized jars and seal. Store in cool place.

Muscadine Jam

Muscadine jam also has a very distinctive musky flavor—much like that of the wild grapes. My personal thanks go to John Egerton of Nashville, the South's food critic and Southern historian supreme, for the following "standard method" for making the jam. He included this method in his glorious and encyclopedic book, *Southern Food*.

Egerton's Muscadine Jam

Squeeze the pulp from the skins, separate the seeds from the pulp and discard the seeds. Cook the skins until they are tender, then recombine them with the pulp and juice. For each cupful, add ¾ cup sugar and boil the mixture, stirring frequently for 10 to 20 minutes, or until the juice becomes noticeably thicker. Put up in ½-pint jars and seal when cool with paraffin or two-piece lids. Each cup of the fruit should make a half-pint of jam.

Pear Preserves

My appreciation goes to the authors of the *Old North State Cook Book* of Charlotte, North Carolina, the source of this Martha Washington recipe for pear preserves. The editors credited Mrs. W. Frank Sample for providing the recipe and had this comment about George Washington's visit to Charlotte in 1791: "[The President] entered the city on North Tryon Street, riding in 'a snow white coach with gilded springs, with his crest emblazoned upon the door.' Four horses drew this elegant vehicle, and his entourage included, besides the coachman and postilion, his valet de chambre, two footmen, four riding horses and a baggage wagon."

If you don't have enough jam to make you happy, cook up some unripe wild grapes or green apples, which supply natural pectin (or use commercial pectin). Don't overcook your jam just because you want to add pectin; it would destroy the fine flavor of the fruit.

—FRANCES HAMERSTROM, *WILD FOOD COOKBOOK*

Charlotte had been one of the centers of fervent and energetic Patriot support during the Revolutionary War. Charlotte's patriotism was typical of the entire Piedmont and Appalachian "backcountry" during that crucial period. Concerning Washington's visit to Charlotte, there was no mention as to whether the first lady was with the president, but probably not. Nevertheless, Martha Washington's pear preserves recipe lives on.

Martha Washington's Pear Preserves

Pears	Water
Boiling lye	Brandy
Sugar (½ pound to every pound of fruit)	

The pears should be very fresh. Wash them and put them into boiling lye for 1 minute. Remove and put them into cold water. Next put them into a prepared syrup of sugar and water, using enough water to dissolve sugar. Then cook them for 15 minutes. Remove and put on plates to cool. Boil the syrup down to one-half the original quantity. Put the syrup and the pears in jars, and add some brandy. Seal while hot.

Crockpot Apple Butter

For an easy way to make apple butter, readers might like to try this adaptation of a recipe passed on to me by Cousin Lib Beach. She and her husband Jack reside near Hendersonville, in the heart of North Carolina's great apple country. Their home sits atop a small mountain at "High Point Lookout" with apple trees all around.

Cousin Lib Beach's Crockpot Apple Butter

A dozen or so tart apples	2 cups granulated sugar
½ cup sorghum syrup	2 teaspoons ground cinnamon
½ teaspoon ground nutmeg	

Peel apples and dice. Place apples in one-gallon crockpot until it's full. Add sorghum, sugar, cinnamon, and nutmeg. Stir together.

Set crockpot on high and cook 1 hour. Take a potato masher and smooth up the apples. Turn the crockpot to low and cook for another 10 hours or so. If the mixture looks too soupy, tip the lid to allow some of the stream to escape. (*Note: It's possible to overcook in some crockpots. Check the mixture after 8 hours. If the apples are turning dark brown, turn off crockpot and let cool.*)

With the completion of the cooking, the apple butter should have a light brown, chunky consistency. To obtain a smooth consistency, run the mixture through a blender. Refrigerate and serve with hot biscuits.

Fat and Lovable Pies, Puddings, and Cakes

Southern desserts are big, fat, and lovable.

—*Courtney Parker,* How to Eat
Like a Southerner and Live to Tell the Tale

~

Stack cake is an all-time mountain favorite. Delicately sweet and spicy, this
cake was usually six or more layers.

—*Carolyn G. Bryan, Sevierville, Tennessee,*
Appalachian Kinfolks Cookbook

~

Gosh plumb, when you cut into them cobblers, they was just as tender
as could be.

—*A. L. Tommie Bass of Sand Mountain,*
Alabama, in Plain Southern Eating

~

No sir, there's nothing like a good half-moon pie straight out
of the skillet.

—*Aunt Tennie Cloer, of Murphy, North Carolina,*
as told to John Parris in Mountain Cooking

Desserts, LaMont Burns has written, "should be like the end of a sermon—heavy enough to stick with you, but light enough to remember the main scriptures."

Sharing the wisdom of his family's cook, Ausiebelle, LaMont struck our sweet tooth sentiments right on the button—the belly button, that is. Folk in the Southern Appalachians, just like other Southerners, have had a love affair with desserts from way back, even though refined sugar was nearly impossible to obtain during hard times such as the Civil War and Reconstruction and also during the Depression. Such times, when the sugar chests ran low, called for "can do" response, nothing unusual for hill country farmers. They went to the woods to lure more honey bees to their homemade bee gums, and boosted their sorghum syrup production. Such "long sweetenin'" sugar substitutes helped keep the mountain kitchen turning out sweet delicacies.

The late Robert Sparks Walker of Chattanooga recalled that sweet cakes made of sorghum were "favorite dainties" at the turn of the century. "These were made in such large numbers that they were often stacked a foot high, but a half dozen or more hungry children could soon devour two or three dozen such stacks."

The word dessert is French in derivation and comes from the verb desservir, which literally means "to clear the table." Certainly a superb dessert is the crowning glory of a proper meal. Often a good dessert has saved a very poor meal from being a tragedy.
—LILY BYRD MCKEE, CASHIERS, NORTH CAROLINA, *HIGH HAMPTON HOSPITALITY*

Indeed, since early colonial days, mountain wives have managed to find ways to put desserts on the table. In the 1890s in east Tennessee, Sarah Amick McQuerry "had little besides molasses and a few precious spices to work with to create sweet dishes." This was according to her great-granddaughter Carolyn Bryan in her *Appalachian Kinfolks Cookbook.*

The 1940 *WPA Guide to South Carolina* gave a similar account: "Long sweet-enin' cookies, molasses pudding…and sweet potato pone may have originated in wartime blockade days, but they are quite as good now as when molasses had to serve for sugar."

This was a replay of Elizabethan England. Up to the early 1700s, British peasants turned to treacle (molasses) and honey since hardrock sugar cones were kept under upper class lock and key.

~

When Appalachian mountain folk remember days gone by, sweets stand out. I asked ninety-year-old Nina Garrett of Gilmer County, Georgia, to give me her fondest food memories.

"Apple and peach pies and puddin's and sweet potato pie!" she declared with a big smile. "That was real good. You see Mother would put plenty of butter in it, and ginger was the spice you put in. We had to beat the ginger and sift it to get the stringy part out. Nobody now would know what it was if they saw a race of ginger. I reckon my dad growed it."

North Carolina's James Villas confirmed the South's sweet cravings.

"If there is another area of the country (or indeed another place in the world besides England) where elaborate, rich, sinful desserts are as popular and beloved as in the South, I'd like to be informed…The number of cakes and pies and cobblers and dumplings…in Mother's black recipe book seems to double from year to year as she continues to gather new ideas from friends."

Pies and Pastries

Pies have had a scrumptious hill country history. Up until this century, it was not uncommon to find fruit pies being served at breakfast. And pies have reigned supreme at social occasions, particularly at all-day singings and dinners on the ground.

Pie-making has been the subject of much improvising. The beauty of attempting to cook a pie is that the housewife could use whatever leftovers she had on hand, particularly in the way of fruit, eggs, flour, or even baked sweet potatoes. Provided she could come up with the right combination and a good pie crust.

One of the keys to pie-making is the matter of pie crusts. Jonathan Swift wrote that "promises and pie-crust are made to be broken." But skilled wives with "light hands" know by instinct how to finger dough. Another key is using flours from soft winter wheat such as those good old Southern standbys, White Lily and Martha White.

In her "Philosophy of Pie Crust," the effervescent and aforementioned Martha McCullough-Williams of Clarksville, Tennessee, declared that "pie-crust perfection" depended on good flour, good fat, good handling, and "most especially good baking." She went on to say that "a hot oven, quick but not scorching, expands the air betwixt layers of paste, and pops open the flour-grains, making them absorb the fat as it melts, thereby growing crisp and relishful instead of hard and tough." Get that? I'm a little confused but it sounds good. She urged the use of "very cold" shortening and water or milk and the use of baking powder or soda to make the crust light. Her "everyday pie crust" formula called for one pound flour, six ounces shortening, and a half-pint of ice water.

> *H*er hand was as light with her pastry as with her husband, and the results as happy.
>
> —ANONYMOUS

With all that as a preamble, here are two pie crust recipes. The first comes from the famed Nu-Wray Inn at Burnsville, North Carolina:

Nu-Wray Pie Crust

3 tablespoons cold water	*3 tablespoons lard*
½ teaspoon salt	*1 cup soft wheat flour*

Put water in bowl, and add salt. Blend lard in water, and mix thoroughly. Add flour, and mix as for any pastry. If kept in icebox several hours, it will be better.

⌒

This second one comes from Louise Woodruff of Walland, Tennessee, near the Great Smoky Mountains. Louise notes that this dough can also be used for fried pies (a recipe that will be upcoming).

Louise's Pie Crust

1 bowlful of White Lily
self-rising flour

½ cup buttermilk
⅓ cup shortening

Sift bowlful of flour and make well in center. Add buttermilk and shortening. Dip in, and mix together with hands to make a very stiff batter. Then let sit for 10 to 12 minutes. Work back down, and roll out thin on floured board to fit pie pan. Pour in pie mixture.

Double-Crust Apple Pie

Nothing is more popular than apple pie in the high-elevation southern highlands where apples of all varieties and colors begin "hitting" from June through November—apples red, apples green, and apples yellow. For baking in pies, firm and tart apples are called for, not "eating apples" such as Delicious or McIntosh that soften too much when baked.

This first "double-crust" recipe is adapted from the *North Georgia Apple Recipes* collection published by the Northeast Home Health Agency. For this pie, apple experts suggest the use of a tart variety such as Stayman or Jonathan or a combination of the two. As an alternative to homemade crusts, you can use two Pillsbury Ready Crusts.

Blue Ridge Double-Crust Apple Pie

6 to 8 tart apples
¾ to 1 cup sugar
2 tablespoons all-purpose flour
Dash of nutmeg
½ teaspoon cinnamon

Dash of salt
⅓ cup sweet sorghum syrup
Pastry for 2-crust 9-inch pie
2 tablespoons butter

It is likely that the most rabid sweet-cravers among us trace our lineage back to the English, whose sweet-eating, in the opinion of the French, amounted to a mindless addiction. They even put sugar into their wine! Queen Elizabeth herself kept a "sucket," later called a sweetmeat, in her mouth most of the time.
—SOUTHERN HERITAGE JUST DESSERTS COOK BOOK

Mother was awful to make egg custards. We loved egg custards. We got them on Sundays. That was our special day. And for Christmas, Mother was bad to make sweet potato pies. She always had something special.

—Bess Dover Pache,
Gilmer County, Georgia

Preheat oven to 400°F. Peel, core, and slice the apples thin. Combine sugar, flour, spices, and salt. Then mix with apples and syrup. Line the 9-inch pie plate with pastry, and fill with apple mixture. Place thin slices of butter over the apples, and then adjust the top crust. Be sure to cut a few slits in top crust to avoid a messy oven! Bake at 400°F for 50 minutes or until done.

Remove from oven when it bubbles through the center. Allow to cool for about an hour. Makes a 9-inch pie.

Dried Apple Stack Pie

Stack pies have been popular in the mountains over the years. Filled with peaches, pears, apples, plums, or persimmons, such ½-inch-thick double-crust pies were made in large numbers, stacked in pie baskets, and taken to picnics, parties, and all-day sing-ings with dinner-on-the-ground. Some of the most popular have been those using dried apples. This recipe comes from Duane Oliver's *Cooking on Hazel Creek* (North Carolina). Accompanying the recipe, Rollins Justice wrote: "The name is said to have originated from baking pies for gatherings and stacking them for convenience and because of scarcity of plates for carrying."

Justice rated this the best of many stack pie recipes he had seen. It was worked up by Pallie Allen and Bessie Gibson in the 1930s from memory. The apple mixture is made up of applesauce made from dried apples. To make a delectable sauce from dried apples, you soak them overnight in water, then stew them in honey or sorghum. The sauce can be refrigerated until time for the pie-baking. On this recipe, Justice suggests when ready for baking, the sauce should be heated up in time for placing in circle dough crusts.

Pallie's Apple Stack Pie

For the crust:

3 cups self-rising flour	½ cup shortening
2 teaspoons baking soda	1 teaspoon vanilla
1 cup sugar	½ cup buttermilk
2 beaten eggs	

Preheat oven to 375°F. In a bowl sift together flour and soda. Add sugar, beaten eggs, shortening, vanilla, and about ½ cup buttermilk or enough to make soft "biscuit dough." Knead as for biscuits. Roll out to 8-inch size using a plate for pattern. On a cookie sheet, bake the circles (layers) in oven at 375°F until golden brown. Stack up circle layers on top of one another, and take to table top.

For the filling: Have 2 cups of dried applesauce good and hot. Flavor it with 1 teaspoon lemon extract. Spread between layers, about 4 layers for each pie.

Egg Custard Pie

This a real favorite in the southern highlands, often cooked for family suppers. Pie authority Susan Purdy says that while it's fairly easy to make a custard pudding, it is far more difficult to bake the same custard inside a pastry shell. The problem is that while flaky pastry requires high heat, creamy egg custard bakes at a low temperature. One solution is to partially prebake the pastry shell, moistureproof it with egg glaze, then add the custard and bake again. In this regard, an old-fashioned wood stove is superior to the electric range, if you would place the pie at bottom of the oven. This recipe is an adaptation from one published in the *Southern Heritage Family Gatherings Cook Book*.

Sweet Potato Custard Pie

¼ cup butter, softened	3 large sweet potatoes, cooked
1¼ cups sugar	and mashed
¼ teaspoon salt	1 cup half-and-half
3 eggs, separated	1 unbaked 9-inch pastry shell
3 tablespoons lemon juice	¼ cup butter or margarine, melted
1 tablespoon grated orange rind	¼ cup firmly packed dark brown sugar
½ teaspoon ground nutmeg	¾ cup chopped pecans

Preheat oven to 425°F. In a large bowl, combine ¼ cup butter, sugar, salt, and egg yolks. Beat well. Add lemon juice, orange rind, nutmeg, sweet potatoes, and half-and-half. Beat until well blended. Beat egg whites at room temperature until stiff peaks form. Fold into sweet potato mixture. Pour filling into pastry shell. Combine ¼ cup melted butter, brown sugar, and pecans. Mix well. Sprinkle mixture evenly over top of filling. Bake at 425°F for 10 minutes. Reduce heat to 350°F. Bake an additional 30 minutes or until a knife inserted in center comes out clean. Cool before serving. Makes a 9-inch pie.

Fried Pies (Half Moons)

The aforementioned Robert Sparks Walker of Chattanooga, Tennessee, author of several superlative books including *Torchlight to the Cherokees*, regarded fried apple pies as "the best-liked food of all." His mother made so many "they would be set in stacks."

The half moon pies, called "mule ears" in some areas of the Carolina Piedmont, are well loved all over the southern highlands. "Aunt Tennie" Cloer told Asheville columnist John Parris, now retired, that the little fried pies "were all the go" when she was a young girl. "Folks…throve on 'em." Mrs. Cloer remembered that when a rail-splitting would occur at their place on Macon County's Sugar Fork River, her mother would cook up over a hundred fried pies to feed the menfolk. She would store the little pies in a hollow gum or a lard can, enabling the rail-splitters to help themselves when hunger pangs struck.

Mrs. Blanche Harkins told *Foxfire* students she preferred dried yellow apples for the little pies. To the delight of youngsters, housewives such as Mrs. Harkins filled the miniature pies with fruits ranging from apples (oftentimes dried apples) to peaches, peach butter, and even blackberry jam. In all cases, a small mound of fruit is heaped onto a half-size rolled-out pie crust. The cook then flips the dough into a half moon, seals at the edges and fries the pie quickly in deep fat. Then she serves them hot, sometimes sprinkling on powdered sugar as a final sweet touch.

This recipe, credited to Mrs. Earle Combs of Richmond, Kentucky, was included in *Kentucky Hospitality*, published in 1976 by the Kentucky Federation of Women's Clubs. Dried peaches can be substituted for apples. As an option, the pies can be baked in a 400°F oven. For a crisper pie when baked, brush first with melted margarine.

Kentucky Apple Fried Pies

1 pound dried apples	*2 tablespoons butter or margarine*
¾ cup sugar	*2 teaspoons cinnamon*

Cover dried fruit in water and soak overnight. Drain and add small amount of fresh water, and cook slowly until tender. Mash the fruit. Add the sugar, butter or margarine, and cinnamon to your taste. Stir well and let the mixture cool. Make your favorite pie crust, using only half the regular amount of shortening. Cut into circles 4 to 6 inches in diameter. Place a generous tablespoon of filling on one side of each circle. Fold the other side over, and seal firmly along the edge with your fingertips or a fork. Fry in about ½ inch of hot lard, turning once. When pastry is browned, remove and drain on paper towels. While pies are still warm, sprinkle lightly with sugar. Yields 16 miniature pies.

Chess Pie

Where did the term chess pie originate? Susan Purdy, author of *As Easy as Pie*, ties it to the word *chest*, pronounced with a Southern drawl, and used to describe pies "baked with so much sugar they could be stored in a pie chest." Such chest-high pie safes with perforated-tin paneled doors were common throughout the region before the days of refrigeration. Another speculation is that the name came as a cook's response—"jes' pie"—to what he was cooking. You take your pick.

Although chess pies are definitely Southern, and very similar to transparent pies and buttermilk pies, they are a relative newcomer to Southern cookbooks, having shown up only since the turn of the century. The late Bill Neal noted that in some places in Tennessee, baked and cooled chess pies would be stacked on top of each other six or seven deep and would be cut as a cake. In most cases, however, the pies are served singly, topped with ice cream or frozen yogurt.

The following recipe is adapted from one Mark Sohn published in his outstanding *Mountain Country Cooking*. The Kentucky chef, TV personality, and author named his dish for Hawksbill Summit, at 4,049 feet, the highest point in the Shenandoah National Park. His rationale was that chess pies are popular with cooks both east and west of the Blue Ridge mountains.

Hawksbill Chess Pie

1 cup evaporated milk	1 teaspoon vanilla
3 eggs	1¾ cups sugar
½ cup melted butter	2 tablespoons all-purpose flour
(not margarine)	1 unbaked 9-inch pie pastry shell

Preheat oven to 350°F. In a mixing bowl, combine and stir together the milk, eggs, butter, and vanilla. In separate bowl, blend the sugar with the flour, then combine and beat it into the milk mixture. Pour mixture into pastry shell. Bake for 45 minutes, or until the center puffs up and a knife inserted near the center comes out clean. Serves 8.

Puddings

Of all the favorite foods I recall from my misspent youth, banana pudding tops the list. I loved it so much, I got sick one time after gorging on the wonderful stuff. Thus it is no wonder that today, I compare every banana pudding I'm served to those puddings Mama fixed back in the 1940s. We always had banana pudding as the grand climax to Sunday dinner, except that time when Mama was attending a Baptist Assembly at Ridgecrest, North Carolina. So you can be sure that one of the upcoming recipes will be for Mother Dabney's banana pudding.

The love of puddings came in our ancestors' genes when they arrived from England. As John Egerton has written, the first colonists arriving in Virginia "brought with them a devotion to puddings, especially sweet ones, and they were the forerunners of the abundance of pies and puddings in modern cookbooks." *Poding, poodying,* and even *pooddynge* was eaten in England as far back as the thirteenth century. But the first printed pudding recipe didn't show up until three centuries later, and it called for bread:

> *take crumbs of bread,*
> *yolks of egges and cowes milke,*
> *with saffron,*
> *seethe them together a lytle,*
> *as if to make a puddinge.*

Pumpkin pudding was one of the earliest puddings enjoyed by early settlers. And little wonder. Pumpkins were the great sustainer. As Edward Johnson called it, the "fruit which the Lord fed his people with till corn and cattle increased."

But it was Indian pudding, boiled cornmeal, butter, eggs, and sugar, topped with syrup—an offshoot of Britain's wheat-based hasty pudding—that enjoyed early success in colonial America. It came to be known as hasty pudding. But a similar dish that took hold in the Appalachians—called mush—was based on boiled cornmeal alone, and was served often with sorghum syrup and at supper with milk. It remained a favorite right up to the early part of this century.

The Second Best Cook

...Next to Grandma, Aunt Cora
  was the best cook—
once she baked six kinds of pie
for a family gathering, and the black ants
got in the piesafe overnight.
You would have thought the last trump
of judgment had come, the way she raved.
She was somewhat mollified by the other aunts'
reassurance that Fanny Farmer herself
had never made lighter pie crust
or tastier gravy to float the tender bits
of home-cured ham and plump yellow eggs.
—From *Spring Onions and Cornbread*,
by poet Bettie M. Sellers of
Young Harris, Georgia
(Poet Laureate of Georgia)

Baked Cornmeal Pudding

This was an authentic old-time Appalachian baked dish that had all the taste-marks of a hasty pudding. Mrs. J. T. Walker, who grew up in east Tennessee, offered this recipe to the Great Smoky Mountains Natural History Association, which published it in 1957. Mrs. Walker's recipe had been handed down from her mother and grandmother, all of whom "were born and reared right here in the foothills of dear Old Smoky." Mrs. Walker remembered the pudding as being delicious, and especially good to serve with any kind of fruit.

Smoky Mountain Baked Cornmeal Pudding

2 cups cornmeal

1 cup all-purpose flour

¼ teaspoon allspice

1 teaspoon baking soda

1 teaspoon salt

¼ cup shortening

2 well-beaten eggs

1 cup buttermilk

1 cup sorghum molasses

Sift meal twice. Thoroughly mix all dry ingredients. Add eggs, milk, molasses, and shortening. Mix all together thoroughly, adding more milk if too stiff. Bake in well-greased pudding pan until a golden brown. Test with toothpick; it comes out clean when pudding is done. Serve hot.

Plum Pudding

Jamestown settlers brought the plum pudding from England, but the American version had no plums in it! Neither did the original British recipe. Plum pudding recipes from the mother country were filled with raisins, just like ours, and the word *plum* was apparently used as a definition of "choice bit." In her recipe for plum pudding, Virginia's Mary Randolph, in her 1831 cookbook, urged cooks to make up their plum puddings before sunrise (apparently to allow the yeast to rise).

While plum pudding didn't make it into many mountain homesteads in the early years of settlement, it was a familiar dish in the Blue Ridge and Appalachian interior in later years, particularly in such places as the homes of James Madison and Thomas Jefferson at Montpelier and Monticello respectively, and has enjoyed currency in the Highlands in the past century. So it is worthwhile for me to include this engaging recipe from Mrs. Randolph's pioneering 1824 cookbook, *The Virginia Housewife*.

Plum Pudding

Take a pound of the best flour, sift it, and make it up before sunrise, with six eggs beaten light; a large spoonful of good yeast, and as much milk as will make it the consistence of bread; let it rise well, knead into it half a pound of butter, put in a grated nutmeg, with one and a half pounds of raisins stoned and cut up; mix all well together, wet the cloth, flour it, and tie it loosely, that the pudding may have room to rise. Raisins for puddings or cakes, should be rubbed in a little flour, to prevent their settling to the bottom—see that it does not stick to them in lumps.

Banana Pudding

Bananas became popular through the Appalachian South in the late 1800s when railroads began shipping in the tropical fruit. They reached most of our Carolina upcountry through the port of Charleston. Fulton, Kentucky, became the banana distribution point for that region when the Illinois Central Railroad in 1880 began shipping bananas out of New Orleans in their new "icebox cars." The Appalachian diet has never been the same since. Bananas became a great hit everywhere, particularly for those Sunday puddings. Every September, townspeople in Fulton, Kentucky, cook up the world's largest banana pudding—a one-ton monster loaded with three thousand bananas—at their big banana festival.

As I said, banana pudding was such a wonderful dish in my preteen years that I over-ate one Sunday and had to lay off bananas for a week or two. But not for long.

With the help of two of my sisters-in-law, Lib and Jeanette Dabney, I here attempt to re-create my mother's banana pudding recipe.

Mother Wincey Dabney's Banana Pudding

4 eggs, separated	7 to 8 bananas
4 cups milk	Vanilla wafers
½ cup sugar	⅔ cup confectioners' sugar
4 teaspoons all-purpose flour	

Preheat oven at 300°F. In large saucepan combine the egg yolks, milk, sugar, and flour. Mix thoroughly and bring to a boil, stirring constantly. Set aside and allow to cool. Into a greased casserole, place sliced bananas and wafers in alternating layers, pouring the mix into each layer and on top. For the topping beat the egg whites, and add confectioners' sugar. Bake at 300°F until lightly brown. Chill before serving. Serves 8.

Cakes

Cakes hold a hallowed place in the memories of most everyone. I remember those delicious smells that came from our kitchen when my mother would bake cakes for special occasions—particularly for Christmas. Made from fresh eggs, newly churned butter, flour, spices, and nuts, plus fresh milk—the sweet and pungent cakes would emerge from the kitchen in what seemed a miracle of creation. And the amazing thing was that up until I was a senior in high school, Mother did all her baking in an old wood-fired stove!

W ho was that let you off at the gate," asked Olivia.
"It was Miss Emma and Miss Etta," said Clay-boy, holding out a
Mason jar of the Recipe. "They sent this. Said it was Christmas Cheer."
"It's bootleg whiskey is what it is," observed Olivia.
"What do you want me to do with it, Mama?"
"I'll take it," said Olivia..."I can use some...for my applesauce cakes."
—EARL HAMNER JR., IN *THE HOMECOMING*

She and other housewives of her era benefited from the arrival in the early 1900s of reliable baking powder. As the late Bill Neal noted, "Cooks were smitten with the airy and fine crumbled qualities of the baking powder layers."

Apple Stack Cake

This is probably the most "mountain" of cakes. The story goes that James Harrod, one of Kentucky's early pioneers and the founder of Harrodsburg, brought the stack cake recipe when he came to the frontier state via the Wilderness Road through the Cumberland Gap.

One story goes that since fancy "in-fare" wedding cakes were beyond the reach of many pioneer mountain families, neighbor wives would bring in cake layers to donate to the bride's family. Author Elizabeth Dunn confirmed the tradition, declaring a bride's popularity was often measured by the number of layers in her cake! As the layers arrived, the bride's family would spread the apple filling between each.

While plain applesauce can be used in such cakes, dried apples offer a much stronger flavor and therefore were the choice of most mountain cooks. (For details about dried apples, consult the Apples chapter and the Art of Preserving chapter.)

This 1800s recipe was used for many years by Mrs. Dolphus Kerley of Waynesville, North Carolina, who died in January 1948, just shy of age ninety. The recipe actually came from her mother, Mrs. Drury Bigham, of the Allens Creek section of Haywood County, North Carolina.

Haywood County Stack Cake

4 cups plain flour	1 cup sugar
1 teaspoon salt	1 cup sorghum molasses
½ teaspoon baking soda	1 cup milk
2 teaspoons baking powder	3 eggs
¾ cup shortening	

For Filling:
3 cups sweetened, slightly spiced applesauce

Sift flour, salt, soda, and baking powder. Cream the shortening, then add sugar, a little at a time, blending well. Add sorghum and mix thoroughly. Add milk and eggs, one at a time, beating well until smooth. Pour ⅓-inch deep in greased 9-inch pans, and bake until golden brown. When cool, stack the layers (around six), and use 3 cups of the applesauce between them. Yields 6 or 7 layers.

Dried Apple Cake

Dried apple cake is another favorite. This recipe originated with Sara Ballew of Murphy, North Carolina. It was passed on to me by her niece, the late Van Barkley, who until her 1997 death attended the same church that I do, Dunwoody Baptist on Atlanta's north side. The secret to the flavor of this cake—as with many apple recipes—is in the dried apples. To enhance the flavor even more, once it's baked and cooled, you should place it in a tight container for twenty-four hours before serving. The cake also freezes very well.

Sara's Dried Apple Cake

1 cup butter	*2½ teaspoons salt*
2 cups sugar	*1 teaspoon baking soda*
4 egg yolks, unbeaten	*1 cup buttermilk*
1 teaspoon vanilla	*4 egg whites, stiffly beaten*
1½ cups all-purpose flour	

Preheat oven to 350°F. In a large bowl, cream butter and sugar until fluffy. Add egg yolks one at a time, and beat well after each. Add vanilla and mix well. Sift together flour, salt, and soda. Add alternately with buttermilk to butter mixture, beating after addition until smooth. Fold in beaten egg whites. Using a greased 8- or 9-inch layer pan, pour contents, and bake at 350°F for 30 to 40 minutes. Cool before frosting.

For Frosting:

1½ cups sugar	*1 cup chopped pecans*
1 stick margarine	*1 cup coconut*
1 small can condensed milk	*1 teaspoon vanilla*
1 cup stewed dried apples	

Mix the sugar, margarine, and condensed milk, and boil five minutes. Add apples, pecans, coconut, and vanilla. Mix well. Frost cool layers.

As far as Christmas at our home, Mother generally made biscuits, a few pies and sometimes she'd make what we call a fruitcake. Actually, it wasn't...like the ones people make now.

She took dried apples and stewed them...And then she'd bake about three common pie-pan cakes—with biscuit dough—and they was about an inch and a half thick. She'd put one of them on the plate, and then she'd take these cooked apples, sweetened, and she'd put a layer of apples...Then she'd put another of these cakes on top of that, and then another layer of apples on it...She generally baked this cake about a week...before Christmas and she'd add some of the apple juice, and oh, Lord, that cake would just get as moist and it'd be just as soft, and you're talking about real eating when you hadn't had no cake or nothing since the Christmas before.

—A. L. TOMMIE BASS, SAND MOUNTAIN, ALABAMA, *PLAIN SOUTHERN EATING*

Moravian Cake

For this basic, old-time recipe, here are instructions for German "Moravian Cake." As mentioned earlier, the Moravians set high culinary and craftsmanship standards after settling North Carolina's vast Wachovia Tract prior to the Revolutionary War. This version comes from Lettice Bryan's 1839 *The Kentucky Housewife*, now available in a University of South Carolina reprint.

Moravian Cake

Sift a quart of fine flour, sprinkle into it a small spoonful of salt, 2 powdered nutmegs, a spoonful of cinnamon, 1 of mace and 4 ounces of powdered sugar. Rub in with your hands 4 ounces of butter and 2 beaten eggs; when they are completely saturated, add 4 tablespoonfuls of good yeast, and enough sweet milk to make it into a thick batter. Put it in a buttered pan, cover it, and set it by the fire to rise, but be sure you do not let it get hot, or the cake will be spoiled. When it looks quite light, add four ounces of sugar, and a handful of flour; sprinkle a handful of brown sugar over the top, and bake it in a moderate oven.

Scripture Cake

The first reference that I could find to Scripture Cake (or "Bible Cake") was in the *Queen of Appalachia Cook Book*, authored by Louisa Roberts Platt of Asheville, North Carolina, around the turn of the century. Mrs. Platt died in 1934 at the age of seventy-one. The cake is said to bring good fortune to those who eat it.

In earlier days, cookbooks often arranged the recipe so that cooks would have to look up the Bible references.

Scripture Cake

Behold! There was a cake baken—1 Kings 19:6 KJV

1 cup Judges 5:25 (butter)

2 cups Jeremiah 6:20 (sugar)

6 tablespoons 1st Samuel 14:25 (honey)

6 Jeremiah 17:11 (eggs)

3½ cups lst Kings 4:22 (flour)

2 teaspoons Amos 4:5 (baking powder)

A pinch of Leviticus 2:13 (salt)

Season to taste with II Chronicles 9:9 (spices)

1 cup Judges 4:19 (milk)

2 cups Nahum 3:12 (figs)

2 cups lst Samuel 30:12 (raisins)

2 cups Numbers 17:8 (almonds)

Preheat oven to 350°F. In large bowl, mix honey, butter and sugar. Beat and add eggs one at a time, beating well with each egg.

In a separate bowl, sift together 3 cups of the flour, plus the spices, salt, and baking powder. Combine with the creamed mixture alternately with milk, starting and ending with flour.

The figs, raisins and almonds should be saturated in the remaining ½ cup flour and mixed into the batter. Into a greased and floured 9x5-inch loaf pan, spoon the batter. Bake in oven at 350°F for 1½ hours. Cool first in pan, then pull and cool on rack.

Black Walnut and Hickory Nut Cakes

Scrumptious black walnut and hickory-nut cakes became a great and continuing favorite throughout the southern mountain states. The nuts were readily available from the magnificent nut trees growing abundantly across the hillsides. Typical of many, Merle

Mother'd make a great big stack of these apple pies out of dried apples, and a great big high stack of pumpkin custards. I'll never forget how she made those custards. She made hers the old-fashioned way. She'd take an egg and beat it and put in the pumpkin, the sugar, flavor, and everything, and just put all that on top of the crust. She made the crust just like any other crust—just rolled it thin as it could be and put in the pan.

—"Aunt Nora" Garland, Rabun County, Georgia, *Foxfire Christmas*

Weaver Garland of near Ticanetley, Georgia, remembered picking up hickory nuts and walnuts for her mother's big year-end fruitcakes.

For this recipe I am indebted to the late Marion Flexner, author of *Out of Kentucky Kitchens*. Marion used to bake this cake in an old-fashioned fluted tin or copper pan. She admitted that while the original recipe called for a boiled white frosting, to her taste, it needs no icing.

Black Walnut/Hickory Nut Cake

1½ cups all-purpose flour	*½ teaspoon baking powder*
½ cup butter, softened,	*1 teaspoon vanilla*
but not melted	*3 egg whites, well beaten*
1 cup sugar	*1 cup finely chopped black*
3 egg yolks	*walnuts or hickory nuts*
1 cup milk	

Preheat oven to 375°F. Sift the flour 3 times and measure out the 1½ cups needed. In large bowl, cream the butter with the sugar. Slowly add the egg yolks and beat well. Add the milk, followed by the flour and baking powder. Add vanilla and fold in the well-beaten egg whites. Next fold in the chopped nuts. Into a greased, floured tube pan, pour the batter, and bake at 375°F for about 1 hour, until cake tests done.

Japanese Fruitcake

This marvelous cake was my mother's favorite (and also mine and apparently the rest of the region's during the 1940s). While the name is somewhat mysterious (with no Japanese ingredients), the cake is a descendant of the traditional English pound cake and, of course, the giant colonial-era fruitcakes that were the rage through the South.

The aforementioned Merle Weaver remembered not only scouring the mountainsides for walnuts and hickory nuts for the year-end cake extravaganza, but eagerly looking on as her mother made baking preparations: "Mama'd save orange rinds forever. And raisins… Grandma used to get raisins when she went to gettin' relief, six dollars a month. Raisins was a big treat you know…great in fruitcakes. Mama would bake her fruitcake in the dishpan. She'd put pebbles in the center. When she got through baking that cake, there'd be enough for us and our kinfolks."

We, too, had enough Christmas cake for our extended family. Mother bolstered it with nuts and raisins and topped it with shredded coconut. The cake—moist and juicy and just plain delicious—was always the centerpiece of our Yuletide season table.

The cake-baking excitement at our house paralleled that of Nannie Jones's home at Mountain View, South Carolina (aptly named since it was in view of Greenville County's Paris Mountain). Here's how Nannie's daughter, Lib Dabney (my sister-in-law), remembered it:

"Nannie baked her cake in a giant pan that measured six inches deep and eighteen inches long. She put fig preserves in her fruitcakes, I guess that made it moist, about a gallon of black walnuts and pecans and brazil nuts and dried fruit, too, plus peaches and raisins. Mama didn't want to cook it fast, either. She would put it in the wood stove in the morning and she would add one stick of wood about every thirty minutes. And she would cook that cake all day long 'til almost midnight." (Nannie Jones, incidentally, lived to the ripe old age of 104.)

Here—on a smaller scale—is my mother's fruitcake recipe in all its mouthwatering, potential glory. The filling should be made first, followed by the cake layers.

Mother Dabney's Japanese Fruitcake

For Filling:

2 cups sugar	*1 fresh coconut, finely grated*
4 tablespoons all-purpose flour	*2 lemons, finely grated*
1½ cups boiling water	*2 oranges, finely grated*

For 3 Cake Layers:

1 cup butter	*1 cup pecans*
2 cups sugar	*3 teaspoons cinnamon*
3 cups all-purpose flour	*1 box raisins*
4 teaspoons baking powder	*1 teaspoon cloves*
1 cup milk	*1 teaspoon nutmeg*
6 eggs	

For the Filling:

In saucepan combine sugar and flour. Mix thoroughly. Add boiling water, then add coconut, lemon, and oranges. Cook mixture on low for about 20 minutes, stirring constantly. Cook until mixture reaches proper consistency but not too runny. Set aside.

For the Cake Batter:

Preheat oven to 325°F to 350°F. In a large bowl, mix butter and sugar in mixer until fluffy. Add flour, baking powder, milk, and eggs (one at a time), and beat everything in as you go. Next add to batter pecans, cinnamon, raisins, cloves, and nutmeg. Pour batter into cake pans and bake at 325°F to 350°F. Bake until golden brown on top. When baked, punch tiny holes in each layer.

Final Step:

Put first layer down (with holes in it) on cake plate. Pour filling on top. Do same with second and third layers, then pour filling over top.

Sorghum Syrup

A Soppin' Delight

My grandfather, Frank Sibley, taught me to poke holes in biscuits and fill them with sorghum syrup, but I never developed his taste for buttermilk or pot liquor.

—Celestine Sibley

~

As I went down to a Georgia town,
With the Georgia boys I courted around.
And the Georgia girls who none surpasses,
They all sweet as sorghum molasses.

— "Sorghum Molasses," Confederate song,
courtesy of Georgia Folklore Archives

~

Pour enough syrup until it says "glub" three times.
—Naomi Smith Walker, a native of Blanch,
North Carolina, describing the amount
of syrup needed for a recipe

Sorghum syrup? La, we loved it! How you eat it is you pour your sorghum on your plate along with a lota butter. Then you mix it up real good. Some would put bacon grease in there instead of butter or add it to the butter and stir it up. And then comes the best part; you sop it up with biscuits. Now some people poured sorghum syrup on corn bread. It's good either way."

Ruth Swanson Hunter of Young Harris, Georgia—who lives just across the holler from Blairsville, the capital of north Georgia's sweet sorghum country—remembered well the days of her family's active involvement with sorghum, all the way from planting a crop of sorghum cane in fertile bottomland to processing and eating the finished product. Pronounced soggum by some, it is known in the mountains as "long sweetnin'." This is in contrast to "short sweetnin'"—refined sugar, which often was in short supply in mountain hard times.

"My granddaddy," declared Mrs. Hunter, "he useta have a mill to grind the juice and boil the syrup. People would bring in their cane to him. Lota families would have a little patch of sorghum cane, just enough for themselves."

In earlier days, no kitchen table in the mountains was complete without its glass cruet of sorghum. Many poured sorghum on badly cooked meats and vegetables to give them a sweet kick. And when the cow went dry, folk would make a butter substitute by mixing sorghum and pork drippings. Sorghum came into its own in colonial America as a substitute for sugar. When sugar became available in the 1700s, it was very expensive, being sold in cones and sliced off as needed. Sorghum also was relied upon as a sweetener during the Civil War when Union blockades halted sugar shipments to Southern ports.

Syrup made from sweet sorghum is primarily a hill country sweetener with a light amber color. Darker-colored "molasses"—made of sugar cane—is mostly a Deep South product coming from Louisiana and surrounding states. While some Appalachian people call their sorghum sweetener "molasses," the precise term is *sorghum* or *sweet sorghum* or *sorghum syrup.*

Sorghum was a key ingredient in moonshine in earlier days. It's one of Appalachia's untold stories. It was during the Prohibition era (1920–33) when whiskey-making progressed to the point where moonshiners, to meet increased demand, turned to sugar to speed up fermentation of what formerly had been pure corn whiskey. The smoother-tasting "sugar whiskey"—corn combined with sugar—zoomed.

During the years leading up to World War II, sugar supplies dropped sharply, forcing moonshiners to turn to sorghum for their mash barrels. The syrup, in shiny tin cans, would arrive at distilleries by the truckload. "I remember seeing stacks of syrup as high as this house," recalled Larry Davis, whose father Willie was a highly regarded corn whiskey craftsman.

In the hills of southwest Virginia I was invited one day to a 'lasses boilin'. To the tune of a fiddle, against the scent of wood smoke and the blue mist of the evaporating juice, we danced our square dances, dominated by the thick, sticky sweet smell of sorghum...

Like participants at a sacrament, we drew near. This year's sorghum, essence of sun and rain and light and earth, was poured, hot still from the evaporators, upon biscuits. We ate and tongues were burned by the heated syrup. But over everything, man and woman and child, and stretching black shadows, hung this sacramental feeling, like a mist of holiness.

There are mountain folk yet today who love to sweeten their coffee with sweet sorghum. A leading member of the sorghum school of sweetening was the late "Tennessee Ernie" Ford, who opined that sorghum-fortified coffee had a sweeter taste for him than with any amount of sugar.

The fragrant aura of sweet sorghum syrup comes into all its luscious glory at the sweet sorghum sopping contest every October in Blairsville, Georgia. The Junior Chamber of Commerce "sop-off" is just one of the attractions at the annual Sorghum Festival that includes a mule-pulled sorghum mill and a steamy and fragrant sorghum boil.

For deep in the heart of man, though he may live in an age of civilization that can build cities like New York and Chicago, deep within him lies the need to celebrate and to worship, uncurbed and undestroyed by the machine.
Here in the mountains of Virginia, with biscuit and sorghum, we held our little saturnalia, but simple though it might be, with a squeaky fiddle for music and smoke from evaporating syrup for incense, it held within this cup of the hills the spirit of all celebration and all earth worship.
In the mountains of Virginia, on a night of October, sanity reigned unconquered.
—Clare Leighton,
Southern Harvest (1942)

Former Georgia governor Zell Miller, who hails from the neighboring community of Young Harris, and who grew up sopping his share of sorghum, is one of sorghum's greatest supporters. But he declares that sopping syrup and butter with biscuits requires a skilled touch.

The way it's done, the governor wrote in his autobiography, "is by taking a helping of butter, covering it well with syrup and blending it with a fork to the consistency of thick cake batter. Then the biscuit is broken in half and dipped into the mixture... The master of this fine art always finishes his biscuit and butter simultaneously—with equal servings on each bite." Quite a feat!

~

The first sorghum cane seed reached the north Georgia mountains in the mid-1800s. It was court week in Ellijay, the county seat of Gilmer County. A stranger pulled up in a one-horse wagon, offering the first ever seed of what he called "Chinese sugar cane." He extolled the cane, saying it would produce in a single season a sugary juice cane with a seed head. The crowd got rowdy, full of disbelief. George Gordon Ward, in his eloquent and authoritative history, *Annals of Upper Georgia Centered in Gilmer County*, told what happened next:

A rough, drunken mob collected around his little wagon and derided him and called him a humbug. General Hansell came by, at the noon hours of the court then in session. He defended the humble peddler and vouched for this product. A scramble for the seed, at ten cents a bunch, followed. Sorghum has been grown here ever since…But this…was gradually superseded by Honey Drip, Texas Ribbon, Sumac, Blue Ribbon and other species. We notice Sarf, Tracy and Texas Seeded are offered for sale now.

Coke Ellington and Stephen Griffith made a wooden mill to crush the stalks and extract the juice…This was the first sorghum mill operated in the bounds of Gilmer County…Boiled and cooked and properly skimmed, it develops a remarkably ripe, delicious flavor. The syrup from some cane is quite red, while from another species, golden or a light honey shade. The red cane seems to stand up well against wind.

If you see any syrup and they call it "homemade syrup," it's jist [sic] cut down and run through a mill with seed, fodder, and all on it. I wouldn't eat a bit of it. I bought some and on the label it said it was stripped cane syrup, but the seed hadn't been cut off. Hit [sic] was bitter. I couldn't eat it. I think I put it in the hog's feed.
—Nina Garrett, Gilmer County, Georgia

The juice was at first boiled in cast-iron wash pots and kettles and was sweet and good enough in flavor, but blackened the teeth. The primitive methods of grinding the cane in wooden mills and of boiling the juice in kettles continued up to and during the Civil War. These early mills, being without guards about their rollers to protect persons "feeding" them, were constantly threatening to handle hands and arms. It was common to hear of someone's having a hand or arm thus crushed.

Cast-iron sorghum mills and evaporating pans of iron and copper did not begin to appear until 1896. Major Frank Williams brought in the first. The new syrup (boiled with evaporator vans) took rapidly with people…Captain Jim Cody, coming into Ellijay soon after sampling his first of the new syrup, declared with enthusiasm it was the next best thing to religion.

~

Throughout the mountains in earlier days, people swore by their sorghum, even when they could afford sugar. And many were finicky about the quality of their product. They wanted only pure cane syrup, with no fodder or seeds boiled along with the cane. Rilla Chastain Nelson remembered that her mother was quite insistent when buying a batch at a particular sorghum mill. She chastised the syrup man for failing to skim off all the bitter, slimy skimmings.

"Mother would stand up there and skim that green skimmings off. Mr. Johnson, he'd stir it in. Mother'd get right on to him, just rare at him. They just almost had a fight. Mother told him she didn't want none of that (skimmings) in her syrup. She wanted it to be real mild. I was worried about Mama getting on to Mr. Johnson like that."

At Linden, Tennessee, on the Cumberland Rim, author Ibbie Ledford remembered that her father was a sorghum-sopping aficionado, also, with high standards. He would stand by the vat, watching for the time when the syrup reached the right color and consistency. At that point, he'd tell the cooks to dip him out a few gallons, "and don't get no bees in it."

The Robert Daniel Pressley farm at Cullo-whee, North Carolina, was big into sorghum syrup. Although Robert's son Frank left the mountains after completing high school at age eighteen, he remembered plenty about his family's sorghum activity.

Aunt Nancy Pankey...is a veteran of hard times in the southern mountains...Many a day, Aunt Nancy told me, she came "weakling in from the field," drank a little water sweetened with sorghum for sustenance, and went back to work.
—Celestine Sibley, *A Place Called Sweet Apple*

Aunt Nancy Pankey

We had our own cane mill. We'd cut a long log with a crook in it—we tried to get locust—to make the sweep that turned the grinding rollers. The heavy butt end was on the short side. We hooked our mule up to the long end with a rope to lead him around. We were very careful not to put too much cane in the grinder at one time. Dad would say to let up: 'That mule is going to give out before we get this cane done.' We had to put it in there steady and that stream of juice a-comin' out. There were a lot of us, the girls were there helping, gettin' that juice and carry-ing it to the vat. My daddy was the head man at the mill but my other brothers were learnin', I was number ten. We had a pan and a furnace built out of rock and red clay and that big long pan set on top of that was made of copper. The pan was ten inches deep and it was in sections.

The making of sorghum is a fall-time ritual across the Southern Appalachians. Here, workman feeds sorghum cane stalks into the horse-pulled sorghum mill while the juice is boiled into syrup in the background. Most sorghum mills were pulled by mules.

We'd put the juice in one section. They skimmed it as it came down through to the skimming pot. We fed those skimmings to the hogs. The syrup would get ready and my Daddy would say, "All right, boys, we got to draw off a batch here now."

We had plenty of syrup all winter long. We used that sorghum syrup for a lota things but mainly at breakfast in the morning with cow butter. We had plenty of that, and biscuits and syrup for breakfast, and our fried meat. We didn't eat that many eggs all the time. About two or three times a week, though, a big platter of eggs would be on the table. We ate a lot of dried fruit, stewed, for breakfast too.

But mountain breakfasts was where sorghum, and to some extent, honey, came into their own. "Breakfast was my favorite meal," Rilla Chastain Nelson recalled. "Mother could make real good biscuits. We always had plenty of butter in the springhouse to go with the sorghum syrup. And we always raised our own meat and had sugar-cured hams. We'd cure it and then can it. Breakfasts were good back then."

~

Long Sweetnin'—once in serious decline, with sorghum mills in Union County, Georgia, for instance, dropping in a decade from thirty to eight—of late seems to be enjoying an Appalachian mini-resurgence, thanks to such events as the Georgia Sorghum Festival.

Another reason may be that nutrition experts are urging us to cut down on overprocessed foods such as refined sugar and return to vitamin- and mineral-rich natural foods such as sorghum and honey.

The cause has received a juicy boost in recent years from a group of once-discouraged eastern Kentucky tobacco farmers. They banded together in a cooperative to market honey and pure sorghum. The Boone County farmers each fall haul their sorghum cane to their cooperative mill at Livingston where the juice is squeezed and cooked, labeled and marketed in attractive jars. They sell their products nationwide under the Golden Kentucky Products label. (*FYI*: They also make a delightful sorghum praline topping fortified with Kentucky bourbon.)

Sorghum is adaptable to many dishes and candies. Here is a recipe sampling.

Sorghum (or Molasses) Taffy

"Molasses-making was a special delight of children living on Hazel Creek," recalled Professor Duane Oliver, who grew up on the North Carolina side of the Great Smoky Mountains. "Not only was the smell of cooking molasses ravishing but there was usually a candy-pulling that produced a very sweet taffy, the only candy that early pioneer children on Hazel Creek knew." Folk also loved to drop ears of green corn into the last batch of molasses. These boiled in the molasses "to make a sticky but delicious and wholesome confection."

On a "molasses pullin'," as many called it, the whole idea was to boil down sorghum syrup to the candy stage (a loaf). Young couples would butter up their hands and pull the cooled taffy loaf from each end, folding it back on itself between them until they had created a delicious taffy.

Bessie Lard ("Muda") Llewellyn of north Alabama and eastern Tennessee remembered pulling candy as a kid. "We'd have gallons of molasses at home. You'd cook it down—you could tell it was candy—and then we'd get a holt of it and stretch it and it'd turn white. The more you pulled it, it would get real blond-looking, and then we'd twist it and it'd get hard."

Ripened sorghum cane stands tall in field in Union County, Georgia, awaiting fall harvest that will result in delicious sorghum syrup.

An overhead view of an East Tennessee sorghum copper boiling pan. Workman cleans off the skimmings from evaporator pan. He will allow the syrup to cook until it reaches what he considers its best consistency.

This first recipe is adapted from *Thangs Yankees Don't Know*, published by the late Bil Dwyer of Highlands, North Carolina, with special thanks to the Dwyer family.

Bil's Taffy Pull Candy

1 cup sorghum	*1½ cups boiling water*
2 cups sugar	*Vanilla flavoring*
½ cup butter	

In a heavy saucepan, melt butter. Add sugar, sorghum, and water. Boil to softball stage (between 234°F and 238°F). Pour into buttered shallow pans. As mixture cools around sides, fold toward center. When cool enough to handle, pull until porous and light-colored. Add flavoring (a few drops of peppermint, cinnamon, or vanilla). Cut into small pieces with a sharp knife or shears.

This second recipe for molasses taffy is adapted from the *Georgia Mountain Heritage* cookbook published by Virginia Underwood of Cherrylog, Georgia. The recipe is credited to Janice Verner.

Fannin County Molasses Taffy

1 cup molasses	4 tablespoons butter
1 cup sugar	⅛ teaspoon baking soda
¾ cup water	½ teaspoon vanilla

Cook molasses, sugar, and water slowly until it reaches the hard ball stage. Stir during the latter part of the cooking to prevent burning. Remove from heat. Add butter, soda, and vanilla. Stir enough to mix. Pour into greased pan. When cool enough to handle, pull until it pours and becomes cool. Cut in pieces with scissors.

Gingerbread

For this snack—loved by children of the mountains and elsewhere—I thank the family of the late Ferne Shelton, of High Point, North Carolina. She included this in *Pioneer Cookbook*, one of a series of cookbooks she published on foods cooked and eaten in colonial pioneer days.

Molasses Gingerbread

½ cup butter	2 cups all-purpose flour
1 cup sugar	1 teaspoon baking soda
2 eggs	1 teaspoon each: ginger, cloves
½ cup molasses	1 teaspoon each: cinnamon, allspice
½ teaspoon salt	1 cup boiling water

I grew up on Sand Mountain. Born in 1884. I was a pretty good size chunk of a boy when I went out on my own at age seventeen after my mother died. Before that I was a runt, pore [sic], and skinny. Yeah, but I growed up tolibly [sic] well.

Before she died, my mother plowed, cut logs—I've seen her pull a crosscut saw for fifty cents a day. And she could shoot a gun bettern'n I could. She brought down many a squirrel.

We grew sorghum cane back then; we tried to raise what you could eat. Everybody had a little patch of sorghum. We ate sorghum and biscuits and we ate sorghum and corn bread many a time. Back then it was hard for us to get biscuits. Wasn't many farmers that eat biscuits.

—WILL SAMPLES, SMYRNA, GEORGIA, AGE 106 WHEN INTERVIEWED BY THE AUTHOR IN 1990

Preheat oven to 375°F. Cream butter and sugar. Add eggs, molasses, and mix well. Add dry ingredients, and blend thoroughly. Stir in boiling water. Pour in greased pan. Bake at 375°F for 30 to 40 minutes or until it tests done in center.

Hot Microwaved Sorghum

Kentucky author Mark Sohn (*Mountain Country Cooking*), likes to microwave this dish as a great biscuit sopper. The idea is that the soda allows the incorporation of air into the syrup, making it milder and thicker.

Sohn's Hot Sorghum

½ cup sweet sorghum, 100 percent pure

⅛ teaspoon baking soda

In a medium bowl, pour the sorghum. Sprinkle the soda, a pinch at a time, over the top evenly. Stir to mix. Microwave on high for 1½ minutes. The sorghum will foam. Stir and serve immediately, or let it cool a bit. Once it cools, microwave again. Stir again and serve.

~

Ethelene Dyer Jones of Epworth, Georgia, holds two quarts of full-flavored Dyer Sorghum Syrup produced by her brother Blueford and other family members. Sorghum syrup such as this has been a mainstay of the Southern Appalachian diet for more than a century.

Honey

Bee Gum Robbery in the Mountains

When any of the Saylor men found a bee tree they cut two parallel
vertical slashes in the bark. This mark let anyone else…know that
the Saylors had claimed this tree.
> —*Sidney Saylor Farr, Berea, Kentucky,* More Than Moonshine

~

If the Lord delights in us, then He will bring us into this land…a land which
flows with milk and honey.
> —*Numbers 14:8* NKJV

Uncle Bud came and robbed our hives for us. He knew how to do it and they
didn't sting him like they did us. You know what? A bee is like a mule. If
you afraid of 'em, they know it. He robbed bees in the heart of the day, at the
noon hour, when all the bees are away; the worker bees most of them are now,
and the rest wasn't as ill. Uncle Bud didn't use no mask on his head. He had a
smoker. He'd go around that gum. He had a homemade knife, like a putty knife.
He prized that cover up. (Those bees will seal it up watertight with beeswax.) If a
bee stung him, he wouldn't fight it. You'd see him reach down and flick him off,
just as calm and cool.

Frank Pressley was remembering the days when honey and bees were a major celebration on the Pressley farm on Cullowhee Mountain, North Carolina, as on farms across
the Appalachians. The wild bees that the Pressleys "robbed" and often "tamed" provided
plenty of honey nearly all year long for the kitchen table at Robert Daniel and Iva Ashe
Pressley's homestead. Frank's remembrances were sharp:

We had some holler log bee gums that was cut off. We put crosses in there
and the bees they'd build on that. The patented 'gum' came out and my brothers
messed with them. We had four or five hives of bees. We had honey any time we
wanted it. If a swarm of bees came over, we'd start clanking on pots and pans and
hollering to make the swarm to settle. We called it 'settling the bees.' I've seen it
a many a time. When they'd settle, Uncle Bud would come and put 'em in the
hive. But he'd hunt that queen out. Once he got that queen out he'd put her in
the gum. I've seen him shake those bees down. They'd be a pod of those bees on

a limb close to the ground. We'd make all that racket to get them down lower. He would shake that pod down on that gum after he got there. He'd make sure the queen was in there. When he done that he put the lid on it and that was it.

Most honey is made by bees. But sourwood [honey] is made by bees and angels.
—CARSON BREWER,
KNOXVILLE, TENNESSEE

They settled some in an old log house, corner of the house that had some boards on it and it boarded up. I seen him get them out of there. The queen came out. He had a hat on and he reached out in the air and caught that bee with his hat—she wasn't flying too fast—and put that queen in that gum. He had a board and those bees would follow that thing but it would take a while but they would crawl right in that gum if that queen was in there.

Coursing the bees—following their bee-line—was how we tracked bees down. I've went many a time and tried to course 'em and found a few myself. But some of 'em would be high. Bees come around creeks and branches and places to get water. You'd watch 'em on flowers, mountain wildflowers, honeysuckles, and sourwood trees. Some of the best honey in the world is sourwood honey. And rattlesnake weed. It had a long, tall white bloom on top of it. We'd follow them with our eye mostly. The direction they'd go in, we'd go that way, too, maybe to a creek. We'd watch bees there and see which way they went. We'd cut the tree down. That was bad sometimes, because the tree when it'd fall, that holler tree would bust and tear up. As long as the honey stayed in the comb, it was okay, but whenever you busted that tree and mixed all that trash up in there with wood in it maybe rotten wood and splinters and stuff, it used up a lot of the honey. If you cut that tree, you'd have to get the honey pretty quick, because it would run out. Us boys would go in there and those bees, wild bees, were bad to sting. But we'd tie our britches leg bottom-around the top of our shoes. We'd get some stings, but we'd put the screen wire on our head and we'd go in there and get all we could of that honey and come out.

~

Scientists say bees and flowers first appeared in the Miocene Age, between ten to twenty million years ago. Records of honey-gathering showed up on cave walls when the Ice Age ended around 8000 BC. Jars of honey were found in Egyptian tombs circa 1400 BC. The Egyptians prized wild honey, considering it magical, and used it in pastries, as a preservative, as a medicine, and as an embalming fluid.

The Greeks followed suit. In preparing Alexander the Great's body for burial, Greek morticians used a jug of honey in a royal rubdown. Perhaps the embalming rationale was based on the fact that honey is the only food known to man that does not spoil. Honey found in Egyptian tombs, for instance, had not spoiled after two thousand years and was said to have been edible.

In biblical times, living in a land of "milk and honey" was considered symbolically a life of joy and abundance. Such a "promised land" was what God promised Moses when the Israelites were going through their forty-year wilderness trek from Egypt.

Honey-based wines—metheglin and mead—were mainstays of the ancient Greeks and Saxons. Early Anglo-Saxon beers were made from honey. Indeed the word *beer* comes from *beo,* the Saxon word for "bee." Signs in some British pubs carry a beehive symbol.

The English brought bees to America as a food resource around

When the queen is found amidst her sting-happy swarm, she is placed in the "patent hive" to attract the other bees. Afterward, the hive will be taken to the finder's farmyard to add to his stands of bees.

1622. From the Jamestown, Virginia, settlement, they spread through the continent throughout the eighteenth and nineteenth centuries. The Amerindians called them "the white man's flies."

Wild bees eventually swept in big swarms through the American interior, setting up colonies mostly in hollow tree trunks and providing pollination for fruits, vegetables, and other crops.

Honeybees—which for a pound of honey fly over 50,000 miles to extract two million flowers—provided Appalachian settlers a delicious additional source for "sweetnin'." Along with sweet sorghum that many loved to call "molasses" (erroneously so), honey filled a sweet tooth gap in those homes that could not afford to buy sugar. Or, in desperate times such as during the Civil War when sugar supplies were totally cut off, honey and sorghum were the region's only source for sweets. Honey was considered the much-loved mountain "long sweetening," along with sorghum syrup as mentioned in an earlier chapter.

Fred Owens ties the bee hive section to the tree stump, leaving the young bees to complete their wildflower honey season. Once a bee tree has been claimed, other mountain bee hunters will leave it alone.

The Appalachians traditionally have been a near perfect place for the bees due to the abundance of wildflowers and blooming trees such as chestnut, sourwood, and locust. While honey from locust had a distinctive taste, mountain people came to love the delicate-tasting sourwood more than any other honey. In *Foxfire 2*, Marie Mellinger called the pale golden sourwood honey "larrupin' good" and added the mountain quote that "a man ain't tasted nothin' lessen he's put his tongue to sourwood honey." Many considered honey good for rheumatism and arthritis and, along with vinegar, a great medicine for insomnia. John Parris quoted Tom Patton of Crooked Creek, North Carolina, as calling honey an excellent remedy in the world to produce sleep. His dose? Two tablespoons of honey mixed with a teaspoon of cider vinegar.

Practically every farm in the southern mountain region boasted at least a few "bee gums"—homemade hives made from hollow poplar logs cut down to hive size and covered at both ends. In the late 1860s, the Smoky Mountain Cataloochee section, for instance, reported the gathering of around 2,000 pounds of honey. In 1900, mountainous Fannin County, Georgia, on the North Carolina line, boasted 2,368 beehives that produced just under 30,000 pounds of honey.

"We had apples, we had bees, we had honey," said Bess Dover Pache of Ellijay, Georgia. "Even my mother could hive the bees. She wasn't afraid of nothin'. She'd put that net over her head and get her smoker and smoke the bees to get the honey out.

I have never tried to find bee trees and get my honey directly from the wild, the way both Indians and bears so soon learned to do after honey bees were introduced from Europe. An oldtimer used to find his bee trees by taking an empty match box and putting a little flour in it. Next he'd catch a bee and put it in the box. After a few moments he'd let the bee go and follow him with his eyes—not too difficult as the bee was white with flour. He'd mark the line and follow. Then he'd catch another bee and repeat the process until he was led directly to the bee tree.

—FRANCES HAMMERSTROM, *WILD FOOD COOKBOOK*

"Mama had an old-timey school bell that came from one of Papa's schools where he taught. Mama would ring that bell and the bees would settle close by and she would put them in the bee gums.

"We had big five-gallon metal cans, we used to call 'em lard cans. We kept the honey in those, seal it up in there; nothing could get to it. Everybody in town [Ellijay] would be waitin' for Papa to bring some honey in. He cut the honey into pound sections and hauled it into town in a two-horse wagon, go about twice a week."

Many mountain people such as Reed Stanley of Cartecay, Georgia, told me they loved to drink a mixture of honey—particularly the sourwood variety—along with vinegar and water. The mountain "switchell" pick-me-up drink called for mixing honey and cider vinegar in equal amounts to be kept in a jar. When you needed a drink, you dropped four teaspoons of mix into a gourd or cup of water.

Cullowhee's aforementioned Frank Pressley for many years has been eating "a teaspoonful of honey every morning, yes sir. And for a long time I took apple cider vinegar and a teaspoon full of honey, mixed together, and put enough water in it so that the vinegar wouldn't be so strong. I'd drink two or three swallers of that. I quit doing that, though. I just eat the honey now. I guess it's good for ye."

Herschel Everett, who grew up in the Coosa district in Union County, Georgia, said that his father always kept honey on the table and after each meal would eat a spoonful. "Just a spoonful. That spoonful of honey was his dessert when he got through eating." Hershel's father kept about forty to fifty bee stands and sold the honey in the Asheville area.

Most mountain people did not use honey much in cooking, rather eating honey directly on hot biscuits or corn bread. The aforementioned Bess Dover Pache recalled that her mother always kept on her table a glass bowl full of honey year-round. "Them days it was pure honey, made from sourwood out of the woods. We kept cans of honey in our smokehouse."

This stand of "bee gums" in the Sugarlands (Tennessee area of the Great Smoky Mountains) is the pride and joy of honey bee expert Steve Cole.

Over the years, mountain housewives developed and adapted some interesting dishes utilizing honey as the base. Here is a recipe sampling.

Honey Apple Pie

One of the delightful ways to sweeten an apple pie was with honey. Lyn Kellner picked up this recipe in the Boone, North Carolina area after discovering that honey complements the taste of apples the same way sorghum complements gingerbread. My thanks to Lyn for this recipe that comes from her out-of-print book, *Taste of Appalachia*.

Boone Honey Apple Pie

Pastry for 8-inch double-crust pie
6 cups sliced tart apples
1½ cups honey
1½ tablespoons lemon juice
¼ cup all-purpose flour

1 teaspoon cinnamon
½ cup chopped black
  walnuts (optional)
1½ tablespoons butter

Preheat oven to 425°F. Roll out bottom crust and place in 8-inch pie pan. Arrange apple slices over pastry. Mix honey, lemon juice, and flour, and pour over apples. Sprinkle with cinnamon and walnuts, and dot with butter. Cover with top crust and seal edges. Cut steam vents in top crust and bake at 425°F for 40 minutes or until apples are tender. Serves 6 to 8.

Honey Muffins

This recipe comes from *Mountain Makin's in the Smokies*, published several decades ago by the Great Smoky Mountains Natural History Association. The recipe is credited to Mrs. W. P. Trotter.

Great Smoky Honey Muffins

2 tablespoons honey	*¼ cup milk*
4 tablespoons melted shortening	*4 teaspoons baking powder*
1 egg	*½ teaspoon salt*
2 cups all-purpose flour	

Preheat oven to 400°F. In large bowl combine honey and shortening. Add well-beaten egg. In separate bowl sift and mix together dry ingredients. Add to first mixture alternately with milk. Beat well. Half fill greased muffin pans, and bake in moderate oven at 400°F for 25 minutes. Yields 12 muffins.

Honey Brownies

Kathleen Kollock loved to make and serve these honey-carob brownies to friends in Clarkesville, located in the northeast Georgia foothills. Her parents, Nancy and John Kollock, also enjoyed sampling the brownies that feature natural ingredients. Noted artist, historian, and painter of mountain scenes, John Kollock created Helen, Georgia's alpine "German look" several decades ago that helped propel the mountain village into a major tourist attraction. My thanks to the Kollocks for this recipe. Kathleen says that sunflower kernels can be substituted for nuts.

Kathleen's Honey Brownies

⅔ cup honey	*½ cup carob powder*
½ cup margarine	*⅔ cup whole wheat flour*
2 eggs	*1 teaspoon baking powder*
½ teaspoon sea salt	*1 cup nuts, chopped*
1 teaspoon vanilla	*3 tablespoons milk*

Preheat oven to 350°F. Cream honey and butter. Beat in eggs, one at a time. Mix in salt and vanilla. Sift together the carob powder, flour, and baking powder, and stir with the nuts and milk into the batter. Pour into an oiled 9-inch square baking pan, and place in oven at 350°F for 30 minutes or until done. Cut into squares while still warm.

Honey Sandwich

Mrs. S. R. Dull—famed foods editor of the *Atlanta Journal*—offered this nice recipe in her authoritative cookbook, *Southern Cooking*. The book quickly became the region's standard cookbook following its initial 1928 edition. My friend Ken Boyd, president of Cherokee Publishing Company, in 1989 brought the book back out in an attractive edition.

Henrietta Dull's Honey Sandwich

| Cream cheese or | Honey |
| cottage cheese | Butter, soft |

Moisten cottage cheese or cream cheese with honey. Spread bread with butter, then the honey mixture. Put on top slice.

Honey Butter

This final honey recipe—similar to Mrs. Dull's honey-butter mixture—was given to me by Frances Gates Hill of north Georgia's Gates Chapel community. It was published in *Sharing Our Best*, a collection published by the Gates Chapel United Methodist Church. This honey butter, by the way, makes an excellent spread for biscuits or toast. "And we loved to all the time eat fresh honey with hot biscuits and butter. But I never did gain weight because of it," Frances declared.

Holley Creek Honey Butter

| ½ cup honey | ½ cup margarine |

Let margarine stand at room temperature until soft. Gradually add an equal amount of honey, beating until the honey is blended with the butter.

I run a bear out of our bee gum stands one time. Me and my son-in-law. The bear—she came around with two cubs behind her. She got up on the beehive and I went around the house and I yelled at her, "You get out of there!" She turned and growled as if to say, "You go—this is mine."

When she growled and hollered, my son-in-law run and got in the car just ahead of me and said, "I beat ye!" We got out of that bear's way. You don't want to get in a bear's way when they got cubs.

We used to help Ed rob bees, that's my cousin. Papa had several bee gums and we had honey on the table all the time.

—Frances Gates Hill, Mountaintown District, Gilmer County, Georgia

The Blessings
With Thanks to the Almighty

The Blessings

With Thanks to the Almighty

"Wait a minute," said Olivia. "We don't ever get in such a hurry around here that we forget to say the blessen. Whose turn is it?"

"It's my turn," four-year-old John said proudly...He turned...to see if all had assumed the proper air of reverence. Satisfied that he had everybody's attention and that each child had his hands folded and placed under his chin, he recited in a sing-song:

Thank you for the food we eat,
Thank you for the world so sweet,
Thank you for the birds that sing,
Thank you, God, for everything. Amen.

—From the novel Spencer's Mountain
by Earl Hamner, Jr.

Would you please ask the blessing?"
Since the days of the earliest settlements across America's Appalachian "Great Southwest," indeed throughout the thirteen original colonies, thanking God at mealtime has been a time-honored and faithfully executed tradition. In earlier days, the assignment usually fell to the father of the house—unless the preacher was visiting.

If your father and grandfather were like mine, economy of language was the greatest of virtues, especially at the table. My dad's usual invocation, spoken quickly, went something like this: "Our Heavenly Father, make us truly thankful for these and all other blessings. Amen."

I've heard other country blessings even more to the point: "Lord make us thankful for what we are about to receive. Amen."

It's amazing that near identical graces can be found spoken all across the South. Such a one is this one that Celestine Sibley's family recites at Sweet Apple, very similar to one spoken over the years at the Milton and John Fleetwood homes in Cartersville, Georgia, and my brother, Rev. Connie Dabney in Augusta, Georgia: "Heavenly Father: Pardon our many sins and make us truly thankful for these and all other blessings. Amen."

From Lakeland, Georgia, came a near identical prayer from Frank Pressley that was spoken six decades ago in Cullowhee, North Carolina by his father, Robert Daniel Pressley: "Dear Lord: Pardon our many sins and give us hearts to be thankful for these and all other blessings. In Christ's name we pray, Amen."

Atlanta Journal sports editor Furman Bisher, whose column in *The Charlotte News* in the late forties ("Bish's Dish") was one of my favorites, grew up on the "short and sweet" school of graces. "I'm grateful for the blessing that ends before the food gets cold," Furman wrote.

Duane Oliver, retired professor at Western Carolina University and unofficial historian of Hazel Creek, told of the preacher running a revival at Tuskeegee, North Carolina, who stayed with various members of the community, and who repeatedly, day after day, was served gritted corn bread. One night, his prayer in church ended with the appeal: "Oh Lord, may we never hear the sound of another gritter on the waters of the Tuskeegee."

Then there was the north Georgia farmer named Stumpey Kelly who was called on to pray in church. Just as he started to pray he remembered going to his smokehouse earlier to fill up his syrup pitcher and leaving the syrup barrel unplugged. He prayed, anxiously, "Oh Lord, my syrup pitcher runneth over." He fled the church with the congregation following. He found his smokehouse running over in syrupy goo. Stumpy waded in, plugged the stopper and said, triumphantly, "A-MEN!"

As I mentioned previously, young folks in my day and age generally were never asked to have any say during grace time. But as our kids were growing up, Susanne and I gave our little ones the opportunity to thank the Almighty at mealtime. Mostly they relished the chance, starting with the usual,

> *God is Great, God is Good.*
> *Let us thank him, for this food…Amen.*

Our brood got to where they liked to improvise. Our oldest son, Earl, for instance, came up with this in February of 1964, at age seven: "Dear God, I want to be on your side, 'cause I like you very much. Amen."

Later, after Earl had spoken a nice blessing, his brother Mark, five, said, seriously, "I feel closer to God."

Thanks to index card notes Susanne recorded up to our kids' adolescent years, we have enjoyed re-reading their blessings and other childhood sayings. In October 1964, Mark, age five, had this blessing: "Dear God, please help LBJ win the war. Amen." (That was the year Mark got to see President Johnson as he stopped at Gainesville on a visit to Georgia.)

That same year, Mark—briefly left alone at the lunch table with his three-year-old brother Scott—engaged in this conversation:

Mark: I gotta have somebody help me with the blessing. Scott, help me: Scott, help me…Dear God…Say *Dear God*, Scott…Scott, say something…

Scott: Mumble mumble…
Mark: Help us be good…
Scott: Mumble mumble…
Mark: Help us be good. What is it?…OH YEAH…AMEN !
Scott: 'Men

Later, when we asked Scott to do the blessing, he had a perfect one: "B'essin', b'essin', b'essin'."

Our granddaughter, eleven-year-old Cheryl Llewellyn of Athens, Alabama, came up with a pretty good variation on an old blessing recently:

> *God is good, God is great,*
> *Please bless this food*
> *That's on my plate.*

~

Young people do, indeed, come up with the durndest blessings. The recently published *Dillard House Cook Book* recalled a delightful blessings story told by the late Henry Dillard.

"Back in the WPA days, Mother started [Rabun] County's first school lunch program. Before she finished, she established six lunchrooms. She prepared the best meals for the lowest cost anywhere. Kids would bring what they could from home, like jelly, jams, cornmeal, and so on, then WPA set up some money to help pay for other food.

"One day they had blackberry pie. Mother asked one little boy named Jack Darnell to say grace, which they did before every meal…Old Jack said: "Oh Lord, look on us this blackberry pie. Open our mouths and eat blackberry pie. One more time we thank you, Lord, for this blackberry pie."

~

Here's a roundup of some traditional (and nontraditional) "blessings" that I've collected and people have sent me from around the region (and England and Scotland):

> *Some hae meat and canna eat*
> *And some wad eat that want it.*
> *But we hae meat and we can eat,*
> *And sae the Lord be thanket.*
> > —Robert Burns

~

> *Lord make us able*
> *To eat all on the table*
> *If there's any in the kitchen*
> *Let it come pitching*
> > —Mountain blessing as quoted by Phila Hach,
> > Clarksville, Tennessee

God bless the owl that ate the fowl
And left the bones for Mr. Jones.
> —Prayer spoken by a Reverend Jones as he
> looked at the chicken being served him.

~

The Lord is good to me
And so I thank the Lord;
For giving me the things I need,
The sun and the grain and the apple seed,
The Lord is good to me.
> —Anonymous English grace

~

Thank you, Jesus, for this day.
Thank you for this food we pray.
Thank you for Mom and Dad,
And don't ever send us nothing bad.
> —Child's prayer spoken in Cullowhee, North
> Carolina, as remembered by Frank Pressley

~

Be present at our table, Lord;
Be here and everywhere adored;
Thy creatures bless; and grant that we
May feast in paradise with Thee, Amen.
> —A John Wesley grace

~

Good food, good meat,
Good Lord, Let's eat!
> —Hurley Badders, Pendleton, South Carolina

~

Supper's ready. Now bow your head,
Say a quick "A-men,"
Then pass the corn bread!
> —Robert Mitchie, *Cooking on the Dixie Range*

Noon-time has come, the board is spread,
Thanks be to God, who gives us bread.
Praise God for Bread. Amen.

—A dining room favorite at the John C. Campbell
Folk School, Brasstown, North Carolina

~

Give us, Lord, a bit o'sun,
A bit o' work and a bit o' fun,
Give us all in the struggle and sputter
Our daily bread and a bit o' butter.

—Inscribed on wall of an old inn
in Lancaster, England

~

Father, thy loving hand supplied
Fresh manna through the olden days.
Supply our daily loaf, and help
Us to accept with fitting praise
This staff of life by which we live.
We ask not to be richly fed,
But Lord, we would evaluate
The miracle of daily bread.

—Patton United Methodist Church,
Franklin, North Carolina

~

Be present at our table Lord
Be here and everywhere adored,
From Thine all-bounteous land our food
May we receive with gratitude. Amen.

—Moravian blessing from Old Salem,
North Carolina

~

Our plates are full,
Our friends are near,
Our hearts are warm,
Our thanks sincere. Amen.

—Hemlock Inn, Bryson City, North Carolina

Give us a good digestion, Lord
And also something to digest.
Give us a healthy body, Lord
With sense to keep it at its best.
Give us a healthy mind, good Lord,
To keep the good and pure in sight
Which seeing sin is not appalled,
But finds a way to set it right…Amen.

—Prayer found in the 1700s
in Chester Cathedral, England

~

Be known to us in breaking bread
But do not then depart
Abide with us, O Lord and spread,
The table in our heart. Amen.

—*The Clemson House Cookbook*

The legendary "Goat Man," Ches McCartney, is pictured with his goat-drawn cart loaded with housewares. Ches and his team of goats were familiar sights across the southeastern hill country, drawing hundreds of curious onlookers. At night, McCartney slept with his goats by the side of the road.

Epilogue

To conclude the narrative begun with the introduction, concerning our family's survival strategy during the Depression years, you might wonder what happened to my parents and siblings in succeeding years.

After five years of "sharecropping" in Greenville County, South Carolina (not far from the gleaming new BMW plant on I-85), my parents were able to return to Lancaster County and Dad eventually resumed his career as a country merchant. My sister graduated from Greenville Hospital's School of Nursing and became a registered nurse; two of my brothers graduated from Furman University and became Baptist ministers; one brother joined the Civilian Conservation Corps (CCC) and later became the owner and operator of a textile plant vending business. My next oldest brother graduated from North Greenville College and became a plant engineering foreman at DuPont's Savannah River Plant. And I, after graduating from Berry College, served a two-year Korean conflict draftee hitch with the U.S. Army in the Far East. I subsequently served as a newspaperman and later became (for twenty-five years) a Lockheed PR representative.

My father and mother—after many years of hard work and sacrifice—died in the 1950s at their country home in lower Lancaster County. Their remains rest in the Midway Baptist Church Cemetery in sight of our old home site. All my siblings except older brother Connie are deceased. Dad's and Mother's old homeplace and my father's crossroads country store and Gulf service station were demolished by the oil company that purchased the property. Before the bulldozers erased the old buildings, I was able to salvage from our homeplace roof a lightning rod weathervane with a beautiful clear glass globe. It has become a family heirloom.

~

And what does the future hold for Southern Appalachian cooking?

I asked my friend Mark Sohn, noted Kentucky chef and author of *Mountain Country Cooking*, to give me his view. Mark, who studied in France and who returned to the U.S. to become a Kentucky public television personality, chef, and author, feels, as I do, that the region's cuisine is "an evolving tradition, and a future in the making." Many mountain stereotypes "that have jumped from our valleys do not reflect the wonder of our Southern Appalachian food."

Friends often ask Sohn to fix them a traditional mountain dinner. "They long for a hand-cooked, home-cooked, slow-cooked meal." He is happy to fill many such requests, realizing that traditional mountain meals reflect the region's heritage and identity and help forge connections to people and places.

I join Mark in rejoicing that people who grew up in the Appalachians look at life differently from mainstream Americans. As a result, mountain people eat a magnificently delightful variety of dishes that are eschewed by folk in other regions…greens, boiled beans, sweet potatoes, and cushaw squash. "We seek our native black walnuts, ramps, grits, persimmons, shuck beans, pear butter and sassafras, custard delights and sweet dumplings. We look for fresh eggs, fresh corn, creases and sweet sorghum. And we gain satisfaction from creating special dishes…black walnut cakes, pawpaw muffins, apple stack pies, and Christmas rocks."

Will Southern Appalachian cuisine survive our hurry-up era of fast foods? In the educated opinion of Mark Sohn, there are sound reasons for optimism. Not only will mountain food and mountain culture endure, they could spread countrywide. After all, there are thirty-eight million "Appalachians" residing across the United States. They form a wonderful cheering squad to spread the word.

Perhaps after reading this volume—if you are not an Appalachian "local"—you may wish to try out some of the recipes in this volume and join the crusade to preserve Appalachian folk traditions, not the least of which are our foodlore and foodways. I fondly hope you will.

Bibliography

Adair, Frances. *A Little Leaven*. Waleska, Ga.: Reinhardt College, 1983.

w, Margaret. *Southern Traditions: A Seasonal Cookbook*. Reprint. New York: Penguin, 1994.

Aidells, Bruce, and Denis Kelly. *Hot Links and Country Flavor*. New York: Knopf, 1990.

Alabama State Planning Commission. *Alabama Guide*. 1941.

Alston, Elizabeth. *Biscuits and Scones*. New York: Clarkson-Potter, 1988.

Amerson, Anne Dismukes. *I Remember Dahlonega*. Dahlonega, Ga., 1990-1997.

Anderson, Jean. *Recipes from America's Restored Villages*. New York: Doubleday, 1975. Reprint, New York: Ballantine, 1987.

Anthony, Emily, and John Anthony. *Sautee Inn Recipes*. Hartwell, Ga.: Callico Kitchen Press, 1992.

Arnow, Harriette Simpson. *Seedtime on the Cumberland*. New York: MacMillan, 1960. Reprint. Knoxville, Tenn.: University of Tennessee Press, 1993.

———. *Hunter's Horn*. New York: Macmillan, 1949.

Atlanta Historical Society. *Tullie's Receipts*. Atlanta: Atlanta Historical Society, 1976.

Auchmutey, Jim. *True South*. Atlanta: Longstreet Press, 1994.

Bartram, Willard. *Travels of William Bartram*. New York: Dover Publishing Company, Inc., 1928.

Bass, A. L. Tommie, and John K. Crellin. *Plain Southern Eating*. Durham, NC: Duke University Press, 1988.

Belk, Sarah. *Around the Southern Table*. New York: Simon & Schuster, 1991.

Berry College. *Favorite Recipes of the Daughters of Berry*. Mount Berry, GA, 1950.

Bivins, S. Thomas. *The Southern Cook Book*. Hampton, Va.: Hampton Institute Press, 1912.

Bodkin, B. A. *A Treasury of Southern Folklore*. New York: Bonanza, 1977.

Borghese, Anita. *Foods from Harvest Festivals and Folk Fairs*. New York: Crowell, 1977.

Brewer, Carson, and Alberta Brewer. *Valley So Wild: A Folk History*. Knoxville, Tenn.: East Tennessee Historical Society, 1975.

Bridenbaugh, Carl. *Myths and Realities; Societies of the Colonial South*. Baton Rouge, LA: Louisiana State University Press, 1952.

———. *The Spirit of '76*. New York: Oxford University Press, 1975.

Brobeck, Florence. *Old Time Pickling and Spicing Recipes*. New York: Gramercy/Crown, 1957.

———. *Pickles and Preserves*. New York: Avenel Books, 1955.

Bronz, Ruth Adams. *Miss Ruby's American Cooking*. New York: Harper & Row, 1989.

———. *Miss Ruby's Cornucopia*. New York: Harper-Collins, 1991.

Brooks, Maurice. *The Appalachians*. Boston: Houghton-Mifflin, 1965.

Brown, Fred. *Dillard House Cookbook*. Marietta, Ga.: Longstreet Press, 1996.

Brown, Fred, and Nell Jones. *The Georgia Conservancy's Guide to the North Georgia Mountains*. Atlanta: The Georgia Conservancy, 1990.

Brown, John Hull. *Early American Beverages*. New York: Bonanza, 1966.

Brown, Marion. *Marion Brown's Southern Cookbook*. Rev. ed. Chapel Hill, NC: University of North Carolina Press, 1968.

Brown, Virginia Pounds. *The World of the Southern Indians*. Birmingham, AL.: Beechwood Books, 1983.

Bryan, Carolyn G. *Appalachian Kinfolks Cookbook*. Sevierville, Tenn.: Nandel Publishing Company, 1990.

Bryan, Lettice. *The Kentucky Housewife*. Cincinnati: Shepard & Stearns, 1839. Facsimile edition, Columbia, S.C.: University of South Carolina Press, 1991.

Bucek, Jay. *Somethin's Cookin' in the Mountains: A Cookbook and Guidebook to Northeast Georgia*. Clarkesville, Ga.: Soque Publishers, 1984.

Bullock, Helen Duprey. *Recipes of Early America*. Heirloom Publishing, 1967.

Burns, LaMont. *Down Home Southern Cooking*. New York: Doubleday, 1987.

Bush, Florence Cope. *Dorie: Woman of the Mountains*. Knoxville, Tenn.: University of Tennessee Press, 1991.

Cagle, Marie, and Lou Nicholson. *Jarrett House Potpourri*. Dillsboro, NC: Jarrett House.

Campbell, John C. *The Southern Highlander and His Homeland*. 1921. Reprint. Lexington, KY: University Press of Kentucky, 1969.

Carter, Susannah. *The Frugal Colonial Housewife*. New York: Dolphin/Doubleday, 1976.

Chiltoskey, Mary Ulmer. *Cherokee Cooklore*. Cherokee, NC: Mary and Goingback Chiltoskey, 1951.

Clark, Thomas D. *The Kentucky*. New York: Farrar & Reinhart, 1942.

Connor, Phyllis. *Old Timey Recipes*. Bluefield, WV, 1975.

Cooper, Nancy Blanche. *Gatlinburg Recipe Collection*. Gatlinburg, TN, 1986.

Cotter, William Jasper. *My Autobiography*. Nashville, Tenn.: Methodist Episcopal Church South Publishing House, 1917.

Cox, Beverly, and Martin Jacobs. *Spirit of the Harvest: North American Indian Cooking*. New York: Stewart, Tabor & Chang, 1991.

Darden, Norma Jean, and Carole Darden. *Spoonbread and Strawberry Wine*. New York: Doubleday, 1978.

Davidson, Donald. *The Tennessee*. New York: Rinehart, 1946.

de Crèvecoeur, J. Hector St. John. *Letters from an American Farmer and Sketches of 18th Century America*. 1925. Reprint. New York: Penguin Books, 1963.

Dean, A. F. *Observations from a Peak in Lumpkin: The Writings of W. B. Townsend*. Atlanta: Oglethorpe University Press, 1936.

Douglas, Ronald MacDonald. *Scottish Lore and Folklore*. New York: Crown, 1982.

Driskell, J. C. *Bridge Roads: Old Brown's Bridge*. Cleveland, Ga.: Ponderell Publishers.

Dull, Mrs. S. R. *Southern Cooking*. 1928. Reprint. Atlanta: Cherokee Publishing Company, 1989.

Dunn, Durwood. *Cades Cove: The Life and Death of a Southern Appalachian Community. 1818-1937*. Knoxville, Tenn.: University of Tennessee Press, 1988.

Dunn, Elizabeth, and Laurie Strickland. *Old Time Southern Cooking*. Gretna, LA: Pelican Publishing, 1995.

Dupree, Nathalie. *Nathalie Dupree's Southern Memories, Recipes and Reminiscences.* New York: Clarkson-Potter, 1993.

———. *New Southern Cooking.* New York: Knopf, 1986.

Dwyer, Bil. *Thangs Yankees Don't Know.* Highlands, N.C.: Merry Mountaineers, 1975.

Dwyer, Louise, and Bil Dwyer. *Southern Appalachian Mountain Cooking.* Highlands, NC: Merry Mountaineers, 1974.

———. *Cookin' Yankees Aint Et Yet.* Highlands, N.C.: Merry Mountaineers, 1980.

Dykeman, Wilma. *The French Broad.* New York: Holt, Reinhart & Winston, 1955.

Egerton, John. *Side Orders: Small Helpings of Southern Cookery and Culture.* Atlanta: Peachtree Publishers, 1990.

———. *Southern Food: At Home, On the Road, In History.* New York: Knopf, 1987.

Elkort, Martin. *The Secret Life of Food.* Los Angeles: Jeremy P. Tarcher, 1991.

Elverson, Virginia. *A Cooking Legacy.* New York: Walker, 1975.

Erbsen, Wayne. *Front Porch Old-Time Songs, Jokes and Stories.* Asheville, NC: Native Ground Music, 1993.

———. *Southern Mountain Fiddle.* Pacifica, Mo.: Mel Bay Publications, 1995.

Exum, Helen McDonald. *Helen Exum's Chattanooga Cook Book.* Chattanooga, TN: Chattanooga News-Free Press, 1970.

Fain, Janet. *Nora Mill Granary Cookbook II.* Sautee, Ga.: Nora Mill, N.d.

Farr, Sidney Saylor. *More Than Moonshine: Appalachian Recipes and Recollections.* Pittsburgh, Pa.: University of Pittsburgh Press, 1983.

Farwell, Harold F., Jr., and J. Karl Nicholas. *Smoky Mountain Voices.* Lexington, KY: University Press of Kentucky, 1992.

Ferris, William, and Charles R. Wilson. *Encyclopedia of Southern Culture.* Chapel Hill, NC: University of North Carolina Press, 1989.

Fitzgerald, Mary Newman. *The Cherokee and His Smoky Mountain Legends.* Asheville, NC: The Stephens Press, 1964.

Flagg, Fannie. *Fannie Flagg's Original Whistle Stop Cafe Cookbook.* New York: Fawcett, 1993.

Flexner, Marion. *Out of Kentucky Kitchens.* New York: Bramhall House, 1949.

Fowler, Damon Lee. *Classical Southern Cooking.* New York: Crown, 1995.

Foxfire Students, eds. *The Foxfire Book of Winemaking: Recipes and Memories in the Appalachian Tradition.* New York: Dutton, 1987.

Frome, Michael. *Strangers in High Places.* New York: Doubleday, 1996.

Fussell, Betty. *I Hear America Cooking.* New York: Viking, 1986.

Gates Chapel United Methodist Church. *Sharing Our Best.* Ellijay, GA, 1978.

Georgia Board of Education. *Georgia Guide.* 1940. Reprint. Columbia, SC: University of South Carolina Press, 1990.

Gilmer County Heritage Committee. *The Heritage of Gilmer County.* Ellijay, GA, 1997.

Glenn, Camille. *The Heritage of Southern Cooking.* New York: Workman, 1986.

Great Smoky Mountains Natural History Association. *Mountain Makin's in the Smokies.* Gatlinburg, TN, 1957.

Grissom, Michael Andrew. *Southern by the Grace of God*. Gretna, La.: Pelican, 1988.

Groff, Betty. *Betty Groff's Pennsylvania Dutch Cook Book*. New York: Macmillan, 1990.

Hach, Phila R. *Official Cookbook, The 1982 World's Fair*. Clarksville, TN: Joe K. Hach, 1982.

Hamerstrom, Frances. *Wild Food Cookbook*. Ames, Iowa: Iowa State University Press, 1989.

Hamilton, Alice McGuire. *Blue Ridge Mountain Memories*. Atlanta: Conger Printing, 1977.

Hamner, Earl Jr. *Spencer's Mountain*. New York: Dial, 1961.

Hardeman, Nicholas P. *Shucks, Shocks and Hominy Blocks*. Baton Rouge, LA: Louisiana State University Press, 1981.

Harris, Gertrude. *Foods of the Frontier*. San Francisco: 101 Productions, 1972.

Hasty, William G. Sr. *I Remember When*. Canton, GA. 1994.

Hayes, Irene. *What's Cooking in Kentucky*. Fort Mitchell, Ky.: T. I. Hayes Publishing Company, 1970.

Hechtlinger, Adelaide. *The Seasonal Hearth: The Woman at Home in America*. Woodstock, N.Y.: The Overlook Press, 1986.

Hemperly, Marion R. *Indian Heritage of Georgia*. Atlanta: Garden Clubs of Georgia, Inc., 1994.

Hess, John L., and Karen Hess. *The Taste of America*. New York: Grossman/Viking, 1977.

Hess, Karen, ed. *Martha Washington's Booke of Cookery*. New York: Columbia University Press, 1981.

Hewitt, Jean. *The New York Times Southern Heritage Cookbook*. New York: Putnam, 1972.

Higgs, Robert J., and Ambrose Manning. *Voices from the Hills, Selected Readings of Southern Appalachia*. New York: F. Unger Publishing Co., 1975.

Hilburn, Prudence. *A Treasury of Southern Baking*. New York: Harper, 1993.

Hill, Annabella P. *Mrs. Hill's Southern Practical Cookery and Receipt Book*. 1820. Reprint. Columbia, S.C.: University of South Carolina Press, 1955.

Hilliard, Sam Bowers. *Hog Meat and Hoecakes*. Carbondale, IL: Southern Illinois University Press, 1972.

Hoffman, Kathryn, and Kay Moss. *The Backcountry Housewife: A Study of Eighteenth-Century Foods*. Gastonia, N.C.: Shiele Museum, 1985.

Hooker, Richard J., ed. *The Carolina Backcountry on the Eve of the Revolution: The Journal and Other Writings of Charles Woodmason, Anglican Itinerant*. Chapel Hill, NC: University of North Carolina Press, 1953.

Horan, Christopher. *English Country Cooking*. New York: St. Martin's Press, 1985.

Houk, Rose. *Food and Recipes of the Smokies*. Gatlinburg, Tenn.: Great Smoky Mountains Natural History Association, 1996.

Housworth, G. Lonnie. *Farm Stories…In Their Own Words*. Conyers, Ga.: Maypop Press, 1994.

Hudson, Charles. *The Southeastern Indians*. Knoxville, TN: University of Tennessee Press, 1976.

Irwin, John Rice. *Alex Stewart: Portrait of a Pioneer*. West Chester, PA: Schiffer Publishing Ltd., 1985.

Jenkins, Emyl. *Southern Christmas*. New York: Crown, 1992.

Johnson City, Tennessee, Junior Service League. *Smoky Mountain Magic*. 1960, 1961, 1969, 1971.

Jones, Evan. *American Food: The Gastronomic Story.* Woodstock, N.Y.: The Overlook Press, 1990.

Kainen, Ruth Cole. *America's Christmas Heritage.* New York: Funk & Wagnalls, 1969.

Kane, Harnett. *The Southern Christmas Book.* New York: McKay, 1958.

Kellner, Esther. *Moonshine: Its History and Folklore.* New York: Bobbs-Merrill, 1971.

Kellner, Lynda W. *The Taste of Appalachia.* Boone, N.C.: Simmer Pot Press, 1987.

Kennedy, Billy. *The Scots-Irish in the Carolinas.* Londonderry, Northern Ireland: Causeway Press; Greenville, S.C.: Emerald House Group Inc., 1997.

————. *The Scots-Irish in the Hills of Tennessee.* Londonderry, Northern Ireland: Causeway Press; Greenville, S.C.: Emerald House Group, Inc., 1996.

————. *The Scots-Irish in the Shenandoah Valley.* Londonderry, Northern Ireland: Causeway Press; Greenville, S.C.: Emerald House Group, Inc., 1996.

Kephart, Horace. *Camping and Woodcraft.* 1917. Reprint. Knoxville, Tenn.: University of Tennessee Press, 1988.

————. *Our Southern Highlanders: A Narrative of Adventure in the Southern Appalachians and a Study of Life Among the Mountaineers.* 1926. Reprint. Knoxville, TN: University of Tennessee Press, 1976.

Killion, Ronald G., and Charles T. Walker. *A Treasury of Georgia Folklore.* Marietta, GA: Cherokee Press, 1972.

King, Daisy. *The Original Tennessee Homecoming Cookbook.* Nashville, Tenn.: Rutledge Hill Press, 1985.

Kirlin, Katherine W., and Thomas M. Kirlin. *Smithsonian Folklife Cookbook.* Herndon, VA: Smithsonian Institution Press, 1991.

Knopf, Mildred O. *Around America Cook Book for Young People.* New York: Knopf, 1969.

Kollock, John. *The Long Afternoon.* Lakemont, Ga.: Copple House, 1978.

Lambert, Walter N. *Kinfolks and Custard Pie.* Knoxville, Tenn.: University of Tennessee Press, 1988.

Langton, William C. *Everyday Things in American Life, 1607-1776.* New York: Scribners, 1937.

La Rowe, John E. *Something's Cooking in the Mountains.* Clarkesville, Ga.: Soque Publishers, 1982.

Ledford, Ibbie. *Hill Country Cooking and Memoirs.* Gretna, LA: Pelican, 1991.

Lewis, Edna. *In Pursuit of Flavor.* New York: Knopf, 1988.

————. *The Taste of Country Cooking.* New York: Knopf, 1976.

Liles, Jean Wickstrom. *Country Living Recipes.* Birmingham, AL: Oxmoor House, Inc., 1982.

Logan, John V. *History of the Upper Country of South Carolina.* Charleston, SC: Courtney, 1859.

Lundy, Ronni. *Shuck Beans, Stack Cakes and Honest Fried Chicken.* New York: Atlantic Monthly Press, 1991.

Lupo, Margaret. *Southern Cooking from Mary Mac's Tea Room.* Atlanta: Cherokee Publishing, 1988.

Lustig, Lillie S. *The Southern Cook Book.* Reading, Pa.: Culinary Arts Press, 1938.

Mahan, Paul E. *Smoky Mountain Wines.* New York: Arco, 1973.

Mankiller, Wilma. *The Chief Cooks Traditional Cherokee Recipes*. Muskogee, Okla.: Hoffman Printing Company, 1988.

Marshall, Lillian B. *Cooking Across the South*. Birmingham, AL: Oxmoor House, 1980.

McCallum, Barbara Beury. *Mom & Ramps Forever*. Charleston, W.V.: Mountain State Press, 1966.

McCullough-Williams, Martha. *Dishes and Beverages of the Old South*. 1913. Reprint. Knoxville, Tenn.: University of Tennessee Press, 1988.

McKee, Lily Byrd. *High Hampton Hospitality*. Chapel Hill, N.C.: Creative Printers, 1970.

McRee, Jannelle Jones. *Down Cooter Creek and Other Stories*. Marietta, GA: Cherokee Press, 1986.

Mellinger, Marie B. *Roadside Rambles*. Clayton, Ga., 1995.

Mickler, Ernest Matthew. *White Trash Cooking*. San Francisco: Ten Speed Press, 1986.

Miles, Emma Bell. *The Spirit of the Mountains*. 1905. Reprint. Knoxville, TN: University of Tennessee Press, 1975.

Miller, Joni. *True Grits: The Southern Foods Mail-Order Catalogue*. New York: Workman, 1990.

Miller, Zell. *The Mountains Within Me*. Toccoa, GA: Commercial Printing, 1976.

Mitchamore, Pat. *Miss Mary Bobo's Boarding House Cookbook*. Nashville, Tenn.: Rutledge Hill Press, 1994.

Moore, Warren. *Mountain Voices: A Legacy of the Blue Ridge and Great Smokies*. Chester, Conn.: The Globe Pequot Press, 1988.

Morley, Margaret W. *The Carolina Mountains*. Boston: Houghton-Mifflin, 1913.

Neal, Bill. *Bill Neal's Southern Cooking*. Chapel Hill, NC: University of North Carolina Press, 1985, 1989.

————. *Biscuits, Spoonbread and Sweet Potato Pie*. New York: Knopf, 1991.

Neal, Bill, and Davis Perry. *Good Old Grits Cookbook*. New York: Workman, 1991.

Nixon, H. C. *Lower Piedmont Country*. Tuscaloosa, AL: University of Alabama Press, 1974.

North Carolina Department of Conservation and Development. *North Carolina Guide*. 1939. Reprint. Columbia, SC: University of South Carolina Press, 1988.

Oliver, Duane. *Cooking on Hazel Creek: The Best of Southern Mountain Cooking*. Hazelwood, NC, 1990.

————. *Hazel Creek From Then Till Now*. Hazelwood, NC, 1990.

————. *Remembered Lives: A Narrative History of our Family*. Hazelwood, NC, 1993.

Oliver, Ted. *Sketches of Union County History III*. Blairsville, Ga.: Union County Historical Society, 1987.

Olstein, Judi. *American Family Cooking*. Exeter Books, 1984.

Page, Linda Garland, and Eliot Wigginton. *Aunt Arie, A Foxfire Portrait*. New York: Dutton, 1983.

————. *Foxfire Book of Appalachian Cookery*. New York: Dutton, 1984. Reprint. Chapel Hill, NC: University of North Carolina Press, 1992.

————. *Foxfire Book of Winemaking*. New York: E. P. Dutton, 1987.

Paget, Russie H. *Clemson House Cook Book: Carolina Up-Country Recipes*. Charlotte, NC: Heritage House, 1955.

Parker, Courtney. *How to Eat Like a Southerner, and Live to Tell the Tale*. New York: Clarkson-Potter, 1992.

Parris, John. *Mountain Bred*. Asheville, NC: Citizen-Times Publishing Company, 1967.

————. *Mountain Cooking*. Asheville, NC: Citizen-Times Publishing Company, 1978.

————. *My Mountains, My People*. Asheville, NC: Citizen-Times Publishing Company, 1957.

————. *Roaming the Mountains*. Asheville, NC: Citizen-Times Publishing Company, 1955.

————. *These Storied Mountains*. Asheville, NC: Citizen-Times Publishing Company, 1972.

Parton, Willadeene. *All Day Singing and Dinner on the Ground*. Nashville, Tenn.: Rutledge Hill, 1997.

Patteson, Charles. *Charles Patteson's Kentucky Cooking*. New York: Harper & Row, 1988.

Pendleton District Historical Commission. *Haygood Mill Corn Meal Recipe Book*. Pendleton, SC, 1976.

Penley, Floe Ellen Turner. *Scrap Cotton*. Long Creek, SC: Tri State Press, 1991.

Penner, Lucille Recht. *The Colonial Cookbook*. New York: Hastings House, 1976.

Perl, Lila. *Red Flannel Hash and Shoo-Fly Pie*. New York: World, 1965.

Phipps, Frances. *Colonial Kitchens, Their Furnishings and Their Gardens*. New York: Hawthorn Books, 1972.

Platt, Louisa Roberts. *Queen of Appalachia Cookbook*. Asheville, NC, early 1900s.

Porch, Ludlow, and Diane Cox Porch. *The Fat White Guy's Cookbook*. Marietta, GA: Longstreet, 1990.

Porch, Ludlow. *The Corn Bread Chronicles*. Atlanta: Peachtree Press, 1983.

Purdy, Susan G. *As Easy as Pie*. New York: Atheneum, 1984.

Raichlen, Steven. *Celebration of Seasons*. New York: Simon & Schuster, 1988.

Raine, James Watt. *The Land of Saddlebags*. Richmond, VA: Presbyterian Committee of Publications, 1924.

Ramsey, Robert W. *Carolina Cradle*. Chapel Hill, NC: University of North Carolina Press, 1964.

Randolph, Mary. *The Virginia Housewife or Methodical Cook*. 1860. Reprint, Avenel/Crown.

Rawlings, Marjorie Kinnan. *Cross Creek Cookery*. New York: Scribners, 1942. Reprint, New York: Fireside/Simon & Schuster, 1996.

Reed, John Shelton, and Dale V. Reed. *1001 Things Everyone Should Know About the South*. New York: Doubleday, 1996.

Ritchie, Andrew Jackson. *Sketches of Rabun County History*. Clayton, GA, 1948.

Ritchie, Jean. *Singing Family of the Cumberlands*. New York: Oxford University Press, 1955. Reprint. Lexington, KY.: The University Press of Kentucky, 1988.

Robertson, Ben. *Red Hills and Cotton: An Upcountry Memory*. Columbia, SC: University of South Carolina Press, 1960.

Root, Waverly, and Richard de Rachemon. *Eating in America: A History*. New York: Morrow, 1976.

Russell, Gladys Trentham. *Call Me Hillbilly: A True Humorous Account of the Simple Life in the Smokies*. Alcoa, TN: Russell Publishing Co., 1974.

Sanders, Dori. *Dori Sanders Country Cooking*. Chapel Hill, NC: Algonquin, 1995.

Schultz, Phillip Stephen. *As American as Apple Pie*. New York: Simon & Schuster, 1990.

———. *Celebrating America: A Cookbook*. New York: Simon & Schuster, 1994.

Sellers, Bettie M. *Spring Onions and Cornbread*. Gretna, LA: Pelican, 1978.

Shelton, Ferne. *Pioneer Cookbook*. High Point, NC: Hutcraft, 1963.

———. *Pioneer Comforts and Kitchen Remedies*. High Point, NC: Hutcraft, 1964.

Sibley, Celestine. *A Place Called Sweet Apple*. New York: Doubleday, 1967.

———. *The Celestine Sibley Sampler*. Atlanta: Peachtree Publishers, 1997.

Signer, Billie Touchtone. *Redneck Country Cooking: Better Eating for Less*. Albany, NY: R&B Books, 1982.

Skinner, Constance Lindsay. *Pioneers of the Old Southwest: A Chronicle of the Dark and Bloody Ground*. New Haven: Yale University Press, 1919.

Smith, Lillian. *Memory of a Large Christmas*. New York: Norton, 1961.

Smith, Mike, and Mike Steed. *Cooking with Lard*. Atlanta: Longstreet Press, 1996.

Smithsonian Institution. *The Smithsonian Guide to Historic America*. New York: Stewart, Tabor & Chang, 1989.

Sohn, Mark F. *Mountain Country Cooking*. New York: St. Martin's Press, 1996.

Solomon, Jack, and Olivia Solomon. *Cracklin' Bread and Asfidity: Folk Recipes and Remedies*. Tuscaloosa, Ala.: University of Alabama Press, 1979.

Spurgeon, Winston B. *Cooking in Old Salem*. Williamsburg, Va.: Williamsburg Publishing, 1981.

Stanley, Lawrence. *A Little History of Gilmer County*. Ellijay, Georgia, 1970.

Stewart, Marjorie M. *Southern Cooking to Remember*. Huntsville, AL: Strode Publishers, 1978.

Strasser, Susan. *Never Done: A History of American Housework*. New York: Pantheon Books, 1982.

Sturges, Lena. *Progressive Farmer Southern Country Cookbook*. Birmingham, AL: Progressive Farmer, 1972.

———. *Southern Living Cakes Cookbook*. Birmingham, Ala.: Oxmoor House, 1975.

Swaim, Douglas. *Cabins and Castles: The History and Architecture of Buncombe County*. Asheville, NC: Asheville and Buncombe County Resources Commission, 1981.

Tartan, Beth. *North Carolina and Old Salem Cookery*. Rev. ed. Chapel Hill, NC: University of North Carolina Press, 1992.

Taylor, Joe Gray. *Eating, Drinking and Visiting in the South: An Informal History*. Baton Rouge, LA: Louisiana State University Press, 1982.

Taylor, John Martin. *The New Southern Cook*. New York: Bantam Books, 1995.

Terrell, Charlene. *Wolfscratch Wilderness: A Backward Walk in Time in An Old North Georgia Settlement*. Roswell GA: WH Wolfe Associates, 1994.

Thompson, Kathy. *Touching Home: A Collection of History and Folklore from the Copper Basin, Fannin County Area*. Blue Ridge, GA: West Fannin County High School, 1976.

Thompson, Kathy and photojournalism students of West Fannin County High School. *In Touch with the Past*. Blue Ridge, GA, 1982.

Tolley, Lynne. *Jack Daniel's The Spirit of Tennessee Cookbook*. Nashville, TN: Rutledge Hill Press, 1988.

Toops, Connie. *Great Smoky Mountains*. Stillwater, Minn.: Voyager Press, 1992.

Townsend, Jimmy. *Wait Jest a Cotton Pickin' Minute*. Jasper, GA, 1983.

Trudeau, Susan. *Georgia Plantation and Historical Homes Cookbook*. Atlanta: Aerial Photography Services.

Underwood, Virginia. *Georgia Mountain Heritage*. Cherrylog, GA, 1981.

Ungerer, Miriam. *Country Food*. New York: Vintage, 1982.

Villas, James, and Martha Pearl Villas. *My Mother's Southern Kitchen: Recipes and Reminiscences*. New York: Macmillan, 1994.

Voltz, Jeane A. *The Flavor of the South*. New York: Gramercy Publishing, 1977.

Walker, Robert Sparks. *As the Indians Left It*. Chattanooga Audubon Society, 1955.

———. *Torchlight to the Cherokees*. New York: Macmillan, 1931.

Wallace, Lily Haxworth. *Rumford Complete Cook Book*. Rumford Chemical Works, 1908.

Ward, George Gordon. *The Annals of Upper Georgia Centered in Gilmer County*. Ellijay, GA, 1965.

Watkins, Floyd E., and Charles Hubert. *Yesterday in the Hills*. Athens, GA: University of Georgia Press, 1963.

Whistler, Frances Lambert. *Indian Cookin'*. Chattanooga, Tenn.: Norwega Press, 1973.

White, Betsy Tice. *Mountain Folk, Mountain Food*. Marble Hill, GA: Recovery Communications, 1997.

White, Rev. George. *Historical Collections of Georgia*. New York: Pudney & Russell, 1854.

Wiggins, Gene. *Fiddlin' Georgia Crazy: Fiddlin' John Carson, His Real World and the World of His Songs*. Urbana, IL: University of Illinois Press, 1987.

Wigginton, Eliot. *The Foxfire Book*. New York: Doubleday, 1974.

Wilcox, Herbert. *Georgia Scribe*. Marietta, GA: Cherokee Press, 1974.

Williams, Samuel Cole. *Adair's History of the American Indians*. Johnson City, TN: The Watauga Press, 1930.

Wilson, Everett B. *America's Vanishing Folkways*. New York: A.S. Barnes, 1965.

Windham, Kathryn Tucker. *Southern Cooking to Remember*. Huntsville, AL: Strode Publishers, 1978.

Witty, Helen. *Billy Joe Tatum's Wild Food Cookbook and Field Guide*. New York: Workman, 1976.

Works Progress Administration. *South Carolina Guide*. 1930s. Reprint, Columbia, SC: University of South Carolina Press, 1988.

Wray, Rush T. *Old Time Recipes, Nu-Wray Inn*. Burnsville, NC: N.p., n.d.

Wright, Louis B. *The Prose Works of William Byrd of Westover: Narratives of a Colonial Virginian*. Boston: Harvard University Press, 1966.

Wrought Iron Range Company. *Home Comfort Cook Book*. St. Louis, MO, 1923.

Photo Credits

Permissions

We have made every effort to trace the ownership of all copyrighted material and to secure permission from copyright holders. In the event of any question arising as to the use of any material, we will be pleased to make the necessary corrections in future printings.

The author gratefully acknowledges permission to quote from the following works:

All Day Singing and Dinner On the Ground by Willadeene Parton, © 1997. Reprinted by permission of Rutledge Hill Press.

American Cooking, Southern Style by Eugene Walter, © 1971. Reprinted by permission of Time-Life Books.

The Annals of Upper Georgia Centered In Gilmer County by George Gordon Ward, © 1965. Reprinted by permission of Mrs. George G. Ward.

An AP dispatch from Gatlinburg, Tennessee, concerning the future of ramps in the Appalachians. Reprinted by permission of The Associated Press.

The Appalachians by Maurice Brooks, © 1965. Reprinted by permission of Houghton Mifflin.

As the Indians Left It by Robert Sparks Walker, © 1955. Reprinted by permission of Chattanooga Audubon Society.

The Back Country Housewife: A Study of Eighteenth-Century Foods by Kay Moss and Kathryn Hoffman, © 1985 and 1994. Reprinted by permission of Shiele Museum, Gastonia, N.C.

Bill Neal's Southern Cooking by William Franklin Neal, © 1989. Reprinted by permission of University of North Carolina Press.

Bushwhackers by William Trotter, © 1988. Reprinted by permission of John F. Blair, Publisher, Winston Salem, N.C.

Call Me Hillbilly: A True Humorous Account of the Simple Life in the Smokiest Before the Tourists Came by Gladys Trentham Russell, © 1974. Reprinted by permission the author.

Camping and Woodcraft by Horace Kephart, © 1917. Reprinted by permission of University of Tennessee Press.

The Celestine Sibley Sampler by Celestine Sibley, © 1997. Reprinted by permission of Peachtree Publishers.

Cherokee Cooklore by Mary Ulmer Chiltoskey, © 1951. Reprinted by permission of the author.

Classical Southern Cooking by Damon Fowler, © 1995. Reprinted by permission of the Crown Publishing Group.

Colonial Housewife by Lucille Recht Penner, © 1976. Reprinted by permission of Hastings House.

Cooking on Hazel Creek by Duane Oliver, © 1990. Reprinted by permission of the author.

Cornbread Chronicles by Ludlow Porch, © 1983. Reprinted by permission of Peachtree Publishers.

Dillard House Cookbook and Mountain Guide by Fred Brown, © 1996. Longstreet Press. Reprinted by permission of the author.

Dishes and Beverages of the Old South by Martha McCullough-Williams, © 1913, 1988. Reprinted by permission of University of Tennessee Press.

Dorie: Woman of the Mountains by Florence Cope Bush, © 1992. Reprinted by permission of University of Tennessee Press.

Down Cooter Creek and Other Stories by Jannelle Jones McRee, © 1986. Reprinted by permission of Cherokee Publishing Company.

Eating, Drinking and Visiting in the South: An Informal History by Joe Gray Taylor, © 1982. Reprinted by permission of Lousiana State University Press.

Fannie Flagg's Original Whistlestop Cafe Cookbook by Fannie Flagg, © 1993. Reprinted by permission of Ballantine Books, a Division of Random House, Inc.

Farm Stories…In Their Own Words by G. Lonnie Housworth, © 1994. Reprinted by permission of the author.

Fat White Man's Cookbook by Ludlow Porch, © 1990. Reprinted by permission of Longstreet Press.

40 Acres and No Mule by Janice Hope Giles, © 1967. Reprinted by permission of Houghton Mifflin.

A Foxfire Christmas, © 1989. Reprinted by permission of The Foxfire Fund, Inc., Mountain City, Ga.

Foxfire Book of Appalachian Cookery. Edited by Linda Garland Page and Eliot Wigginton, © 1992. Reprinted by permission of University of North Carolina Press.

Foxfire Book of Winemaking by Foxfire students © 1987. Reprinted by permission of The Foxfire Fund, Inc.

Gatlinburg Recipe Collection by Nancy Blanche Cooper, © 1986. Reprinted by permission of the author.

Georgia Mountain Heritage by Virginia Underwood, © 1981. Reprinted by permission of the author.

Georgia Scribe by Herbert Wilcox, © 1974. Reprinted by permission of The Cherokee Publishing Company.

I Hear America Cooking by Betty Fussell, © 1986. Reprinted by permission of Penguin/Putnam.

In Pusuit of Flavor by Edna Lewis, © 1988. Reprinted by permission of Alfred A. Knopf, Inc.

I Remember Dahlonega by Anne Dismukes Amerson, © 1990-1997. Reprinted by permission of the author.

I Remember When by William G. Hasty Sr., © 1994. Reprinted by permission of the author.

Jack Daniel's The Spirit of Tennessee Cookbook by Lynn Tolley and Pat Mitchamore, © 1988. Reprinted by permission of Rutledge Hill Press.

Jericho by James Dickey, © 1974. Reprinted by permission of Oxmoor House.

The Kentucky Housewife by Lettice Bryan, © 1839 & 1991. Reprinted by permission of the University of South Carolina Press.

Kinfolks and Custard Pie by Walter N. Lambert, © 1988. Reprinted by permission of University of Tennessee Press.

Marion Brown's Southern Cookbook by Marion Brown, © 1968 by Marion Brown. Reprinted by permission of University of North Carolina Press.

Miss Mary Bobo's Boarding House Cookbook by Pat Mitchamore, © 1994. Reprinted by permission of Rutledge Hill Press.

Mom and Ramps Forever by Barbara Beury McCallum, © 1968. Mountain State Press, Charleston, W.V. Reprinted by permission of the author.

More Than Moonshine: Appalachian Recipes and Recollections by Sidney Saylor Farr, © 1983. Reprinted by permission of University of Pittsburgh Press.

Mountain Cooking by John Parris, © 1978. Citizen-Times Publishing Company, Asheville, N.C. Reprinted by permission of the author.

Mountain Country Cooking by Mark F. Sohn, © 1996. St. Martin's Press. Reprinted by permission of the author.

Mountain Folk, Mountain Food: Down-Home Wisdom, Plain Tales and Recipe Secrets from Appalachia by Betsy Tice White, © 1997. Recovery Communications, Inc. Reprinted by permission of the author.

Mountain Makin's in the Smokies, © 1957. Reprinted by permission of The Great Smoky Mountains Natural History Association.

Mountain Voices: a Legacy of the Blue Ridge and Great Smokies by Warren Moore, © 1988. John F. Blair, publisher. Reprinted by permission of the author.

The Mountains Within Me by Zell Miller, © 1976. Reprinted by permission of the author.

Mrs. Hill's Southern Practical Cookery and Receipt Book by Mrs. Annabella P. Hill, © 1820. Reissued by University of South Carolina Press 1955. Reprinted by permission of University of South Carolina Press.

My Mother's Southern Kitchen by James Villas with Martha Pearl Villas, © 1994. Reprinted by permission of the Author's literary agent, Robin Straus Agency, Inc.

New Southern Cooking by Nathalie Dupree, © 1986. Reprinted by permission of Knopf, a Division of Random House.

North Carolina and Old Salem Cookery by Beth Tartan, © 1955, 1992. Reprinted by permission of University of North Carolina Press.

Old Time Pickling and Spicing by Emyl Jenkins, © 1952. Reprinted by permission of The Crown Publishing Group, Random House.

The Original Tennessee Homecoming Cookbook by Daisy King, © 1985. Reprinted by permission of Rutledge Hill Press.

Our Southern Highlanders by Horace Kephart, © 1946, 1949. Reprinted by permission of University of Tennessee Press.

Out of Kentucky Kitchens by Marion Flexner, © 1949. Reprinted by permission of Dr. John Flexner, Nashville, Tenn.

Pioneers of the Old Southwest by Constance Lindsay Skinner, © 1919. Reprinted by permission of Yale University Press.

A Place Called Sweet Apple by Celestine Sibley, © 1967. Reprinted by permission of Peachtree Publishers.

Plain Southern Eating by A. L. Tommie Bass, edited by John K. Crellin, © 1988. Reprinted by permission of Duke University Press.

Red Hills And Cotton: An Upcountry Memory by Ben Robertson, © 1942, 1960. Reprinted by permission of University of South Carolina Press.

Redneck Country Cooking by Billie Touchtone Signer, © 1982. Reprinted by permission of the author.

Roadside Rambles by Marie B. Mellinger, © 1996. Reprinted by permission of the author.

Roaming the Mountains by John Parris, © 1955. Citizen-Times Publishing Company, Asheville, N.C. Reprinted by permission of the author.

Sautee Inn Recipes by Emily and John Anthony, © 1992. Reprinted by permission of the authors.

Shuck Beans, Stack Cakes and Honest Fried Chicken by Ronni Lundy, © 1991. Reprinted by permission of Atlantic Monthly Press.

Shucks, Shocks and Hominy Blocks by Nicholas P. Hardeman, © 1981. Reprinted by permission of Lousiana State University Press.

Side Orders by John Egerton, © 1990. Reprinted by permission of Peachtree Publishers.

Singing Family of the Cumberlands by Jean Ritchie, © 1955. Geordie Music Publishing, University Press of Kentucky. Reprinted by permission of the author.

Smithsonian Folklife Cookbook by Katherine S. Kirlin and Thomas M. Kirlin, © 1991. Reprinted by permission of Smithsonian Institution Press, Washington, D.C.

Smoky Mountain Magic by the Junior Service League of Johnson City, Tenn., © 1960-1971. Reprinted by permission of the authors.

Somethin's Cookin' in the Mountains by John E. LaRowe, © 1982. Soque Publishers. Reprinted by permission of the author.

Southern Appalachian Mountain Cooking by Bil and Louise Dwyer, © 1974. Merry Mountaineers Publishers, Highlands, N.C. Reprinted by permission of Bill Dwyer.

Southern Cooking by Mrs. S. R. Dull. © 1989. Reprinted by permission of The Cherokee Publishing Company, Marietta, Ga.

Southern Food: At Home, On the Road, In History by John Egerton, © 1987. Reprinted by permission of Alfred A. Knopf Inc., a division of Random House.

Southern Heritage Family Gatherings Cookbook, © 1984. Reprinted by permission of Oxmoor House.

The Southern Highlander and His Homeland by John C. Campbell, © 1921. Reprinted by permission of the Russell Sage Foundation.

Nathalie Dupree's Southern Memories, Recipes and Reminiscences by Nathalie Dupree, © 1993. Reprinted by permission of Crown Publishing Group, Random House.

The Southern Mountain Fiddle by Wayne Erbsen, © 1996. Mel Bay Publications, Inc. Reprinted by permission of the author.

Spoonbread and Strawberry Wine by Norma Jean and Carole Darden, © 1978, 1994. Reprinted by permission of the authors.

Spencer's Mountain by Earl Hamner, © 1961. Reprinted by permission of the author.

Food and Recipe Index

Y

People and Places Index

C

Cabbagetown Families, Cabbagetown Food (Edwards), 79
Cades Cove, Tennessee, 24, 84, 103, 396
Cadiz, Kentucky, 124
Call Me Hillbilly (Russell), 67
Call, Claude, 281
Campbell, John C., 3–4, 304, 455
Campbell, Will, 99
Cannon, Oscar, 48, 188, 254, 364
Canton, Georgia, 88, 98, 106, 158
Caperton, Mrs. Jane Bouie, 403
Cardwell, Glenn, 212, 356
Carolina Housewife, The (Rutledge), 121
Carpenter, Aunt Arie, 69, 81
Carrboro, North Carolina, 344
Carroll County, Virginia, 303
Cartecay, Georgia, 69, 87, 116, 129, 159, 302, 315, 445
Cartersville, Georgia, 7, 215, 451
Carver, Buck, 158–59
Castleberry, Margaret, 81
Celebration of Seasons (Raichlen), 361, 378
Chappel, Alex, 21, 134, 376
Charles Patteson's Kentucky Cooking, 182
Charlotte, North Carolina, 118, 130, 411–12
Chastain, Harley, 156, 315
Chastain, Lucinda McClure, 342
Chattanooga Audubon Society, 127
Chattanooga, Tennessee, 59, 113, 347, 396, 419
Cherokee Cooklore (Chiltoskey), 321, 336
Cherokee County Recipes and Recollections (Stancil), 25
Cherokee County, Georgia, 25, 34, 46, 85, 88, 106, 294, 173, 301, 342, 397
Cherokee Indians, 25, 36, 294
Cherokee Nation, 24–26, 113, 215, 321, 393
Cherokee Trading Path, 13
Cherokee, North Carolina, 26, 74, 184, 321, 327, 335, 375
Cherrylog, Georgia, 232, 345, 374, 382, 438
Chickamauga River valley, 127
Child, Lydia Maria, 107

Chiltoskey, Goingback and Mary Ulmer, 321, 336
Choestoe District, Union County, Georgia, 36
Christian, Jack, 158
Church of England, 125
Church, Mrs. Henry, 396
Civil War, 22, 27, 69, 95, 124, 136, 230, 252, 262, 365, 376–77, 413, 432, 434, 444
Clark, Thomas, 41, 121, 223
Clarkesville, Georgia, 108, 113
Clarksville, Tennessee, 329, 415, 453
Classical Southern Cooking (Fowler), 203, 278
Clay County, North Carolina, 369
Clay, Henry, 144
Clemson House Cook Book-Carolina Country Recipes, 377, 456
Cleveland, Colonel Benjamin, 22
Clinton, Sir Henry, 23
Cloer, "Aunt Tennie," 413, 419
Cloer, Charlie, 90
Cloer, Ralph, 90
Cobb, Irvin, 144
Cobbett, William, 265
Cochran, Hattie, 299, 400
Cocke County, Tennessee, 229, 281
Cohutta Mountains (Georgia), 7, 27, 58, 153, 284, 408
Coker, J. R., 242
Cole, Steve, 446
Collins, Ebb, 49
Collins, Jebb, 49
Collins, William, 207
Colonial Cookbook, The (Penner), 334
Colonial Cooking, 205
Columbus, Christopher, 339
Combs, Mrs. Earle, 419
Connor, Phyllis, 340
Cooking on Hazel Creek (Oliver), 83, 107, 127
Cooper, Nancy Blanche, 210, 298, 327
Coosawattee River, 24
Cope, Andy, 254–55, 394
Corn, Mrs. Elvie, 275
Cornstalk, Chief, 20
Cosby, Tennessee, 229, 281–82

E

East Ellijay, Georgia, 58, 76, 173, 233, 260, 338, 351

Eating, Drinking and Visiting in the South (Taylor), 27, 171, 189, 233

Edwards, Azilee, 79

Egerton, John, 53, 73, 112, 124, 130, 145, 195, 208, 211–12, 216, 251, 291, 303, 308, 326, 339, 402, 411, 421

Egyptians, 86, 442

Elberton, Georgia, 61, 157, 195, 197

Eldreth, Bessie Mae, 370

Elisha, Blueford, 36

Elizabethan England, 176, 184, 238, 353, 414

Ellijay Times-Courier, 126

Ellijay, Georgia, 32, 58, 76, 117, 126, 159, 173, 193, 209, 233, 255, 260, 281, 285, 338, 351, 444

Elliott, Frank, 284–85

Elliott, Sue Parker, 284

Ellis, Tandy, 224

Elsberry, Mrs. Gerrie, 91

Emory University, 65

English settlers, 365

Epworth, Georgia, 440

Ernst, Mrs. L. R., 147

Etowah, 203, 215, 334

Euharlee Farmers Club, 217

Everett, Herschel, 394, 445

Exum, Helen, 41

F

Fain, Janet, 80

Fannie Flagg's Original Whistlestop Cafe Cookbook (Flagg), 212

Fannin County, Georgia, 45, 47, 50, 178, 183, 243, 282, 299, 317, 400, 444

Farmer, Hazel, 11, 71, 91–92, 104, 232, 249, 408

Farmer, Mrs. Lillian, 105, 119

Farr, Sidney Saylor, 5, 65, 105, 111, 120, 138, 171, 271, 332, 334, 337, 340, 441

Faucette Lake, 45, 59

Faulkner, William, 131

Feast of Scotland, A (Warren), 135

Federal Road (through Cherokee Nation), 24

Ferguson, Patrick, 21–23

Fields, Eli, 151–52

Flagg, Fannie, 187, 209, 212

Flexner, Marion, 103, 224, 428

Floyd County, Virginia, 292, 391

Fontana Dam, 84, 341

Food and Recipes of the Smokies (Houk), 100, 294, 325, 373

Foods of the Frontier (Harris), 341

Forsyth County, Georgia, 177

40 Acres and No Mule (Giles), 5

Fowler, Damon Lee, 102, 304

Fox, Gene, 49

Foxfire series, xii, 67, 69, 80, 157, 167, 178, 210, 254, 312, 394, 419, 427, 444

Franklin Hedden Dyer sorghum mill, 36

Franklin, Benjamin, 15, 100

Free, Simmie, xvii, 7, 14, 134, 141–42

Freeman, "Aunt Martha," 105

French and Indian War, 14

French Huguenots, 14, 17

Frome, Michael, 14, 155

Frymire, Dick, 62, 65, 163

Fulton, Kentucky, 423

Fulton, Mrs. Lyman A., 212

G

Gainesville, Georgia, 81, 87

Garland, Merle Weaver, 427–28

Garrett, Nancy Brookshire, 132

Garrett, Nina, xvii, 69–70, 78, 87, 128, 132, 177, 353, 384, 414, 434

Garvey, Jane, 157

Gastonia, North Carolina, 162, 358

Gates Chapel United Methodist Church, 119, 310, 448

Gates Chapel, Georgia, 448

Gates, Sam, 176, 236

Gatlinburg Recipe Collection (Cooper), 210, 327

Gatlinburg, Tennessee, 210, 246, 283, 327, 339

Genesee Farmer, 406

Georgia Country Life (Bayett), 188

Michie Tavern (Virginia), 357

Michie, John, 357

Middlesboro, Kentucky, 211

Milledgeville, Georgia, 24

Miller, Elliott, 110

Miller, Governor Zell, 29, 136, 140, 169, 281, 367, 375, 397, 433

Miller, Joni, 115, 189, 339

Mills, Nora, 103, 114, 328

Millsaps, Bill and Wilma, 287

Mint Julep, The (Harwell), 143

Miracle, Janice, 211

Miss Leslie, Directions for Cookery, 312

Miss Ruby's American Cooking (Bronz), 311

Missionary churches, 45

Mitchamore, Pat, 213, 342

Mitchell County, North Carolina, 342

Mom & Ramps Forever (McCallum), 286, 288

Monongahela National Forest, West Virginia, 282

Montgomery County, Tennessee, 207

Moon, Gid, 131

Mooney, Ruby Fowler, 106, 112

Moonshine: Its History and Folklore (Kellner), 56

moonshiners, 22, 24, 63, 131–132, 134, 136–37, 151, 157, 377, 432

Moore, Warren, 11, 28, 85, 372

Moravian Germans, 18–19, 128, 338, 344

More Than Moonshine (Farr), 5, 65, 105, 111, 138, 441

Morris, Judge Newt, 252

Moss, Dr. Bobby Gilmer, 23

Moss, Kay, 162, 358

Mount Berry, Georgia, 119, 174, 405

Mount Vernon (Virginia), 137, 206

Mountain Cooking (Parris), 83, 281, 371, 413

Mountain Country Cooking (Sohn), 99, 122, 184, 293, 317, 347, 420, 440

Mountain Folk, Mountain Food (White), 344, 397

Mountain Spirits (Dabney), 3, 20, 134, 141, 152

Mountain View, South Carolina, 323, 428

Mountain Voices (Moore), 11, 28, 85, 372

Mountains Within Me, The (Miller), 169, 287, 367

Mrs. Donahoo's Boarding House (Cartersville, Georgia), 7

Mrs. Hill's Southern Practical Cookery and Receipt Book, 259

Mrs. Winner's chicken, 116

Mud on the Stars (Huie), 118

Mulinix, Rufus and Martha, 220

Mulinix, Vic and Marty, 220–21

Murfreesboro, Tennessee, 41

Murphy, North Carolina, 413, 425

Murray County, Georgia, 310, 396

Murray, Maynard, 109

Museum of the Cherokee Indian (Cherokee, North Carolina), 74, 327

My Mother's Southern Kitchen (Villas), 145, 149, 276

Myers, Bonnie, 343

Mynders, Alfred, 231

N

Nabors, Floyd and Vernie, 116

Nacoochee Valley, Georgia, 305, 346

Nashville, Tennessee, 73, 216, 411

Native Americans, 5, 18, 54, 229, 231, 295

Native Indian Wild Game, Fish & Wild Foods Cookbook, 255

Neal, Bill, 75, 97, 110, 120, 130, 144, 147, 206, 254, 313, 329, 344, 358, 403, 420, 424

Neal, Earl, 49

Nelson, John D., 228

Nelson, Rilla Chastain, 315, 318, 434, 436

New Southern Cooking (Dupree), 409

Nicholas Creswell, 190

Noe, Cotton, 279

Nolichucky River, 21

Nora Mills (Georgia), 114

Norcross, Georgia, 170

Norris, Frank, 85

North Carolina and Old Salem Cookery (Tartan), 73, 173, 295, 403

North Georgia Apple Recipes, 400, 416

Proctor, Moses, 84, 238, 368
Proctor, Patience, 84
Progressive Farmer, 74, 78
Pulaski, Tennessee, 71, 368
Purdy, Susan, 418, 420

Q

Quakers, 17
Quala, 26, 335
Queen Anne, 18
Queen of Appalachia Cook Book (Platt), 426
Queen Victoria, 189
quilting bees, 40

R

Rabun County High School (Georgia), 157
Rabun County, Georgia, 44, 255, 282, 365, 379, 397, 427
Rabun Gap, Georgia, 225, 230
Raichlen, Steven, 361, 378
Raine, Rev. James Watt, 6, 126
Raleigh, Sir Walter, 295, 381
Ramp Cove, Cullowhee, Mountain, North Carolina, 283
Ramp Cove, Rabun County, Georgia, 282
Ramp Cove, Swain County, North Carolina, 282
Ramp Festival, 281–82, 287–88
Randolph, Mary, 70, 120, 149, 191, 297, 330, 422
Rawlings, Marjorie Kinnan, 104, 385, 401
Ray, J. H. (Duck), 43
Reach of Song, 71, 232
"Rearguard of the Revolution," 21
Red Hills and Cotton (Robertson), 95, 301
Redneck Country Cooking (Signer), 78
Reece, Byron Herbert, 263
Reed, Doug, 318
Reed, John Shelton, 206
Reeves, M. E., 174
Reid, Mrs. Gunther, 347
Resaca, Georgia, 72, 162, 226, 270, 383, 405
Revocation of the Edict of Nantes, 18
Richards, Alvin B., 218

Richmond, Kentucky, 419
Riddle, Betty, 140
Riley, James Whitcomb, 385
Ritchie, Andrew Jackson, 235
Ritchie, Jean, 31, 35, 169, 389, 391
Ritchies, The, 35
Roadside Rambles (Mellinger), 379, 386, 392
Robbinsville Ramp Festival, 288
Robbinsville, North Carolina, 35, 240, 287
Roberts, Guy, 252
Robertson, Ben, 70, 95, 97, 301
Robinson, Estelle Keever, 348
Rome, Georgia, xvi, 105, 115, 278, 403
Roosevelt, Theodore, 20, 299
Root, Waverly, 226, 363
Rorabaugh, W. J., 132
Ross, Cherokee Chief John, 321, 335
Ross, John, 113, 321, 335
Rossville, Georgia, 113
Royal, Anne, 131
Ruddell Mill, 59
Rumford Chemical Company, 77
Rumford Complete Cook Book, 77
Russell Sage Foundation, The, 17
Russell, Gladys Trentham, 395
Rutledge, Sarah, 121

S

Saine, John Will, 40
Saine, Sam, 40
Salacauga, Alabama, 376
Salem, North Carolina, 455
Salisbury, North Carolina, 13, 19, 121
Samples, Will, 439
Sand Mountain (Alabama), 13, 61, 129, 168, 413, 426
Sapp, Julian, 253
Sautee Inn, 298, 305, 346
Schronce, Arty, 348
Schronce, Gordon, 348
Scotch-Irish Presbyterians, 39, 101
Scotch-Irish settlers, 23, 75, 125
Scottish Lowlanders, 15
Scuppernong River (North Carolina), 157